Raccoon (Photo by Dr. Donald R. Gunn)

WILD MAMMALS OF CANAD

Wild Mammals of Canada

by FREDERICK H. WOODING

Foreword by
R. YORKE EDWARDS
DIRECTOR, BRITISH COLUMBIA PROVINCIAL MUSEUM

"Mammal Watching," A Special Chapter by
DR. DAVID R. GRAY
ASSOCIATE CURATOR OF VERTEBRATE ETHOLOGY,
NATIONAL MUSEUM OF NATURAL SCIENCES

Drawings of Mammals by
PETER KARSTEN
DIRECTOR, CALGARY ZOO

Drawings of Tracks by
KAREN FIRN WOODING

McGRAW-HILL RYERSON LIMITED
Toronto   Montreal   New York

This book was written for and is dedicated to my grandson, Matthew Taylor Wooding, in the passionate hope that wildlife, in all its forms, will be to him an enduring source of fascination, understanding and respect.

1 2 3 4 5 6 7 8 9 10 BP 9 8 7 6 5 4 3 2

Designed by Robin Brass
Printed and bound in Canada

Canadian Cataloguing in Publication Data

Wooding, Frederick H., date
    Wild mammals of Canada

Includes index.
Bibliography: p.
ISBN 0-07-082973-X

1. Mammals—Canada. 2. Mammals—Northeastern States. 3. Mammals—Northwestern States. I. Title.

QL721.W66   599.0971   C82-095032-7

CONTENTS

FOREWORD

When Fred Wooding told me he was writing a book on mammals, I was impressed. When I heard he was doing it so people would know more about the lives and times of these intelligent creatures, and so people would also know how rapidly some of them are disappearing, I was suddenly personally involved.

Much of my life has been spent prying into the private lives of wild animals, and through the years they have given me full measure of both adventure and delightful experiences. I have become increasingly alarmed at how rapidly people continue to destroy the places that many of our most spectacular mammals must have to survive. Like Fred Wooding, I concluded that informing people about the beauty, fascination and drama of what they are losing was the only possible remedy.

For years I have dreamed of a book, widely read, that gave glimpses of the lives of these wild creatures, and also made clear their present survival problems. Here now is such a book by an author who did not just dream about one — he accepted his publisher's suggestion and he wrote one.

There is nothing new about the vanishing of the mammals, for it has been going on for centuries. What *is* new is the wildly quickening pace. Anyone in North America with some gray in his hair and happy memories of walking in rural or wild places has personal knowledge of mammals disappearing due to urban sprawl, industrial development, natural resource exploitation, government poisoning programs, and a host of related destructive causes. I know countless fields that are now without woodchucks, marshes that are now no longer marshes so, sadly, without mink and muskrats, forests now without deer, canyons now without bighorn sheep. I have wandered on mountains that were the most exciting places I have known because

they were home to grizzly bears. They are just ordinary mountains now, for the bears are gone as part of the long retreat that began in Mexico, moved through the full depth of the United States, and now continues into Canada. The great caribou vanishing tragedy, in contrast, is largely a Canadian production. Their numbers dwindle in all their forest ranges near man; the famous Arctic herds began to decline later, but now slip toward extinction just as surely as southern resource exploitation invades the far north.

Not all mammals retreat before the steady spread of man's influence on the landscape, but those that do form a long list of distinguished travelers on Spaceship Earth: muskox, bison, elk, caribou, bighorn sheep, pronghorn, badger, marten (sable), fisher, otter, mink, wolverine, most whales, grizzly bear, kit fox, prairie dog and wolf, to name some. Some others are of less concern, not because they are unaffected, but because they seem able to survive in some man-made landscapes. Examples are most of the squirrel family, the coyote, white-tailed deer, mule deer, cottontail, jackrabbit, raccoon and black bear.

Wild mammals are living miracles, like all living things, because of the apparently huge odds against such complex things ever existing on Earth at all. They are also our closest kin on this planet. I am a mammal. You are a mammal. Superficially we may look different from them, and they may look very different from one another, but it is part of the miracle that we are all constructed inside, where it counts, on the same fantastically complicated plan.

That the bat has specialized in flying, while the seal has specialized in swimming and man has specialized in walking, does not alter the obvious common architecture in all three. It is also probably true that in the mammals other than us there exists something of the feelings, the values, the capabilities that combine to make us human. We now know, of course, that those mammals that *appear* to be most like man are not the only ones having elements, however rudimentary, of being somewhat "human." The whales are the best example. They do not in any way look human (except perhaps for their eyes) but we are discovering that some kinds have an astonishing amount of intelligence.

We are really just beginning to discover this world that we now dominate, but we destroy it much more quickly than we discover it. We have just about exterminated some species of whales, yet there are still educated people who believe that whales are fish! How many wonders will vanish forever, quite undiscovered, to leave us with only our old and mindless beliefs?

Wild mammals are not only our fellow travelers through time and space; they can be memorable parts of our individual lives. Encounters with them are among my most unforgettable experiences. Looking back, I have had happy days searching for elusive caribou on the top of the world where great domes of mountains roll up out of forest into alpine tundra, and watching moose bob for lily roots in summer lakes or lethargically survive in mountain valleys white with winter as the deep cold periodically splits trees with loud reports like rifle shots. There was a wolf that chased a white-tailed doe almost into my canoe at the edge of a northern lake, and there were mole tunnels in rich southern soil that revealed secrets about how small mammals live that "swim" through the earth in their hunt for food and other needs. I have watched from a few inches at night the big-eyed beauty of flying squirrels, perhaps my favorite mammal, attracted to a bird feeder in a suburban garden, and I have walked for days, every nerve alert and fully aware of every detail around me, the adrenalin flowing because I was not alone, a fact made clear by the fresh tracks and diggings of grizzly bears. Mammals are everywhere around us: in our gardens and fields the kinds that can live near man, in wild places the many that cannot.

My home is by the sea, so my city garden is unusual in having seals, mink and an occasional otter at its edges. But as in many gardens, there are also mice living on nasturtium seeds and a big raccoon that inspects the grounds every night, starting with the garbage pails. In other cities it is not unusual to have skunks, foxes, cottontails, gray squirrels or coyotes as garden assets. These, quite literally, can live with man.

Many large mammals, and some small ones too, are unable to cope with changing North America. They vanish from watershed after watershed, county after county, mountain after mountain, with no alarm raised as long as someone knows some place where they are still to be found. When we ring the alarm it is close to the last mountain, the last valley, the last county to have them, and it is much too late.

When I first discovered the scientific literature on mammals, I read a learned paper called *The Close of the Age of Mammals*, which pointed out that the great flowering of seemingly countless species of mammals during the Ice Age was over, and we were left with a poor remnant of that spectacular parade surviving in only a few places with great herds, places like Africa, the prairies, and the Canadian Arctic. That article was written in the early 1900s. In 70 years or so we have made much progress at losing also the "poor remnant."

The Age of Mammals really does seem to be closing down. How far it closes is for us humans to decide. There is much to be done to inform people of the worth of what is being lost and of the root causes of the problems.

These wild creatures of Earth are part of our heritage. Far more than old buildings restored or battlegrounds preserved, they are the living evidence of where we came from and how we got there. Fred Wooding's book takes a large step toward informing North Americans about the mammals around them, and why they are worth knowing, and worth having as wild lives living in their chosen kinds of wild places.

The *saving* is especially important, for as the author of this book often quotes with concern: "Extinction is forever."

R. Yorke Edwards
Director, British Columbia Provincial Museum
Victoria, B. C.

AUTHOR'S NOTE

In struggling to find words that would express adequately my indebtedness to the many people who supported me in the writing of this book, I faced, I think, the most difficult part of the whole project. As I look at the undertaking retrospectively, I marvel at the encouragement I received, the way in which so many scientists—some themselves striving to meet publishers' deadlines—took the time to chart my paths of research and, as if that were not enough, to read and evaluate the manuscript as, section by section, the book took shape. I marvel, as well, at the immediate and generous response when the call went out for photographs to illustrate the text and, when it became evident that a book of this kind needed, as well, other illustrations depicting—as photographs could not easily do—the nature of mammals in their wild environment.

The rationale behind this book has been explained by Yorke Edwards in his foreword and by David Gray in his chapter on "Mammal Watching." To say much more would be redundant, but I must add that were it not for my own deep concern for the future of our wildlife resources, a project of this magnitude would never have been undertaken. If our mammals are to survive against the forces of increasing urbanization and industrial development, new and appropriate conservation and management measures will have to be taken without further delay.

I have tried to do a careful, responsible book, but the subject is so vast, so complex, and there are still so many different points of view that I expect to be confronted with disagreement (friendly, I hope) with some of the facts presented. But however the book is received, I must accept full responsibility for any errors that are uncovered.

The list of those whom I must thank is lengthy, but I think my first words of appreciation must go to these five people: R. Yorke Edwards, Director of the British Columbia Provincial Museum, who bravely and generously undertook to read the whole text as it developed and who, throughout, encouraged and counseled me; Dr. Valerius Geist, Faculty of Environmental Design, University of Calgary, who went far out of his way at the outset of the project to urge me on; Charles Guiguet, Victoria biologist and outdoors man, who offered invaluable advice; Dr. David R. Gray, Associate Curator of Vertebrate Ethology, National Museum of Natural Sciences, Ottawa, whose help and friendship meant, and continue to mean, so much; and Peter Karsten, Director of the Calgary Zoo and one of North America's most accomplished wildlife artists, who contributed the splendid drawings which illustrate these pages. The photographs in this book were, for the most part, generously provided by people who share the same concerns for the well-being of wildlife, but several deserve special mention because it was they who, at the beginning, set the example for other photographers to follow. I mention especially Dr. Donald A. Gunn, Bill Lowry, Dr. Gray, and Dr. Geist. To the other photographers my gratitude is equally sincere.

The scientists who read the text, in addition to those already mentioned, were all specialists in their field and their help can never be repaid: Dr. N. S. Novakowski, Coordinator of Wildlife Research, Canadian Wildlife Service, Ottawa; Dr. William O. Pruitt, Jr., Professor of Zoology, University of Manitoba; J. C. Holroyd, Parks Canada, Calgary; Dr. Ian Stirling, Canadian Wildlife Service, Edmonton; Dr. R. L. Peterson, Director of Mammalogy, Royal Ontario Museum, Toronto; Dr. Milan Novak, Ontario Ministry of Natural Resources, Toronto; George B. Kolenosky, Ontario Ministry of Natural Resources, Maple; Dr. J. David Henry, Biological Consultant, Waskesiu, Saskatchewan; Dr. Stephen Herrero, University of Calgary; Mme. Françoise Patenaude-Pilote, Laval University, Quebec City; Dr. Michael A. Bigg, Department of Fisheries and Oceans, Nanaimo; Dr. C. G. van Zyll de Jong, Curator of Mammals, National Museum of Natural Sciences, Ottawa; Dr. John B. Theberge, University of Waterloo; Dr. Peter B. Bromley, Virginia Polytechnic Institute and State University, Blacksburg, Virginia; Dr. A. T. Bergerud, University of Victoria; and Dr. B. T. Aniśkowicz, Shawville, Quebec.

I want also to thank those scientists who provided me with papers containing new findings arising from their own field studies, and to thank, as well, those who allowed me the use of their personal libraries.

Finally, I acknowledge a debt of gratitude to Karen Firn Wooding for undertaking the painstaking job of preparing the mammals' tracks, to Rachel Mansfield, Vice-President of McGraw-Hill Ryerson, for patiently awaiting the completion of the manuscript (well beyond its due date), to Colleen Darragh, my editor at McGraw-Hill Ryerson, who helped to keep me at my desk, and to Robin Brass, who, as the publisher's editorial consultant, advised me understandingly and well.

Frederick H. Wooding
Qualicum Beach, B. C.

NOTE ON MEASUREMENTS

The reader should understand that where figures are given for the dimensions of animals, the areas of their ranges, the elevations at which they occur and so on, these figures are approximate. Individuals vary, and indeed whole populations of a species may be larger in one range than in another. The dimensions on the drawings of tracks too are approximate and are given to allow the reader to gauge the general size of the tracks and to make comparisons.

ACKNOWLEDGEMENTS

Appreciation is extended to the following authors and publishers who granted permission to quote brief extracts from their books:

Dr. John A. Livingston. *One Cosmic Instant: A History of Human Arrogance*. McClelland and Stewart, 1973.

Dr. W. O. Pruitt, Jr. "The Wolverine." *Alive in the Wild*, edited by Victor H. Cahalane. Prentice Hall, 1970.

Dr. Valerius Geist. *Mountain Sheep: A Study in Behavior and Evolution*. University of Chicago Press, 1971. *Mountain Sheep and Man in the Northern Wilds*. Cornell University Press, 1975.

Dr. Randolph Peterson. "The Moose." *Alive in the Wild*, edited by Victor H. Cahalane. Prentice Hall, 1970.

Shirley E. Woods, Jr. *The Squirrels of Canada*. National Museum of Natural Sciences, 1980.

John Madson. *Gray and Fox Squirrels*. Winchester Group, Olin Corporation, East Alton, Illinois, 1964.

A. W. F. Banfield. *The Mammals of Canada*. University of Toronto Press. National Museums of Canada, 1974.

Victor H. Cahalane. *Mammals of North America*. Macmillan Publishing Co., Inc., New York. (Copyright 1947 by Macmillan Publishing Co., Inc., renewed 1975 by Victor H. Cahalane).

Dr. David R. Gray. "The Marmots of Spotted Nellie Ridge." *Nature Canada*, Jan/Mar, 1975.

Dr. David R. Gray and Heather Hamilton. "Hare Revelations." *Nature Canada*, Jan/Mar, 1982.

The author wishes also to thank Mr. David Maclellan, Editor of the *Canadian Geographic*, The Royal Canadian Geographical Society, for permission to use the chapter on muskox which originally was published in slightly different form in the *Canadian Geographic*, Feb/Mar, 1979.

ORDER ARTIODACTYLA

THE HOOFED MAMMALS

Between 8,000 and 12,000 years ago, when the last great Ice Age was drawing to a close, the northern part of this continent was inhabited by an amazing variety of wild mammals. Among these creatures were giant woolly mammoths, mastodons, saber-toothed tigers, camels, horses, tapirs, caribou, moose, elk and a host of smaller mammals including foxes, badgers, lynx, lemmings and ground squirrels. And, as archeological digs have revealed, man himself.

Then a remarkable change took place: two major groups of mammals vanished from this vast North American refugium. One was a group of odd-toed mammals: horses and tapirs, of the order Perissodactyla. The other was a group characterized by elongated, flexible trunks and great tusks: the woolly mammoths and mastodons, of the order Proboscidea. What happened to bring about the elimination of these beasts is a matter of conjecture; how it was that mammals belonging to eleven other orders continued to survive and evolve as part of North America's present-day mammalian life remains unanswered.

A popular view is that the disappearance of the perissodactyls and the proboscideans was caused not by sudden climatic changes or geological upheavals but by the wholesale slaughter of them by primitive man. Many of the mammals—the horse, for example—belonged to species that had evolved in North America millions of years before. Horses were only restored to this continent in the 1500s when they were brought here by Spanish conquistadores, thus ending an absence of nearly 8,000 years.

Although Dall's sheep are eagerly sought by trophy hunters, they are becoming increasingly the wilderness favorites of amateur and professional photographers. These magnificent animals are found in northwestern Canada and Alaska. (Photo by Dr. Norman M. Simmons)

Fortunately for this continent a number of very desirable orders were spared, particularly the even-toed (or "cloven-hoofed") mammals of the order Artiodactyla—elk, deer, moose and caribou (family Cervidae), bison (buffalo), goats, muskoxen and sheep (family Bovidae), and the pronghorn (family Antilocapridae). It should be mentioned that wild boar (family Suidae) and the peccaries (family Tayassuidae), which occur in the United States, are also artiodactyls, as are domestic cows, sheep, goats and pigs.

The artiodactyls are exceedingly diverse in their general morphology and behavioral patterns. In fact, as Dr. Valerius Geist has pointed out, "an even number of weight-bearing toes is one of the few things that members of the order have in common." In other words, each representative has four toes on each foot, of which two are hoof lobes and two are dew claws. It is the third and fourth toes that form the cloven hoof and it is these that bear most of the animal's weight. The dew claws are smaller and higher on the legs and are also used to support weight when the animal sinks into soft or muddy ground.

Superficially members of each family look somewhat alike, although the antlers of the cervids and the horns of the bovids readily set these two families apart. The horns of the pronghorn make it different in turn from the others.

All members of the order are ruminants ("cud chewers") and have a four-chambered stomach. The food (mostly vegetable matter such as grasses and woody material) is briefly chewed and quickly swallowed into a chamber known as the *rumen*, where fermentation takes place. It is regurgitated, chewed again and reswallowed, this time into a second chamber known as the *reticulum*, where for up to 18 hours it goes through additional digesting and a process that filters out foreign matter. Then it is once again regurgitated, chewed and finally swallowed to make its way through the digestive tract for eventual elimination.

They are medium- to large-sized mammals. Their habitat is varied and ranges from open plains to deep forests, alpine meadows, rocky plateaus and cliff-sides well beyond the tree line, to the barrenlands and Arctic tundra. They are strong, fleet of foot, and capable of

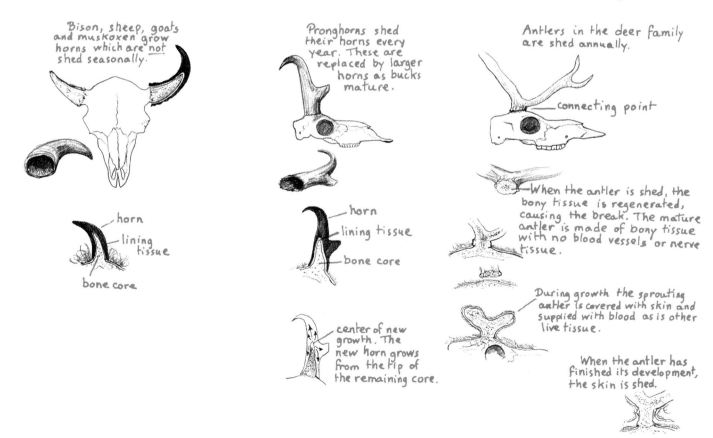

Bison, sheep, goats and muskoxen grow horns which are not shed seasonally.

horn
lining tissue
bone core

Pronghorns shed their horns every year. These are replaced by larger horns as bucks mature.

horn
lining tissue
bone core

center of new growth. The new horn grows from the tip of the remaining core.

Antlers in the deer family are shed annually.

connecting point

When the antler is shed, the bony tissue is regenerated, causing the break. The mature antler is made of bony tissue with no blood vessels or nerve tissue.

During growth the sprouting antler is covered with skin and supplied with blood as is other live tissue.

When the antler has finished its development, the skin is shed.

withstanding extremes of temperatures. Some, other than during the mating season, are loners; others are gregarious.

Call them what you will—artiodactyls, cloven-hoofed mammals, even-toed mammals, ruminants or cud-chewers—these creatures are among the most important and most valued of all forms of wildlife. But they continue to be under enormous pressure from man, just as they were in primitive times. We need only point to the near-extinction of the bison and the precarious status today of muskoxen and some herds of caribou to deplore our lack of responsible stewardship of this part of our natural heritage.

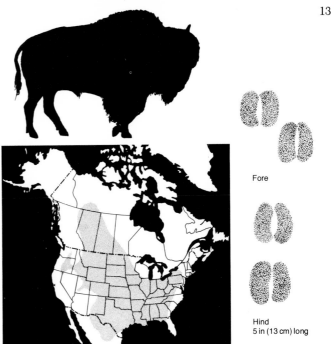

Fore

Hind
5 in (13 cm) long

American bison (Former range. Now exists as semi-wild herds in a number of parks and reserves. There are also some privately owned herds.)

FAMILY BOVIDAE

Bison bison

American Bison*

Few recent North American wild mammals have come closer to extinction than have the plains and wood bison. And few others have commanded a more dominant place in the history and folklore of this continent. These remarkable creatures are a species of wild cattle that is believed to have evolved from ancestors that reached this continent about 100,000 years ago from the Old World.

The bison prospered in their environment and eventually spread throughout most of the continent where they found a wealth of forage in the great open plains and prairies and, farther north, in the rich park-lands and coniferous forests. As recently as the middle of the 18th century, it is believed, the North American bison population numbered between 40 and 50 *million*!

When the ancestors of the Indians and Eskimos (Inuit) arrived from the Old World, the bison faced the first threat to their survival. The newcomers were in need of food, clothing, utensils and shelter and the bison provided all of them. Many thousands (some historians say in excess of 2 million) were killed each year, and there was much waste. What had been done by Neanderthal people in Paleolithic times was repeated in North America: mass slaughter was practiced by

stampeding several hundreds of the beasts over cliffs to meet instant or lingering death. It mattered little, so enormous were the herds.

It was much the same when Europeans arrived on the continent. The bison provided the same basic needs for the early fur traders, explorers, colonizers, railway workers, road builders and others who made their way across the Canadian prairies and the United States midwest. Many of the routes followed by the white man were, in fact, trails carved out by the bison themselves.

The diaries of these early travelers tell almost incredible stories. When Lewis and Clark were ascending the Mississippi in 1804, they saw bison "in such magnitude that we cannot exaggerate in saying that at a single glance we saw 3,000 of them before us." But this was a small herd compared with that seen in September 1874 by Sir Cecil Denny during the original westward journey of the North West Mounted Police (now the Royal Canadian Mounted Police). Just east of the Cypress Hills in what is now Saskatchewan "we came," he wrote, "to places, where, as far as the eye could reach, thousands and tens of thousands were in sight; the country was fairly black with them."

---

* Bison is the name preferred by scientists. The name "buffalo" more appropriately belongs to species of Old World bovidae, e.g., the water buffalo found in the far east and India.

But it was the massive extermination of these magnificent animals that still vibrates so disgustingly in North American history, and many written accounts are almost impossible to believe. Here, for example, is an extract from the 1889 writings of the zoologist, Dr. William Hornaday, concerning the organized slaughter of 1870-74:

"Probably never before in the history of the world, until civilized men came in contact with the buffalo, did whole armies of men march out in true military style, with officers, flags, chaplains, and rules of war, and make war on animals. No wonder the buffalo has been exterminated. So long as they existed north of the Missouri in any considerable number, the half-breeds and the Indians of the Manitoba Red River settlement used to gather each year in a great army, and go with carts to the buffalo range. On these great hunts, which took place every year from about the 15th of June to the 1st of September, vast quantities of buffalo were killed and the supply was finally exhausted. As if Heaven had decreed the extirpation of the species, the half-breed hunters, like their white robe-hunting rivals farther south, also killed *cows* in preference to bulls so long as a choice was possible, the very best course calculated to exterminate any species in the shortest possible time."

Before the last spike of the Canadian Pacific Railway was driven home at Craigellachie, British Columbia, in 1885, the Canadian population of bisons was reduced to less than 1,000 animals. In the United States it was just over 500.

Not all historians agree, however, that humans were the major cause of the near complete disappearance of the bison, despite indisputable evidence that humans were guilty of unbelievable acts of butchery. There are those who contend that natural predators and the elements played a significant part. Wolves and grizzly bears then, as now, appear to have been the only animals capable of killing a beast of such strength and stature and both carnivores were plentiful at that time. Unusually severe winters of heavy snows and long successions of blizzards, fires that raged in every direction across miles of dry prairie land, and mass drownings during river crossings when floods were rampant also are believed to have caused enormous mortality. In dealing with the history of the bison, the whole truth surrounding their near-extinction may never be known.

Whatever the causes, by 1885 the vast grasslands and northern forests were virtually silent. No longer were the Metis hired for pennies a day to supply meat for the militia and travelers on their way to the West. No longer were there animals to be hunted for their hides, or taken for the pemmican so easily made from their flesh. No longer did brigades of more than 1,500 hunters, with their wives and children, 1,000 or more dogs, and over 1,000 Red River carts set out in the spring from Fort Garry on bison hunts. Gone too were the escapades in the United States of Buffalo Bill Cody, under contract to the Kansas Pacific Railway to supply food for the construction crews. Buffalo Bill was committed to place before the cook tents 12 bison each day, and within 18 months is said to have killed 6,400 animals!

The West had become quiet and lonely, for the thundering sounds of hundreds, even thousands of these animals, as they galloped across the land to escape their tormentors, had become but a memory, a memory that finally turned into history as the last homesteaders themselves passed on. But for a long time monuments to these animals marked some landscapes as far as the eye could see: the bleached bones of those slaughtered—grotesque reminders that human beings had failed to understand that wild creatures, in all their forms, had the same right of survival as they did, and that this right was being denied them.

The turn of the century, fortunately, marked the end of the decline, for by then conservation measures were being applied. A law passed by the Dominion government in 1893 provided for the protection of the remaining Canadian herds, although it did not become fully effective until 1897 when the North West Mounted Police were charged with its enforcement. This arrangement continued until 1911, when the protection responsibilities were turned over to game wardens. Subsequently rigidly controlled preserves were set up, among them being Wood Buffalo National Park in the Northwest Territories and Elk Island National Park in Alberta.

In the United States equally serious efforts were taken to preserve the bison, a notably successful example being the National Bison Range in Montana. Yellowstone National Park also has bison that were there before the park was established and these have since been protected. There are, in addition, privately owned herds of plains bison on ranches in the United States and Canada. These privately managed herds are held for aesthetic or scientific purposes, although some are bred like domestic cattle for specialty meat markets

About two centuries ago 40 to 50 million bison (buffalo) roamed North America. Wanton slaughter and the advance of civilization brought them to the brink of extinction. They are now protected. (Photo by J. C. Holroyd)

or for the value of their heads and hides.

But while the plains bison was recovering numerically, the small numbers of pure wood bison (*Bison bison athabascae*) continued to cause concern. A remnant population of about 300 animals, living in an area straddling the border of Alberta and the Northwest Territories south of Great Slave Lake, continued to prosper however, and by 1922 the population had increased to upwards of 2,000. It was this area that was set aside in 1922 as a preserve under the name of Wood Buffalo National Park.

Unfortunately a smaller preserve known as Buffalo National Park, at Wainwright, Alberta, had become overcrowded with plains bison and the government, apparently not realizing the consequences of the action, between 1925 and 1928 moved 6,673 of them by train and river barge into Wood Buffalo National Park. These animals interbred with the resident wood bison and within six years the bison population had grown to 12,000 animals. Of the total, however, only about 2 per cent survived as pure wood bison.

In 1958, however, 200 animals found in the Nyarling River area of Wood Buffalo National Park were identified as *B.b.athabascae*. Of these, 18 were translocated and came under rigid protection in a newly-established preserve northwest of Great Slave Lake, named the Mackenzie Bison Sanctuary. In addition, 23 wood bison were moved to Elk Island National Park where they are held in a fenced-in area. These actions on the part of the authorities have had gratifying results and today the known population of wood bison, as a distinct subspecies, totals 900 individuals: 750 in the Mackenzie Bison Sanctuary and 150 in Elk Island National Park. At the present time studies are being made of other northern sites to which transfers may be made for the purpose of developing new herds.

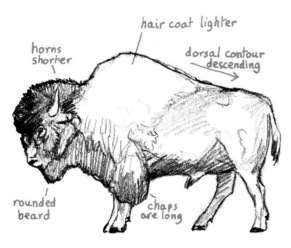

horns shorter

hair coat lighter

dorsal contour descending

rounded beard

chaps are long

Plains bison

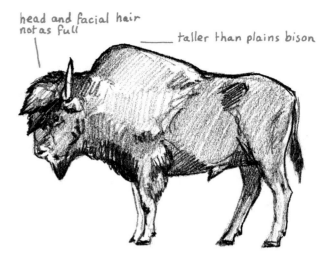

head and facial hair not as full

taller than plains bison

Wood bison

One such transfer has already been made to the Nahanni Butte area of the Northwest Territories, but the success of this transfer has yet to be determined.

This increase, although significant, is not enough to consider the future of *B.b.athabascae* secure. As a consequence it has been declared "endangered," a fact recognized by the Committee on the Status of Endangered Wildlife in Canada and the Convention on International Trade in Endangered Species. The wood bison is also listed in the "Red Data Book" by the International Union for the Conservation of Nature. All three of these steps serve notice on the world that the wood bison, found only in Canada, is still in danger of joining the long list of wild creatures that are now extinct.

Both subspecies of bison are impressive looking animals, although aside from certain cranial differences they are so similar in appearance that comparisons are sometimes difficult to make. The wood bison is generally a little larger overall, somewhat darker in color and its coat is woollier. It is not unusual, in fact, for an adult wood bison to stand 7 feet (2.1 m) or more in height and weigh over a ton (1,000 kg). A large adult plains bison would stand 6.5 feet (1.98 m) in height and weigh over 2,000 pounds (900 kg). Cows of both subspecies are substantially smaller and lighter in weight.

The plains and wood bison have massive-looking heads, short necks, humped shoulders and short tails which end in tufts of hair. In each the head, neck and shoulders are covered with long, woolly hair which is brownish-black in color and ends in a beard up to a foot in length. The hind quarters are not blanketed, but are covered with short thick hair, giving the animals a semi-naked appearance.

During the mating season, which lasts from July to September (it reaches its peak in mid-August), the deep guttural roaring of the bulls can be heard for miles. Long drawn-out confrontations between competing bulls are common occurrences but these contests are engaged in primarily to establish dominance. They usually take the form of harmless head-to-head shoving matches. The female when bred undergoes a gestation period of 9½ months at which time she will give birth to a single calf. Although she will move away from the main herd for the purpose, the mother will drop her young in any comfortable spot. Within 2 or 3 days the stiff-legged, reddish-tan youngster is able to follow the herd. It will change in color to brownish-black when about 3 months of age and will suckle with diminishing frequency for about 7 months.

Bison are primarily grazers and because of their ability to subsist on forage of poor quality they can exist more readily in short-grass country (even during the winter) than can domestic cattle and other large ungulates. Their massive, powerful heads can easily sweep the ground clear of packed or ice-encrusted snow to get at vegetation.

With the approach of spring the pelage of bison

begins to molt and large amounts of ragged hair are removed when the animals roll in dust bowls or rub against trees. During this time their hides become almost bare, and mosquitoes and other blood-seeking insects make their lives miserable. It is not uncommon to come across depressions in the ground up to 15 feet across and nearly a foot deep made by bison rolling and thrashing on their sides to seek relief from their tormentors. When rain turns these depressions into mud bowls, the bison wallow in them and then let the mud dry on their hide as a protective covering. By fall, however, the coat is restored, the insect scourge is ended and the grasses and other ground vegetation are lush and plentiful.

Bison have few natural enemies capable of killing them, and probably the most dangerous are wolves and grizzly bears where they are present. Calves that have become orphaned or that have strayed away from the herd are easy prey. Bison live an average of 12 to 15 years, although a few may survive beyond 20 years. It is thought that cows have a longer lifespan than do bulls.

Bison bulls often "horn" the ground before combat.

Oreamnos americanus
Mountain Goat

The first thing to be said about *Oreamnos americanus* is that it is a superb mountaineer—a skillful, dauntless and unflappable mountain dweller whose ability to move with ease up and down cliff faces, up and down smooth rock surfaces, and to leap 10 feet (3 m) or more across deep chasms from one promontory to another is a source of constant amazement to scientists, backpackers, hunters and other hardy souls who venture up and beyond the timberline of the great ranges of Alberta, British Columbia, Yukon, southern Alaska, and parts of Washington, Idaho and Montana.

Why, in the course of evolution, mountain goats were destined to inhabit such a sparse and desperately rugged environment, is as unanswerable as why muskoxen, polar bears and the little lemmings were destined to inhabit the equally harsh environment of the high Arctic. But all these creatures, and many others, survive and prosper in such places and have done so for thousands of years.

Mountain goats, although classified as members of the family Bovidae, are not true goats. They are really antelopes, and their closest relatives are the serow and goral of Asia and the chamois of the European Alps.

My first experience with mountain goats was a sighting at about the 5,000-foot (1,500-m) level on a mountain a few miles north of Whitehorse, Yukon, during a flight from there to Dawson City, Old Crow and Inuvik. Field glasses provided a good look at about 30 animals, at least a dozen or so being quite young kids. The roar of the aircraft must have disturbed them because several of the adults raced down the face of what seemed to be a sheer precipice. It was a display of incredible agility.

Mountain goats frequently browse through alpine meadows as they move to salt licks at lower levels, but one normally has to be above the treeline, at elevations of 4,000 feet (1,200 m) or so, to see them. Although they favor higher elevations, deep snows along the Coast Range often force them to seek food almost at sea level.

The mountain goat is well equipped for survival. An undercoat of very fine wool, about 3 or 4 inches (8-10 cm) thick, covers virtually the whole body down to a few inches above the hooves. This in turn is covered by an outer coat of long white hair, and both provide excellent insulation against the extremely cold winter tem-

Mountain goats spend most of their time in sparse and treacherous habitats well above timberline, but frequently browse in alpine meadows. Their generally inaccessible ranges help to assure their survival. (Photo by Michael E. Wooding)

peratures. Goat-like, both nannies and billies carry a double beard of longer hair on the chin and throat. The guard hairs on the neck and shoulder are long and thick and give the animal a decidedly humped appearance.

The slender 8- to 10-inch (20-25 cm) horns of the mountain goat are not shed but are occasionally broken in fights or deformed at birth or later from disease. In their prime, they are black and shiny. The horns of both male and female extend upward from the long, narrow head and curve backward to very sharp tips. In the male the curves near the tips are gradual; in the female the curves are more pronounced. The spread between the tips is about equal to the length of the horns.

Like all artiodactyls, the mountain goat is an even-toed ungulate. In this case the split, or cloven, hooves are broad and short and are covered by horny outer shells so hard and tough they can by themselves support the animal's weight. The foot pads are made of a tough, rubbery substance so that when the feet are pressed down hard, these pads, working in conjunction with the horny outer shells, provide a strong, sure footing. It is a remarkable example of two elements perfectly designed and working together. This partly explains the animal's ability to negotiate smooth surfaces and steep angles and to move along cliff ledges only inches wide.

The combination of a large, heavy-set body, fairly short legs and highly specialized hooves—plus an inborn ability to move with relative ease in a seemingly impossible habitat—gives the mountain goat a special place among the larger mammals. To an observer, however, this ease of movement can be deceiving. Actually goats have a healthy respect for the paths they follow and, in exposed areas especially, unless frightened or trying to elude a predator, they move slowly and choose their footing deliberately and with care.

Female goats become sexually mature in their second year and male goats in their third. Mating takes place between November and December. Unlike species such as elk and muskoxen, male mountain goats do not establish harems. During the rutting season, moreover, the males woo the females in a subservient and always cautious manner, being careful to avoid the nannies' very sharp horns should they try to repulse sexual advances. As is customary among animals during the rut, there is a high degree of pent-up emotions and ill-temper; fights among males, therefore, are common.

Mountain goat combatants do not clash head-on as do other bovids, but seek to strike at each other's rears and bellies. Although most battles are harmless shams, confrontations causing serious injury do occur. Death sometimes results when the rapier-like horns pierce internal organs.

It has been generally recorded that gestation takes 178 days, the young being born from May to June. An extensive study of goats on Mount Wardle, Kootenay National Park, B. C., by John C. Holroyd of the National Parks Service, has revealed, however, that gestation in that area has taken as long as 191 days.

The nannies, which mate each year, give birth to one kid (sometimes twins), generally in a high, inaccessible, sheltered place such as in a cave or under a large

front hoof of mountain goat (side view)

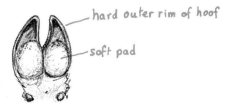

— hard outer rim of hoof

— soft pad

underside of hoof

Mountain goats are superb mountaineers but sometimes suffer injury or death when caught in rock slides or avalanches. (Photo by J. C. Holroyd)

rock overhang on a cliff. The newly-born kid, about a foot (30 cm) long and 6 to 7 pounds (2.7-3.2 kg) in weight, comes into the world covered with a white, woolly overcoat. Mother and child remain in their shelter for about 10 days, then both join the herd.

For several weeks, as the kid grows and gains experience, it stays constantly within a few feet of its mother. During this time it learns to follow its elders along knife-edged ridges, to climb the dizziest crags and to jump over sheer drop-offs. Within 3 months it reaches a weight of about 40 pounds (18 kg) and is accomplished in mountaineering. Holroyd, on one occasion during his Mount Wardle studies, watched a nanny and her kid in interesting behavior. "Several times," he wrote, "the nanny mounted a large rock and then jumped across a gap of about 4 feet. After each time the nanny did this, the kid would climb up and repeat the same jump, although much more awkwardly. The kid was not more than 3 days old. . . ." Whether the nanny was actually giving the kid a lesson in mountaineering or they were merely playing is a matter of conjecture.

It is usual for the young of the year before to remain with their mothers, but when new births are about to occur these yearlings are chased off and form temporary groups of their own. Contrary to popular belief, they do not always become part of mixed herds. As Holroyd has found, they often return to their mothers to continue as part of the family. He reports, however, that if they threaten their young brothers and sisters, or even come too close to them, the nannies treat them in the same aggressive way they would treat any other intruder.

Those who have watched mountain goats in high altitude habitats have seen amazing feats of acrobatics. Victor H. Cahalane, for example, in *Mammals of North America*, has this to say: "It is a careful mountaineer, rarely taking a step until certain about the trail beyond. If, because of some emergency, the goat chooses a narrow, crooked ledge that 'peters out,' it doesn't get panicky. Perhaps it is possible to back away slowly until it can turn around, but if that is impossible, it cautiously rears up on its hind legs. With its weight pressed against the cliff, the goat carefully turns inward and around and then drops down on all fours, or it may grab a rock shelf with its short forelegs and pull itself up to a higher level."

But accidents sometimes happen. A miscalculation, a weakened ledge, an unexpected rock slide, or in

Mountain goat

3½ in (8.9 cm) long

winter an avalanche, cause injury or death.

Mountain goats, in prime condition during the winter months when their outer coat is long and white, are handsome animals. But during the shedding period their appearance is less than attractive. Shedding of the winter coats begins in late spring or early summer, and as it progresses large patches of hair and wool hang from the goats in great disarray. The animals at this stage are dirty and have the color of grey limestone. Shedding is usually completed by the end of July and by then the new coat of hair is beginning to show. For most of the summer the new coat is quite yellow in color, but with the cleansing help of snow in the late fall and early winter, it becomes clean and white again.

British Columbia's Spatsizi country, according to Yorke Edwards, is often referred to as the "land of the red goats" because the pelage of the animals is markedly dyed by the dust of the red rock that predominates there.

Mountain goats browse heavily on sub-alpine fir which is common at and above the timberline and this, Edwards suggests, is a key to their widespread survival. Also included in their diet are grasses, forbs, shrubs, buffaloberry and western hemlock. Feeding goes on throughout the day, most heavily at dawn and dusk.

During May and August they move temporarily from their rocky ramparts to the dry limestone licks sometimes found close to well-traveled highways. It is during this time, when they are in the lower meadows or on treed hillsides, that they can be susceptible to attack by predators. Mountain goats are competent in defence, however, and successful attacks by their most likely enemies — grizzly bears, cougars, wolves, coyotes and lynx — are the exception rather than the rule. Occasionally one hears reports of eagles carrying off very young kids.

Mountain goats are strictly western mammals, and are found in Canada only in the mountains of Alberta, British Columbia and the Yukon, and in the United States, in Alaska. Although Banfield writes that no subspecies of mountain goats are recognized in Canada, Hoefs, Lorties and Russell (submission to a symposium held at Kalispell, Montana, in 1977) suggest that *all* mountain goats in the Yukon are of the subspecies *O.a. columbiae*, characterized by larger size and narrower skull. Subspecies are, of course, often cause for disagreement among experts. The total population of mountain goats in western Canada, Yukon and Alaska is said to number about 100,000 animals.

Defying a deep chasm, this mountain goat was caught by the camera lens as it jumped from one ledge to another — a demonstration of remarkable agility. (Photo by J. C. Holroyd)

Ovibos moschatus
Muskox

From 1,500 feet the scattered dark spots on the low-lying Keewatin plains north of Baker Lake seemed nothing more than natural landmarks. Only when the pilot of our twin-engine Otter aircraft motioned us to use our field glasses did we discover that what we were looking at was in fact a small herd of muskoxen. Although there are more than 10,000 of these mammals on the Canadian mainland and Arctic islands, their remote and harsh environment makes sightings of them a rare and memorable experience.

The suggestion that we circle at a lower altitude for a better view was declined. It was calving time and the noise of the aircraft and its threatening appearance could cause harmful stress to the animals. Our pilot was a rare breed of man whose love of the north country was equaled only by his understanding of, and respect for, the wild creatures that make it their home.

There is good reason to be concerned about the well-being of muskoxen — as there is for the well-being of all wildlife — for, although now thought to be secure, they were on the verge of extinction as recently as 1917. At that time the Canadian government prohibited their killing and thus prevented the tragedy. Even so, biologists continue to keep a close watch on all populations since mortality, mainly through winter starvation, can be alarmingly high.

Muskoxen from time to time have suffered from large-scale die-offs, such as the virtual disappearance in 1948-49 of some 200 animals on Prince Patrick Island, and the alarming decline in 1973-74 of muskoxen on Melville and Bathurst islands. Similar conditions have prevailed in neighboring Greenland. There in 1953-54, for example, unusually deep snow, much of it covered by an icy crust, made it impossible for the animals to dig through to ground vegetation. Hundreds died of starvation.

Muskoxen are among the oldest surviving herbivores and can trace their ancestry back about a million years. They evolved, it is believed, on the tundra of north-central Asia. The history of their survival is part of the history of the evolution of the earth itself. In ancient times great icefields covered much of the northern hemisphere. As the icefields advanced and retreated, the levels of the oceans fluctuated and massive changes in the earth's surface occurred. One of the changes was the creation of a dry "land bridge" where

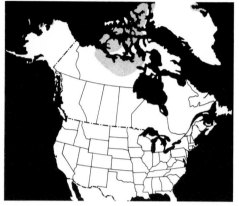

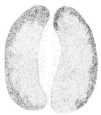

Hind
4 in (10 cm) across
4 in (10 cm) long

*Muskox (Present range. Original range more
extensive, from north coast of Alaska to half
way down west coast of Hudson Bay)*

the Bering Strait now separates Alaska and Siberia.

This land bridge had an enormous influence on our continent. Not only did wildlife, such as muskoxen, cross from Asia but also humans. Anthropologists generally agree that Eskimos (Inuit) and Indians came by this route from Asia. Muskoxen are believed to have made their way across nearly 100,000 years ago, and there is indisputable evidence that Eskimos were present in what is now the Yukon some 10,000 years ago.

Although early man hunted muskoxen for food and clothing and used their horns for a variety of purposes, particularly hunting bows, the existence of the animals was not seriously threatened until the coming of the fur-traders and explorers and the introduction of firearms. Muskox hides, with their thick wool and long hair, made excellent sleeping robes and sleigh rugs, so thousands upon thousands of the animals were killed for their well-haired skins. Thousands more were killed for food.

By 1917 some populations had been so depleted that the Canadian government passed legislation (the Northwest Game Act) that gave the muskoxen virtually complete protection. Until relatively recently even the native people were forbidden to kill them. Today hunters from several Arctic settlements are permitted to kill a total of about 250 muskoxen each year. As a result of stringent conservation measures, the Canadian population of these animals is now believed to be more than 10,000, of which 1,500 or so are on the mainland and the rest are distributed throughout most of the islands of the eastern Arctic.

Convinced that herds of muskoxen could again be established in areas where they had long been extinct, or had never been present, authorities in the late 1800s arranged numerous transplants. Some stocks from Greenland (where there are now well over 10,000 animals) were sent to Norway and its Arctic archipelago, Svalbard, and to Sweden and Iceland. Of these transplants, only those to Norway and Svalbard were successful—a notable achievement nonetheless.

There have been other successes. In 1935 a Greenland herd kept at the University of Alaska was set free on Nunivak Island off the west coast of Alaska and has since grown steadily. From these stocks some animals were later taken back to mainland Alaska to form the basis of a "cottage" industry for the harvesting of muskox wool. The Nunivak transplant has been so successful that more than 200 animals have been returned to the mainland and are now roaming free along Alaska's north slope.

In 1967, 15 muskoxen from Ellesmere Island were moved to a site near Fort Chimo, Quebec, and their progeny have been released in the province's Ungava region as free animals. In the 1970s, 10 Canadian muskoxen from Banks Island and 40 muskoxen from Alaska's Nunivak Island herds were sucessfully transported to the Soviet Union and are now believed to be well established. Muskoxen had been extinct in that country for some 2,000 years.

These are splendid examples of man's concern for the well-being of our creatures of the wild. Although much larger funds are required for research and for the application of management programs, what has been accomplished is a tribute to the scientists who have interested themselves in this work.

Superficially muskoxen resemble the plains and wood bison, but they are more closely related to sheep and goats. Their only close relative is the takin of southeast Asia. The muskox, like the caribou, is a relatively small animal, although its thick, shaggy coat and long mane make it appear larger than it really is. At shoulder hump an average bull (the cows are always smaller)

stands about 5 feet (1.5 m). Length is about 7 feet (2.1 m). Because of the difficulty in weighing wild muskoxen, there are considerable differences in published weight estimates. While most range from 600 to 700 pounds (270-320 kg), one estimate is 800 pounds (360 kg) and another, for a captive bull, is 1,433 pounds (650 kg). Recent studies in the Arctic islands suggest that typical weights are less: 500 to 700 pounds maximum (230-320 kg).

The coat of the muskox, which is black-brown to dark brown, drops raggedly around the whole animal to knee level. Underneath the long outer hair is a thick covering of finer wool not unlike cashmere. It is this finer hair that provides the main insulation for the animal and enables it to withstand the bitterly severe winter weather of the mainland and Arctic islands. During spring and summer, the inner coat is gradually shed, making the animal appear quite bizarre for a time, but it is all restored by fall.

These three muskoxen bulls, part of the Bathurst Island, N.W.T., herd, assumed a defense formation at the approach of what they perceived to be an enemy—in this case a friendly scientist-photographer engaged in field studies. (Photo by Dr. David R. Gray)

Another interesting feature is the large eyes, which project out beyond the face in bony sockets. In front, almost hidden by the wool, is a pre-orbital gland that is rubbed against the leg in defensive and offensive situations, producing a chemical signal to other muskoxen. During the rutting season the bulls have a strong odor.

In addition to the pronounced shoulder hump and shaggy coat, another distinguishing characteristic is the set of heavy horns. They provide formidable armament in defense against enemies and in fights between bulls. Emerging in the young at about 6 months of age, the horns take at least 6 years to mature. The horn on each side of the forehead extends from a solid boss or knob of

Herd of muskoxen ringed up in a defensive circle. Calves are pressed to the sides of the adults.

muskox skull (side view)

Adults will leave the defensive circle to charge approaching wolves.

muskox skull

A threatening bull approaches his opponent with a stiff walk and his head swaying sideways.

bone and horn about 4 inches (10 cm) thick, curves downward toward the face, then up and out, ending in slender tips. Stretching the imagination a bit, they might be said to resemble a British sergeant-major's waxed moustache. The horns of the cow muskox are more slender. In older animals of both sexes the horns are darker in color.

The legs of the muskox are short and stocky and the hooves, especially those in front, are large, giving the animal better stability in snow and enabling it to paw more easily through snow to feed on ground vegetation. Muskoxen normally are slow and deliberate in their movements, but when necessary they can run with surprising speed and climb difficult rocky inclines

with agility. On the run, they usually keep a closely packed formation. Their sight, hearing and sense of smell are highly developed.

Unlike caribou, muskoxen do not migrate, although in their search for food they do travel considerable distances within both their summer and winter ranges. In the short summer months they are on the coastal and inland plains and around the shores of lakes and rivers where there is an abundance of Arctic vegetation such as willow (their favorite food), grasses, sedges and flowering plants. During this time they feed constantly to build up body fat and other reserves of energy to sustain them through the long and bitterly cold months ahead.

When winter comes they move into larger herds, but generally remain in the same feeding areas. Should food supplies become inaccessible because of deep snow or icy conditions, they may move to higher ground where almost constant winds keep the vegetation relatively free of snow. For several of the winter months in this exacting environment, the sun does not appear above the horizon. Throughout this period

there is an awesome silence—a silence broken only by human voices and barking dogs in isolated settlements, by the howling of wolves, the whistling winds of a raging blizzard, or the occasional brief drone of a passing aircraft. From 20°F (−7°C) the thermometer can plunge in a matter of hours to −40°F (−40°C). It is remarkable that muskoxen and other Arctic animals, as well as man, can survive these desperate winters.

Mating takes place from late July to early September while the animals are still on the summer feeding ranges. At that time the lead or herd bull, whose dominance has been established after vicious ramming clashes, head-to-head pushing and wrestling, takes possession of a herd of several adult cows, along with

Although muskoxen cows may give birth to a calf every year, production is often low and irregular. The young are born during late spring and early summer when snow still covers the land and temperatures are well below freezing. (Photo by Dr. David R. Gray)

calves, yearlings, heifers and a few subordinate bulls. Throughout the rutting period the herd bull's dominance may be challenged by other bulls in the herd.

Although cows do not become sexually mature until they are 4 years old, during the rut the bulls will nevertheless "test" females as young as 2 years. Mature cows can produce a calf every year if conditions are right, but calf production is often low and irregular. There is no record of the birth of twins in the Canadian population. When the rut is over, the animals regroup for the winter into larger mixed herds of up to 60 or more.

Calves are born from late April to early June when the snow is still deep and the temperature may still be very low. Although they emerge with a heavy coat of fur, they must be dried immediately by the mother to prevent freezing. Within minutes they can stand upright and within hours they can move with the herd. Their mothers' milk nourishes them for the first few weeks, but soon after birth they begin to feed on vegetation as well. Calves suckle regularly during their first summer. Some suckle during the entire first year, but this is discouraged by the mother, especially if in the meantime a new calf has been born.

Field studies have shown that bulls tend to be aggressive throughout all seasons, but particularly so in late summer. The physical confrontations can be exciting entertainment to those who observe them. Almost as if they were conforming to some sort of Marquis of Queensberry rules, the battle lines are usually drawn between two evenly matched bulls. At the sound of the gong, so to speak, the combatants rub their pre-orbital glands against their forelegs, and in a slow, strutting style approach each other until they are virtually face to face. Seconds later both back slowly away, with heads swinging from side to side. Then they charge in a head-on clash, the impact of which can sometimes be heard a mile away. This wondrous performance is repeated a number of times and then, if both combatants are still aggressive, a more vicious pushing or wrestling match follows.

One or both animals may sustain injuries ranging from superficial to severe. Sometimes the tip of a horn is broken—a permanent reminder of a battle won or lost. Generally the defeated one takes off and joins another herd or wanders about alone.

Studies carried out in recent years at the High Arctic Research Station, established in 1968 on Bathurst Island, N.W.T., by the National Museum of Natural Sciences and the Polar Continental Shelf Project, have substantially broadened our knowledge of muskoxen and have enabled scientists to counter a good deal of faulty information that had accumulated about the species.

Dr. David R. Gray, Associate Curator of Vertebrate Ethology at the National Museum of Natural Sciences, spent the winter of 1970-71 at the station and his published findings have been invaluable. Of particular importance are his observations of muskox behavior in defense formations—a behavior pattern seen when the animals are under attack by wolves or other natural enemies, or disturbed by low-flying aircraft. Even in the most recent literature, this defense formation has been erroneously described.

It is accurate to say that when forced to assume the defense formation, the animals' first concern is to protect their rears. A single muskox will always try to back up against a boulder or an incline, and two or more will form a line facing the enemy, with their flanks or rumps pressed together. But, as Dr. Gray has written, "when the threat comes from above as is the case of aircraft disturbance or when the enemy on the ground circles the herd, a rough, solid circle is formed."

The common belief is that only the bulls form the circle, with the cows and calves contained within it. Dr. Gray's studies show that the circle most frequently is made up of *both* sexes, with the calves pressed close to their mothers' sides for protection. Both bulls and cows will leave the formation to charge attacking wolves.

Another important observation recorded by Dr. Gray is that low-flying aircraft can pose serious threats to muskoxen. Numerous ground observations have shown that the animals may stampede *after* the passing of aircraft and that young calves, if left behind and unprotected, become easy prey for wolves. Stampeding, he also reports, can lead herds away from areas of rich vegetation to areas where food is less abundant.

As man moves farther and farther north with his aircraft, snowmobiles, drilling rigs and the like in his search for oil, gas and minerals, the future of muskoxen becomes more and more beset by hazards. The Thelon Game Sanctuary, established in 1927 in the central Barrens of the mainland, is the only large area where both muskoxen and their habitat are fully protected. It is not too soon to pass additional legislation to assure the survival of these wonderful Arctic mammals.

Ovis canadensis

Bighorn Sheep

Scattered throughout the western mountain ranges of North America are six species, and nearly 40 races, of wild sheep. Of these, two are found in our region — the bighorn sheep (*O. canadensis*) and the thinhorn sheep (*O. dalli*), and each in turn has several subspecies. The two subspecies of the bighorn sheep are the Rocky Mountain bighorn (*O. c. canadensis*) and the California bighorn (*O.c. californiana*).

Descendants of mammals that evolved some 2.5 million years ago during the Pleistocene era, wild sheep reached this continent about 100,000 years ago from the Old World, during an interglacial period when dry land joined what is now Siberia and Alaska. Time, as reckoned in "eras," "periods," and "ages" is mind-boggling. For example, the Pleistocene was not an age of constant ice, but one of perhaps a dozen alternating cycles of ice advances and warm "interglacials" extending over the most recent four million years or so of Earth's geological history. It was during this period that many changes of importance to mammals, including man himself, occurred: many mammals became extinct and new types evolved.

Dr. Valerius Geist, of the University of Calgary, reminds us that between the extinction of the dinosaurs and the arrival of the modern Eurasian mammals lie some 70 million years. During that time America evolved its *own* fauna. Later there were also periodic exchanges of mammals between this continent and Asia — exchanges accelerated by the Ice Ages. Sheep and their kind were among the last of the species to migrate from Asia to America.

Wild sheep adapted well to the North American climate and terrain, although their ranges and densities of population have changed as a result of human incursions. Nonetheless bighorns are still found as far south as the tip of Baja California. The thinhorn sheep are the only representatives of the sheep in Yukon and Alaska. Both North American species of wild sheep have close relatives in Siberia.

The best known of the sheep group is the Rocky Mountain bighorn, which is commonly seen where highways cut through the mountains of western Canada and the United States. They are often seen just west of Banff, Alberta, on the trans-Canada highway and along the Banff-Jasper highway. The Rocky Mountain bighorn is larger and paler in color, and its horns are more

The tip of the horn is often "broomed" off in older bighorn rams. (Photo by Dr. David R. Gray)

These handsome little animals are 2-week-old bighorn sheep. (Photo by J. C. Holroyd)

3½ in (8.9 cm) long

Bighorn sheep

covers the rump, and there is also white around the mouth and nostrils. The hide is covered with two layers of hair, the undercoat being short, thick and wool-like, and the outer coat being longer, thicker and coarser. Sheep are darkest in late summer and early fall when they are growing their new winter coats.

As in other members of the Bovidae family, the hooves of the bighorn are cloven and the foot pads are rough, thus giving good traction in steep and rocky ranges. Ram bighorns weigh an average 250 pounds (114 kg), but larger specimens may weigh as much as 280 pounds (127 kg). The average weight of ewes is 130 to 150 pounds (60-70 kg), and exceptional ones may go as high as 200 (90 kg). A commonly accepted report that one Alberta ram *dressed out* at 365 pounds (166 kg) is considered the figment of someone's imagination.

Bighorns are grazing animals, and throughout their mountain habitat they live on grasses and forbs, their favorites being bluegrass, junegrass and wheatgrass. When they change to browsing, it is usually because their normal feed is not available.

Although late November and early December is the usual rutting period, in some areas mating may begin as early as October and carry on through December. Females become sexually mature between 2 and 3 years, and the rams between 15 and 30 months.

Dr. Geist has carried out comprehensive field studies of three kinds of wild sheep: the Rocky Mountain bighorn, in Banff National Park, the Stone's sheep, in the Cassiar Mountains, northern British Columbia, and the Dall's sheep, in the St. Elias Range, Yukon. These studies (*Mountain Sheep—A Study in Behavior and Evolution*, University of Chicago Press, 1971) reveal a social behavior among mountain sheep that, as he describes it, "must come as a painful surprise to anyone who applies our moral codes to animal behavior...for there is little in sheep behavior our society would condone cheerfully." Reprehensible though their conduct may be (by human standards) Dr. Geist shows understanding and reminds us that "it is a time-tested, evolutionary success and illustrates one way in which highly aggressive animals can live together with a minimum of harm to each other."

The male herds, which isolate themselves for most of the year from the herds of females and immature young, are homosexual, the dominant ram simulating the sex act and the subordinate ram simulating the role of the receptive female. But contrary to normal custom even in heterosexual relationships, the dominant ram

tightly curled than those of the California bighorn.

Bighorns were first recorded by science in 1804 when Duncan McGillivray, a companion of the explorer David Thompson who was doing survey work in Canada's Rocky Mountains, shot one above the Bow River just east of Banff. Lewis and Clark recorded in their journals for 1806 that they had seen bighorns — "animals of immense agility."

The most remarkable feature of these mammals is their high spiraled horns, which swing back and outwards from the crown to form a near-circle, ending just below the eyes in sharply curved tips. In large specimens the horns, brown in color, have been known to reach a weight of 25 to 35 pounds (11-16 kg). The horns of the female are smaller and less curved.

The bighorn is a large, rather heavy-set animal with a straight back, slender legs, long narrow muzzle, a small dark tail and short pointed ears. Its eyes are large, and it is beardless. The pelage is not unlike that of the deer, but varies in color depending on habitat. A typical specimen may be described as mainly brown, turning to white on the belly and inside of the legs. A large white patch, which accentuates the small tail,

This bighorn ram carries a superb set of high-spiraled horns. The species was first recorded by science in 1804 when one was shot near Banff, Alberta. (Photo by Dr. Valerius Geist)

reserves the right to *act* sexually. The subordinate's role is to act *aggressively* — in other words, to get the "action" going.

Throughout the months of self-imposed isolation from the ewes and juveniles, rams frequently vie for positions of dominance — an interaction that becomes almost frantic when intermingling again occurs during the October to December period of rutting, or when a large, strange ram joins the group.

The mating period is a time of periodic quarreling and physical combat. Although the sex drive becomes almost a craze in the rams, a peculiar behavior pattern is that they frequently court each other! Whatever sex attracts them until natural mating takes place with the ewes, the key to success is dominance, and from time to time over a period of two months the sounds of fighting echo and re-echo throughout the vastness of the mountains. Real fights resulting in broken horns and bodily injury do occur, but they are rare.

The duels take many forms and seem to follow established patterns. The common attack is the one in which two rams, standing first side by side in opposite directions, tap sideways at each other with a front hoof. After repeated strikes of this kind, they back away about 20 feet, still facing each other. Running on their hind legs they then charge, at the last moment dropping on all fours to crash head on with a vicious impact. These battles may be brief or may last for hours, and not infrequently horns are broken, there are bloody gashes, and skulls are fractured. Horns, once broken off, are never replaced.

The normal time of gestation of bighorn sheep is 170 to 180 days and the young, weighing 6 to 11 pounds (3-5 kg), are born in sheltered, isolated places away from the herd. Geist reports that there are no strong mother-lamb bonds, and although suckling may continue for 4 to 6 months, whatever emotional ties remain (or ties based mainly on suckling) soon disappear after that and the lamb begins an adult life. By the time winter arrives they are only about a quarter less the size of their mothers and may weigh 80 or so pounds (36 kg).

Like some other members of the Bovidae family, sheep are spectacularly agile in coping with the rugged mountain terrain, but whereas goats are climbers rather than jumpers or runners, sheep run and jump. The principal enemies of mountain sheep are wolves, coyotes, grizzly bears and wolverines, but probably the most dangerous of all is man himself. Trophies are still eagerly sought by sportsmen with high-powered rifles and telescopic sights—weapons that, in the hands of experts, render most animals virtually defenseless except for the protection their own rugged environment affords them.

If spared starvation, the predation of natural enemies, including man, the ravages of disease, death in conflict with each other, and accidents through rockslides and avalanches, rams may reach an age of 20 years and ewes an age of 24 years. The average, however, is considerably lower, probably 9 to 10 years, for those that reach adulthood. There is a high mortality among infants.

*   *   *

While wild sheep have managed to hold their own throughout their range, some types have either disappeared or have been substantially reduced in numbers. The Badlands bighorn of the United States (*O.c. auduboni*) has become extinct, while the population of Cali-

fornia bighorn (*O.c. californiana*) qualifies it as an endangered species.

California bighorn differ from the Rocky Mountain bighorn in that their overall covering is darker, they have less white on the face, and there is a more open curl to their horns. Some races are said to have a longer than normal mating season, but this has not been confirmed. Here, as in most species, the differences between subspecies are not evident to most people.

Thinhorn Sheep

Thinhorns live north of the bighorns in the mountainous west of North America. The differences between the thinhorn sheep and the bighorn lie not in their horns alone, but in their size, body covering, and in several other distinctive morphological characteristics. Behavioral patterns, habitat preferences and mating are also dissimilar.

There are three distinctive races or subspecies: *Ovis dalli dalli*, the well known Dall's sheep; *O.d. stonei*, the Stone's sheep; and *O.d. kenaiensis*, the Kenai sheep. The latter is a white sheep, virtually identical to the Dall's, and is found on Alaska's Kenai Peninsula, which juts out in the Gulf of Alaska between Prince William Sound and Cook Inlet. All three are apparently much the same except for superficial and variable coloration and some anatomical measurements of interest to scientists.

Ovis dalli dalli
Dall's Sheep

High up the almost vertical walls of the South Nahanni River's First Canyon are a score of ancient caves, some of which snake their way into the very heart of the Tlogotsho Mountains. A few years ago scientists who penetrated far into one of the caves found the remains of about 90 Dall's sheep. Carbon dating of some of the bones showed them to be about 2,000 years old.

How the sheep got there in such large numbers, and what caused them to die there, remains unsolved. What is abundantly clear, however, is that we have as yet removed only a thin veneer of the heavy layer of mystery covering the evolution of the far north and its fauna and flora.

The South Nahanni is one of many northwestern

3½ in (8.9 cm) long

Dall's sheep (shown here) and Stone's sheep are also known as "thinhorns." They inhabit the mountains of western North America and frequent alpine meadows close to precipitous, rocky escape areas. (Photo by Bill Lowry)

Thinhorn sheep

areas where Dall's are found. Their heaviest concentration in Canada is in the Yukon Territory. In the Northwest Territories they inhabit the Mackenzie ranges west of the Mackenzie River. They also occur over a wide area in Alaska.

On a rafting trip down the South Nahanni a few years ago, my companions and I had frequent glimpses of these sheep in the Ragged Range near Rabbitkettle Lake and at about the 1,500-foot (460 m) level near the Flat River. The sight of them stirred the protoplasm in a way I had never experienced before, for there is an emotional mystique about these marvelous creatures — their natural majesty, their wonderful curled horns and their pure white coats, all accentuated by the remoteness of their environment.

Three of our party — my son Mike and his friends Ken Palmer and Karl Norbeck — were determined to achieve a "close encounter" and on a rest day near the Flat River they left camp to climb a slope where Dall's had been seen the day before. In an alpine meadow at 1,000 feet (300 m) they encountered a group of about six and, being downwind, were able to approach to

within 50 feet (15 m). It was all done very stealthily, for Mike was shooting 16 mm moving picture film and wanted close-ups. When a couple of hundred feet of film had been exposed, the three stood up, expecting the sheep to run away immediately. But contrary to all reports that they "spook" easily, the animals remained where they were, one or two looking at the hikers while the others continued to graze. They moved only after a couple of loud shouts and a bit of arm waving, thus proving not always to be the skitterish animals they are said to be.

These white sheep rank among the most prized of North America's big game animals. Hunters regard their handsome heads, with their sleek curved horns, as more impressive than those of the Rocky Mountain bighorn. To kill one in the remoteness of the far north rates as a rather special achievement, for the hunt calls for wilderness skills, patience and an endurance that comes only from top physical condition. Aside from the trophy head, the flesh (even during the rutting season) is said to be delicious. Years ago, when market hunting was legal in the Yukon, cuts of sheep sold for 50 cents a pound in Whitehorse, twice the price of cuts of moose and caribou!

The Dall's sheep is smaller than the bighorn, and its face is shorter and more pointed. The horns, with well scored annual growth rings, are the color of dried lemon peel and more slender. The hooves are also yellowish. Body coloring is over-all white, sometimes with black hairs on the tail. During the mating season, the animal is ragged in appearance and its hair frequently dirty looking. A mature ram will weigh about 200 pounds (90 kg) and the female somewhat less.

The habitats of Dall's sheep are alpine meadows and open ridges adjacent to precipitous, rocky escape areas. There, sometimes in herds of 50 or more ewes and lambs, the rams having segregated themselves and moved to other meadows, they graze on grasses and sedges. In the winter, rams, ewes and yearlings descend to lower levels.

The mating season begins about the middle of November and continues to the middle of December, and in about six months the single lambs are born. If they are able to survive their first year, their chances of a long life are good.

In the spring the herds move to snow-free areas, frequently as much as 40 miles (64 km) away, where there are new vegetation and salt licks. As summer progresses, and the snow-line retreats, the sheep move to higher meadows and ridges and these are sometimes at the very lip of large icefields. Such a one was reported by Geist, the outskirts of the St. Elias Range in the Yukon where "Dall's sheep roam in large bands over dry, dusty mountain slopes in sight of the huge glacier that stretches for hundreds of miles and fills the interior of the range."

Man has perhaps been the most serious enemy of Dall's sheep, but during movements across the alpine tundra on their way to winter ranges, they are subject to attack by wolves. Other predators are grizzly bears, lynx, wolverines and coyotes.

Ovis dalli stonei

Stone's Sheep

This subspecies is considered to be a blood brother of the Dall's but is quite different in coloring. In fact, Geist describes it as looking, "with its white rump, belly, leg trimmings, gray head and neck and black body, like a Dall's sheep in evening dress. It is a most attractive animal." But coloring and patterning vary greatly and range from black to silver, brown, yellowish or pure white. The muzzle is always white and the rump carries a white patch. The horns are generally

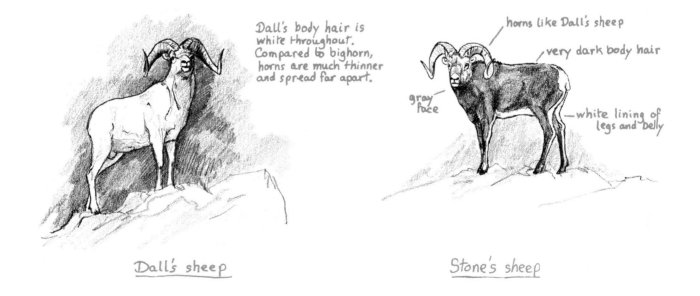

Dall's body hair is white throughout. Compared to bighorn, horns are much thinner and spread far apart.

Dall's sheep

horns like Dall's sheep

very dark body hair

gray face

white lining of legs and belly

Stone's sheep

Handsome Dall's sheep, such as this fine specimen, are highly prized by sportsmen. Some trophy hunters claim their sleek, curved horns are more impressive than those of the bighorn. (Photo by Dr. Valerius Geist)

dark brown, and the age rings are prominent. In some regions, animals intermediate in appearance between Dall's and Stone's sheep are called Fannin or saddleback. Behavioral patterns—habitat, feeding, mating—are similar to the Dall's.

Stone's sheep, the last of the Canadian sheep to be found and described by science, live in the wildest parts of northern British Columbia—north of the Peace and Skeena rivers, east of the Coast Range glaciers, and east to the foothills of the Rockies. It was named in 1897 for Andrew Stone of Montana, who donated three specimens to the American Museum of Natural History. Stone shot them near the Stikine River.

FAMILY ANTILOCAPRIDAE

Antilocapra americana
Pronghorn

Hundreds of thousands of years before man invented the heliograph, a signaling system able to be seen for a distance of several miles had evolved in a mammal living only in North America. The mammal was the pronghorn, an amazing creature smaller than most mature deer, that in scores of millions used to range the rolling prairies of this continent from Canada to Mexico.

The "heliograph" of the pronghorn is a large double patch of hair on the rump. By means of remarkable muscular controls, it can be flared instantly into a reflective white disk. When activated it serves as an effective means of communication, primarily to warn others of impending danger. Scores of motorists traveling along rural roads as well as busy highways of the Canadian and United States midwest have seen this phenomenon. My own experience was unforgettable.

A trip across the continent in 1978 took us westward through the southeastern part of Alberta. It was open rolling country. At one point as we drove over a rise, six browsing pronghorns in a field about 500 yards ahead and to our right suddenly assumed a position of alert. Their rump patches, often called rosettes, reflected brightly in the morning sun. But that was not all. The animals stayed where they were as we came abreast of them—legs stiff, heads high, large black eyes glistening in the light—seemingly unafraid even as we slowed to a stop to watch them. All but one then resumed browsing.

When we began moving on, that animal moved with us, increasing its gait as we accelerated. Periodically making long, graceful leaps, it was still alongside when our speedometer registered 47 miles (75 km) an hour. It kept this up for at least 2 miles (3 km). Then, in a sudden burst of speed and a series of remarkable leaps, it crossed the road in front of us and in an instant turned around to stare at us as we went by. We had seen at first hand three of the pronghorn's notable characteristics: its legendary "heliograph," its speed and its curiosity.

Actually the 47-mile-an-hour race between us was normal. Although reports of maximum speeds vary, Geoff Taff of Foremost, Alberta, who has clocked a group running at about 60 miles (97 km) an hour, records one incident in which a pronghorn doe attained a speed estimated by him as being nearly 70 miles (112 km) an hour! This compares with the speed of Africa's cheetah, which has the reputation of being the fastest mammal in the world.

The pronghorn's running is a marvelously smooth and seemingly effortless movement, especially when it is punctuated by graceful bounds of 15 feet (5 m) or more. But speed is an inherited capability, for even 2-week old fawns can reach 35 miles (56 km) an hour. They often do this when, perhaps in their sheer joy of being alive, they romp with other youngsters in the herd.

Although pronghorns can leap high and for considerable lengths, they almost always crawl *under* fences (even if the low strand is only a foot or so above ground) rather than jump over them. They do this without any apparent loss of speed.

Pronghorns are noted for the way the white hairs on the rump can be flared into a reflective disk. (Photo by Bill Lowry)

The pronghorn occupies a special place in North American animal life. Fossil remains leave little doubt that many present-day mammals descend from ancestors that reached this continent during the Pleistocene epoch perhaps a million or so years ago, by way of the land bridge that once connected Siberia and Alaska. But the pronghorn is different. It evolved on this continent. Scientists believe that the present mammal is a descendant of many types, some of which were only about 2 feet (60 cm) high at the shoulder and some of which carried horns much larger and shaped differently than those of today.

Although traditionally it has been placed in the Antilocapridae family, recent anatomical work carried out by taxonomists suggests that it actually belongs to the Bovidae family, sheep, goats and muskoxen. Dr. Peter T. Bromley, a graduate of the University of Calgary and an authority on pronghorns, has taken a fresh look at the racial status of this mammal. In a personal communication, he writes that "the common ancestor for African antelopes and American pronghorns lived long before the emergence of the Bering land bridge in the Pleistocene. Perhaps such an ancestor lived at a time when North American and *western* Europe were

connected. In the late Eocene and early Miocene (perhaps 50 millions years ago) the climate of the northern hemisphere was warmer and more humid than today. At this time deciduous, broad-leaved forests extended from eastern China to western Europe and all across North America. Perhaps a small, forest-dwelling bovid lived in this general habitat. Then as the continents drifted apart and grasslands evolved independently on the continents in response to a general cooling and drying of the world climate, the astonishing array of American and African antelopes evolved during the Miocene and Pliocene. Climatic changes were more severe in North America than in Africa during the late Pliocene and Pleistocene. Consequently, extinction of large mammals was more common in America than in Africa. We are left with one plains antelope, while in Africa many species survive."

Dr. Bromley emphasizes that the foregoing is speculative. He expresses the hope, however, that before long someone will discover the missing link between the Old World bovids and the New World pronghorns.

A subject of much scientific study is the unusual nature of the pronghorn's horns. These grow upward directly above the eyes out of a frontal bone, and emerge as bony cores around which grow black outer sheaths. Averaging 10 inches (25 cm) in length, they carry one forward-pointing prong about half way up and a higher prong that curves backward to a rather sharply pointed tip. It is these outer sheaths, which recent research has shown to be a solid substance made up of a modified form of skin growth, that are shed each year. For many years literature has wrongly described this growth as one of consolidated hairs, although hairs are present around the base and some even grow inside and through it. Incidentally, shedding also occurs in members of the deer family, but what they shed are antlers—very different structures.

The mating behavior of the pronghorn is sometimes misunderstood. Whereas bovids generally establish "harems," each mature pronghorn male claims a "territory" of up to half a square-mile containing his band of does and fawns and better than average food supplies. Meanwhile the 1-, 2- and sometimes 3-year-old bachelors band together and roam around the periphery of the territory. Should any of them enter the area they are immediately chased off by the defending buck. This territorial and "band roving" situation continues until after the rut. In late October the horn sheaths are cast off and both sexes band together into winter herds. They remain together until March, when food again becomes plentiful and accessible.

The territorial pattern does not apply, however, in arid, short-grass prairies or cold deserts where forage is scattered and not quickly replenished. In such situations, territories would not be practical, so free-moving harems are established by dominant males.

Mating takes place in the latter part of September and early October. One observer has described the bucks as "amorous, combative and possessive." The following May or June twins are born weighing 4 to 10 pounds (1.8-4.5 kg) each. They are able to stand and nurse an hour after birth and grow so rapidly that by the third month they are nearly the size of their mothers.

The twins are dropped by the mother in separate bedding-down places, often as far as 50 to 70 yards (45-65 m) apart. The separation gives the mother a better

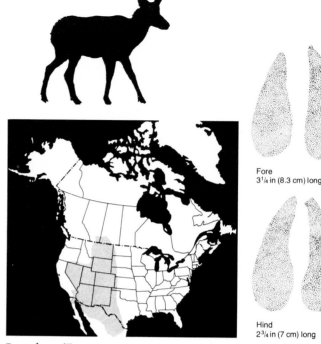

Fore
3¼ in (8.3 cm) long

Hind
2¾ in (7 cm) long

Pronghorn (Former range more extensive)

chance to protect them from predators, particularly coyotes, wolves and eagles, their most dangerous enemies. Fawns, by the way, are practically odorless for several days after birth, a period long enough to ensure their safety while they gain sufficient strength to join the herds.

Pronghorn fawns are not spotted, as are deer fawns, but carry a coat of gray-brown in which the pigments of later coloring show faintly. What will soon become the famous heliograph is at this stage dull in color and tipped with grayish brown. Nonetheless, a couple of hours after birth the rump muscles are strong enough to flare the rosette.

Throughout the winter, as mixed herds, pronghorns move to areas that not only provide the best food but also offer the best opportunity to spot encroaching predators. At this time their summer coat of fine hair has been replaced by a thick covering of coarse hair that provides insulation against the severe cold and high winds that sweep the Prairies. This coat is shed during March and April.

Most ungulates use their forefeet to paw through

horn sheath

lining tissue

bone core

male pronghorn with one horn shed

Pronghorn

Male has black cheek patch.

When pronghorn is alarmed, the long rump hairs are bristled, producing a white flash.

snow for food, but pronghorns are less inclined to do this. If snow hides forage plants, they seek other places where the ground is bare and the food is more readily available. Some herds spend all their lives in the same area if food is plentiful, but others travel as much as 50 miles (80 km) to and from their winter and summer ranges. Food is made up of forbs such as clover, alfalfa, lupin and wild pea vine, and browse such as sagebrush and saltbrush. Grasses such as timothy, foxtail, bluegrass and sedge are also included in their diet.

All living creatures require water to survive. It is interesting, however, that while most animals drink intermittently, most pronghorns do so only once each 24 hours. Some, however, are said to go without water for a week at a time, while others never drink in the conventional way but rely on moisture in such plants as cacti.

Pronghorns have more scent glands than are found in most other animals. These glands are on the rump patches, on the face at the base of each horn, on the lower back, and on each hind leg near the hock. There are even small glands between the toes of each foot. It

is thought that the glands on the rump and feet give off signals understood by other animals in the herd. The largest glands in the bucks are at the base of each horn; these are most active during the rutting season and are in some way a part of sexual behavior. One gland, the subauricular, is particularly active during the rutting season and, according to Dr. Bromley, "it is used to mark vegetation as territorial signposts, much as we would erect fences."

The pronghorn is one of the most beautiful of animals. Barely 3 feet (1 m) high at the shoulder and weighing not much more than 140 pounds (64 kg), it has a large head, long pointed ears and eyes that are bigger than those of a horse. The body is chunky, the legs are short and slender, and the tail is short and pointed. It walks on the tips of its two-toed, pointed hooves. Females are a little smaller.

Complementing the attractive body conformation is a color pattern reflecting nature at her creative best. Pronghorns have a distinctive combination of color bands, horn development, and neck, mane and tail coloration. A typical specimen would be light tan or brownish-red on the back and on the sides of the legs, white on the belly and lower part of the neck, and, of course, white on the rump rosettes. Bands of alternating tan and white show below the black-tipped ears. Unlike the female, the male has a black patch on the lower jaw just below each eye; these patches, which readily identify the sexes, increase in size as the animal grows older.

A few hundred years ago, before Europeans devastated the pronghorn as they did the bison, North American prairies must have sparkled on sunny days with "heliograph" flashes. A few generations later, as civilization spread across the western continent, the pronghorn declined drastically. In 1908 it was estimated that fewer than 20,000 animals remained. The reduction had been abetted by a very severe winter the year before; cold and heavy snows wiped out whole herds.

Alarmed that the pronghorn was in danger of extinction, governments on both sides of the border took remedial action. In Canada, in 1915, the National Antelope Park was established at Nemiskan, southern Alberta, and this remained a protective area until 1947. The park status of this land was terminated that year when it became evident the herds had been restored in numbers sufficient to assure their safety. Today it is estimated that pronghorns in Canada number more than 31,000. In the United States they have increased over much of their former range and are game animals of considerable importance in most western states. Limited hunting is permitted in Canada. In both countries populations are monitored carefully and the number of animals harvested by hunters is regulated on the advice of wildlife biologists.

Beautiful in appearance and fleet of foot, the pronghorn is one of the most inquisitive of animals. Its hearing and sense of smell are highly developed, it is an accomplished swimmer, and it has wide-angle vision that alerts it to movements as far as 2 miles (3 km) away. Its curiosity, despite its timidity, contributed to its near-extinction years ago; although the pronghorn is provisionally removed from the endangered species list, the trait remains, with its attendant risks. Those pronghorns that manage to survive the precarious first few weeks of life may live up to 13 years, which for most ungulates is considered to be a long lifespan.

FAMILY CERVIDAE

Rangifer tarandus
Caribou

About 20 million years ago, during the Miocene period, there evolved on this continent a group of mammals that were the progenitors of the present-day North American deer. There is no way of knowing how many forms of deer developed during that long period of time, but there must have been numerous species and subspecies. Eventually, however, this great variety of deer in North America became simplified by many extinctions until it leveled off at the three distinct groups recognized today: 1) the white-tailed deer and the mule deer, which carry the genus name *Odocoileus*, 2) moose, which carry the genus name *Alces*, and 3) caribou, which carry the genus name *Rangifer*. Elk (wapiti), which carry the genus name *Cervus*, are Old World deer. All belong to the family Cervidae, all are ungulates (even-toed animals), ruminants (cud chewers) and all have several subspecies.

There were many casualties during the evolutionary process, and among the primitive North American deer to become extinct was the 30-inch-long (77 cm) Blastomeryx. It had no antlers; instead, from near the front of the mouth there protruded large canine tusks. An equally grotesque European deer to disappear was Megaloceros, an Irish deer — often wrongly referred to as the "Irish elk" — whose antler spread, as shown in remains found in bog deposits, was as much as 11 feet (3.4 m) from tip to tip!

While North American deer were consolidating themselves on this continent, other animals were migrating back and forth across the Arctic land bridge which, from time to time during the long intermittent periods of glaciation, connected the Old World with the New. Among Old World species which took up residence in the New World were elk, muskoxen, plains and wood bisons, and bears, to name a few. But the New World, of course, had many indigenous species of its own — moose, camels and horses for example — and many of these in turn, traveled to the Old World where they settled in and are found today. This "two-way traffic" came to an end with the termination of the last great Ice Age and the return of the Bering Sea.

Of all species of large North American mammals,

Peary caribou are found only in the Canadian Arctic archipelago. Hunting pressure and northern development are contributing to their alarming decline in numbers. (Photo by Dr. David R. Gray)

few have been the subject of more controversy than has *Rangifer tarandus*, the caribou. These remarkable creatures are among the most advanced of the deer family, but just where they evolved is still a matter of conjecture. According to one authority, Dr. Valerius Geist, they could have originated in Alaska, in the mountains of northern Asia, or in the land corridor that once connected Eurasia and North America where the Bering Sea is now.

Bones found in deposits dating back about half a million years indicate that they made their first appearance in the middle Ice Ages. In any case, that caribou were known in Europe in ancient times is evident in rock paintings believed to date back to about the 25th millenium BC. Notable examples of these can be seen in the Tamgaly defile near Alma Ata in Kazakhstan, U.S.S.R., and in caves in the Dordogne district of southern France. In early times caribou adapted read-

ily to domestication and even today the nomadic Lapps, as well as other northern European people, use them as a source of milk and to pull sleds.

Caribou have also been a vital resource from the very beginning of human life in our own far north. They still are, although this dependency has lessened substantially with the impact of southern influences. Many thousands of Eskimo, however, from Alaska in the west to Baffin Island in the east, rely on caribou as an important source of food. The animals' hides are still used for some articles of clothing. Caribou are also important to the Indian people, especially those in the Northwest Territories, Ungava and Labrador. In Newfoundland, where, like fish, caribou have traditionally been a source of protein food, large numbers were harvested each year. Over-hunting was a major cause in reducing the caribou population in that province; there the numbers fell from about 40,000 animals in 1900 to about 2,000 in 1930. Management programs have since restored the herd to slightly more than 25,000.

The Swedish botanist Linnaeus (1707-78), originator of the binomial method of naming plants and animals in Latin, gave the caribou their first specific name. But as scientific study in the broad field of mammalogy became more sophisticated, taxonomists found what they believed were enough physiological differences in caribou throughout their whole northern circumpolar range to justify distinguishing several distinct species. This was followed by the naming of subspecies —so many, in fact, that some taxonomists were accused of splitting hairs.

About 30 years ago it was thought that four distinct species and nine subspecies were resident in Canada alone. Thanks to the work of such scientists as Hall, Kelson and Banfield however, there has been international acceptance of the thesis that all caribou, including those of Europe and Asia (where they are known as reindeer), are a single species, *Rangifer tarandus*, and that in North America there are four indigenous subspecies and one European transplant.

Acceptance of the single species thesis has helped to simplify matters, as has the fact that *R. tarandus* comprises two identifiable groups—the "barren-ground caribou" and the "woodland caribou." There remains, however, the complex problem of sorting out the subspecies within the two groups, with their various populations and their constantly changing migratory habits.

BARREN-GROUND CARIBOU

This group inhabits the far northern boreal forests and the Arctic tundra. The long treks of some of the herds from their winter feeding grounds to summer calving grounds are among the marvels of the animal world. These are the recognized barren-ground subspecies:

R. t. granti (Grant's caribou), found in the Yukon and Alaska. The combined population of all herds is about 330,000 animals.

One of the best known is the Porcupine herd, now numbering less than 110,000 animals, which winters in the forests of the interior of the Yukon and Alaska and which migrates each year to and from the Arctic coastal

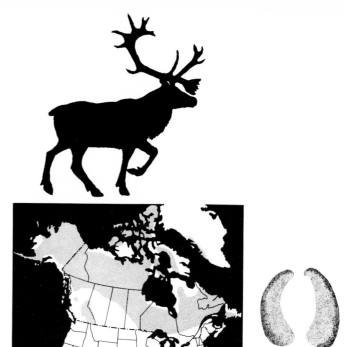

Caribou

Fore
5 in (13 cm) across
3—5 in (7.6—13 cm) long

plains along the Beaufort Sea and northeastern Alaska, a return journey (as the crow flies) of about 800 miles (1,287 km). In 1977 concern for the protection of the Porcupine herd played a major role in denying the application of an international consortium to build a natural gas pipeline from Prudhoe Bay, Alaska, to the Mackenzie Delta, thence along the Mackenzie Valley to southern Canada and the northern U.S. states.

R. t. groenlandicus (barren-ground caribou) wander about a range that now extends from southern Hudson Bay to the Mackenzie River. The total number of this subspecies, although greatly reduced in recent years, is estimated at about 700,000 animals.

R. t. pearyi (Peary caribou), indigenous to Canada, are found only in the Canadian Arctic Archipelago. *Peary Caribou, A Status Report* (Gunn, Miller and Thomas), published in 1979 by the Committee on the Status of Endangered Wildlife in Canada, states that the "purest stock is found on the western Queen Elizabeth Islands, where the population declined by about 90% between 1961 and 1974. A series of winters with crusted deep snow and groundfast ice restricted forage availability causing malnutrition that led to high winter mortality and zero or low reproduction. Their precarious existence in one of the harshest environments in the world is under additional pressure from hunting and disturbances associated with increasing industrial activities. Thus, the Queen Elizabeth Islands stock of Peary caribou should be recognized as 'endangered'." The report further states that due to heavy and increasing hunting pressure the populations on the mid-Arctic Prince of Wales and Somerset islands should be classified as "threatened."

About 20 years ago the total population of Peary caribou was slightly more than 24,000 animals. The herds today number less than 3,000. This subspecies is a small, pale animal with narrow, upright antlers.

R. t. tarandus (reindeer). A herd of this European subspecies, brought originally from Siberia to Alaska, was transplanted from that state to the Mackenzie Delta for the purpose of creating a caribou and muskoxen industry to improve the economic condition of the native people living there. The movement of these animals over 1,400 miles (2,254 km) of mountains, alpine slopes and tundra is one of the great epics of northern history. In an incredible forced march starting in December 1929 from Kotzehe Sound, 3,450 caribou began the long journey to a holding station north of the present town of Inuvik. Many died along the way, many were killed by predators or strayed from the herd, and many were born. In March 1935, 2,382 animals reached the destination. The name of Andrew Bahr, the Lapp herder who supervised the undertaking, will probably live as long as caribou roam the northern ranges. The herd prospered and today numbers about 15,000. The animals for nearly 50 years have provided greatly needed food and clothing for the native people. Pantocrin, a substance derived from their processed antlers, is used medically as a heart stimulant.

WOODLAND CARIBOU

There is only one subspecies, *R. t. caribou*. These animals, the largest of the species, are forest dwellers whose northern range extends to the Mackenzie Mountains in the Northwest Territories and Yukon as far north as the 65th parallel. Some races, such as those in Ungava, form large herds and migrate long distances. Others confine their annual movements to only a few miles — the distance from alpine meadows to wintering grounds at lower levels; or, at still lower levels, from more open flatlands to the protection of the forests.

Caribou

Caribou give the impression of being very large animals, but their bodies are actually not.

Antlers are developed by **both** sexes, which is not the rule in other deer.

Antlers in females are much smaller than in males. Some females do not produce antlers.

white neck mane

underside of hoof

Caribou hoof, as in moose, has a large surface to distribute the weight on soft ground and snow. Caribou hoof is more rounded.

At their best, the antlers of both male and female caribou are impressive. Note the wide sweep of the antlers on the bull at the right. (Photo by Dr. A. T. Bergerud)

Although not as numerous as they once were, herds are still found in all Canadian provinces (except Prince Edward Island, Nova Scotia and New Brunswick, where they have been extinct for more than 50 years) as well as in the Yukon and southeastern parts of the Northwest Territories. The total population today numbers about 243,000 animals.

Woodland caribou were at one time abundant in Ontario, but their range in that province has been seriously pushed back through predation, hunting and altered habitat. Contraction of a disease common in white-tailed deer, the parasitic worm *Parelaphostrongylus tenuis*, to which caribou are particularly susceptible, also contributed to the decline. They met a similar fate in Maine and Minnesota, where they are no longer present.

An isolated population—a herd of about 20 to 30 animals—has been able to survive in the Selkirk Mountains of southeastern British Columbia and in northern Idaho. A small woodland subspecies known as *R. t.*

dawsoni inhabited Graham Island in the Queen Charlottes, but it became extinct about 1910. Other populations live in the mountains of central and northern British Columbia.

*   *   *

In every significant respect but two, caribou are similar to other members of the Cervidae family.

One exception is that males *and* females carry antlers. But, as is typical in all forms of life, some caribou are different. While antlers are carried by nearly all females in northern populations, those in Ontario, Quebec and Newfoundland are frequently without them. Disregarding the exceptions, the presence of antlers in female caribou is unique among deer.

The second exception is the snapping or clicking sound which is made when the animals are walking or running. This curious characteristic is often audible at a considerable distance when large herds are on the move. It has yet to be fully explained, although most authorities attribute it to the slipping of tendons over sesamoid bones in the feet. This characteristic is sometimes noted in elk and red deer.

There are, of course, differences among caribou in

size, habitat, color patterns, dietary habits, antler development, herding, migration behavior and the like —differences to be expected in animals of such great numbers and occupying such vast and varied geographical areas.

Color patterns vary greatly in both woodland and barren-ground caribou and in their various populations. The general coloring, however, is clove-brown, except for the neck, mane and parts of the belly, which are creamy white. The face is a darker brown and the snout is whitish, as are the thick hairs inside the very small ears and the underside of the short tail. A band of white hair grows around the legs just above the hoofs. This overall coloring changes in the spring to a dirty, grayish-white. *R. t. groenlandicus*, whose environment for much of the year is marked by severe cold and darkness, are mostly white with bluish gray on the back.

As in most animals, the coat of the caribou adjusts to the seasons. The adult males are the first to molt and this change in pelage takes place in the spring and early summer. Then follows the molting of the yearlings and sub-adults, and finally the molting of the adult breeding females. The process, which for a time gives the animals a ragged, even unsightly appearance, is over by mid-summer, except for some breeding females whose molt may not be completed until late August. When the new winter pelage of soft, thick underfur and long stiff guard hairs grows in, the animals—especially the bulls, proudly carrying a great rack of polished antlers —are striking in appearance.

The antlers of the caribou, in both males and females, are handsome appendages when they are at their best. The main beam of a fully developed rack in a mature bull sweeps backward, outward and upward, spreads widely and ends in flattened palms. A single brow tine grows forward over the face and is "shovel" shaped; a second tine, also somewhat palmated, rises just above the brow tine and points in a more upward position. This description is a generalization, for there are great variations in caribou antlers—so much so that Banfield's studies of a thousand or so skulls have shown that no two sets are the same and that even "on any animal one [antler] is seldom the mirror image of the other."

The oft-repeated claim that caribou use the vertical palmated tine to shove away snow covering lichens and other ground food must not be taken too seriously. Aside from the fact that this tine never extends past the muzzle (which would make its use as a shovel an acro-

Caribou calves are born on windswept rocky uplands during May and June. Unhappily, 23 per cent or more die within their first month. (Photo by Dr. A. T. Bergerud)

batic achievement), the caribou's large front feet with their sharp-edged hooves do the job quite effectively.

Most references to caribou suggest that the animals are well equipped for the harsh and rugged environment they live in. This is not wholly true. One significant deficiency in their make-up is their inability to cope successfully with the fearsome flying insects so prevalent in the far north.

Fred Bruemmer, naturalist-author-photographer, has spent a good deal of his northern career in the study of this mammal. This is his graphic description of the annual warble fly infestation:* "While mosquitoes and black flies may harass the caribou, the insect they really fear is the warble fly, a rather attractive hirsute animal looking like a bumblebee that's been on a diet. It has a

---

*Another fly that causes panic among caribou is the nose fly, also a bee-like insect. The nose fly deposits eggs in the animals' nostrils and the maggots are not only very painful but in sufficient numbers may cause death.

loud, distinctive buzz and caribou react violently to this noise. They break into a frantic gallop, twitch and shake vehemently, and race off again in wild desperation. Apparently these evasive maneuvers do not help much, because nearly all adult caribou are infested with warble fly larvae. They tunnel along under the skin of the caribou, bore their way through it when full grown, drop to the ground and pupate, leaving the skin so full of holes and scars that it looks as if it has been peppered with buckshot. The Eskimos once regarded the inch-long, oval, cream-colored larvae as a gustatory treat, and Stefansson, ready to try anything, ate some and reported they tasted like gooseberries."

But in other ways caribou are indeed well adapted to their environment. Although not large in comparison with most other deer, they have long legs and disproportionately large, nearly round hooves which are splayed and often wider than they are long. The dew claws, which grow on either side of the legs, are large and close to the ground; they provide additional support for the animals, particularly when they are traveling on soft surfaces.

Changes of season are accompanied by marked changes in the structure of the hooves. In summer the outer edges shrink, exposing fleshy foot pads which bear the animals' weight and which are well suited for travel over boggy tundra and muskeg. In winter the pads shrink and hair grows between and over them for warmth and protection. The hooves now extend beyond the pads, and their outer edges, which are hard and sharp, facilitate travel over solid or slippery surfaces. The size and sharpness of the hooves also help the animals to dig through snow and crust for food. During migration, the hooves provide strong thrust as the caribou swim across lakes and rivers.

Wherever they may be and whatever the season, caribou are constantly on the move, grazing and browsing as they go, pausing only for longer periods when food resources are unusually plentiful. The most mobile, and in many respects the most interesting, are the barren-ground subspecies of Alaska and northwestern Canada. With the approach of spring different populations of these animals gather together in enormous numbers along the fringes of the boreal forests where they have spent the winter. Led usually by pregnant cows, yearlings and sub-adults, with adult males bringing up the rear, they begin their long journey to the calving grounds on the rough, inhospitable uplands in northern Yukon and northeastern Alaska, and the summer feeding valleys bordering the Beaufort Sea.

The movement of a caribou, to use a cliché, is sometimes a study in contradictions. One moment, as it walks at a slow pace, its head drooping, it looks awkward and disconsolate. Suddenly it will straighten up, lift its great antlered head high and move away at a regal trot, its legs raised high and moving in long fast strides. But a galloping caribou, which can sometimes reach speeds of 35 to 49 miles (56-79 km) an hour in short bursts, is again awkward-looking. When not moving, it is commonly seen with its head in a dejected, down position, looking, as one writer described it, like a "wildlife bum."

The caribou is a strong swimmer. Many lakes and rivers, some of the latter in spring flood, have to be crossed during the migration journey. Undeterred by currents or the distance to be traveled, the animal plunges in and the buoyancy of its heavy waterproof coat easily keeps it afloat. It can swim about 6 miles (10 km) an hour.

After weeks of travel through mountain passes, across lakes and swollen rivers, and over icefields and soggy tundra, the caribou of the Porcupine herd reach their first destination — the calving grounds. During the last week of May and the first two weeks of June the pregnant does gradually break away from the main herd. There, in the windswept rocky uplands, each gives birth to a single fawn. The youngsters weigh from 12 to 20 pounds (5-9 kg) and come into the world with a fawn-colored coat of crinkly fur-like hair.

The birth of a calf is a perilous time, particularly when the weather is severe. The mother, exhausted after her long trek and the ordeal of parturition, must work quickly to dry the coat of her youngster so it will attain its maximum insulation against sub-zero temperatures and penetrating winds. Newly-born calves are able to follow their mothers within an hour of their birth. Within 48 hours they have so adapted to their new environment that they are able to join and keep up with the main herd, even when rivers are to be crossed. Were it not for this high degree of *immediate* mobility, mortality among calves would be very high. Even so, Dr. A. T. Bergerud, one of North America's foremost authorities on *R. tarandus*, reports that 23 per cent or more of the calves die before one month of age.

The Porcupine herd returns to the meadows of the North Slope when the calving season is over. But it is not until August and September, when the insect season has ended, that they are able to build up the body fat needed for the long journey back to the wintering grounds and to help sustain them during the austere months ahead.

The annual rut occurs during October and early November when the migrations are nearly over and the animals are once again back in the area of the tree-line. Barren-ground caribou do not normally form harems for breeding purposes as do the woodland group. Instead, their selection of estrous females is on more of a "catch as catch can" basis. During this time, bulls of both subspecies are aggressive and short-tempered, and there is a good deal of rushing about, thrashing of trees, sparring and head-to-head pushing. Some snorting and heavy panting accompanies these performances, and some encounters end in death or serious injury to the combatants.

With the ending of the rut the animals return to a more placid relationship. The bulls, gaunt and bedraggled after their exhausting sexual encounters, soon move away from the females and gather into separate herds and, as they move about, they shed their antlers. Their main concern now is to restore the thick reserves of fat that were depleted during the rut, and this they do by feeding heavily on sedges and lichens. These may form their only diet, for by now the deciduous foods of summer—the leaves of willows, birches and aspens—are gone. Barren-ground caribou have a highly developed sense of smell and can detect the presence of food lying under as much as 7 inches (18 cm) of snow.

For the next few months, until it is time to regroup into large herds for the return journey to the calving grounds, the caribou live quietly in and along the edges of the boreal forests, constantly moving about in their quest for food. With the arrival of spring the long migration into the tundra will begin again, thus perpetuating a cycle of life as incredible as any to be found in all the wild kingdom.

Throughout all seasons of the year barren-ground and woodland caribou are aware of the constant, haunting presence of predators. Wolves follow the large herds wherever they go, searching for animals that are easy to kill; these include healthy animals, especially calves, as well as animals that are sick or old. By culling out so many of the weak and infirm, wolves in some areas serve an essential role in helping to keep caribou herds in healthy balance. Grizzly bears, lynx and wolverine are also predators to be reckoned with, as are—but only on rare occasions—golden eagles, which prey on very young calves.

Man is the caribou's second most serious predator—justifiably in the case of the native people and others who rely on the animals for food. But with the increasingly easier access to wilderness areas resulting from new transportation corridors and industrial development, big-game hunters are taking a heavier toll of the animals each year. Dr. Bergerud estimates that at one time there were three to five million caribou in North America; today, there are less than one million.

The "opening up" of the Canadian north and Alaska is perhaps inevitable, but whether it can be accomplished in such a way as to accommodate successfully both man and wildlife remains to be seen. New knowledge of the sensitive total biome is essential if safe and rational policies are to be evolved. The role of the wildlife specialist in this challenge has never been more vital.

To come across any big-game animal in the wild is an exciting experience, but nothing can equal the astonishing sight of thousands of migrating caribou. It was early May when, for the first time, I saw this phenomenon. I was on a mid-morning flight from the Prudhoe Bay oil complex and our route took us parallel with the North Slope, across the Brooks Range for a brief stop at Old Crow, a native settlement, then on to Inuvik in the Mackenzie Delta. Just north of Old Crow, at the start of the tree-line, we saw them. They formed a wide, almost unbroken line that stretched for miles. The estimates of the number of animals in the long trek ranged from 10,000 to 15,000 bucks, cows and yearlings.

There are those who have witnessed spectacles such as this from ground level and at close range, and I shall always envy their good fortune—while being grateful for my own. Dr. Bergerud summed up his own emotions appropriately when he wrote "such sights, or even knowledge thereof, add perspective to our lives, a tonic and humbling experience. Surely our stewardship on Earth requires our continued coexistence with this splendid animal."

Odocoileus hemionus

Mule Deer

The mule deer (*Odocoileus hemionus*) is a westerner, occurring from southeastern Alaska south as far as northern Mexico and Baja California. In Canada, it is present in southern Yukon and in the southern Northwest Territories east to Great Slave Lake, and across an extensive range from coastal British Columbia (islands and mainland) to southwest Manitoba. While it can be found in a variety of environments, including semi-arid desert regions, its favorite habitat is the edges of mountain forests from lower to middle elevations. Blacktailed and Sitka deer on the Pacific coast are two of the eleven distinct forms of *O. hemionus* recognized in North America.

A distant relative of the mule deer is the more widely-known white-tailed deer, *O. virginianus*, a more abundant animal found over an extensive range in southern Canada west to central British Columbia, and throughout most of the United States, Central America and northern South America.

The mule deer and the white-tailed differ physically in these respects: the mule deer is stockier, its ears are larger and its tail is cylindrical, shorter and black-tipped, while the tail of the white-tailed is long, bushy and fringed with white. The main beam of the antlers on each side of the mule deer's head branches into a "y" and each arm of the "y" forks again. The main beam of the white-tailed deer's antlers does not fork.

There are, of course, less obvious morphological differences, such as differences in shape and size of the metatarsal glands on the outer side of the lower legs. The pit of the orbital gland (ahead of the eye) is deeper in the mule deer and is reasonably diagnostic. The configuration of the skulls and nature of the teeth differ very little, however, and it is difficult to distinguish between the skulls of the two animals.

An interesting difference in the behavior of these deer is that the mule deer, when frightened, speeds away with its tail *down*, whereas in a similar situation white-tailed does and fawns often carry their tails up; buck white-tails do this less frequently.

The gait of the two deer, except in one mode, is quite different—and that exception is the gallop. Both gallop in a similar manner, and do so when chasing one another and when trying to escape from bothersome flies. In other modes the mule deer displays a fast, bouncing, stiff-legged action, whereas the white-tailed has a more loping style. The white-tailed is particularly adept at making long leaps, especially when clearing obstacles. Mule deer in a hurry make remarkable bounding jumps even when there is nothing in the way to be jumped over.

The average fully mature male mule deer of the Rocky Mountain race weighs between 200 and 250 pounds (90-115 kg) while does are appreciably smaller. The average length is 55 to 70 inches (140-180 cm), and the average height at the shoulder ranges from about 35 to 42 inches (90-107 cm). Bucks in rare instances reach a weight of around 400 pounds (180 kg).

The antlers are shed between mid-December and mid-January and new growth does not take place until early spring. At that time they appear as dark protrusions on the frontal bone of the head. Antlers, however, differ from true bone in that they are not nourished by internal blood vessels and nerves; their nourishment comes from a covering of tissue commonly referred to as "velvet." When this velvet dries in late summer, it is rubbed off, leaving the antlers hard and shiny.

The animal is now at its majestic best, its antlers full grown and its coat thick, sleek and beautifully patterned. Its body covering is predominantly grayish (tawny or yellowish-brown during summer). The face between the eyes and the black, moist muzzle, is whitish, as are the cheeks, the insides of the ears, the lower part of the legs, and the rump. The short tail is also white, except for the tip, which is black. A dark patch is present on the forehead.

This description, however, must be considered as a generalization. It cannot, in any event, be considered as constant for the mule deer which range over a wide area of the Rocky Mountains. Dr. Geist found that individuals in just one area showed great diversity in coat markings and body conformation. For example, in some deer the rump patch was white while in others it was yellow; some deer had a single white throat patch while many had a distinct second patch. The hair on the tip of the tail in some was black, in some it was white, and in others it was white with a mixture of black. These diversities, he found, were of a permanent nature.

Dr. Geist's studies of mule deer have substantially modified a number of traditional beliefs concerning behavioral customs of this animal. The modifications, too numerous to list here, include such matters as feeding, predator avoidance, group etiquette, communication, dominance displays, courting and mating.

Mule deer are westerners. Their name derives from the fact that their ears are at least two-thirds the length of their heads. (Photo by Dr. Valerius Geist)

Whether the studies reflect commonalty in mule deer behavior elsewhere throughout their North American range will require further research, but the Rocky Mountain range is a large one containing many animals and the findings must, therefore, be considered of prime scientific interest.

Mule deer mate between late October and early December (most commonly between November 15 and December 10) and the young—usually twins, but sometimes one or three—are born in early June. The female's period of oestrus lasts for about 24 hours, and should she not mate successfully she will come into "heat" again. This accounts for the fact that fawns are sometimes born between March and November.

The courting behavior of all members of the Cervi-dae family is closely associated with the urinating of the females. During courting the buck "tests" the female's urine by mouthing the ground cover she has doused. This "testing" procedure continues until the urine, presumably by taste, indicates that the female has reached oestrus and is ready for breeding. This pattern, of course, is not constant: males, being polygamous, "canvass" other females; females, unless restrained, may be attracted to other, more dominant males. In any case, it is always the female's urine that determines the proper time of breeding.

Before the rutting season bucks often spar with each other—contests characterized by engaging antlers and pushing back and forth. These are not fights, but "sporting" engagements in which injury is rare, and in which there are no "winners" or "losers." Even during the rutting season itself, fighting to establish dominance is rare and differences are most often settled quickly when one "out-intimidates" the other. When serious fights do occur, the main weapons are the antlers, and wounds are sometimes inflicted. Front legs are used as weapons only when antlers are absent or are in the early stages of growth. Mule deer, unlike moose, do not kick with their hind feet, nor do they bite as elk may do. Success in fights not only proves superiority, but also increases the possibility that only the strongest and healthiest males will father the new generations.

Another rutting behavior of mule deer is what is known as horning. This is carried out by rubbing an antler against bushes, tree trunks, hanging branches and the like and is believed to be sexually stimulating. The sound of this action, when done vigorously, serves as a signal of male dominance. It occasionally attracts other bucks.

When the breeding season is over, the bucks gradually leave the female ranges and about a month later they shed their antlers. With the coming of winter, however, deer of both sexes and all age groups migrate to lower mountain levels. There, in mixed herds, they gather in areas where food is available and the snow covering is soft and not too deep. At this time, their antlers having been shed, it is almost impossible to differentiate bucks from does.

The diet of the mule deer for the next few months consists of a wide variety of fibrous foods, among them fallen leaves, twigs of willow, dogwood, aspen, Douglas fir and western cedar, salal and shriveled fruit of snowberry. In coastal areas, where there is a heavy rainfall, thick growths of shrubbery provide nutritious fod-

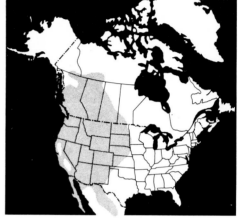

3¼ in (8.3 cm) long

Mule deer

der, especially in very old and open forests as well as in burns and logged-off areas.

But survival depends on more than food. It depends also on shelter from extreme cold and deep snow. When heavy snows cover ground forage or make access to other food difficult, deer may starve to death; food shortages, along with severe cold, make the animals vulnerable to such predators as cougars, bears, lynx, bobcats, wolverines and coyotes. Often, in escaping from enemies, mule deer take to water, sometimes swimming for several miles.

Dr. Geist writes colorfully of his field studies of mule deer in winter. "I have accompanied mule deer during a number of blizzards," he recalls. "Although they accept very low temperatures and withstand being buffetted by powerful winds, a combination of both makes them respond. They chose pockets of serenely calm air, for instance, in dense mature Douglas fir forest. Here the only evidence of the blizzard was the violently shaking crowns, a drizzle of tiny glimmering snow crystals, the periodic loud plop of snow mass detaching from a lower branch and hitting the snow blanket on the ground, the odd splinter of a branch and

Sparring between mule deer bucks is common before the rutting season, but these are "sporting" engagements in which injury to either animal is rare. (Photo by Dr. Valerius Geist)

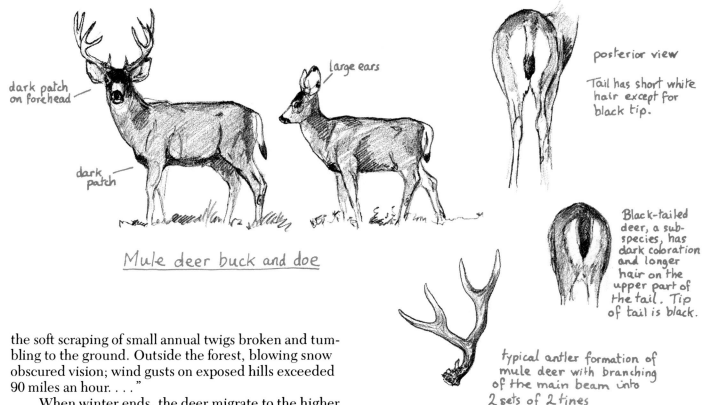

dark patch on forehead

dark patch

large ears

Mule deer buck and doe

posterior view

Tail has short white hair except for black tip.

Black-tailed deer, a sub-species, has dark coloration and longer hair on the upper part of the tail. Tip of tail is black.

typical antler formation of mule deer with branching of the main beam into 2 sets of 2 tines

the soft scraping of small annual twigs broken and tumbling to the ground. Outside the forest, blowing snow obscured vision; wind gusts on exposed hills exceeded 90 miles an hour. . . ."

When winter ends, the deer migrate to the higher elevations where the fawns are born, 6 to 7 pounds (2.7-3.2 kg) in weight, eyes open and alert, and carrying a red coat in which there are irregular rows of white spots on the back and sides (with extra spots in between). A few minutes after birth they are able to stand and begin to suckle. Fawns are always dropped where there is foliage tall and dense enough to hide them from predators. A thorough licking by the mother—a cleansing procedure which also enables her to identify her own—leaves the youngsters practically odorless and thus less likely to be discovered by passing enemies. For nearly a month the fawns remain quietly in hiding and see their mother only when she comes to feed them.

By the end of the first month the fawns are strong enough to leave their hiding places and to remain with their mothers. Their diet of milk is now supplemented by the tender new spring vegetation, and growth is rapid. By the middle of summer they are sturdy and sure-footed, and by autumn they have lost their baby spots. Their first molt, leaving them with a thick gray coat of inner and outer hairs, occurs in fall before winter sets in. By the time they are 18 months of age they are often sexually mature.

Appealing though they are, fawns found in their hiding places should *never* be disturbed. Nor should they even be fondled. A doe rarely deserts her young and one must always assume that she is still in charge and probably not far away. If, however, it is known *for certain* that a fawn has been orphaned, it may be given protection, but the game authorities should be notified as quickly as possible. Deer, in any case, do not make good pets for long. When they are sexually mature and enter their periodic rut, they can be extremely dangerous.

The black-tailed deer, *O. h. columbianus*, is also known as the coast deer or Columbia blacktail. This mule deer subspecies is resident in Canada along the coast and islands of British Columbia, on Vancouver Island as well as all of the islands of the Strait of Georgia. In the U. S. it is found in forests along the Pacific coast as far south as central California. It is also found in Alaska. Black-tailed deer are good swimmers and move freely from island to island to mainland. Semi-dwarf races occur on some islands. During summer most

50

black-tailed live at higher elevations and return to lower elevations for winter.

The sitka deer, *O.h. sitkensis*, is almost identical in appearance to the black-tailed, but is smaller in size. It is found in forested areas along the Pacific coast and islands north to the Alaska panhandle. It was introduced many years ago to the Queen Charlotte Islands and continues to prosper there.

Odocoileus virginianus
White-tailed Deer

Of the genus *Odocoileus*, the white-tailed deer is by far the species best known to most North Americans. Long before Europeans reached this continent it was a major source of food for a large proportion of the Indian people; it provided them also with skins for clothing and utensils and later became a means of exchange for the goods of the white trader. In those early days in North America the white-tailed was resident mainly in the east and south, but as colonization spread so did the deer. Today they are found in every province of Canada (except Newoundland) and almost all of the continental U. S. (but not Alaska). White-tailed deer are also residents of Mexico and much of northern South America. They are most abundant, however, in southern North America; in Texas the number per square mile is estimated to be more than 160 in some localities.

White-tailed deer are exceptionally handsome animals and are avidly sought by sportsmen not only for their meat but for their trophy heads and antlers. Since they are a highly successful species, thinning out of stocks by hunters and predators keeps their populations under control, and thus ensures an end result of healthy, vigorous animals.

In the fall of the year, when the first frosts occur and the delicious, nutty odor of the open forests fills the air, the white-tailed bucks, does and juveniles are at their best. Fattened by a summer of browsing, they have now grown out of their thin coats of reddish fawn into their thicker winter coats of grayish blue. The bucks' solid antlers, free of velvet, are fully grown; the does, their bodies well-rounded after months of feeding, are ready for the double stresses of winter survival and producing new fawns; the growing youngsters, on their part, have lost their baby spots and have become almost as large as their mothers.

The rutting period of the bucks—the time when their sexual urges are aroused—begins in late October and continues to about mid-December. Does, however, are responsive (estrous) for only about 24 hours during a 3- to 4-week period, normally from November 15 to December 10.

Unlike elk, white-tailed do not form harems but the bucks mate with receptive does as they find them. The mating season is a frenetic one and a single buck will sometimes breed the same doe more than once before seeking other females to conquer. Fighting among bucks belonging to the same group occurs only occasionally, since dominance and superiority have already been established. Once in a while, however, a younger buck may attempt to replace an older more dominant one. Serious fighting is more likely to occur when mature bucks meet as strangers to each other. These fights between combatants of *equal* size rarely last longer than a minute and are most common just before and during the rut, especially when a nearby doe is the prize to be won. On such occasions antlers may be broken and on rare occasions even locked; the result of locking is a lingering and painful death for both. Sparring matches, which occur only among *unequals*, are common but these, as in the case of mule deer, are "sporting" activities without "winners" or "losers."

Following the rut, and with the arrival of winter, the white-tailed "yard up" where there is protection from cold and deep snow and where there is a good food supply. Some, however, form large, loose herds in the open prairie far from the protection of woods and bushes.

Because of their diverse international habitats, types of browse vary. In the east where there are large populations of white-tailed the main winter food consists of the buds and twigs of red maple, cedar, dogwood, sumac and the like. If too many deer feed in the same area and food supplies become depleted, the animals turn to the less palatable and less nutritious needles and sprouts of evergreens such as balsam and white pine, as well as lichens and dead leaves. Shortages of proper food often result in starvation and disease, and by spring surviving animals are usually thin and gaunt and their coats are shaggy and tattered. A new diet of lush grasses, sprouting leaves, forbs and water lilies, however, quickly restores their health.

Most fawns are born between late May and mid-June, but some come into the world in April or in succeeding months as late as September. In any case the gestation period is from 205 to 210 days. A young

White-tailed deer head the list of the most popular large game animals of North America. They are elusive creatures, however, and masters at camouflaging their presence — which makes them challenging quarry. (Photo by Dr. Donald R. Gunn)

doe, giving birth for the first time, usually bears a single fawn. Mature does normally have twins, but triplets and even quadruplets are not unknown.

For the first two weeks after their birth the new fawns, although able to move about freely on their long thin legs, remain relatively quiet in the sheltered spots where they hide themselves. They are beautiful little creatures, weighing about 7 pounds (3 kg), and are garbed in a silky, reddish coat carrying many large white spots. Each youngster occupies a separate bedding place of its own choosing. Thoroughly cleansed by the mother at the time of birth, they are practically odorless and if they lie perfectly still and quiet their presence generally goes undetected by predators such as coyotes, wolves, cougars and free-roaming dogs. During the hiding period, the mother returns every two or three hours to nurse them. About the third week the fawns are strong enough to follow their mothers. While they continue to suckle until they are about 4 months old, they learn to supplement their diet with a variety of vegetation, including such delicacies as fiddleheads, blueberries, asters, goldenrod and mushrooms.

Fawns for the first year do not carry antlers, although bases from which antlers will eventually grow begin to form on the heads of the males when they are about 4 months of age. It is not, as a rule, until the fourth or fifth year that maximum growth is completed. Females do not carry antlers, but there have been rare instances when they have appeared on does suffering from glandular disorders.

White-tailed are to hunters what steelhead and brown trout are to anglers—elusive. Those familiar with the behavior of these deer are amazed at the animals' ability to conceal themselves and to disappear rapidly once they have been sighted and aroused. Few animals are equipped with such remarkable hearing, eyesight and sense of smell. It is said that they can hear movements of other animals, including man, from incredible distances, that they can spot the slightest movements also from great distances, and that they can smell the presence of a man from nearly a quarter of a mile away. Dr. Geist, however, believes that despite their well-developed faculties, white-tails tend to disregard much of this distant information. Even in crunchy snow, he says, they may let a hunter approach very closely, but in such situations the hunter is usually not aware of the animal's presence. White-tailed are masters at camouflage. This comparative indifference to things heard, smelled or seen is not characteristic of mule deer.

The common gait of white-tailed differs from that of mule deer. Instead of being stiffed-legged and bouncing, it is more flowing and graceful. When fleeing, they usually move low over the ground in a succession of three or four leaps, make long broad jumps, then change to a steady canter. The agility of these animals is amazing and many an observer has been left spellbound at the sight of them zigzagging through brush, over rocks and tangled masses of deadfalls in almost effortless flying leaps. From a standing position they can clear fences and similar obstacles with hardly any apparent flexing of their muscles. If running to

Fore
3 in (7.6 cm) long

White-tailed deer

escape predators, they can reach speeds of nearly 40 miles (65 km) an hour in a steady gallop. Long jumps have been measured at nearly 30 feet (9 m) and high jumps at nearly 9 feet (2.7 m). They are accomplished swimmers, and there is one record of a white-tail having crossed a 5-mile-wide (8 km) lake, during the course of which it attained a speed of 13 miles (21 km) an hour!

White-tailed are not nomadic and, if the habitat is satisfactory and the food supply adequate, they may remain within a summer area as small as 40 acres (.16 km²). In winter they may extend their range to 300 acres (1.2 km²) or more.

"Within its home range," wrote Dr. Banfield, "the deer is familiar with every tree, hollow, brook and trail. It is reluctant to leave its home range, even when hunted by dogs, and usually runs in circles through its familiar territory. In tagging studies it has been found that bucks are recovered an average 6.7 miles [10.7 km] from the initial tagging spot, and does an average of 3.7 miles [5.9 km], although one buck traveled 165 miles [264 km] after being tagged. As a rule they 'home' to their original territories after being moved up to twenty

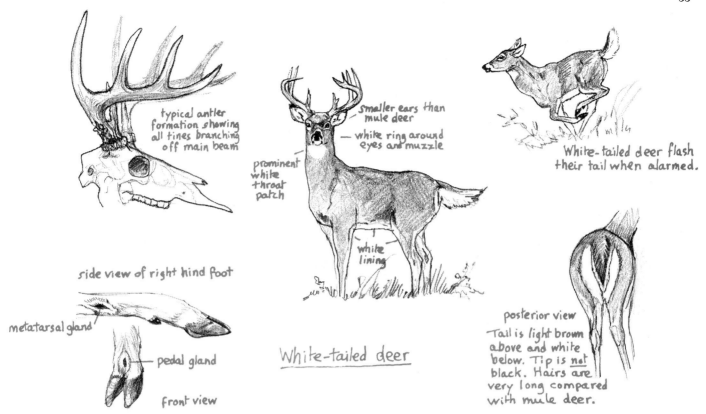

typical antler formation showing all tines branching off main beam

smaller ears than mule deer

— white ring around eyes and muzzle

prominent white throat patch

White-tailed deer flash their tail when alarmed.

side view of right hind foot

metatarsal gland

pedal gland

front view

white lining

White-tailed deer

posterior view

Tail is light brown above and white below. Tip is **not** black. Hairs are very long compared with mule deer.

miles [36 km], but beyond that distance they usually scatter. Deer populations (in Canada) have been calculated as being up to thirty-four animals to a square mile."

The white-tailed, although closely related to the mule deer, has a number of different physical characteristics. Two major differences are its ears, which are noticeably smaller, and its tail, which is noticeably bushier and longer. The tail of the white-tailed is brown at the base and then generally black for a third to a half of its length. The edges and the tip carry long white hairs. The under part of the tail is snowy-white, as is the rump area, but this narrow area is not considered to be a "rump patch" of the type displayed by the mule deer and the pronghorn.

The tail of the white-tailed, however, like that of the pronghorn, is an effective communications device, for when it is raised and the white hairs are flared outward and in an up and down motion, it and the white rump act as light reflectors. This serves as a signal to its young and to other deer that danger is at hand. When the deer is trying to escape detection, the tail is pressed close to the rump and the white fringes are turned inward so that only the dark dorsal hairs show.

The antlers of the white-tailed differ from those of the mule deer in that, instead of projecting upward and slightly backward, they curve upward, forward, outward and then forward over the face; the main beam, furthermore, does not fork as in the mule deer.

Color varies but normally in summer is reddish fawn on the sides and white on the belly. The outer winter coat, under which is a soft undercoat, is grizzled gray and is longer and stiffer than the summer pelage. A white band encircles the snout behind the nose, the inside of the ears is white, and there is white around the eyes, on the chin and on the throat.

Scent glands are present between the two toes of all four hooves, on the outside of each lower hind leg, and at the hock on the inside of each hind leg. These glands play an important part in communication and are especially active during the rutting season. All of the glands are larger and more active in dominant deer than in subordinate deer.

Of the 30 recognized subspecies in North America, three occur along the borders of Canada and the United States. They are:

54

O.v. borealis, commonly known as the northern woodland white-tailed. Not only is it the largest in size, it also has the largest range. In Canada it is found in New Brunswick, Nova Scotia, Quebec and Ontario, and in the United States it is found in all of the New England states, as well as New York, Michigan, Wisconsin, Minnesota, Illinois, Ohio, Pennsylvania, New Jersey, Delaware and Maryland. This deer is normally darker in color than the other subspecies.

O.v. dacotensis, commonly known as the Dakota white-tailed. This is also a large deer and the favorite of many hunters who seek it for its trophy-sized head. In Canada it is found in Alberta, Saskatchewan, and Manitoba, and in the United States it occurs in North and South Dakota, Nebraska, Kansas, Wyoming and Montana. Its pelage is a little lighter in color than that of *O.v. borealis*.

O.v. ochrourus, commonly known as the northwestern white-tailed. It too is a large deer with widespread antlers. In Canada it occurs in Alberta and British Columbia, and in the United States in Montana, Idaho, Washington, Oregon, Nevada, Utah and California. Its winter pelage is grayish brown.

Alces alces
Moose

In size, appearance and behavior moose are among the most remarkable of North America's wild animals. They are the largest living antlered creatures on earth, sometimes standing 7 feet (2.1 m) high, weighing up to 1,500 pounds (680 kg), and carrying broad-bladed antlers that may be more than 60 inches (150 cm) in width and weigh more than 85 pounds (39 kg). But even these statistics may be moderate. Ernest Thompson Seton, in his *Life Histories of North American Animals*, tells of one Alaskan moose "recorded by a competent authority," that measured 7 feet 8 inches (2.33 m) in height and another, verified by a photograph, with antlers that measured 78$\frac{1}{2}$ inches (2 m) and weighed 93$\frac{1}{4}$ pounds (42 kg). A contemporary scientist, Dr. Randolph L. Peterson, Curator of Mammalogy, Royal Ontario Museum, in his highly respected *North American Moose*, supports the probability that in Alaska bulls reach a weight of 1,800 pounds (816 kg)!

Whatever the variables may be, even the *smallest* adult moose is huge. In North America the only other wild animals exceeding them in weight are the plains and wood buffalo, which weigh between 2,000 and 2,200 pounds (900-1000 kg). Neither, of course, belongs to the deer family or is antlered.

Moose originated in North America, but during the Pleistocene epoch, when periods of glaciation caused the seas to recede, a land corridor was exposed where the Bering Sea is today and across it Old and New World animals spread and mingled and sometimes colonized a continent where they had never lived before. The North American animals that were near the connecting "land bridge" lived north of the great continental glaciers in a large ice-free region called a "refugium," which covered part of Alaska and Yukon. At one time (about 20,000 years ago) this refugium contained many types of animal life, some creatures as small as lemmings and ground squirrels, others as large as camels, mastodons and woolly mammoths. Moose were among New World mammals that established themselves in the Old World.

As changes in geology and climate occurred, some of these North American animals, such as camels, mastodons and mammoths, became extinct. Some, among them lemmings and Dall's sheep, remained in the north. Others moved southward to become residents of what are now Canadian provinces and U.S. states, and even into South America. Moose, like lynx and wolverines, chose northern habitats. Today they are well established throughout most of their range, which includes not only North America but the countries of Northern Europe and Asia. The Canadian range of the moose extends from Newfoundland to British Columbia, but only rarely west of the B.C.'s Coast Range. It is found in the Northwest Territories, Yukon and Alaska. In continental United States it occurs in Maine, Minnesota, Montana, Wyoming, Idaho, Utah, northwest Colorado and Washington.

To people living in remote areas, moose are an important source of food. Indians, for example, in some areas have traditionally relied on them for their meat supplies, and the hides of the animals are still used for outer clothing, as well as for mittens, moccasins and leggings. But their primary importance to humans is their conversion to food. In the Yukon, for example, about 80 per cent of the moose killed for their meat are shot by resident hunters. In Newfoundland, on the other side of the continent, where they were introduced more than a century ago, from 8,000 to 10,000 moose are taken each year. Early explorers, such as Hearne and Tyrell, relied on moose not only for food

but for their hides, especially in the making of dog harnesses.

The moose, in some respects, is a study in contradictions. Despite its great size and formidable appearance, it is a shy and harmless creature that wants only to go its way, unmolested and unmolesting. Only during the frenetic season of the rut does its placid temperament change. But not always, as Dr. Peterson found out.

During one of his many field studies, Peterson deliberately confronted a bull seeking a mate. Hearing the grunting of the animal as it swam across a channel between two islands in Lake Superior, he hurried to a place along the shore where he thought the creature would emerge. When the bull reached land, Peterson stepped directly in front of it. There were only about 10

Moose originated in North America but established themselves in the Old World during the Pleistocene epoch when a land corridor existed where the Bering Sea is now. Despite their great size and formidable appearance, they are shy and harmless creatures. (Photo by Wayne Lankinen/Valan Photos)

Moose

body hair dark except for legs

Males have dark faces, females light brown to tan.

bell

front hoof

underside of hoof

yards separating the two. This was no "after you, my dear Alphonse" situation. It was a display of human courage to determine the behavior of a large animal whose only aim in life at the time was to fulfill its overwhelming sex drive. How, Peterson wanted to know, would it respond to surprise and interference?

The first reactions of the moose were predictable: lowered ears, bristling shoulder hairs and expanding and contracting nostrils. It was a menacing sight. When the bull took a few steps forward, Peterson, heart pounding, was ready to beat a hasty retreat, a procedure that probably would have found him up a tree with an angry animal snorting and pawing fiercely at the ground below. Instead, he remained where he was. A moment or so later the moose turned and walked away, crashing through the underbrush and grunting as it went. Peterson followed, and after a few steps made a similar grunting noise. The animal stopped and looked glaringly back at his pursuer.

"For an instant I felt he might turn and charge," Dr. Peterson recalls. "But with a nasal snort he slowly turned his majestic head and resumed a deliberate walk. Not at all belligerent, he appeared merely disgusted with my interruption of his main purpose—to find a suitable, if not specific, cow in an amorous mood."

This kind of courage, understandable in dedicated scientists, is not recommended for the ordinary wilder-

ness traveler. The harmless encounter just recounted could as easily have been a viciously angry one. All members of the deer family, it should be stressed, are potentially dangerous at rutting time, a factor not always taken into account by people who adopt fawns as pets. The enchanting "bambi," when it reaches maturity, can turn into a killer during the time of sexual arousal.

While bull moose are aggressive and vocal during the mating season, the females are no less uninhibited in annoucing their readiness to cooperate in lovemaking. Their passionate calls, a series of low, resonant bawlings, stir any bull within hearing distance into frenzied, immediate action. Abandoning instinctive caution, the responding bull will thrash through the forest, coughing, bellowing and grunting as it works itself into a peak of sexual anticipation.

When more than one bull responds to the same beckoning cow, what follows may be little short of mayhem. From time to time evidence can be seen of what must have been devastating confrontations—churned-up, blood-stained earth, bushes uprooted and branches torn off trees. These fights sometimes leave one or both bulls so seriously injured that mating, for a while at least, has little attraction. Antlers may become locked and the animals' inevitable death is horribly slow and agonizing. Death sometimes comes more quickly, for, if wolves or bears are waiting on the sidelines, they quickly move in and kill the exhausted and defenseless warriors.

Unlike elk, moose are not herding animals and thus do not assemble harems. Instead, when a bull finds a receptive female, it will stay with her up to 10 days, then leave to search for another female. Occasionally a bull will stay with its mate for the whole breeding season from late September to the end of October.

Courting is truculent and violent and is accompanied by remarkable physical and olfactory performances. A common bull behavior is to make hollows in the ground by pawing up the soil, soaking it with urine and then wallowing in it. These are known as "rutting pits" and presumably do for moose what French perfume does for humans. In Europe these pits are known as "soil" or "gross." So exhausting is the breeding period for the bull that it may lose as much as 20 per cent of its body weight.

The reproductive potential of moose, Dr. Geist points out, is directly related to the quality of the habitat. When the habitat is favorable and there is an abundance of food, calf survival is exceedingly high; otherwise it may be low. This view is shared by Yorke Edwards, who writes that during the 1950s in Wells Gray Park, north of Kamloops, B.C., (a favorable range) one quarter to one third of moose pregnancies resulted in twins, and the young there seemed to face no survival problems. Triplets do occur, but these are rare. The gestation period for moose is from 240 to 246 days.

Following the rut, bulls and cows tend to separate. Clothed now in heavy winter coats, both sexes are content to spend their time quietly browsing and chewing the cud. Those in the high country migrate to lower elevations where there is less snow, better shelter from the intense cold, and greater food supplies. Such areas are often used by a number of moose—bulls, cows and yearlings. These "yards" offer reasonable protection from predators, but when snows are deep, particularly in the late spring, older and weaker animals, as well as the young, are often killed by wolves and bears. Starvation also takes its toll. To meet food requirements, adult

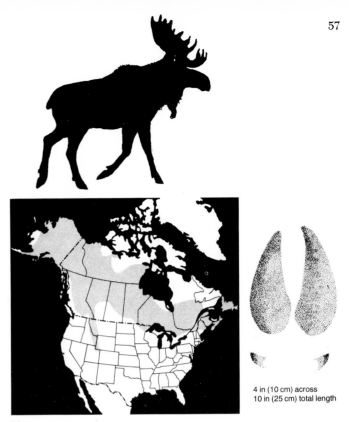

Moose

4 in (10 cm) across
10 in (25 cm) total length

moose need from 40 to 60 pounds (18-27 kg) of fodder each day.

Calves, born during late May and early June, weigh from 25 to 40 pounds (11-18 kg) and are somewhat grotesque miniatures of their mothers. They are awkwardly long-legged and have very large ears on heads that are outsized in relation to their bodies. But these youngsters, reddish-brown in color, are remarkable. Within a few days they can run faster than a man and can swim strongly. Their rate of growth is extraordinary, for at the age of 3 months they will weigh 150 to 200 pounds (70-90 kg) and when a year old will weigh 400 to 600 pounds (180-270 kg). By this time antler growth is apparent, frequently showing as two or three points. Full antler development is attained when they are 2½ years old, but maximum growth is not reached until the seventh to tenth year. Only bulls carry antlers and these are shed between mid-December and early January. Growth of the new antlers begins the following April.

The calves remain with their mothers throughout the first year, but with the birth of new calves imminent, "protective custody" comes to an end. Now is the

Moose calves remain with their mothers for about a year. With the approaching birth of a new calf, each yearling is rejected and must fend for itself. (Photo by J. C. Holroyd)

time for the yearlings to fend for themselves. The separation, for the youngsters at least, is a traumatic one. Knowing only the companionship of their mothers and others their own age, they are bewildered and frightened when suddenly chased off. Any attempts to return are repulsed. Realizing the finality of the rejection, the yearlings are forced to face the wilderness alone or seek the company of other moose. Shortly afterwards, the mothers bed down in a thicket, often in the safety of an island, and there in late May or early June produce their new calves.

Moose in some areas spend part of their time in swamps and in the shallow bays of lakes and rivers, generally where there are water lilies and similar foods and where, by wallowing in deep mud or submerging in the water, they can find relief from the hordes of blood-sucking flies that pester them and other animals. They sometimes dive to depths of nearly 20 feet (6 m) to seize mouthfuls of bottom-growing plants. This is the scene most frequently captured on film and canvas and which gives the impression that the animals are semi-aquatic. This, however, is not necessarily the case. As Dr. Geist reminds us, many ranges, particularly in the west and north, support only minimum areas of wetland and, where there are relatively dry habitats, moose survive quite satisfactorily.

Most of the time, and especially during the days when flies are less bothersome and the weather is cooler, moose frequent the boreal forests and burned-out areas where there are stands of second-growth trees, feeding on twigs, leaves and bark of willows, aspen, maple and birch. Their winter diet is also made up of woody plants, although at that time they have a liking for evergreens such as balsam and fir; in western Canada and U.S., willows, serviceberry and red osier dogwood are favorite foods, as are the leaves and twigs of false box (*Pachystima*) when they can be pawed free from the snow-covered ground.

While moose have been driven out of some of their original ranges by human encroachment, or thinned out by hunting intensity, they are secure in most of the ranges they occupy today. In fact, as a result of management programs and the animals' own capacity to survive, in terms of sheer numbers they are considered to be a "howling success," not only in North America but in the U.S.S.R. Some authorities estimate that the total North American moose population is upwards of 300,000; others put the figure at more than half a million in Canada alone.

Because they are solitary rather than herding animals, moose in their western and northern ranges are seldom encountered by wilderness travelers. In fact it is estimated that rarely is there more than one moose per square mile. In areas where there are deep accumulations of snow, however, as is so often the case in eastern North America, as many as a dozen or so moose may come together to form the "yards" previously referred to. In such winter concentrations there may be a dozen within a square mile.

Moose have wide-spreading, cloven hooves that enable them to travel over uneven ground without difficulty, and their long, spindly but powerful legs carry them with ease over fallen trees and through tangled undergrowth. The popular notion that moose have poor eyesight is debatable, for there is now evidence that their eyesight is exceptionally good. They are, as well, powerful swimmers and there are records showing nonstop journeys as long as 12 miles (19 km). Despite their size they can run as fast as 35 miles (56 km) an hour.

There is no mistaking this monarch of the wild, for

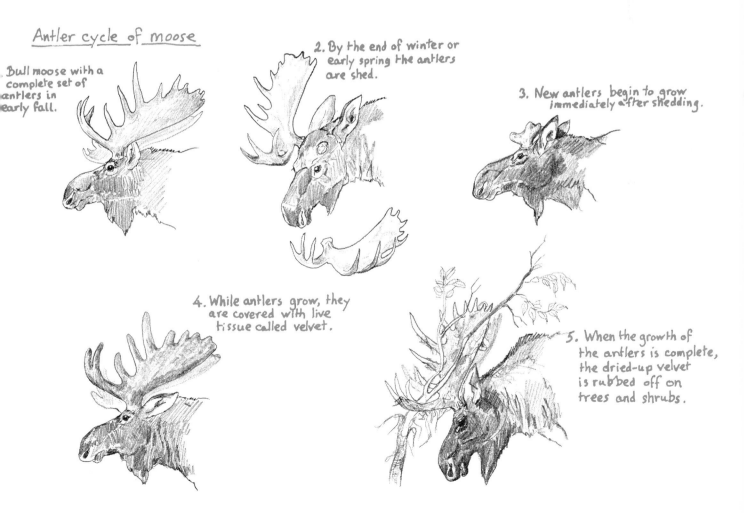

Antler cycle of moose

Bull moose with a complete set of antlers in early fall.

2. By the end of winter or early spring the antlers are shed.

3. New antlers begin to grow immediately after shedding.

4. While antlers grow, they are covered with live tissue called velvet.

5. When the growth of the antlers is complete, the dried-up velvet is rubbed off on trees and shrubs.

it occupies a unique place in the North American animal kingdom. Aside from its size, its ponderous and less than handsome head, its humped shoulders and great rack of mahogany-colored antlers, it carries an appendage which serves no known purpose—the fur-covered "bell," sometimes a foot long, that hangs from its throat. The moose has everything necessary to make it a ferocious, dangerous beast, but, except in the rutting season, *Alces alces* is one of the most harmless of all big-game animals.

There are four subspecies of moose in North America, and three subspecies in Europe (where they are known as "elk.") Moose in the wild have a lifespan of from 17 to 22 years. In East Prussia, according to Dr. Peterson, there is a record of a tagged calf that lived for 27 years.

Dama dama
Fallow Deer

This is an Old World deer, native to the Mediterranean and Asia Minor, and introduced not only to a number of other areas of Europe, but recently to North America as well. In Canada it is present only on the Gulf Islands of British Columbia—on James Island, where it was probably first introduced, and from where transplants were made to Sydney and Saltspring islands. Occasionally it reaches the Saanich Peninsula of Vancouver Island to which it sometimes swims from James Island. In the United States small herds, some as small as 10 individuals, are present in Alabama, California, Georgia, Kentucky, Maryland, Nebraska, Oklahoma and Texas. It is unlikely that the total North American fallow deer population exceeds 3,500. Herds in Canada, and a few in the United States, are controlled by private landowners.

Dama dama averages about 5 feet (1.5 m) in length and 3 feet (1 m) in height at the shoulders, approximately the same measurements as for the small coastal mule deer. The antlers of this animal have a large brow tine and the tops are palm-like, rather as in the moose. They are carried only by the bucks and are shed in the spring.

The fallow deer has protective seasonal coloration. In summer it is fawn-colored on the sides and back, with numerous white spots. The underparts are creamy-white, and the long tail is brown on top, white underneath and black at the tip. In winter the fallow deer is uniformly grayish-brown and the spots are absent.

This species is gregarious, with the tendency to move about in separate small herds. The bucks remain apart from does during most of the year, but rejoin them in October when it is time to mate. Each buck generally breeds several does. The fawns—usually one, but sometimes twins—are born the following June.

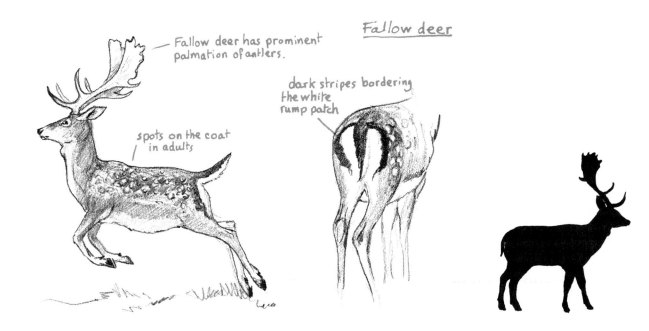

Fallow deer has prominent palmation of antlers.

Fallow deer

dark stripes bordering the white rump patch

spots on the coat in adults

Cervus elaphus

Elk (Wapiti)

It was the end of August, and the Rocky Mountain high country had taken on the feel and smell of approaching autumn. The alpine meadows, still ablaze with the late summer bloom of wild flowers, reflected like millions of diamonds the dew yet to be absorbed by the heat of the morning sun.

At a lower level, where a small lake gave life to a generous growth of aquatic plants, a moose submerged its massive head to seize mouthfuls of succulent water lilies. A fox sparrow, one of the mountains' most accomplished songsters, mingled its melody with the wheezy but easily identifiable voice of a boreal chickadee. A flock of harlequin ducks, which earlier in the year had forsaken the rocky, wave-battered shores of the Pacific to find breeding and nesting grounds in the mountains many miles to the east, took flight, their voices sounding squeaky and shrill over the fluttering of their wings.

A herd of elk, 18 in number, emerged quietly from a grove of aspen, alternately grazing and browsing as it moved. Of the herd, ten were cows, seven were calves, and one was a bull, a large animal carrying a set of antlers that, in human terms, was of undoubted trophy quality. The "herd bull," as such a beast is called, shepherded his harem with an alert, nervous dominance.

At first the sound was muted, then it became an increasingly high-pitched roar, or "bugle," that ended in a shrill scream and a number of grunts and barks. The sound reverberated for several seconds, and it was as spine-tingling in those mountain wilds as the maniacal laughter of a loon on a remote Ontario lake. The bull trotted stiffly to the front of the herd, his head and swollen neck held high. A few minutes later a big, six-point bachelor came over a rise about 100 yards (91 m) away. He stared at the herd bull, then began horning a nearby bush, his antlers sending bits of broken branches in all directions. The herd bull, sensing a challenge to ownership of the harem, roared in defiance and he too began the horning ritual.

Visibly palpitating, they approached frontally, turned sharply, circled, then trotted parallel to each other about 10 paces apart for nearly 200 yards (183 m). Each avoided the other's gaze, as if to suggest that neither was really there at all. Suddenly both turned and looked at each other directly. Both then swept their antlers over the ground. After thrashing some nearby bushes and uttering brief "bugles," they marched off

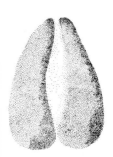

Fore
2½ in (6.4 cm) across
4 in (10 cm) long

Elk (Former range much more extensive, reaching to Great Lakes)

again. Most of the action was a prolonged sham performance, but with all the appearance of a horrendous battle about to begin.

The real clash came when the herd bull, having decided to end the affair, lowered his head and assumed a crouch position; his opponent did the same. Both animals, evenly matched, then crashed head on, engaging their antlers in a shoving contest that, to the accompaniment of throaty noises and heavy breathing, went back and forth for almost half an hour until the herd bull forced his opponent to his knees. There was a quick disengagement, time for the aggressor to regain his feet, then turn abruptly and beat a hasty retreat. The herd bull followed, making several long jumps in pursuit; then he stopped and "bugled" loudly as the other disappeared into heavy forest growth. Victorious, he trotted back to the harem. The activities of the herd continued as if nothing had happened.

"Bloodless" battles such as this are not motivated by any magnanimous desire on the part of either combatant to *avoid* injuring its opponent. Recent scientific field studies leave little doubt that in confrontations of this kind each animal knows that win or lose, by inflict-

Growing antlers of bull elk are covered with a spongy substance encased in soft, hairy skin. When this "velvet" drops off, the antlers are hard and shiny. (Photo by Dr. Valerius Geist)

ing wounds it must face the certainty of angry retaliation. This the animals try to avoid, somehow sensing that injuries to themselves are debilitating and could lessen ability for their own later self-defense and breeding activity. And so it is much better to "defeat" the enemy by a display of greater strength and endurance. The use of dangerous weapons such as horns and hooves might result in victory—but at too high a cost.

This was a typical elk encounter before and during the rut. In either elk engagements the behavioral patterns might be somewhat different. A young buck, for example, overrating his own physical stature, might be scared off by a harem-master who, hissing and grinding his teeth and holding his head high, would simply rush

at the intruder. In another situation, when two evenly-matched males are involved, a fight might get out of hand, blind rage take over, and deep, fatal wounds be inflicted by plunging antlers. But bloody and mortal battles of this severity are believed to be rare.

Victory over this one opponent did not mean that the herd bull's dominance was secured. As the days passed, others would take up the challenge. In other contests, hinds (females) would seize the opportunity to run off, thus reducing the size of the herd or even breaking it up. In some instances, herd bulls might be ousted by superior bulls and the losers would have to compete for mastery of other herds. The struggle for dominance would continue until the end of October. At that time the rut would have ended, as would sexual aggressiveness.

With the onset of cold and snow, large bulls segregate from the cow herds and go in small groups, or as single animals, to winter apart. Adult cows, calves, yearlings and sub-adults of both sexes unite to form herds. This is particularly so in preserve areas. They remain together until spring, when the cows seek isolated places where they can safely give birth to their young—single calves mostly, but occasionally twins. The young are large at birth, weighing from 19 to 45 pounds (9-20 kg).

During the summer months the hinds and their young, in bands of 25 or so, spend their time on alpine meadows or low-level wooded hillsides. The stags, carrying magnificent antlers, form their own separate bachelor groups. With the coming of autumn and sex-

ual arousal, they form into harems and life continues as before.

The elk—or wapiti as it is often called—is one of North America's most majestic animals, "the most highly evolved Old World deer existing, the most recent to arise and the latest to colonize a continent void of Old World deer," writes Geist.

At one time widely distributed throughout northern Europe and Asia, and in North America over much of Canada, Alaska and continental United States, as well as part of Mexico, elk are now absent from most of these ranges due to intensive hunting, starvation and disease, and the loss of their habitat as colonization spread. At one time in North America, vast herds literally darkened the western plains much as did the great American bison. Today the largest stocks are found in the forested Rocky Mountain regions of western Canada and the U.S.

This small group of mature bull elk was photographed in a heavily forested area where there was ample food and protection from the harsh winter elements. (Photo by J. C. Holroyd)

Elk

dark neck

tan-colored rump patch

—short tail

"Imperial" elk have seven tines branching off the main antler beam.

"Royal" elk show six tines on their antlers. Numbers of tines on left and right antlers are not always equal.

The elk is the largest of the Old World deer, falling midway between the moose and mule deer. An exceptional mature male may have a length of up to 10 feet (3 m) and a height of 5 feet (1.5 m) at the shoulders, and may weigh up to 1,000 pounds (450 kg). The average female is about 25 per cent smaller.

What characterizes the male of the species is its spectacular set of antlers. These arise from large burrs high on the head, and at their ultimate growth may reach a length of 6 feet (1.8 m) with a spread of 47 inches (1.2 m). Each of the two antlers consists of a main beam with long, branching tines, or prongs. The main beams grow outward, upward and backward, curving inward at the tip. The tines increase in number until, in a prime animal, there are 6 or 7 on each side. When a male has a complement of 12 "points"—6 tines on each antler—it is known as a Royal Stag, while a male with 14 "points"—7 tines on each antler—is known as an Imperial Stag.

These massive appendages, present only in males, are solid, bone-like structures which begin their growth in early April or May. By July they reach their maximum size in relation to the age of the animal. For example, the antlers on a 1-year old may attain a height of up to 18 or 19 inches (46 cm), those on a 2-year old may reach a height of 24 inches (60 cm) or so, while bulls older than that may grow antlers of Royal or Imperial dimensions.

When the antlers are growing each year, they are composed of a spongy substance encased in a covering of soft, hairy skin commonly known as "velvet." Through this skin, blood vessels provide the antlers with the nutrition necessary for development. In late August and early September the "velvet," no longer serving a useful purpose, either drops off or is rubbed off. By this time the antlers are fully developed and are hard and shiny. It is also at this time, and especially before and during the rut, that the antlers help to establish each bull's dominance—or lack of it.

Late the following winter, generally from February to early April, the antlers are shed, falling off of their own accord. Loss of the heavy gear leaves the animals light-headed and sometimes ludicrous in appearance. As Banfield writes, "if only one antler is dropped, the animal goes about with its head on a tilt." This naked state lasts only a short time, for antler growth begins almost immediately and is a rapid process.

Complementing the majestic structure of the elk, especially the bulls, is their over-all coloration. This pelage of short hair is glossy and tawny on the back and sides, changing to a darker shade on the face, neck, belly and legs. But there is another distinguishing characteristic—the large, buffy heart-shaped patch on the rump, around the edges of which runs a distinctive brown line. The winter pelage consists of longer guard hairs over warm underfur and is generally grayish-brown on the back and sides and chocolate brown elsewhere. There are two annual molts, a major one in the spring and a less noticeable one in autumn.

Most elk spend their summer in alpine meadows at high elevations, although some remain at lower levels, generally near wooded areas close to water. Their summer diet consists mainly of forbs and grasses. With the coming of winter they seek the protection of lower-level forested valleys and feed mostly on browse.

Severe winters, intense cold and deep snow often make foraging difficult. In the Banff area in the winter of 1947, for example, many animals resorted to eating the cambium layer of trees. The scars left on the trees as a result of this food shortage are still to be seen.

Elk are susceptible to predation and disease, and many die from starvation in severe winters. Wolves, grizzly bears and cougars are their main enemies, not to mention man. Young unprotected calves are sometimes killed by black bears and wolverines. In captivity, elk may live for up to 20 years.

Although the name "elk" is most commonly used, the Shawnee Indian name "wapiti" has also been retained. Elk was the name given to this deer by English settlers who mistook it for Scandinavian elk.

Elk at birth weigh 19 to 45 pounds (9-20 kg). When mature they may weigh as much as 1,100 pounds (500 kg). This youngster is 10 days old. (Photo by J. C. Holroyd)

ORDER CARNIVORA

THE MEAT EATERS

North America can lay claim to being the home of both the smallest and the largest members of the diverse and marvelous order of carnivores. These distinctions belong to the least weasel — 6 to 9 inches (15-23 cm) in length, including tail, and 1¼ to 2 ounces (35-57g) in weight — and the great brown bear of Alaska — a type of grizzly bear that has been known to reach the staggering weight of more than 1,600 pounds (720 kg)!

Carnivorous means "flesh eating" and the carnivores are generally referred to as the meat eaters. But this is only partly true, for while all of them make meat (fresh or carrion) the major part of their diet, many consume significant amounts of vegetation, fruits, nuts, wild honey, invertebrates, birds' eggs, and even at times (notably in the case of some bears) just plain junk — odds and ends of refuse piled up in garbage dumps. So in a very real sense most carnivores can also be called omnivores.

Carnivores in North America are divided into five groups: those belonging to the family Canidae — coyotes, foxes, wolves and their kin; those belonging to the family Ursidae — the bears; those belonging to the family Mustelidae — martens, weasels, mink, wolverine, skunks, otters, and their kin; those belonging to the family Felidae — cougars, bobcats, lynx and their kin; those belonging to the family Procyonidae — raccoons and their kin. The semi-terrestrial seals, sea lions and walruses, while also carnivorous, belong to a different order — Pinnipedia.

Carnivores, being meat-eaters, are equipped with the most powerful jaws and teeth of all mammals. Thus endowed, they can grasp, bite, crush, tear and slice. If

Wolves in different habitats are known by different names. This is an Arctic wolf, an intrepid animal which has adapted to the harsh environment of the far north. (Photo by Dr. David R. Gray)

the prey is too large to consume at one sitting—deer, sheep or moose, for example—and has to be eaten over a period of days, it may be dragged away to a more protected place to be feasted upon whenever the captor feels hungry.

A quaint bit of folklore biologists are fond of telling is the story of the fisher (*Martes pennanti*) that hit the jackpot with its discovery of the frozen body of a moose. Determined to take full possession of the huge carcass, it began feasting vigorously and when it had hollowed out a large enough cavity in the dead animal's abdomen, it moved in as a permanent resident. As it continued to eat, however, the cavity became larger and larger and finally the inevitable happened: the fisher literally ate itself out of house and home!

Most carnivores have well developed senses. The bears, for example, have a particularly keen sense of smell. Those nocturnal in habit have marvelous night vision (raccoons, ferrets). Some are fleet of foot (a grizzly can outrun a man). Some are accomplished tree climbers (wolverines, martens). Some swim powerfully and for long distances (polar bear). Some make their homes in burrows (badgers). Some hibernate for varying periods of time (bears and striped skunks). Some are loners (mink) and some make up closely knit family groups (wolves and coyotes). Some are homebodies and live in areas of only a few acres (least weasels), and others are roamers and travel hundreds of miles (wolves, when following migrating caribou). All the Mustelidae have scent glands and use them to mark their territories or to communicate in other ways, particularly during the mating season. Nearly all carnivores wear coats of fur that are highly valued in the manufacture of various kinds of wearing apparel.

Unfortunately man has so pushed back the natural habitat of these creatures and so reduced their populations that many of them, before the end of this century, will be added to the endangered species list. Unless care is taken, some may even be extinct.

FAMILY CANIDAE

Canis latrans
Coyote

Like its distant cousin, the wolf, the coyote has traditionally been one of North America's most maligned animals. While it would be difficult to defend it in some areas where its excessive depredations have been proved beyond all doubt, particularly in its killing of sheep, cattle, poultry and other farm stock, in broad terms this animal is much more an asset than a liability.

Discounting the damage done to livestock, there is ample evidence that most of the larger wildlife it kills—deer, antelope, mountain sheep, for example—are sick, injured or old. By thinning out these casualities the coyote, like the wolf and other carnivores, is simply discharging its role in the natural scheme of things. In the wild there is no room for the disabled, and the coyote's predations do much to keep wildlife populations healthy and mercifully under numerical control. If, in the process, it also preys on healthy individuals that, too, must be considered its right—its right to feed itself and its family.

Man has not always moved wisely in his management of predatory animals such as the coyote. The Grand Canyon National Game Preserve, established in 1906, is an example. To protect the mule deer population there (a personal concern of the preserve's founder, President Teddy Roosevelt) the government encouraged the killing of wolves, cougars, bobcats and coyotes. The mule deer prospered as their traditional enemies disappeared, and in 8 years their numbers increased from about 40,000 to more than 100,000.

What was not forecast was the capacity of the preserve to cope with other items making up the animals' diet. There was a dramatic turnaround as too many deer were forced to compete for too little food. Heavy damage was inflicted on the preserve's ecology and eventually thousands of deer died of lingering starvation. Fortunately restorative measures were taken in time and today the preserve and its deer are in a healthy, balanced state. The disaster, it became evident, would not have occurred had predator control been more wisely planned or, in the opinion of some, if the size of the deer population had been left to find its natural level. The cost was heavy to both the preserve and its ecosystem. Aside from the subsequent loss of deer, during the control period 7,388 predators were destroyed. The suffering of these creatures can only be left to the imagination.

Large animals, whether wild or domestic, make up only a small part of the coyote's diet. Rabbits, mice, ground squirrels, small birds and, to a significant extent, carrion are also consumed, as are insects, berries and fruits of various kinds. But farmers who have suffered severe losses from the depredations of coyotes sometimes have just cause to demand the animals' permanent removal from their vicinity. Cahalane, for example, writes about one coyote in the United States having killed 26 ewe lambs in three days! If this story is true one has to assume that the animal was either rabid or demented. Its behavior, certainly, must not be regarded as typical.

It is unwise to render a blanket guilty verdict as far as their kills of deer are concerned. This contention is supported by the Ontario Ministry of Natural Resources, whose paper "Wolves and Coyotes in Ontario" (1978) reveals that there are "no authentic reports of coyotes attacking deer in this Province, and the deer that are eaten are those which have been disabled by sickness, injuries, or hunters' bullets." The Ministry concedes, however, that *occasional* kills cannot be ruled out.

The evolution of coyotes and wolves—both members of the dog family—can be traced to late Eocene and early Oligocene times, 40 to 50 million years ago. They were, it is believed, present on this continent (where they originated) during the days when other prehistoric mammals such as sabre-tooth tigers and mastodons also roamed the land. The name "coyote" is Spanish, from the Aztec Indian word *coyotl*. Its correct pronunciation is "ki-ó-tee." Nineteen races are recognized at present in North America.

Coyotes are considerably smaller than wolves. Male coyotes of the prairies, for example, average about 26 pounds (12 kg), while male coyotes of Ontario may reach a weight of 40 pounds (18 kg). Females are always smaller. The coyote has a narrow chest, long legs and a slender muzzle. Its black nose-pad is about the size of a 25¢ coin and its ears, like those of the jackal, are disproportionately large and pointed. Its feet are smaller than those of a dog of comparable size and its tail, about half the length of its body, is bushy. A coyote when running or standing carries its tail low and close to its hind legs. A wolf when running carries its tail in a horizontal position.

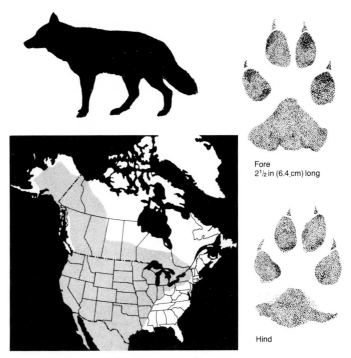

Fore
2½ in (6.4 cm) long

Hind

Coyote (Has increased range eastward in historical times)

The back and sides of the coyote are gray to dull yellow, the outer hairs of the fur on the back and tail being broadly tipped with black. The throat is white, and the chest and belly are white to pale gray. The backs of the ears are reddish and the muzzle is grayish. Despite this general description, there is much variation in coloration and in some cases individuals may be almost black or all white. Generally speaking, however, there is a wider range of coloration in wolves than in coyotes.

In some rural areas female coyotes have intermingled with domestic dogs and hybrids have resulted. These animals are called "coydogs" and are generally larger. While coydogs and coyotes live happily enough together, there are significant differences. For example, pure coyotes, like wolves, mate only once a year, whereas female coydogs are capable of mating twice a year. The various breeds of domestic dogs crossing with coyotes can produce in the offspring a varied range of coloring.

The coyote's breeding time runs from late January to late March, the peak period being late February to early March. About 63 days later the pups are born,

Coyotes originated in North America some 40 to 50 million years ago and were present on this continent when sabre-toothed tigers, mastodons and other prehistoric mammals roamed the land. (Photo by Dr. Valerius Geist)

usually five or six and sometimes, but rarely, as many as 12. It is almost certain that in broods as large as that some of the weaker babies will not survive. Dens may be either dug by the parents themselves or, as is more often the case, made by enlarging burrows dug by other animals—groundhogs, foxes, badgers, marmots, for example. Dens may also be made under hollow trees, in river banks or rock cavities, or even in deserted buildings.

The pups, born blind, gain their sight when about 8 to 14 days of age. Coyotes come into the world about the same time as do fox pups and as infants they look much alike. Parent coyotes, like parent wolves, share in the responsibility of feeding and rearing the young. Weaning begins when the pups are about 8 weeks old and at that time their diet includes partially digested food which the mother or father regurgitates at the den site. The young, introduced now to solid food, begin to learn to hunt on their own. Coyotes become sexually mature when they near their second birthday.

Both coyotes and wolves are most active during evening and early morning hours, but it is not unusual for them to range freely during the day as well. While wolves are noted for their night-time howling, coyotes are barkers. In fact the scientific name *Canis* is the Latin word for dog, while *latrans* is the Latin word for "barking." Hence *Canis latrans*.

Wolves "in concert" usually perform when they are together in packs, and a lonelier and eerier sound is difficult to imagine—unless it is the vocalizing of coyotes. Coyotes frequently bark and "yip yap" when wandering about alone. When this happens other coyotes within hearing may follow suit and there is soon a chorus of voices, the singing in some cases ending in a loud, drawn-out howl. They also may sing as a family group, their barking and howling carrying for miles as a rather falsetto uproar.

Coyotes inhabit wooded country, open farmlands and prairies, alpine tundra and swamplands, and are frequently found within areas of human habitation, even large cities where there are greenbelts and parklands. In mountainous country they often range well above the treeline, even in the dead of winter.

Coyotes have lived for as long as 10 years in the wild and 18 years in captivity.

Canis lupus
Wolf

Long before Mother Goose had drawn up her list of "good guys" and "bad guys," the pre-eminence of the ubiquitous wolf as the master criminal in the animal world had been established. In art, folklore, music and religion, some of it going back to ancient times, *Canis lupus* has been portrayed as a villain. It was described as a creature that slunk silently through the dark forests in search of prey, froth drooling from its heavily-dentured mouth, its large yellow eyes the very essence of evil. So powerful was this reputed evil in *Canis*, in fact, that it was once a popular belief that some humans, willingly or unwillingly, could change into a wolf and consume human flesh and blood. They were called werewolves or *loup garous*. Clergy, during ceremonies leading to their consecration as bishops, are still exhorted to "be to the flock . . . a shepherd, not a wolf." *Little Red Riding Hood* and *Peter and the Wolf* have retained their popularity in children's literature and music.

Some grown men who spend a good deal of time in the wilderness admit that the night-time howling of wolves never fails to send shivers up and down their spines. Recent studies carried out on Alaska's North Slope have established that under ideal conditions the howling of wolves is sometimes so resonant that it can be heard by human ears at a distance of more than 10 miles.

It is only in recent years that the true nature of wolves has become known. There is now overwhelming evidence that wolves, except in self-defence, near starvation or when suffering from rabies, are not the villains they were believed to be; nor are they, in normal circumstances, a threat to the safety of human beings. There are always exceptions of course. For example, although a wolf "profile" published by the Canadian Wildlife Service claims that there are no records of wolves *killing* humans in Canada or the United States, Dr. Banfield, in his *Mammals of Canada*, records an attack in 1942 by a wolf on a railway section man in northern Ontario. The man was working on a speeder used to inspect tracks when the animal jumped on him, even though the speeder was traveling at about 10 miles (16 km) an hour.

"The force of the impact knocked him and the gasoline speeder off the track," relates Dr. Banfield. "He reached for an axe and defended himself until a freight train came along and the crew jumped off and killed the wolf."

The wolf, had it not been thwarted, presumably would have seriously mauled or even killed the man. Could this attack, almost without precedence, have happened because the animal was rabid? A more recent incident, reported in the Victoria, B.C., *Colonist*, tells of an engineer for a logging company taking refuge in a tree because he was being followed by wolves. He was "treed" for four hours before fellow workers arrived and chased the animals away. Was this deliberate aggression or curiosity? Even domestic dogs have a tendency to chase people who run from them. Jim Curran, the northern Ontario editor who for years carried out a campaign in defence of wolves, was probably right

The tail of the wolf serves communication purposes.

tail curved slightly upwards

A loosely held tail reflects no particular mood — the wolf is relaxed. Here the tail is slightly raised and curved upwards, indicating the beginning of a threat.

Tail held high serves to assert dominance.

loosely held tail

Tail tucked under signals submission.

when he made the imperishable statement that "any man who says he's been et by a wolf is a liar."

Wolves were resident over almost all of North America, including Alaska and the Arctic, when Europeans began colonizing the continent. In some parts of Europe, wolves preyed on sheep and other domestic animals (as they still do in some areas of North America) and memories of these depredations, along with myths and legends that had been handed down from generation to generation, created in the early settlers a very real fear of the animals. Almost as soon as the first log cabins were built the settlers undertook a war of harassment of wolves, a war that was to last for nearly 300 years.

The first Canadian wolf bounty was paid in 1792 in Ontario (then Upper Canada) and the system was eventually adopted throughout the rest of the country. It was not until 1973, 181 years later, that all of the provinces as well as Yukon and the Northwest Territories, had repealed the bounty. In some areas, notably in British Columbia, where wolves as well as coyotes are said to be excessive killers of livestock, special legislation can permit controlled extermination. There are also county-sponsored bounties on wolves, as well as coyotes, in some provinces.

Bounty systems were also in effect in the United States where as early as 1630 the Massachusetts Bay Company paid one shilling for 12 wolves and one pound sterling for 280 wolves! It is little wonder that the exter-

mination programs carried out on this continent for so many years have radically, and in some instances permanently, changed the animal's historic ranges.

The situation today is a sad one: wolves are almost extinct in the United States except for those in Alaska, and protected populations in parts of northern Minnesota and Isle Royale National Park in northern Lake Superior. Wolf research is continuing in other areas bordering that lake. George Kolenosky, Ontario Ministry of Natural Resources, advises that a pack of 10 or 12 wolves is now resident in Lincoln County, Wisconsin. It is possible that remnant populations exist in some Rocky Mountain states. A smaller animal known as the red wolf is resident, but is near extinction, in some southern states.

There are no wolves at all in the Canadian Maritime provinces or on the island of Newfoundland. Although they are resident in all other provinces, as well as Yukon and the Northwest Territories, large areas where they once thrived are devoid of them. The total wolf population in Canada is now estimated at approximately 33,000 animals.

In Europe the story is even more appalling. While there are large populations in Russia, only Greece, Rumania and Yugoslavia appear also to have viable numbers. There may be a few wolves in Italy, Spain and Portugal, but their numbers are believed to be small. In Finland, for example, where wolves once prospered, only about 15 are believed to have survived, and in

Sweden there are only a few individuals in widely separated areas. The extermination of the wolf, so often without justifiable cause, is another example of man's failure to recognize fully the right of all forms of wildlife to exist in their natural state as part of the earth's ecosystem.

There is no denying that wolves are handsome animals. At a quick glance one might mistake a wolf for a German shepherd dog (or vice versa!) but even when of similar size the wolf's larger head, longer feet, heavier paws and bushier tail are obvious differences. Adult wolves in Alaska and the Northwest Territories mainland frequently weigh more than 100 pounds (45 kg). On average, however, male wolves weigh about 80 pounds (36 kg); females are 10 to 20 per cent smaller. A wolf weighing 118 pounds (54 kg) was officially recorded in Ontario but repeated references to a creature 7 feet (2.1 m) in length and weighing 170 pounds (77 kg) have yet to be verified. Wolves, by the way, belong to a group which also includes dogs, foxes and coyotes. The African jackal is also a member of this family.

Unlike their cousins the foxes, whose family ties in most species are limited to the breeding season, wolves are inclined to form family units. Dr. John B. Theberge, Associate Professor of Ecology, University of Waterloo, and an international authority on wolves, said in a personal communication that "yearling wolves often break family ties and become loners, eventually pairing with other lone wolves and thus establish new packs; even mated pairs, however, occasionally break up. This dispersal is most evident in exploited wolf populations that have not reached a carrying capacity."

This social structure is a complex one and is still not fully understood. Studies made of wolves in the wild and captivity show that in each unit the subservient members seldom challenge their leader, nor do they often challenge those that precede them in rank. This acknowledgement of the chain of dominance accounts for the fact that wolves in packs rarely fight among themselves.

The size of wolf packs varies, but a typical unit would consist of the two parents, four to eight pups, and adolescents of previous matings. Groups significantly larger than that are likely made up of packs that have united for a short time but will soon go on their way as separate units.

Female wolves mature sexually when about two years of age and males mature in their second and third

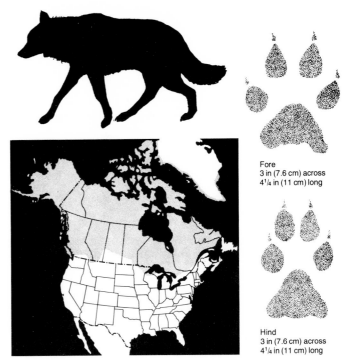

Fore
3 in (7.6 cm) across
4¼ in (11 cm) long

Hind
3 in (7.6 cm) across
4¼ in (11 cm) long

Wolf (Exterminated from southern Canada and most of U.S.A.)

year. Mating, which occurs only once a year, takes place between late February and April (depending on the latitude) and 63 days later the pups are born. The average size of a litter is 5 or 6, but in some instances the number may be 7 or 8 and (but rarely) even up to 14.

Denning sites may be among the roots of fallen trees, in hollow logs, rock crevices or outcrops, in abandoned beaver houses and fox holes, or, in the Keewatin Barrens, in burrows dug into "eskers"—ridges of glacially deposited sand. Most dens contain at least two entrances, and the passages to the nursery chambers may be anywhere from 7 to 30 feet (2-9 m) in length. The average length is about 12 feet (4 m). The nursery chambers contain no bedding.

Wolf cubs are born with a furry, sooty-gray or dark brown coat, and each weighs about a pound (0.5 kg). Their eyes open in 10 to 13 days and are slate blue. In about 3 months their eyes turn yellow as in adults. At 3 weeks or so, the cubs leave the pitch-black nursery area to make their first hesitant, stumbling forays outside. They continue to suckle until they are about 2 months old and by that time they are gangly, awkward, 15-pound (7 kg) youngsters with long legs and large feet.

Wolves are residents of the wild and, like humans, must eat to survive. And to survive is as much their right as it is ours. (Photo by Bill Lowry)

Now they are ready for solid food, but until they can forage successfully on their own, the mother provides most of their food by regurgitating at the den site, dropping meat and other food she has carried home in her stomach and partly digested on the way. Solid food also is occasionally brought to the pups. When the parents go hunting, other wolves will often "baby sit" the pups until they return.

The rearing and educating of the young is a process in which the whole pack plays a part, and it is an example of family unity and affection in which much time is devoted to fun and games. Most observers believe, however, that the "fun and games" aspect of pack activity serves other important purposes. Dr. Theberge writes that "play provides the mutual interaction necessary for pups to form a bond with their own species, a bond that later allows for cooperation in hunting, mating and care of the young. During this period pups also learn individual characteristics of their

littermates, parents and other wolves in the pack; the groundwork is laid for social hierarchies that enable wolves to resolve disputes without fighting."

When the den has been permanently vacated, the family moves to a new location, an acre or so in size, from which the animals range over their previously declared territory. These territories, identified by means of urination and defecation "posts" (tree stumps, grassy hillocks, rocks, for example) may be anywhere from 50 to 260 square miles (130-673 km²) in extent, depending on latitude and nature of the terrain, and on the type and abundance of prey species living within them. Territorial rights are respected by wolves of other packs, so violations are seldom in the nature of incursions. It is a system of "land claims" also used by animals such as cougars and other members of the Felidae family.

While wolves eat a variety of small animals such as muskrats, hares, voles, lemmings and raccoons, by far the largest part of their diet is made up of deer, caribou, elk, moose and beaver. It has been the wolves' high kill of members of the deer family that has helped to give *C. lupus* such a shady reputation; that and the now thoroughly discredited claims that wolves are a threat to human life. Even the argument that, except in isolated areas, they seriously endanger livestock has been shown to be ill-founded. Scientists have long known that kills of deer, elk, caribou and moose are usually those animals that are young, sick, injured or of advanced age. The proportion of young of all four species killed can at times be substantial, but more so in the case of deer and migrating caribou.

Wolves are not especially adroit as killers. On even terms most animals can outrun them, and they give up easily if the race is too demanding. Success depends on forcing their prey into a position of disadvantage, such as chasing deer into deep snow, into swamps, or on hard surfaces such as frozen lakes. When hunting as a pack, they often encircle their quarry, and once surrounded the animal may be doomed. But not always. Isle Royale studies have shown that while moose are often encircled, the wolves in most cases actually leave. Any healthy moose on the defensive is not to be lightly reckoned with.

Wolves do not normally kill more than they can eat, but if edible parts are abandoned they are eagerly finished off by foxes, fishers, martens or wolverines. Often the wolves themselves will return to feast again on their kills. In the Arctic, ravens, herring gulls and

This hauntingly beautiful photograph shows a pair of wolves (male in the foreground) making their way across the Arctic tundra. (Photo by Dr. David R. Gray)

barren ground grizzlies feast on whatever is left of caribou carcasses. A host of other creatures also benefit, such as shrews and suet-eating birds. Since animal matter is recycled in many ways, in the wild there really is no such thing as "waste."

Wolf predation of deer and other large animals helps to maintain a proper balance between animals and their available food supplies. Numerous census counts show beyond doubt that when, for example, deer populations exceed the food supply many of the animals die of starvation. By killing the weak, and some prime animals too, and so favoring healthy prey populations, wolves serve nature and man and for this we should be grateful.

Because of size differences, color variations and habitat, wolves are known by a number of descriptive common names such as gray wolf, timber wolf, black wolf, white wolf, great plains wolf and Arctic wolf. The subspecies, *C.l. irremotus*, a large whitish animal, is

on the endangered list. A few individuals still roam the mountains of southwestern Alberta and southeastern British Columbia. At the time of writing, U.S. scientists were focusing their attention on this subspecies and evidence is now accumulating to suggest that there may be some of the animals in Montana. It is not known if there are any in Wyoming. The common names for *C.l. irremotus* are northern Rocky Mountain wolf and Montana gray wolf.

The number of subspecies of *C. lupus* once recognized in North America has been substantially reduced and may even be reduced further. Of the 23 currently listed, the most common are the Mackenzie Valley wolf (*C. l. occidentalis*), the eastern wolf (*C. l. lycaon*) and the Hudson Bay wolf (*C.l. hudsonicus*). The endangered red wolf of the southern United States, thought by some to be a distinct species (*C. rufus*), is commonly classified as a subspecies of *C. lupus*.

Despite the centuries-old hatred of this animal and the concerted efforts to eliminate it, the wolf continues to hold its own over large areas even though it has been forced out of many of its old ranges and many subspecies have disappeared or are in danger. Occasionally statements are made that there may be as many wolves in North America today as there were when the white man first arrived, but this is unlikely.

What we are beginning to understand is that while we have a responsibility to implement control measures whenever wolves conflict with the best interests of human society—not a few individuals, but human society—blanket condemnation of these creatures is no longer acceptable. In the natural order of things wolves are neither "good" nor "bad." They are simply residents of the wild which, like humans, must eat to survive. And to survive is as much their right as it is ours.

Alopex lagopus
Arctic Fox

At first glance the little white-cloaked animal with the long bushy tail looked for all the world like a large Persian cat, curiously misplaced on the lonely Arctic tundra. It was barely visible against the background of snow, but when it turned its head the black of its eyes and blunt little nose left no doubt as to its presence. Its forward movement, as it sniffed the snow surface, was cautious and halting. Suddenly it pounced and its two front feet began digging furiously. In seconds a tiny white creature, squeaking in terror and desperately trying to wriggle free, was securely held in the hunter's mouth. The lemming, weighing barely 3 ounces (85 g), fur included, soon disappeared, its role in the wildlife food chain fulfilled.

This act, one of thousands of similar incidents that occurred that day, was only a part of the larger drama being performed on the vast Arctic stage. A few hours later the scene changed. The white fox, *Alopex lagopus*, its appetitie satisfied with other lemming meals, made its way under the snow-hardened cornice overhanging an esker. Suddenly there was a loud snap and a cry of pain from the fox; its leg was securely held in the Eskimo's trap. But this was not to be the man's prize, not this time, because before the week was over a wolf came upon the fox's frozen body and once again a ravenous appetite was appeased.

The Arctic fox occurs throughout a circumpolar range. In North America it is resident from northern Alaska to coastal Labrador, and north to virtually all of the Arctic islands. It is resident in the Pribilofs, the Aleutians and other islands off the coast of Alaska. Its southern range extends to northern Manitoba, although individuals sometimes are found in northern

Unlike most wild animals, Arctic foxes have little fear of humans. After sizing up the photographer this individual proceeded to attend to a more pressing matter—an itch. (Photos by Dr. David R. Gray)

Newfoundland and even as far south as Cape Breton Island. These Atlantic Coast occurrences are animals that have become isolated on southward-flowing ice packs that are eventually moved shoreward by the currents.

The Arctic fox, sometimes called the white fox, averages about 7 pounds (3 kg) in weight (about that of the Arctic hare), although some specimens occasionally grow much larger. A typical fox would measure 30 to 45 inches (80-114 cm) in length, and its long, very bushy tail might be more than a third the length of the whole body. It has a round head and a blunt nose and its ears are short and rounded. Its eyes are golden yellow.

Like its cousins the swift fox and the gray fox, its legs are short, but in all three the long thick fur which covers the body makes them appear bigger than they really are. The soles of the feet are fully furred, providing additional insulation against the severe cold. So well insulated is the Arctic fox, in fact, that only the coldest and stormiest of weather forces it to seek shelter. When this occurs, the animal generally digs itself into a snowbank or seeks protection under the windswept overhang of a snowdrift. Like all foxes, it curls itself into a little ball and wraps its tail around its body. In this position, protected by its long thick covering of fur, the fox can maintain its body heat when the temperature plunges as low as $-40°F$ $(-40°C)$.

Despite the vastness of the far north, it would be exceptional for a traveler not to encounter these little creatures at some stage of a journey, whether in winter or in summer. This would apply especially from late May to the end of June, for it is during that time that the six to eleven pups born to each mated pair emerge from their underground nursery. When several families are resident in the same area, the commotion caused by the yapping, yipping, barking, whining youngsters and adults is so resonant that it can be heard across the clear northern air for a mile or so. These sounds are not, however, like domestic dog sounds, but are more highly pitched and undulating.

Arctic foxes are normally solitary animals and it is only during the mating season or when they are lured to a common feast—such as the carcass of a stranded

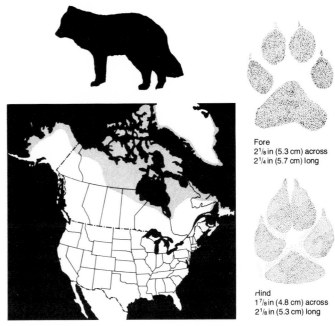

Fore
2¹⁄₈ in (5.3 cm) across
2¹⁄₄ in (5.7 cm) long

Hind
1⁷⁄₈ in (4.8 cm) across
2¹⁄₈ in (5.3 cm) long

Arctic fox

whale or the remains of an animal killed by a wolf or polar bear—that they may appear to be social animals. As a breeding pair they are gentle and solicitous toward each other, although the dog fox will put up a good fight to gain possession of a vixen. As feasters, they scrap noisily among themselves but these scraps are rarely serious. For the most part *A. lagopus* wanders about the land alone.

Arctic foxes mate between February and April and the young are born during May and June. Dens are usually dug in the dry sandy soil of eskers, river banks or small hillocks, although some give birth to their young in holes on rocky slopes. Many of the dens have been in use for several hundred years and over such long periods of time new tunnels to nursery areas have been excavated. Banfield writes that some dens may have as many as 60 entrances but that the average number is 12.

The young are blind when born, weigh about 2 ounces (57 g), and are clothed in dark brown fur. Their growth is rapid and by the third or fourth week they begin leaving the den for their first exploratory trips in the open. When they are 5 to 6 weeks of age they are weaned, and by this time the guard hairs that will provide them with their thick, luxurious outercoat begin to show prominently. During these early days, the parents display unusual affection and concern for their cubs. As is common among Canidae, the dog fox shares the responsibility for providing food, and this is especially so when the vixen is lactating.

The appetite of an average litter is astonishing and according to S. W. Speller "for . . . 11 whelps just starting to eat solid food, about 30 lemmings are required per day. The demand increases to over 100 lemmings per day just before the whelps leave the den. About 3,500 to 4,000 lemmings are consumed by the adults and young during the denning period."

The affectionate care of the parent foxes is short-lived, for when the young are barely 4 months old, they are abandoned. When they are 8 to 10 months old, they become sexually mature. Their average lifespan is 8 to 10 years.

For most populations of Arctic foxes, other than those living along sea coasts, lemmings are the main source of food. The Canadian Wildlife Service, in fact, says that in the central portion of the District of Keewatin, lemmings make up 90 to 95 per cent of their food intake. But wherever foxes occur their success in obtaining lemmings is greatly affected by the population fluctuations of these little tundra rodents. When lemmings are plentiful — in the millions — foxes, as well as wolves, ermine, wolverines, owls, hawks, glaucous gulls and peregrine falcons, thrive. When cyclic "crashes" occur, resulting in depleted food supplies, hardship follows and the reproductive rate of the other species often declines. Arctic foxes are then forced to abandon traditional hunting areas and often migrate long distances in their quest for food. A remarkable overland migration occurred in 1922 when a scarcity of lemmings forced the foxes to move south. Hundreds made their way to the north shore of the Gulf of St. Lawrence where their foraging devastated colonies of nesting eider ducks.

Arctic foxes are what is known as dimorphic animals: that is, they occur in two distinct forms, white and blue. The reasons for these color phases are not fully understood, but diet is believed to be the controlling factor. Arctic foxes whose main diet is made up of lemmings, along with other Arctic voles, ptarmigan and carrion (supplemented in summer with feasts of ground squirrels and the eggs and fledglings of birds) are predominantly white. Those that are resident along coastal areas and rely heavily on marine life such as

mollusks, crustaceans and various forms of echinoderms — in addition to whatever food may be cast up by the tide, fish that come in to spawn, and the eggs and chicks of nesting seabird colonies — are predominantly blue. The blue phase is more common in populations in the Aleutians, Pribilofs, Greenland and Iceland. This coloration, however, is sometimes found in all populations regardless of habitat. Throughout the whole circumpolar range of *A. lagopus*, white foxes vastly outnumber the blue variety. Supporting the theory that diet influences color is the fact that in Iceland, where there are *no* lemmings, the foxes are all of the blue variety, whereas in Greenland, where lemmings occur only in isolated areas, the ratio of blues and whites is approximately even.

The color changes for both types occur at the times of molting, the first occurring in the spring and the second in late summer. In the transformation from their winter to summer coats, their long, dense fur is replaced with a shorter, thinner covering. The glistening white pelage of the white fox is gradually replaced with hair that is dark brown on the animal's back, tail and legs, and fawnish on the belly and flanks. The bluish-gray of the blue fox undergoes a less dramatic change and in most cases simply assumes a darker shade. The colors change again when the winter coats

This Arctic fox, a resident of Bathurst Island, N.W.T., is shown in its summer pelage. (Photo by Dr. David R. Gray)

In winter the coat of the Arctic fox is made up of long, luxuriously soft, dense fur. (Photo by Dr. David R. Gray)

of underfur and guard hairs grow in. The white fox, like the winter ptarmigan, becomes snow white, while the blue fox assumes a slightly paler blue color.

An interesting characteristic of Arctic foxes is their lack of fear of humans. Passers-by have noted that the animals will come out of their burrows and stare at them, or follow them on the trail. Sometimes they gather around the fringes of a campfire, and the more daring ones will try to steal food. Fred Breummer (*Encounters with Arctic Animals*), relating his experiences at Cape Churchill, said that "when we walked out with a flashlight, they stopped and stared, greenish eyes glowing in the dark, then scurried away. If we turned off the torch and sat quietly on the porch, they came back, and scampered all about us, like gray furry goblins in the light of the moon."

Trapping is still an important source of income for northerners, especially for the Eskimo people, and the most marketable of Arctic fox furs are those taken during the winter months. During those months the pelage is glistening and luxuriously thick. One trapper, living on Victoria Island in the western Arctic, is reported to have earned nearly $50,000 in one season.

Vulpes vulpes
Red Fox

If all the stories, true or concocted, of the intelligence and craftiness of the red fox were brought together, the material would form the basis of a sizable book. There was, for example, the fox that stole one egg every day from a farmer's hen house and, when it had a dozen or so on hand, enjoyed the luxury of having two of them each morning for breakfast, sunny-side up! And then there was the fox, a pack of dogs in hot pursuit, that ran to the top of a cliff, side-stepped into a bush at the edge of the precipice at the last moment, and joyfully watched the dogs plummet to their deaths. One fox, also hard pressed by hounds, is said to have run onto thin ice, knowing very well that the heavy hounds would crash through and drown. As good as any is the story of the fox, just yards ahead of a pack of yowling barking dogs, that plunged headlong into a haystack where a friendly skunk and her family were known to make their home, a fact the dogs were unaware of. The fox came out to safety on the other side, but the dogs were thoroughly sprayed by the skunk and the chase came to an abrupt end.

While all of these stories, including the marvelous *Reynard the Fox* stories written for children, stretch anthropomorphic licence beyond the limit, there is little doubt that the animal has a mind of its own and skill to match it. Making its trail difficult for dogs and other predators to follow calls for premeditated craftiness, and the fox excels at this: when, for example, it walks along fences, enters a hollow log part way and back-tracks over its trail, criss-crosses brooks or runs along a stream—each maneuver designed to kill its scent or otherwise frustate its pursuers. Or are these tall tales too?

This animal, a member of the dog family (Canidae), for better or for worse has been recognized by man since ancient times. St. Luke, in alluding to the artful and cruel conduct of King Herod, likened him to a fox, and the fox was castigated in the *Song of Solomon* —"take us the Foxes, the little Foxes, that spoil the vines." This was a reference to the fox's fondness for grapes. In a fable, Reynard was said to remark about grapes he couldn't reach that he didn't want them anyway because they were probably sour.

Like the Atlantic salmon, *V. vulpes* is referred to repeatedly in European literature, especially in English literature about country life and such sporting activities as riding to hounds. Typifying the great sporting events of England are the famous Quorm and Belvoir hunts in the Midlands, events that led Oscar Wilde to refer to them as "the unspeakable in full pursuit of the uneatable." The fox, in art, is the central theme of rare and priceless tapestries and paintings, many of the latter reproduced on place mats and as prints.

Of the four species of foxes, in North America, *V. vulpes*, with its nine subspecies, is one of the most widely distributed of all North American wild animals. Populations are resident in every province and state except for coastal British Columbia and offshore islands, Florida and the other deep southeast states, some parts of the Great Plains, and some parts of the southwest Rocky Mountains. They are present in Alaska, Yukon, and the Northwest Territories, and some individuals have managed to establish themselves on Baffin Island and Southampton Island in the eastern Arctic. They are also widely distributed throughout Europe, Asia and North Africa.

The red fox is a small but beautiful creature, dog-like in appearance, that averages about 42 inches (1.1 m) in length (tail included), 14 inches (36 cm) in height (at the shoulder) and 12 pounds (5.5 kg) or so in weight. Its outer coat is long and silky and its tail, which is a third the length of the body, is exceptionally bushy. The underfur of the body is long and thick and is gray with buffy-colored tips. The throat, chest and belly are white, as are the inside of the ears. The nose, the outside of the ears along the edges, the feet and lower parts of the legs are black. The foot pads are furred. A distinguishing characteristic is that it is the only fox whose tail is white-tipped.

Although most specimens answer to this description, a variety of color phases occur, even in the same litter. As a consequence, there are rare individuals known as cross fox, silver fox and black fox.

The cross fox is reddish-yellow and gets its name from the broad black bands that run down its back and across its shoulders. The silver fox is black, its outer guard hairs silver-tipped. The black fox is simply that— black. When fox fur was at the height of its popularity, silver foxes were bred in captivity and for a time formed the basis of a small but highly lucrative business. Foxes are still killed for their fur and the fox farming that became widespread in the 1920s still persists, but on a small scale.

A rare and curious form of red fox is the Samson fox, a creature completely devoid of outer guard hairs.

The name derives from a story in the *Book of Judges*, which tells how Samson used foxes to do mischief to his enemies. "And Samson went and caught three hundred Foxes, and took fire-brands, and turned tail to tail, and put a fire-brand in the midst of the two tails. And when he had set the brands on fire, he let them go into the standing corn of the Philistines, and burnt up both the shocks and also the standing corn, with the vineyards and olives." Whatever good qualities may be ascribed to Samson, a love of animals was not one of them, for the guard hairs were scorched off the backs of the poor creatures. Thus did "singed" foxes come to be called Samsons.

The red fox is at home in a wide variety of habitats, ranging from the northern tundra well beyond the tree-line (where the largest specimens are found), to mountainous country, prairie lands, hardwood and softwood forests, farms and the greenbelts of cities and towns. One fox, whose audacity made newspaper headlines, lived for a time at Yankee Stadium in New York where, between games, it fed on rats that grew fat on the peanuts, popcorn and other food dropped by the patrons.

Whatever their habitat, foxes normally confine their roaming to specific territorial areas. These vary in size, depending on the density of the fox population itself and the availability of food, but the average is believed to be 1 to 4 square miles (3-10 km²). Limited though these areas may be, the nightime wanderings of some individuals may be as much as 20 miles (32 km). The average sunset to sunrise movements, however, are probably from 5 to 10 miles (8-16 km). Young foxes, when they leave their parents in the autumn to live

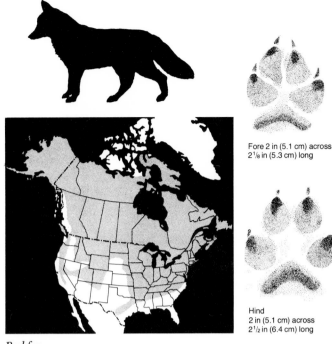

Red fox

Fore 2 in (5.1 cm) across
2¹⁄₈ in (5.3 cm) long

Hind
2 in (5.1 cm) across
2¹⁄₂ in (6.4 cm) long

independent lives, may travel more than 100 miles (161 km) before they find their own mates and establish their own home ranges.

The time of mating varies according to geography and in some areas may be between the end of December and the end of March, in others in late January through February. Male and female are known to establish a relationship before the female comes into heat, but it is only just prior to and during the mating, and after the young have been weaned and go their separate ways in the fall, that the two adults enjoy each other's company—and even this may be for only parts of the day or night.

Dr. J. David Henry, who has extensively studied red foxes in Prince Albert National Park, attributes this mainly detached relationship to their predatory habits. Vixen and dog fox will share a common or "family" territory and will keep in touch with each other by means of scent marks. But because they are, of necessity, solitary hunters they are unable to associate closely. As a rule, the prey they kill (they prefer mice and rabbits) is small, alert and quick in its reactions, and must be stalked stealthily in cat-like fashion. Generally it is large enough to provide just one meal.

Red foxes often catch mice in tall grass in this fashion.

The red fox, one of the most intelligent of all wild animals, is sometimes a nuisance around farms, but its consumption of rodents and insects makes it an ally, not a foe. (Photo by Dr. Donald R. Gunn)

Dr. Henry says that the length of the animal's lunges at its prey is usually from 2 to 6 feet (0.6-1.8 m). There have been occasions, however, when he has observed a lunge of 15 feet (4.6 m)—from a standing start! Foxes, he adds, when stalking a prey *downhill* have been observed by him in air-borne lunges a distance of 25 feet (7.6 m).

Vicious fights, sometimes resulting in serious lacerations, frequently occur among males vying for the same female. Then the dog fox, despite the fact that it has won a mate and the two have become a seasonally permanent unit, is inclined to be promiscuous and may breed several other females. It is not uncommon, as a result, for two litters to share the same den—a remarkable display of tolerance and goodwill by both vixens.

Most red foxes prefer to make their dens under-

ground and for this purpose will either dig their own or enlarge dens formerly occupied by other animals such as ground squirrels and groundhogs. Others make their nurseries in the hollow of trees, in protected caves or rock overhangs, or where there is a dense growth of bushes. Foxes, incidentally, are among the few carnivores that can actually dig out their own burrows.

Underground dens normally have more than one entrance, but the main one, sometimes marked by a large mound, usually faces south to get the benefit of the warmth of the sun and to avoid prevailing westerly winds. A clear view is also preferred so that approaching predators can be more quickly seen. The floor of the nesting chamber, which may be as much as 15 feet (5 m) back and 10 feet (3 m) down, is generally well padded with insulating material such as grasses and leaves.

Foxes (an average litter of seven) are born after a gestation period of about 53 days. At birth they weigh 3 to 4 ounces (85-113 g) and carry their first undercoat of brown- or gray-colored fur. As they mature, the long silky guard hairs grow in to completely hide the under-coat. The cubs' eyes open when they are about two weeks old. The vixen remains constantly with the babies for the first two weeks; the father, although rarely entering the den during that time, leaves food for her at the entrance. When she finally leaves for short periods of time to exercise and to forage on her own, the father takes over protective duties and is very solicitous toward the young.

For about 3 months the cubs make the den—or perhaps other nearby dens—their home, venturing outside more and more frequently to play, to eat small animals brought to them by their parents, and to learn to hunt and kill on their own. They are completely weaned in 8 weeks.

The senses of the red fox are well developed, especially hearing and smell. Their diet is diversified and is not, as some people are led to believe, directed primarily toward the farmers' henhouses. Generally speaking, while foxes prefer mice and rabbits, when grasshoppers are abundant they gorge on them, as they do on other insects. Wild fruits are favorites—apples, blackberries, blueberries, grapes and cherries. They will eat frogs, muskrats, worms, grass, nuts, ground-nesting birds and their eggs, and carrion. They like ground squirrels. While attracted to game birds such as quail, grouse and pheasant, usually they are simply not fast enough to catch them. Whenever they can, they will raid a farmer's chicken or duck enclosure. Some-times they kill piglets. But one must come quickly to the defense of foxes in relation to their forays on domestic poultry and the like. While they enjoy an occasional chicken, they feed much more heavily on small rodents and insects that, if uncontrolled, could cause great damage to farmers' crops. The farmer with a fox in residence has an ally, not a foe.

With the arrival of autumn, the family unit begins to break up as the pups, now well developed and capable of looking after themselves, wander farther and farther away from the den site. Eventually they answer the urge to establish their own territories, and these may be near by if available, or many miles away. The dog fox and the vixen also lose interest in each other and finally separate, often to reunite a few months later.

Foxes do not hibernate and like Arctic huskies are able to withstand the cold winter temperatures. To protect themselves in sub-zero weather, they curl up on the ground and virtually wrap their thick tail around themselves, thus protecting their nose and feet from frostbite. Seton, in fact, believed that foxes, as well as coyotes, would not be able to survive the winters were it not for their brushes.

The red fox, a shy and nervous animal, is most active at night although it may sometimes be seen during the day when it patrols its territory or when it is on a hunting expedition. But as it seeks food, it too is sought. Its worst natural enemies are coyotes and bob-cats. The agility of the fox generally enables it to out-run, and outwit, wolves.

*Vulpes velox**

Swift Fox

This species, once present in southwestern Saskatche-wan, southern Alberta and southeastern British Colum-bia, is now believed to be extinct in Canada, although the Canadian Wildlife Federation suggests that a few individuals may remain in the Cypress Hills of south-western Saskatchewan. It is, however, still present in its midwest United States range but in some states it is recognized as endangered and is therefore protected. Its decline has been caused by loss of habitat and by indiscriminate predator-control programs. It inhabits short-grass country and other arid areas.

The swift fox is not much bigger than a well-developed house cat and measures about a foot (30 cm) in height at the shoulder and about 24 to 32 inches (61-81 cm) in length and weighs 3 to 6 pounds (1.4-2.7 kg). Its forehead, back and tail are grizzled gray, the sides are buff-yellow, the underparts are white, and the legs, shoulders and back of the ears are buffy. The tail is well furred and cylindrical and tipped with black, and a prominent black mark occurs below the eyes on each side of the snout.

This mammal is solitary and mostly nocturnal. It makes its den in open country where it either excavates a burrow itself or expropriates one made by a badger or marmot. The burrow is generally about 3 feet (1 m) below the surface and up to 10 feet (3 m) in length with one to seven entrances. The entrances (or exits) are easily identified by the mounds of earth on the surface.

The time of mating ranges from December through to February, depending on the area, and the couple often remains together for life. Two to seven pups are born after a gestation period of 50 days. When

*Considered by many taxonomists as a subspecies of the southern kit fox (*V. macrotis*).

The swift fox is exactly that — swift. It can run, for short distances, as fast as 25 miles (40 km) an hour. (Photo by Peter Karsten)

the young are about 3 weeks old, they leave the den at which time the mother teaches them how to hunt. Small mammals, birds, insects, grasses, berries and sometimes fish make up their diet. In winter the swift fox caches its excess food under the soil. Like its relatives, it is active all year. One characteristic of special interest is the speed it attains when running from a terrestrial predator: it can move for short distances as fast as 25 miles (40 km) an hour. Its natural enemies are coyotes and golden eagles.

Urocyon cinereoargenteus

Gray Fox

This animal is unique among canids in that it climbs trees and moves about in them with remarkable ease. It is relatively rare in Canada, being found only in southern Manitoba, a small southern area of northwestern Ontario, southern Ontario and possibly the Eastern Townships of Quebec. It is present in most of the United States except the central states of the mid-west (an approximation).

The gray fox is grizzled gray on the face, back and sides, changing to red near the belly, which is white. The throat and chest are white, encircled with a band of red. The front edges of the hind legs are also white, as are the inside of the ears. The tail, long and thick, carries along its top to its tip a prominent black stripe. Adult males weigh about 7$\frac{1}{4}$ to 13 pounds (3-6 kg), measure in height about 14 to 15 inches (36-38 cm) at the shoulder and are about 32 to 45 inches (81-114 cm) in length. Females are always smaller.

The habitat of this animal is generally forested or brushy areas. It seldom digs its own den, and although it will move into one formerly occupied by a red fox or a woodchuck, it will also take up residence in a hollow log or a rock crevice. Mating takes place from late January to March. Three or four pups are born in the spring and after a weaning period of 3 months they are able to forage for themselves. The food of the gray fox includes numerous species of rodents, as well as birds, insects, plants, fruits and vegetables.

The gray fox is mostly nocturnal, although it occasionally is seen during the day. Its main enemies, aside from man, are dogs and bobcats.

FAMILY URSIDAE

Ursus americanus

Black Bear

The black bear is the smallest North American member of the Ursidae family. But small in this case is a relative term only, for males of the species at maturity reach an average weight of 300 pounds (136 kg), a length of 5 feet (1.5 m) or so, and a height of up to 4 feet (1.2 m). In exceptional cases males have attained a weight of more than 600 pounds (270 kg). Females are considerably smaller and weigh on average 150 pounds (68 kg).

Black bears are among North America's best known wild animals—the quarry of big game hunters, stars of television programs, and panhandling entertainers of thousands of people who annually visit national, state and provincial parks. Unlike the unpredictable grizzlies—animals to be feared in the wild—the blacks, with encouragement, are more inclined to accept a social relationship with humans. This relationship is generally an unsatisfactory one for, having lost their fear of man, some animals go on a rampage of destruction in campsites and cottages in their search for food. At such times they can be extremely dangerous. In wilderness areas, however, black bears avoid contact with man and will rarely attack humans except when with cubs, when they feel threatened with no means of escape, or in spring when hibernation is over and they are hungry and irritable.

Black bears are found mainly in wooded areas of North America where there are thick growths of deciduous and coniferous trees. Some, however, prefer alpine meadows and hardwood swamps, but they avoid arid desert country and the open barrens beyond the Arctic treeline. Wherever they occur, they add a desirable quality to the wilderness and are as much a part of it as the chattering of squirrels, the sweet perfume of spruce trees or the melancholy cry of the loon.

The versatility and intelligence of black bears are well known. They can climb up and down trees with remarkable agility, they can relax happily while stretched out 50 feet above ground on a branch only a few inches in diameter, they can swim strongly and for several miles at a stretch, they can run as fast as 35 miles (56 km) an hour for short distances. They rear and train families with patience that would do credit to the wisest of human parents.

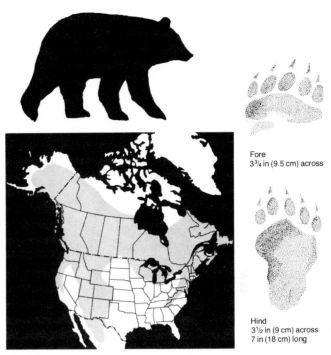

Black bear

Fore
3¾ in (9.5 cm) across

Hind
3½ in (9 cm) across
7 in (18 cm) long

In their quest for food they balance their diet with a menu ranging from carpenter ants and grasshoppers to wild honey, a variety of grasses, sedges, berries and nuts. They relish mice, squirrels, chipmunks, ground squirrels, young deer, spawning salmon and the decaying flesh of dead animals. Some observers claim that when feasting at a garbage dump they consume just about everything in sight: paper, cardboard, aluminum foil and even pieces of wood, hardly a diet for an animal officially classified as a carnivore! As a result, black bears are generally regarded as omnivores.

A great deal of study has been carried out on the biology and behavior of bears and a significant scientific and popular literature has been developed around them. But this is all new compared to the prominent role bears have played in the ancient mythology and totemistic beliefs of the Indians of the Pacific northwest. Evidence of this is found in the carvings and decorative art portraying full-face, and profiles of, squatting bears. A bear cult also has been practiced for many years by the Ainu people of Hokkaido, northern Japan, and an image of a squatting bear was found in Anyang, China, which experts have dated at about 1,300 BC.

Male black bears in the wild are solitary animals, preferring to remain aloof from others of their kind except for the mating season in June and July, when both males and females are boisterous and affectionate. Some observers, during this brief period of togetherness, have seen them standing in an upright position, hugging each other or exchanging playful cuffs. When mating has been completed, the two separate. Sexual maturity for both is reached during their third or fourth year, although sometimes it is later in life.

After mating, female bears experience what is known as "delayed implantation." In other words, implantation of the fertilized egg in the uterus does not take place immediately after copulation as is customarily the case with most other animals, including humans. The reasons for this are still under study, but George Kolenosky, a bear specialist with the Ontario Ministry of Natural Resources, offers this intriguing suggestion: "Probably this delay allows the bear's system time to gauge whether implantation should occur or not. If food supplies during the summer were adequate, and the female was able to accumulate sufficient fat reserve to successfully produce and feed young, then implantation occurs. If conditions were not favorable, the fertilized egg does not implant. In essence, the delay can prevent unnecessary expenditure of body energy."

With the coming of fall and its crisp short days, black bears, now well fattened after a summer of almost constant feeding and covered with a glossy coat of warm thick hair, seek out their den sites. Unlike grizzlies and polar bears, which go to some lengths to establish comfortable winter homes, black bears are more easily satisfied. Any protected area—a hillside hole or cave, a hollow under a fallen log, or a place under the overhang of a ledge—will do. When the choice is made, the bottom area of the den is lined with grass, leaves and the like, but this extra effort to be warm and comfortable seems to be made primarily by females, no doubt for the benefit of the young which will be born the following late January or early February. Some black bears, however, will excavate to depths of 4 and 5 feet (1.2 and 1.5 m) when constructing winter dens and will rake leaves for distances of 90 feet (27 m) or so for lining and, possibly, camouflage.

Dens may be made in other ways. For example, it is known that some bears have used drainage culverts while others, in Yellowstone National Park, have made their winter homes in the steam-heated fissures of hotspring formations. Whether they have demanded room-service is unrecorded.

Bears do not go into deep sleep as do some other mammals, and for the most part their hibernation, which generally lasts until spring, is a state of lethargic torpidity. It is not uncommon for a hibernating bear to be aroused sufficiently on warm winter days to leave its den for short excursions before returning to resume its sleep.

The birth of the young—usually one the first time, and then two or even up to five thereafter—occurs when winter is at its peak and the den is still blanketed with snow. The cub or cubs are born naked, blind and toothless and weigh about half a pound (0.2 kg). By the time spring has arrived, they weigh about 10 pounds (4.5 kg), their eyes are open, permanent teeth have begun to appear, and they carry a thick coat of soft woolly fur. When the family emerges from the den in spring, the young are fat, boisterous and eager to take on the new world around them.

Few animals in the wild show greater affection for their offspring than do female bears, whether black, grizzly or polar. Training begins immediately after the den is abandoned. One of the first lessons taught black bear cubs is the need to scamper to safety up trees when commanded to do so and to remain there until permitted to come down. This defensive maneuver is used primarily when there is danger of attack by itinerant black bears or when grizzlies, which seldom climb trees, appear on the scene. Adult blacks have a great fear of grizzlies and will run from them.

While some females will adopt orphan or stray cubs, others will have nothing to do with them. Victor Cahalane, the noted American biologist, tells of one such cub that was consistently chased up a tree by a female it had been trying to suckle. The youngster was found a few days later by its mother when she happened to recognize its scent on the bark of the tree where it had sought refuge. "Rising up on her hind feet," Cahalane wrote, "she grunted urgently and affectionately to him to come down. The reunion was very touching. She fondled him and talked to him with comforting sounds. Then she cleaned him and sat down to nurse him and his sister at her breasts."

The family unit remains intact for about a year and a half. By that time the yearlings are well able to look after themselves and the mother is ready to mate again. Although well trained in the art of finding food and in defending themselves, the young ones face a period that is fraught with danger. If they have learned their

Black bears inhabit most of North America with the exception of arid desert country and open barrens beyond the treeline. They are especially fond of wilderness areas with thick growths of deciduous and coniferous trees. (Photo by Wayne Lankinen/Valan Photos)

lessons well, they will avoid contact with humans, grizzlies and adult blacks. If they survive this period of adolescence, they stand a good chance of living up to 10 to 14 years. Captive bears have lived to 30 years but such longevity is rare.

Black bears are well organized socially, particularly in the matter of territorial rights. Most females remain within well defined ranges varying from 6 to 12 square miles (12.5-31 km²) in area. Males, however, tend to wander over greater areas. Their ranges, being much larger, often overlap the ranges of several females. Both sexes follow the practice of mutual avoidance, except

flat dorsal contour   light muzzle

Black bear

shoulder hump

beard

long claws

Grizzly bear

streamlined body adapted to swimming and diving

Polar bear

during the mating season and on rare occasions when a few unrelated families or individuals may share a particularly luscious berry patch.

Like grizzlies and polar bears, black bears are bulky and thickset. They are normally black in color, with a light brownish muzzle and a white patch on the throat or across the chest. There are, however, as with grizzlies, marked color differences within families and races. The most interesting of these are the "white" or so-called Kermode bears of northern coastal British Columbia. It is possible, as Yorke Edwards suggests, that these bears are part of a population of black bears showing unusually frequent albinism.

Black bears are found in every province of Canada except Prince Edward Island, as well as the Yukon and Northwest Territories. There are large populations in Alaska. In continental United States they occur over an extensive, but irregular range. (See range map).

A recent finding, as reported in the *Journal of Mammalogy* by Lynn L. Rogers, is that black bears shed their foot pads during hibernation. This is of interest, as in most mammals "cells of the foot pads are lost *as a result of activity* and are replaced simultaneously by new cells produced in underlying epidermal layers." (Bloom and Fawcett, *A Textbook of Histology.*) Mr. Kolenosky, who has pursued this study, writes that at the time of shedding "the pads are still quite tender, and this may partially explain the reluctance of bears to move any great distances shortly after spring emergence. . . ."

Ursus arctos
Grizzly Bear

No other terrestrial carnivore other than the polar bear equals the grizzly in size or strength. It is hard to believe that a wild animal, weighing at birth a mere 14 ounces (400 g) and measuring less than 10 inches (25 cm) in length, can grow to a weight of 600 to 800 pounds (270-360 kg) and a length of nearly 9 feet (2.7 m). In exceptional cases, grizzlies have been known to reach 1,500 pounds (680 kg), and one Alaska brown weighed a record 1,656 pounds (752 kg).

Grizzlies at one time ranged across the western half of North America from Alaska, Yukon and the Northwest Territories south to California and Mexico, east in Canada to Manitoba and northern Ontario and in the United States east to the Missouri River. It is possible they may in very early times have been as far east as Ohio and Kentucky.

These frontiers have been so pushed back, mainly as a result of human population spread and consequent predations by man, that the animals are now found in significant numbers only in Montana, Wyoming, Idaho, British Columbia, Alberta, the Mackenzie River Basin of the Northwest Territories, Yukon and Alaska. Relic populations may survive in Washington and some other western states and it is believed that a few remain in Mexico. Recent evidence has confirmed that grizzlies once again are resident in the Ungava Peninsula, and there are also indications that some animals have made their way eastward across the tundra to Hudson Bay and northern Manitoba.

While taxonomists are still striving to reach agreement as to the number of *Ursus arctos* subspecies, there is increasing belief that in North America it can be properly reduced to two: *U. a. horribilis*, the common subspecies, and *U. a. middendorffi*, the big brown bear found on Alaska's Kodiak Island. Some taxonomists in Europe consider that the European brown bear is a third subspecies, *U.a. arctos*. This appears to be a temporary compromise; at least it offers a more realistic number than the 86 species and subspecies listed by name in 1918.

Because of their wilderness habitat and low population densities, accurate counts of grizzlies are virtually impossible. About 200 years ago, it is thought, 100,000 grizzlies roamed continental United States, but today the population numbers less than 1,000, most of them in national parks where they are protected. The Alaskan population, although increasingly threatened, may be around 18,000. No one is certain of the total Canadian population but the most recent estimate is 20,000, most of them found in British Columbia and Yukon. About 350 grizzlies live in national parks in Alberta and British Columbia and are also protected.

In appearance the grizzly can be an awesome creature. Standing on all fours or upright on its hind legs, it can be unbelievably huge, and its great strength is shown not only in its large head, long dished face, short thick neck and stocky powerful legs, but also in the hump of muscle on the shoulders. This hump, in fact, is a fast way of identifying the grizzly; the hump is absent on the black bear. In the Rocky Mountains the races are relatively small—females, for example, weigh only about 300 pounds (135 kg)—so there can be some difficulty in knowing whether a bear only briefly seen was a grizzly or a brown-colored black bear.

The grizzly's rounded, well-furred ears are small relative to the size of the head and are placed well back and wide apart. The eyes are small and set close together. The mouth has large teeth—the usual carnivorous assortment for cutting, holding or crushing. The fur varies in color from blackish-gray through a variety of browns to creamy yellow. In some areas, especially the Rocky Mountains, grizzlies often show hairs that are white- or silver-tipped.

Another feature is the huge front paws, each armed with five long and slightly curved claws which, unlike those of the cat family, are not retractile. These claws register clearly in the tracks left in soft ground.

Black bears have a flat profile.

Grizzlies have a dished profile.

Toe nails of front paws are shorter and darker than in grizzly bears.

Grizzlies have long curved nails light in color.

While there is every reason to fear the grizzly, there is also a pressing need to understand its personality and its instincts for self-preservation and the safety of its young. (Photo by J. C. Holroyd)

The trails used by grizzlies as they move from one range to another are sometimes well defined and often run almost as straight as a survey line, even through the roughest country. Bears in the same area tend to follow the same trail, stepping in the same tracks as the bears before them. If traffic is heavy these tracks become fairly deep depressions. Occasionally, as they travel, the animals reach up as far as they can to claw bark from trees or tear off chunks of the tree with their teeth. Whether this action is to leave territorial signs or simply to stretch and relax their muscles is a matter of conjecture. Some years ago, when I visited the late Jim Stanton, an internationally known grizzly bear guide who lived at the head of Knight Inlet, B.C., I was taken into the rain forest and shown a tree that carried deep, wide claw marks at least 10 feet (3 m) from the ground. It took little imagination to realize how massive the animal must have been.

Grizzly bears occur in all major biogeoclimatic regions of the west including forested slopes, alpine meadows, river flood flatlands of mountainous regions, coastal rain forests, brushlands, river valleys and Arctic tundra. Where they live is influenced not only by the availability of food and suitable denning sites but by the animals' sensitive aversion to the presence of humans. Wherever man encroaches, particularly where there is use of firearms, grizzlies retreat deeper and deeper into the wilderness. In some park areas, however, where there are open garbage dumps and campsites where food is left unprotected, grizzlies have grown less timid and it is often these animals that pose the most serious threat to humans.

Grizzly bears mate between late May and early July, but not until they have reached an age of about five or more years. The courting period may last a month, during which, after copulation, there occurs delayed implantation, the period in which pregnancy takes place but the embryo is temporarily prevented from attaching to the uterus.

In October or November (times vary according to the location) the female enters her den to begin winter hibernation, but this is more a state of lethargy than the deep sleep of other denning animals such as ground squirrels and marmots. Sometime during January or February, or even as late as March, one to four (usually two) cubs are born. The young, remarkably small in relation to the size of the mother, weigh about a pound (0.5 kg) at birth and are covered with silky, dark fur. Growth is rapid and by the time they are 6 months old they weigh close to 60 pounds (27 kg). It should be noted, however, that the reproduction rate of grizzly bears is extremely low, which applies, but somewhat less so, to black bears as well. In the case of the grizzly there is generally a 3- to 4-year interval before the female produces her next litter.

The dens used by grizzlies, as well as black bears, are usually prepared in advance of occupancy. They may be excavated on steep slopes, or they may be in existing hollows under the roots of large trees or in caves on a hillside. Generally they face north or east where there is less sunlight to thaw the snow covering the den entrance. Melting snow would make the den uncomfortably damp and minimize the insulation provided by the lining of evergreen bows and thick layers of dried grasses.

As a rule black bears den at relatively low levels and in well-forested areas. Grizzlies, on the other hand, den at about the 7,200-foot (2,200 m) level. They tend to feed on open slopes in the spring and in the subalpine meadows during the summer. In Banff National Park, the dens are most frequently near the treeline.

Males and females without cubs emerge from their dens in early spring, but females with cubs generally keep themselves and their young in or close to their dens until late April or early May. When they emerge for the first time, the cubs are clothed in rich dark fur and weigh about 20 or 25 pounds (9-11 kg). Like all young animals, they are playful and, when not sleeping or feeding, they spend their time in whatever rough-house behavior they can devise. The doting sow, often the brunt of the cubs' "attacks," is a patient mother but she does not hesitate to administer a severe cuffing if

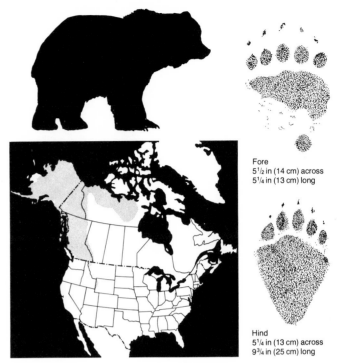

Grizzly bear

Fore
5½ in (14 cm) across
5¼ in (13 cm) long

Hind
5¼ in (13 cm) across
9¾ in (25 cm) long

conduct gets out of hand. Lessons in discipline and prompt obedience are taught as soon as the cubs are old enough to understand. As the weeks go by the cubs continue their rapid growth and by the time they are 6 months old they weigh close to 40 pounds (18 kg). During this time they are gradually weaned and an increasingly important part of their diet is made up of solid foods.

Although scientifically classified as carnivores, grizzlies are primarily omnivores. The diet of a typical grizzly includes a wide variety of vegetation such as grasses, fungi, skunk cabbage and licorice roots, and berries such as blueberies, elderberries, salmonberries and highbush cranberries. When available, they eat insects, ground squirrels, mice, marmots, and spawning or spawned-out salmon. They will also occasionally kill large animals such as elk, deer, moose, black bears, mountain goats and, from time to time, domestic cattle. When a large animal is killed, the grizzly will move it to a protected place, and after gorging itself, will sometimes cover it with earth, branches, leaves and grass and then bed down in a nearby spot where it can keep watch over the remains. Carrion is also eaten and in this connection Andy Russell describes grizzlies as "the clean-up squad of the wilds—they fulfill the function of vultures in more southerly latitudes." Despite their fondness for meat, however, he believes that about 85 per cent of their food in the Rocky Mountains is vegetable; but this appears to vary from region to region and with the time of year.

Mother and cubs remain together for about two years and as long as the cubs are with her, and particularly if they are still suckling, she will not mate. In some instances, according to Dr. Frank Craighead, who has spent a lifetime studying grizzlies, suckling continues for up to 24 months. The usual life expectancy of adults in the wild appears to be 10 to 15 years, although some have been known to live as long as 30 years.

The grizzly is very much a solitary animal and even the mating season, while loving and very passionate, is a short-lived romance. After copulation, which may be repeated several times, both go their separate ways. Much research, often involving tagging and the use of electronic transmitters, has recently gone into learning more about the movements of specific bears. As a rule it has been found that although home ranges vary in size, most stay within a 20-mile (32 km) limit. There are records, however, of grizzlies having traveled more than 100 miles (185 km) from the place of their birth.

Aside from their great size and enormous strength, grizzlies are endowed with other exceptional attributes —acute hearing and sense of smell. Offsetting these, however, is their extremely poor eyesight. Craighead, for example, claims that they are too short-sighted to discern a man much beyond 100 yards (90 m). Weak vision does not lessen their ability to successfully attack their prey. They can outrun a horse, and they can run at a fast clip for half a mile or so without stopping.

While there is every reason to fear the grizzly, there is also a pressing need to understand better its personality—its timid and retiring nature, and its instincts for self-preservation and the safety of its young.

Dr. Stephen Herrero, of the Faculty of Environmental Design and Department of Biology, University of Calgary, has been in the forefront of those scientists determined to defend this great animal and to prove that human beings and grizzlies can co-exist, especially in national parks where man and beast are most likely to confront each other. Dr. Herrero's research into man/bear conflict in those areas in the U.S. and Canada now designated as national parks revealed that during

the 97-year period between 1872 and 1969, only 5 persons were killed by these animals and only 77 sustained injuries. Since 150 million people visited the national parks during that period, the 5 fatalities represent only *one death for each 20 years*, or *one death for every 30 million visitors*.

Subsequent data collected by Dr. Herrero show that during the following three years (1970-73), 23 persons came into direct contact with bears and sustained minor or major injuries. Of this total two died as a result of wounds. This suggested that as more and more people began to visit the national parks during the 1970s injury rates increased somewhat. Ten of the injuries were sustained in Yellowstone and Mt. McKinley National Parks and 13 in Banff, Jasper, Glacier and Revelstoke National Parks.

What the fatalities of the next decade will be is anyone's guess, but in July 1980 a young man and woman camping in Montana's Glacier National Park were mauled to death in a pre-dawn attack while they were asleep in their tent. This bear also destroyed the tent and tore up the campers' belongings.

While the evidence gathered by scientists shows clearly that attacks on humans are numerically infinitesimal, one should not lose sight of the fact that grizzlies *are* dangerous—but then, so are rattlesnakes, white sharks and tsetse flies. The point is, when in the wilderness, and especially when in national parks where grizzlies are known to frequent garbage disposal sites, one must exercise common sense. Approaching bears to get a "better look" or to photograph them, leaving food unprotected at campsites, coming between a mother and her cubs or otherwise acting in a provocative way is to court a confrontation that could have disastrous results. No one should venture into grizzly country without thorough knowledge of the precautionary rules available from government sources.

Travelers in grizzly country should always be on the watch for bear signs such as droppings and fresh tracks. Bears also exude a strong odor. Bears generally go out of their way to avoid humans, so talking, singing, rattling pebbles in a can and making other noises may scare them off. Campers and backpackers should take special precautions to secure their food properly at campsites, to avoid areas where fish, such as migrating salmon, attract bears, and meadows where wild berries are plentiful. But perhaps the first essential precaution is to consult with park authorities or forest rangers about known or suspected locations of bears and so avoid those areas. Grizzlies, incidentally, are most active from dusk to dawn.

Explicit instructions are readily available for human behavior in a bear encounter. Here is what British Columbia wildlife experts advise: "A bear rearing up on its hind legs is probably taking a more careful sniff to make certain of who or what you are. The signs of an attack are growling, with ears laid back. Running or waving of the arms will only provoke a bear. If the bear is close, back away slowly, talking as calmly as possible, towards a tree or behind rocks and into a gully. Do not do anything suddenly. Should a charge be unavoidable, protect your stomach, thigh and neck by lying down on the ground in a hunched position with knees drawn up to the chest and hands clasped over your neck. The bear may try to maul you but it will do less damage if you can manage to lie still. Usually the bear will retreat immediately after the attack. But never run unless you are able to climb a *tall* tree with plenty of time to spare."

It is commonly believed that adult grizzly bears cannot climb trees, but it is also known that there have been exceptions. Dr. Andy Russell advises that he knows of three such climbs, and there is also on record the case of a photographer who, from the "safety" of a limb, tried to attract the attention of a sow with cubs by making noises resembling the squeaking of a rabbit. The grizzly climbed nearly 15 feet (4.5 m) up the tree and hauled the man down. The man, guilty of deliberate provocation, was seriously injured. This and other instances may be exceptional, but it must always be remembered that, even without climbing, a grizzly standing on its hind legs can reach up to 10 or 12 feet (3-3.6 m).

There are those who wish the grizzly bear removed completely from all areas frequented by humans, and those who would have it destroyed wherever it exists. But to do either would be to commit a heinous crime, not only against one of the most magnificent of all wild animals, but against the very substance of our wildernesses. Grizzlies and humans *can* co-exist, but it is for humans—the more intelligent of the two—to set and abide by the rules of common sense behavior.

Stephen Herrero, a compassionate as well as passionate defender of grizzlies, speaks for many wilderness travelers when he says: "The grizzly bear is a symbolic and living embodiment of wild nature, uncontrolled by man. Entering into grizzly country presents a unique opportunity to be part of an ecosystem in which man is not necessarily the dominant species. Through humility, caution, and often worry in such wild areas, I feel that I have developed and discovered parts of myself that might otherwise have lain dormant."

Ursus maritimus

Polar Bear

It is late October. Throughout the circumpolar vastness of the northern hemisphere, pregnant female polar bears ready themselves for winter hibernation. Having mated the previous April or May, they are restless, knowing that the birth of their young is fast approaching and that little time is left to find suitable denning locations.

By now the last of their summer coat has been shed and replaced with a thick blanket of outer guard hairs and dense underfur. Under this covering of waterproof insulation are deep layers of fat, enough to sustain them during their six-month period of semi-consciousness and to help produce the nourishment required by the cubs (usually twins) that will come into the world in December or early January. Pregnant females are the only members of the *Ursus maritimus* species that den up for such long periods of time.

Mature males, non-pregnant females and young of both sexes seek shelter during the winter mainly for periods of rest or to wait out winter storms. Their dens

Grizzly bear with salmon

may be occupied (almost always by single bears) for only a few days, or for as long as three or four months. They may be constructed in heavy snow drifts in much the same way as maternity dens, or under snow ridges, under ice in dried up river beds, or even in protected areas in the lee of icebergs.

Maternity dens are usually made on slopes of hills or in valleys where there is a southern exposure. In such locations, snow driven by northerly winds accumulates in heavy drifts and these help to provide a greater insulation. As a consequence, the inside temperature may register as much as 37° F (21°C) warmer than the temperature outside. Southern exposures also provide longer periods of balmy spring sunshine—ideal conditions for brand new, vigorous cubs to bask and play in.

Maternity dens are excavated and occupied by females two or more months before their cubs are born. Entrance ways, according to Dr. C. Richard Harington, Curator of Quaternary Zoology, National Museum of Natural Sciences, Ottawa, average about 6½ feet (2 m) long, nearly 2 feet (0.6 m) wide and nearly 2 feet (0.6 m) high. Most of the entrances are slightly lower than the one or two (four have been reported) rooms beyond. Sizes of these rooms vary, but on average they are between 6 and 7 feet (1.8-2.1 m) long, nearly 5 feet (1.5 m) wide, and a little more than 3 feet (1 m) high. Alcoves or recesses, thought to be used by the cubs, are commonly found in dens occupied by family units.

Field studies have shown that dens, whether occupied by families or single bears, are remarkably clean. Dr. Harington, in his examination of numerous dens, found only minor traces of urine or excrement. On the other hand, he writes, relatively large amounts of excreta were found within 40 yards (37 m) of three den entrances. Most dens have ventilation holes and often the quickest way of locating a den is to watch for small black spots on the surface of the snow; when it is very cold and there is no wind, wisps of vapor may often be seen rising from these holes.

Normally, most polar bears restrict their terrestrial wanderings to areas beside or near the sea, for it is from the sea that they derive their main food—the ringed and bearded seals. Most maternity dens are located at or near sea level within 5 miles (8 km) of the coast. Some, however, may be as far inland as 30 miles (48 km) and at elevations of up to several hundred feet.

Although pregnancy actually takes place at the time of mating in April or May, it is not until much later

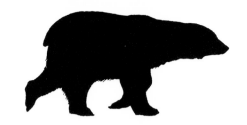

9 in (23 cm) across
12 in (31 cm) long

Polar bear

that the embryo, held back by what is known as "delayed implantation," is allowed to attach to the uterus.

The newborn cubs weigh less than 2 pounds (0.9 kg) and are blind and helpless. At one time it was thought that they were born naked, but recent research shows that they carry a coat of very fine hair. Within 6 weeks they gain their sight and their sturdy little bodies are covered with a coat of woolly fur. By March or April they attain a weight of 2 pounds (0.9 kg) or so. At this time the mother and her family emerge from the den, although for the next couple of weeks they remain close to it and frequently re-enter it. Polar bear cubs suckle for a remarkably long time and are not fully weaned until they are about 2½ years of age. (Those in the southern Hudson and James Bay area, however, may be weaned when they are 1½ years of age.)

As soon as the mother renews her strength after her long sojourn, and the cubs are able to travel, the family leaves on its journey to the sea. During the journey there are frequent rest and feeding periods, the cubs not only suckling but nibbling at vegetation pawed free by the mother from the still-frozen ground. The trek, which may take a week or so, is an exciting time for the family. During most of their waking hours the youngsters wrestle or try to outrun each other and seldom miss a chance to investigate anything that to them is new and interesting. Throughout it all the mother remains patient and solicitous.

When the cubs are ready and able to make their own kills of seals has been the subject of much study. Their long dependency on their mother's milk, and the lack of scientific data confirming the time at which yearlings and two-year olds were capable of surviving on their own, raised questions vital to the enactment of protective legislation.

Two scientists of the Canadian Wildlife Service, Dr. Ian Stirling and Paul B. Latour, carried out extensive field studies and their findings have been of great value to all countries with polar bear populations. A major conclusion is that "cubs which remain with their

Polar bears are not plentiful and their status is constantly monitored. Every two years a five-nation team of experts representing Canada, U.S.A., Norway, Denmark and the U.S.S.R. meets to recommend policies for the conservation and management of the species. (Photo by Bill Lowry)

mothers until they are weaned have a higher probability of survival than those that do not and this interpretation lends support to the management concept of *total protection of family groups and the harvesting of independent bears only.*"

Polar bears are more marine mammals than they are land mammals, for a large part of each year is spent at sea as they wander across the endless stretches of fractured ice in their hunt for seals. They are excellent swimmers though their "dog paddling" style makes for slow progress. They are capable of swimming long distances and there are reports (Dr. Thor Larsen) of some having traveled non-stop across more than 200 miles (322 km) of Arctic water. When ice packs have melted, drifted to shore or moved out to sea, most polar bears will have returned to land. Some, however, remain on ice packs or on icebergs and may be carried hundreds of miles south by currents. When this occurs, they face a long trek back by land.

The hunting behavior of the polar bear shows patience and cunning. In large areas of sea ice, seals must keep holes open if they are to breath. Once a hole

has been found, the bear will wait almost motionless, perhaps for hours at a time, for its prey to appear. With one sweep of its huge paw and bite of its powerful jaws, it can kill a seal weighing 500 pounds (227 kg). This kind of hunting, according to Dr. Stirling, accounts for 80 per cent of polar bear hunting in summer and about 99 per cent in winter. In both seasons ringed seals make up 80 to 90 per cent of their diet.

Another hunting technique is to approach silently and pounce on seals basking on the ice, killing them before they can escape to the sea through their breathing holes. A hunting method of some bears during summer is to swim under an ice floe and heave up to the surface through the breathing hole before the unsuspecting victim has a chance to escape. In early spring many baby seals, commonly called "whitecoats," are killed while still in their snow caves.

Dr. Stirling records two observations he made of polar bear behavior during midsummer studies on Devon Island, N.W.T., in 1973. These incidents not only suggest a way in which young bears may be helped to survive, but also leave little doubt that polar bears are by nature very clean animals. "When more than one bear fed on a carcass at the same time, it became severed into two or more pieces after the skin and fat were removed. In all the instances observed, large pieces of the seal were left on the ice by the bears that first fed there. All of these carcasses were scavenged by other bears and it seems likely these remains could be important to the survival of subadults, or cubs orphaned unnaturally early, before they have become completely self-sufficient. Another important feature of feeding behavior was washing. After an initial feeding period of 20 to 30 minutes, a bear typically went and stood with its forepaws at the edge of, or actually in, a pool of water. The bear then licked off the upper and lower parts of the paws and its face, alternating between rinsing and licking. The washing procedure was repeated every 5 to 10 minutes thereafter. At the termination of feeding, up to 15 minutes might be spent in a final washing. From its frequent occurrences in all observations, it is apparent that washing is an integral part of feeding behavior in the polar bear."

For the most part polar bears gain their winter sustenance from the fat already stored up in their bodies. This reserve of food is acquired during the late summer and early fall when they also feed on the carcasses of marine mammals washed up on the shore, as well as on lemmings, sea birds and their eggs, and a wide variety of vegetation and wild berries.

Sometimes, when extremely hungry, family groups will eat nearly every scrap of a seal carcass, leaving nothing behind but bones and blood-stained ice. If edible parts remain after such a feast, they are quickly eaten by Arctic foxes, ravens and gulls. In places of human habitation hungry bears will eat almost anything. In fact, Dr. Harington reports that some have eaten rope, canvas and even cardboard.

The polar bear is in every sense an extraordinary animal. An average male specimen at maturity measures from 8 to 10 feet (2.4-3 m) in length and may weigh over 1,200 pounds (545 kg). In 1970, Dr. Stirling and Dr. Charles Jonkel weighed one bear, tranquilized for tagging purposes, at 1,450 pounds (658 kg)!

Aside from their coloring (white in winter and yellowish or gold-colored in summer) and habitat, polar bears differ from the brown grizzlies in a number of important ways. For example, *Ursus maritimus* is a longer animal in body as well as in length of head, neck and legs. Whereas the grizzly has a typically "dished" face, the profile of the polar bear is more "Roman." The polar bear does not have the grizzly's pronounced shoulder hump. Its hair, although sometimes shorter than that of the grizzly, is thick all over its body, even around its huge paws. Its tail is longer and its ears are shorter. The very strong claws of the polar bear are brown in color, and not as long or as curved as those of the grizzly.

It has long been known that polar bears have an extraordinary sense of smell and that their hearing is well developed. It is only recently, however, that studies have indicated that their eyesight is probably as good as that of humans. Another important recent finding is that polar bears, while solitary animals except for brief periods of mating and for females with cubs, do not have just one nomadic population. There are, rather, distinct sub-populations. Dr. Stirling, who is a world-renowned authority on *Ursus maritimus*, estimates that up to 10 sub-populations of various densities and migratory habits may be present, for example, in the Canadian Arctic.

One of the most important studies undertaken in recent years involves the impact of northern development on polar bears and other animals, particularly the disturbances that might be caused by the movement, by pipeline or tankers, of oil and gas. These matters are still under critical examination, but since it is known that the various sub-populations seldom range far from denning areas, there is concern for the security of the environment in the eastern Canadian Arctic where there is the greatest concentration of denning sites. These have been identified by Dr. Harington as southern Banks Island, Simpson Peninsula, eastern Southampton Island, and eastern Baffin Island. Oil spills in those areas, depending on winds and currents, could also endanger the lives of bears living in northwestern Greenland. In the western Arctic, where polar bears live out their lives on pack ice sometimes many miles from the coast, oil and gas exploration poses potential danger, particularly in the areas of the Beaufort Sea and Prudhoe Bay.

Polar bears have a slow rate of reproduction. For example, Dr. Stirling's studies show that in the eastern Arctic the bears reach an age of 4 years before they breed for the first time, while those in the western Arctic and Alaska do not breed before they are 5 years of age. Since females will not mate while lactating, the most rapid rate at which they reproduce is only once every 3 years. In most areas many polar bears live up to 10 to 15 years, although some live beyond 20 years. Consequently a female may only give birth to two or three litters in her lifetime. Female polar bears, incidentally, average about half the weight of males.

Again, there are exceptions: the oldest and largest polar bears found in North America are those in the Hudson and James Bay areas of Manitoba, Ontario and Quebec. In Manitoba the ages of several bears have been recorded at over 20; one old-timer, in fact, was over 30 years of age. Age determination is made by counting the annual rings formed in the teeth.

Polar bears frequent the area near the port of Churchill, Manitoba, where they forage for food in garbage dumps. Although they are considered a nuisance and attempts have been made to air-lift them to distant points (from which they generally manage to return), they have become a tourist attraction and are now tolerated on a controlled basis.

The world's wildlife has never been under such intensive study as it is today. In the case of the polar bear, Canada has a Federal-Provincial Technical Committee for Polar Bear Research and Management, which meets annually. Internationally, a five-nation team of experts (Canada, U.S.A., Norway, Denmark and the U.S.S.R.) meets every two years under the auspices of the International Union for the Conservation of Nature, to analyze independent and co-operative research and to recommend policies for the conservation of the species. As a result the polar bear is probably the best managed of the Arctic large mammals.

The polar bear is not considered an endangered species in Canada, but continuing protective legislation is imperative. The killing of these bears in some areas is totally prohibited (U.S.S.R.), in others permitted only for Eskimos and Indians, and in other areas (Canadian Northwest Territories) permitted on a rigidly controlled small scale as an Eskimo-guided hunt for white non-residents. The kill by white non-residents is considered a part of the Eskimos' total quota for that particular area. The United States Marine Mammal Protection Act, passed in 1972, allows only native people to kill polar bears in Alaska for subsistence purposes.

Man is the main predator of polar bears, although there are reports of them having been killed by large walruses and killer whales. A healthy bear, unless surprised or cornered, will normally move quickly away from people or dogs. Their movement when unmolested is a slow, lumbering walk. When galloping they can reach speeds of up to 18 miles (29 km) an hour, but because of their heavy insulation their bodies overheat, so fast speeds cannot be sustained. As Dr. Stirling has observed, "they can run in short bursts only, but they may keep moving, if pressured—alternately walking and trotting, for many miles."

From time to time there are reports of humans being killed by polar bears. I recall one incident with nightmarish clarity. During a film-making expedition to the Beaufort Sea, our oil-company aircraft landed at a man-made island where drilling operations were under way. Three snowmobiles, each carrying two men armed with powerful rifles, were just leaving the campsite to hunt down a bear that only that morning, barely 400 yards (365 m) from the camp itself, had attacked and devoured a worker. The anger, fear and sense of horror that prevailed at the camp were feelings I have no desire to experience again. The bear was destroyed the following day. In fairness, however, it must be pointed out that the animal was a thin, subadult male, and it was starving. Fortunately, incidents such as this are very rare.

The thick, luxurious coat of the raccoon was at one time much in demand by the fur industry but, happily for this intelligent and engaging animal, is no longer fashionable. (Photo by Dr. Donald R. Gunn)

FAMILY PROCYONIDAE

Procyon lotor

Raccoon

Throughout the winter, regardless of the weather, the patio table we used as a feeding station was busier than Saturday at a supermarket. Daylight brought the first of the shoppers, a mixture of pine siskins, redpolls, tree sparrows and purple finches. Then would come the chickadees and juncos, an occasional pair of evening grosbeaks and cardinals and, whenever we added cracked corn to the menu, the mourning doves.

The sound of whirling wings seemed constant as things unknown to us "spooked" the visitors and they would come and go in sudden bursts of flight. There was squabbling and vying for position, of course, but they were always compatible gatherings. For example, individuals of each species (with the exception of the grosbeaks and the cardinals) were once seen on the feeder *all at the same time!*

It was the Carolina wren, a rarity in our part of the world, that prompted us to make up molds of suet and sunflower seeds. A beautiful creature, it heralded its sporadic visits with the familiar *toodlewee, toodlewee, tawee, cherrrrr,* but came to the feeder only when the other birds had departed. Whether the mixture was to its liking or not, we never knew, for every night the moulds were removed by "person or persons unknown."

After a week of thievery we were on the point of suspending this kind of hospitality. Then we were alerted late one night by a subdued noise on the patio. Dousing the lights, we went to the door and there he was, in the full reflection of the moon — the biggest, handsomest raccoon we had ever seen! He stared momentarily at us and, showing not the slightest concern, delicately lifted the mold from the table. Holding it in his mouth, he ambled away without so much as a backward glance.

Our first impulse was to say "no more, old boy," but a lifetime of affection for this animal made us realize that, no less than the birds, he too had a right to some of the finer things of life. And so, except when blizzards were raging or it was simply too cold to venture out, the big fellow paid frequent nocturnal visits and carried back to his den whatever delicacies as we left out for him.

We were more than rewarded early that summer when "he" arrived toward dusk one day with four kits. Mother and children remained on the patio for a full five minutes, the kits stumbling over each other and chattering away in purrs and chuckles. One loud purr from the mother as she looked our way seemed to mean "thanks—on behalf of all of us!"

Raccoons, resident in almost all of southern Canada except Newfoundland, are members of the Procyonidae family and as such are related to the ring-tailed cats of southwestern United States and the kinkajous of Latin America. They occur in all continental U.S. states except Alaska and some parts of the Rocky Mountain and southwestern states. Their range also extends to South America. Although classified as carnivores, they actually are omnivores and include in their diet birds and their eggs, small mammals, crayfish, minnows, frogs, nuts, berries and corn on the cob.

The species name *lotor* means "washer" (from the Latin *lutoris*) and it is commonly thought that they wash their food before eating it. This is not the case. Glen Sanderson, who has made a special study of raccoons, reports that they "are *feelers* rather than *washers* and that repeated handling of food items, with or without water, is exploratory behavior." Recent investigations, he says, have found that wetting the palms increases the sensitivity of the raccoon's hands.

There is no mistaking the raccoon: a sharply pointed face with a pronounced black mask running across the eyes from cheek to cheek, large erect ears; an overall chunky body thickly covered with long fur, and a bushy tail prominently ringed with wide black bands. Another distinguishing characteristic is the mischievous face which, along with the large black eyes, makes it a rather beautiful creature.

Nature writers have waxed lyrical over raccoons and have given them top billing as fun-loving, highly intelligent animals capable of relating to humans in an affectionate, companionable manner. They are also described as "masked bandits," "inquisitive, meddlesome night-time thieves," "scrappy fighters" and "rogues." Anyone who has kept a raccoon as a pet will agree with all of these descriptions, and have a few of his own!

Raccoons thrive in rural and wilderness areas where there is running water and an abundance of big elms, maples and other deciduous trees. Dens are usually created out of cavities begun originally by other forest dwellers or by natural causes, and may vary in alti-

These two young "masked bandits" were born in a tree cavity, but others may come into the world in caves, woodchuck holes or abandoned birds' nests. At birth raccoons weigh about 2½ ounces (70 g) but they grow rapidly and in about 5 weeks will weigh about 1½ pounds (700 g). The pups remain with the mother for a year. (Photo by Mark Nyhof)

tude from near ground level to as high as 70 feet (21 m) up.

If den trees are not available, they have been known to establish homes and raise their kits in caves, woodchuck holes and even the abandoned nests of large birds. In urban areas, if tree habitat is not available, they are not averse to using boathouses, garages, and attics of houses—whether the houses are occupied or not. A friend of mine, Robin Brass, tells me that in his east Toronto neighborhood raccoons have been known to climb down chimneys! In these situations, their popularity drops to zero and for everyone's sake they should be chased off without delay.

The average lifespan of raccoons in the wild is 7 to 8 years. When adopted and cared for as pets, they have been known to live as long as 14 years. Although it takes about 2 years for the male to become sexually mature, the female can successfully mate at the age of one. The male is polygamous and may mate with several females during February and March. Some females, however, have been known to reject *all* suitors during a season; but once mated the female will refuse the advances of all other males.

The kits, from one to seven, are born 63 days later and enter life lightly furred, the face mask and tail rings showing only as pigmented tracings on the skin. Blind at first, they gain their sight in about 3 weeks. Although they weigh a mere 2½ ounces (70 g) at birth, they grow rapidly and in about 5 weeks reach a weight of 1½ pounds (700 g) or so. The kits feed on their mother's milk for the first 2½ months, but after they leave the den to begin their nightly foraging they develop a diet of solid foods. Mother and children remain together for about a year.

Raccoons are said to have a vocabulary of about 15 different sounds and many nuances of each. Most of them are pleasant, some almost bird-like, and others are spine-chilling screams. But it is the extraordinary intelligence of these animals, their capacity to solve problems, and their engaging sense of wonder that endear them to humans. Stories of how they use almost human-like intelligence in opening doors, unscrewing jars, turning on taps and outwitting hunting dogs, and even their fondness for music, are legion.

When winter comes and food gets scarce, raccoons simply call it quits and settle down in their dens to sleep a good deal and live off stored-up fat. Sometimes a number of them will hole up together to assure protection from the cold, but they do not hibernate as do

Right fore
1¾ in (4.5 cm) across
2¼ in (5.7 cm) long

Left hind
4¼ in (11 cm) long

Raccoon

ground squirrels, woodchucks and chipmunks. During mild spells they frequently leave their dens either to bask in the sun or search for food. In any case, the January to March mating season brings them out, at least for brief periods of good weather.

Raccoons are mainly nocturnal mammals in the wild, but if tamed as pets they adjust to human time schedules. On both the Atlantic and Pacific coasts wild raccoons, when undisturbed, frequent flats and beaches to feast on marine life left stranded at ebb tides and consequently are on the move during both daytime and night-time hours.

Raccoons once supported a fairly significant fur industry, but this has become of minor economic importance with the decline of public interest in the fur. The flesh of the raccoon, incidentally, is edible and said to be especially tasty when roasted.

FAMILY MUSTELIDAE

Martes americana
Marten

"This interesting creature appears to be the least sociable of this unsociable family. Otters will meet to enjoy their slide in a merry party. Skunks will gather for warmth, the smaller weasels will help each other in distress or in hunting, but, as far as I can learn, no man ever yet saw two adult martens meeting with feelings other than those of deadly hate; the one essential supreme exception to this is doubtless found in the moment of sexual congress."

Seton's reference to *Martes americana* reflects the opinion generally held of this wilderness creature. However true the reference may be, it perhaps leaves a wrong impression of this handsome and beautifully-furred animal, certainly to man one of the least offensive members of the North American wild kingdom. It also ignores the fact that, whatever "hate" there may be in the animal's nature, the female of the species appears to excel in the love and attention she gives to her young.

The marten, about the size of an average house cat, has remarkable attributes. Solitary in habit, it is totally self-reliant. Yet, despite its "hateful" personality, stories abound that baby martens respond to gentle and affectionate treatment and make excellent pets.

Martens are expert climbers.

This animal, sometimes called "pine marten" or "American sable," was at one time common in most of the coniferous forests of North America—a range remarkably similar (perhaps only coincidentally so) to the combined ranges of the red and Douglas's squirrels, two of its favorite foods. While its range remains much as it was recorded by Seton nearly 75 years ago, populations are greatly reduced or even eliminated when logging destroys the old forests essential to the species' survival. As a consequence, it has become rare in much of its traditional United States range. In Canada it is no longer present in Prince Edward Island, in Nova Scotia it is rare and fully protected, and in Newfoundland it is officially listed as an endangered species. Despite these declines, however, there are still areas in Canada and the United States where the marten thrives and where controlled killing for its fur is permitted; these may be generally defined as wilderness areas where intrusion by man, other than trappers, is minimal.

The chances of seeing a marten in the wild are slight, for it is by nature a furtive being with a hearty distaste for anything foreign to its natural element. If you were to encounter one and were able to observe it at leisure, you would be impressed by its slender, attractive appearance and its extraordinarily lithe movements. Some years ago, in a rain forest far up the coast of British Columbia, I had a look at one but the encounter was too brief to make anything but cursory mental notes. Here, however, is how Tom Northcott describes it:

"The marten has a long, slender body, small head with large round ears, dark brown eyes, a short pointed muzzle, and a bushy tail about half as long as the body. . . . Males average 20-25 inches [50-64 cm] total length, including tail, and weigh up to 3 pounds [1.4 kg]. Females average 18-22 inches [46-56 cm] and weigh about 2 pounds [.9 kg]. Legs are short, but the feet are large and furred. The hairy pads may help the marten grip when scaling trees. . . . Unlike others of the weasel family, the marten has semi-retractable claws, probably an adaptation to tree climbing.

"The soft rich fur varies from a pale buff to a variety of reddish and dark browns: the head is lighter in color than the rest of the body. On the throat and chest, there is a yellowish orange patch and the edges of the ears are white."

The marten, usually nocturnal in habit, is a remarkably versatile animal, as much at home on the ground as it is in trees. In its arboreal environment it is a sure-footed, skilled aerialist, outclassed in speed and dexterity only by its slightly larger cousin, the fisher. But, being essentially a carnivore, it spends a good deal of its time on or near the forest floor hunting for mice, rabbits, shrews, voles and other prey species. This diet is supplemented with deer, elk and similar carrion, with birds and their eggs, reptiles, fish, insects, fruits, berries and nuts. Red squirrels and chipmunks are also part of its diet. Most references to marten food preferences include blueberries, and observers say that after feasting on this fruit the animal's lips become decidedly blue, as do their droppings.

For the greater part of the year the marten remains a solitary forest dweller, but sometime between June and September (depending on the geographical area) the nasty disposition of males and females mellows sufficiently to make mating possible in an atmosphere of temporary gentleness. The female's receptiveness lasts for only 2 weeks, though during that time she may accept the advances of several males.

Once the breeding season is ended, however, the sexes separate and the female bears the full responsibility for creating a nest and rearing the young. The phenomenon known as "delayed implantation" (experienced by other small carnivores such as fisher and ermine, and by certain large carnivores such as bears) occurs in the marten. As a consequence, there is a long period of gestation, and the young are not born until the following March or April. The average litter is three or four, but occasionally it may be five or six.

Favorite den sites for martens are cavities in trees, and they may be high up or close to the ground. The young are born in a nest well padded with leaves, moss and grass. Weighing about an ounce (28 g) their tiny bodies are covered with fine yellow (sometimes white) hair, their eyes are sealed and for a time the infants are apparently unable to hear. After the fifth week their eyes open, and at the end of the sixth or seventh week they are weaned. By now their baby fur is being replaced with a dark brown coat, thick and luxurious.

Martens become fully grown when they are nearly 4 months of age and about that time they separate, each going its own solitary way. Mating does not occur until they are over 2 years of age and, because of the "delayed implantation" phenomenon, it is not until about their third birthday that young females produce their first litters.

This non-hibernating animal is one of the most rugged of all forest dwellers and only the most severe

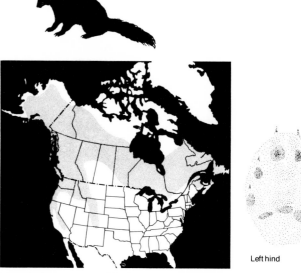

Left hind

Marten (Exterminated by logging and agriculture in eastern provinces and New England)

winter weather prevents it from being active every night, and occasionally during the daylight hours too. So swift and subtle are its movements, whether hunting on the ground or moving about in trees, that its presence is generally undetected by humans. In winter, it often tunnels its way beneath the snow when it suspects the hidden presence of mice, shrews, rabbits and the like. But martens are not always able to escape the watchful eyes and sensitive hearing of other forest dwellers, and their presence—as well as the menacing presence of birds of prey—is loudly announced by squirrels and songbirds.

The marten has a pair of scent glands under its tail and a scent gland under the skin on the belly, but the scent is not as objectionable (to humans) as those of the skunk and ermine. Release of the secretion, by rubbing the abdominal glands on tree branches and other objects, marks its territory. Both sexes do this frequently before and after the mating season. The use of the scent glands is an important means of communication since other than cooing sounds when with their young, or snarls, growls or even screams when threatened or irritated, they are relatively silent in the wild.

Despite their suspicious, furtive nature, martens are remarkably curious about anything that to them is out of the ordinary. So inquisitive are they, in fact, that they have been known to approach within a few yards of a wilderness cabin or the temporary shelter of a trapper. This trait often leads to their easy capture in traps or death from a small-bore rifle.

Home ranges of martens vary according to geography, but if Ontario's Algonquin Park can be used as a reference, a typical female confines herself to about a square mile (2.6 km²), while a male may move about in an area as large as 3 square miles (8 km²). Whatever the range sizes may be, studies have shown that they are generally larger during the mating season.

The lifespan of the marten in the wild is 6 to 8 years, but in captivity it may be much longer. Seton, in fact, recorded one captive's lifespan of 17 years. Trapping probably accounts for the heaviest mortality among martens, but the little animal is sometimes also preyed upon by fisher, lynx, coyotes, golden eagles and great-horned owls, and as always in the wild, starvation can drastically reduce populations when prey species are scarce.

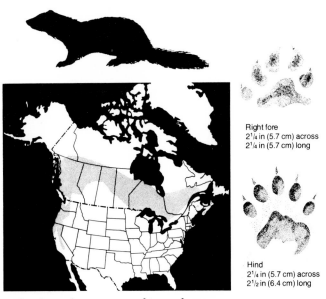

Right fore
2¼ in (5.7 cm) across
2¼ in (5.7 cm) long

Hind
2¼ in (5.7 cm) across
2½ in (6.4 cm) long

Fisher (Largely exterminated in southeast Canada and most of U.S.A.)

Martes pennanti

Fisher

Although the fisher is not considered endangered, it does qualify as one of the rarest, and certainly one of the most seldom seen, of our boreal forest animals. This creature was once relatively secure over a wide transcontinental range, but its numbers have been drastically reduced as a result of human encroachment, particularly through deforestation and trapping. It would be a sad day indeed if the fisher, as has happened to its little cousin, the black-footed ferret, became listed as one of the "10 most wanted" of North America's endangered species.

The fisher, commonly known in some areas as "pekan," structurally resembles another mustelid, the marten, but is nearly twice the latter's size. A comparison might be: fisher = small dog or, because of its long and very bushy tail, a fox; marten = small domestic cat. Comparative weight would be: male fisher, 5 to 13 pounds (2.3-6 kg); male marten, 1 to 4 pounds (0.5-1.8 kg). Females of both species are considerably smaller. Coloring also helps to identify the two. The fisher is very dark brown or even black overall, with perhaps some small irregular white spots on the chest and belly, whereas the marten is dark brown to blond overall, particularly light around the head, and with prominent orange or buff patches on the throat.

No one knows how the fisher got its name, but it may have been so called by early settlers after a European polecat known as "fitch" or "fichet"; or it may have been confused with the mink, which does include fish in its diet. In any case, *M. pennanti* has no detectable piscatorial habits, even though it favors habitats where there is free-flowing water, presumably with populations of fish. Although not an aquatic animal, when necessary it is an accomplished swimmer.

The fisher is one of the most solitary of wilderness animals, and for its size one of the most courageous in defense of its life and one of the fiercest in subduing its prey. It is primarily nocturnal in habit, although there is evidence that it sometimes moves about during daylight hours. It is also arboreal and a frequently quoted Seton observation is that "the squirrel is considered a marvel of nimbleness, but the marten can catch the squirrel, and the fisher can catch the marten."

There are differences of opinion regarding its arboreal habits, some writers claiming that it travels for considerable distances by jumping from tree to tree, others claiming that most of its traveling is on the ground. It is, however, a long-distance traveler, often journeying (mostly by night) distances of up to 100 miles (161 km).

The fisher, a solitary wilderness dweller, is one of the rarest of North American wild mammals. It is mostly nocturnal in habit. (Photo by Bill Lowry)

Its normal home range, however, is thought to be about 10 miles (16 km) in diameter.

The fisher mates in March and April, but because of the long period of delayed implantation of the embryo into the uterus, the young are not born until March or April of the following year. The litter size may range from one to five, but three is about average. The young, born blind and helpless, are slow to develop and do not acquire their sight until they are about 7 weeks old. The mother nurses them from 3 to 4 months, at which time they are weaned and begin to hunt on their own. The family breaks up in the fall and the nursery den (usually made in the hollow of a tree or in a crevice in rocks) is abandoned. Sexual maturity is reached in about 2 years. Females breed again within 3 to 18 days after giving birth.

The fisher, like the marten, lives mainly on small mammals such as squirrels, chipmunks, mice and voles. It will also eat carrion, small birds, berries and other vegetation such as leaves and lichens. Porcupines and snowshoe hares, however, are its favorite prey. Porcupines often destroy valuable timber by eating the inner bark of trees and prevent new growth by eating seedlings. Since porcupines make up a large part of the fisher's diet, the fisher is generally regarded by foresters as an ally and has been introduced into some areas as an aid in controlling porcupine populations.

The commonly held belief that the fisher kills the porcupine by flipping it over on its back and ripping open the unprotected belly is no longer given full credence. It may happen occasionally, but normally the fisher bites its prey repeatedly about its face and head by dashing back and forth at it. Death for the porcupine can be slow and painful.

The fisher often follows traplines, stealing bait or feeding on captured animals. If trapped itself, it may chew through its leg to free itself; self-mutilation to gain freedom is not uncommon among fur-bearers.

The fisher, a rare but valuable fur-bearer, is believed to have a lifespan in the wild of from 8 to 10 years, perhaps nearly 15 years. *M. pennanti* is native only to North America. Its present Canadian range includes the boreal forests of all provinces except the Maritimes and Newfoundland, although about 30 years ago the species was re-introduced into Nova Scotia and New Brunswick and may have become established there. In its northern range it occurs in the southern portion of the Yukon and in the southwestern Northwest Territories. Loss of habitat has critically reduced its U.S. range and today it occurs spottily only in some parts of the Rocky Mountains, California, New England and New York.

Mustela erminea

Ermine*

It was just after daybreak and the beginning of another fall day on Vancouver Island. "Randale Farm" was the scene of quiet splendor—mist lying in the lowlands, the white homestead and out-buildings standing in sharp relief against the background of towering Douglas firs, the herd of Black Angus ready for milking, and the air pungent with the incomparable bouquet of autumn.

Suddenly the silence was shattered by the panic-stricken cackling of a hundred chickens and by the frantic beating of wings. Inside a low, free-standing build-

*The common name "ermine" is not accepted by all naturalists. Some prefer to call it "stoat," but there is a growing preference for the more logical name "short-tailed weasel." Furriers, of course, prefer the name ermine because it more elegantly describes the fur used in royal robes and other costly apparel.

ing, pandemonium had broken loose as a long-bodied, short-tailed animal slew half a dozen birds and tore pieces of flesh from each of them. Finally it seized another by the neck, moved quickly to an open window and fled with its prey across the field to a nearby woodlot.

Mustela erminea, the ermine, was new to the neighborhood and had begun a habit that a few weeks later led to its own demise from the pellets of the farmer's shotgun. Had it stayed with its normal diet of small birds and mammals, it might comfortably have lived out its full lifespan of 5 or 6 years; perhaps with luck it might even have survived for 10 years, as ermine in the wild sometimes do. The ermine is not the only member of the Mustelidae family with a fondness for poultry. Long-tailed weasels and skunks also consider them delicacies.

The ermine makes its home in a variety of habitats, and while it is often found in farmlands, it normally favors boreal forests, woodlands, brushlands, river banks and lakeshores where there is good cover, as well as barns, woodpiles and stone fences. Some live in mountainous country at elevations of up to 10,000 feet (3,000 m).

The ermine occurs in all parts of Canada including Newfoundland and most other large offshore islands. It is absent from southern Alberta and southern Saskatchewan. Its range in the United States is more irregular: in the east in Michigan, Pennsylvania and Iowa; in the west from Washington south to California. It also occurs in Colorado and northern New Mexico.

The ermine measures about 10 to 17 inches (25-43 cm) in length, including tail, and weighs about 2 to 7 pounds (1-3 kg). The males are almost twice the size of the females. (A far northern subspecies, *M. e. semplei*, is considerably smaller.) In appearance the ermine has a long lean body, a small narrow head and blunt nose, a long neck, short ears, and short legs, each foot having five claws.

The pelage of the ermine is short and fine in summer and is dark brown. The underparts are creamy white, and the brown tail is tipped with coarse black hair. The hairs on the feet are white. The winter pelage, which grows in over a period of several weeks during the late October and November molt, is snowy white except for the tip of the tail, which remains black; the rump and part of the tail sometimes are stained yellow from the discharge of glandular musk. The winter coat is longer and thicker and at that time is in prime

3/4 in (1.9 cm) across
1 in (2.54 cm) long

Ermine

condition. Only in regions where there is snow and cold temperatures, however, does the ermine turn white; in warmer areas where there is little or no snow and where temperatures are more moderate, the pelage retains the brown color. The year's second molt occurs in March and April.

The ermine, which is active and alert throughout all seasons of the year, is primarily nocturnal although daytime excursions are not unusual. It makes its home underground, usually in dens usurped from ground squirrels, gophers and other small burrowers, and sometimes above ground in hollow logs, barns, stone fences and woodpiles. It is an agile climber and will not hesitate to climb trees in pursuit of squirrels and chipmunks, although, according to Peterson (*Mammals of Eastern Canada*), it avoids going higher than 10 or 15 feet above ground. It can swim when necessary but its paddling movements are clumsy. When pursuing prey on the ground, it moves, back arched, in bounds of 5 or 6 feet; in a straightaway, its maximum speed is only about 8 miles (13 km) an hour. Its senses of smell, hearing and sight are well developed; in fact, it uses its keen sense of smell in hunting, especially during the hours of darkness.

Although a solitary little animal, the ermine drops its antisocial manner when responding to the mating urge, usually in July and August. The long (8 to 9 months) time of gestation is due in part to delayed implantation and so it is not until the following April or May that the four to nine young are born.

The nursery is usually underground in a burrow with two or three approaching tunnels. The nest itself is made of fur from animals killed by the parents and to the fur are added bits of grass and leaves. At birth the very tiny babies carry a mane of fine white hair on the neck and a few white hairs along the back, and their ears and eyes are sealed. In about 5 weeks the ears and eyes are opened and at that time the coat is fully grown. The young, weaned during the fifth to sixth week, are then able to accompany their mother on hunting expeditions. Like all young creatures, baby ermine are playful and during their tussles with each other they squeal and squeak, and when quiet they purr. Angry adults, especially the mother when standing in defense of her family, hiss, scream and bark. The young grow very quickly and at 7 weeks the males are often larger than their mother. Sexual maturity is also reached at an early stage (normally within 2 or 3 months). A young female is capable of giving birth to a family about the time of her first birthday; the young males do not mature, however, until they are about 8 months of age, and so they mate first as 1-year-olds.

The ermine seems to be constantly seeking food and while its main diet consists of small rodents, along with small birds and their eggs, fish, frogs and snakes, it will tackle prey considerably larger than itself, such as rabbits and hares. It is commonly believed that each adult consumes one-third to half its weight in such fare every 24 hours.

The killing technique of the ermine is no more savage than that of other carnivores and, mercifully, is usually quick. Once a prey is within reach, the ermine pounces with lightning speed on the victim's shoulder and bites through its neck, usually at the base of the skull. At the same time it wraps its serpentine body around the victim, using its forelegs to secure its grip and its hindlegs to scratch wildly.

In turn, while it has fewer enemies than most mammals, it maintains a constant alert against attack by martens, wolverines, fishers, coyotes and foxes, hawks, owls, and bald eagles. Man, of course, has been a traditional foe, for ermine remain on the list of trappers' prized species.

Despite its diminutive size, *M. erminea* has, as Seton described it, "the unloveliest disposition of all our wild animals," and he added that "outside of their strength and courage, we find in them little to admire. Most other animals have a well-marked home region and friends, but the ordinary life of a weasel is that of a wandering demon of carnage."

Up to a point there is truth in Seton's remarks, for the ermine is at times a reckless hunter that seems to kill for the sheer joy of killing. It is true, however, that a portion of its prey is stored away for future use, that many of the rodents it kills are undesirable within the boundaries of human habitation, and that raids on poultry are infrequent. But most writers follow the Seton condemnation—"murderer," "little brown terrorist," "game hog," for instance—and few indeed are those who attribute to the creature any virtues.

But since all creatures have the right of survival, mammals such as members of the weasel group should not be condemned out of hand. All too often human standards are used in making judgements and all too often they are unfair. There are those, fortunately, who recognize the weasel's place in the scheme of things and defend its right to prosper.

Ermine (short-tailed weasel)　　　Long-tailed weasel

Mustela frenata

Long-tailed Weasel

Superficially the only difference between the long-tailed weasel and its immediate cousins, the short-tailed weasel (ermine) and the least weasel, is the fact that it is the largest of the three species. In most other respects—conformation, coloring, habitat and behavior—it is basically similar.

It does not, however, occupy the same North American ranges. It occurs in Canada only along the southern boundary (with northern extensions into Saskatchewan, Alberta and the eastern half of British Columbia), but its United States range takes in all of the states except Alaska, Arizona and southeastern California. Its more southerly range extends to Bolivia. The ranges of the short-tailed weasel and the least weasel, on the other hand, take in most of Canada and Alaska, but only limited sections of the northern states (see range map for each). This large weasel is strictly a New World species, whereas the other two have a broad circumpolar distribution and are known in Europe, Asia and North Africa. The short-tailed weasel is also found in Greenland.

M. frenata rarely exceeds 20 inches (50 cm) in length, approximately 10 inches (25 cm) of which is its well-furred tail, and weighs an average of about 10 ounces (284 g). Its body is typically weasel-shaped— long and slender, with short legs, small flattened head, short rounded ears, and small beady eyes. The pelage is dark brown above and white to yellowish-white underneath, and throughout all seasons the tip of the tail is black.

As is characteristic of weasels, there are two annual molts, the most pronounced change occurring during the fall in individuals living in northern areas or at higher altitudes where in winter the weather is cold and snow conditions prevail. These animals change from brown to pure white, except for the tip of the tail. The second molt occurs in the spring.

Why the tail retains its black tip is one of Nature's secrets, but this is the rather quaint explanation given in a venerable volume called *American Animals: A Popular Guide to the Mammals of North America North of Mexico, With Intimate Biographies of the More Familiar Species*:

"I am inclined to think that this black point serves its owner in a variety of ways, though at first thought one might think it would prove conspicuous on the white surface of the snow and in contrast with the intense white of the remaining fur. But if you place a weasel in its winter white on a new-fallen snow in such a position that it casts no shadow, you will find that the black tip of the tail catches your eye and holds it in spite of yourself, so that at a little distance it is very difficult to follow the outline of the rest of the animal. Cover the tip of the tail with snow and you can see the rest of the weasel itself much more clearly; but as long as the black point is in sight, you see that, and that only.

"If a hawk or owl, or any other of the larger hunters of the woodland, were to give chase to a weasel and endeavor to pounce upon it, it would in all probability be the black tip of the tail it would see and strike

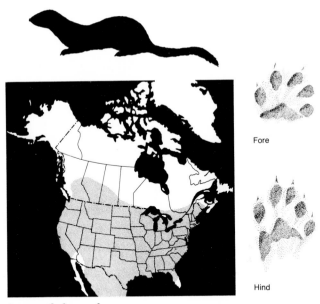

Long-tailed weasel

Fore

Hind

at, while the weasel, darting ahead, would escape. It may, moreover, serve as a guide, enabling the young weasels to follow their parents more readily through grass and brambles."

The long-tailed weasel makes its home in shallow burrows (usually abandoned by or expropriated from other small mammals), in rock or brushy fence rows, in barns when mice or rats are present, or among the roots of trees. It may have several homes, any one of which will serve as a nursery when the young are born in April or May.

This weasel, like others of its kind, is a solitary creature, and while it is occasionally abroad during the day, its main period of activity is at night when it moves about in search of food such as mice, squirrels, chipmunks, shrews, rabbits and other small creatures. Caught in the glare of a car's headlights or the beam of a flashlight, the black eyes reflect a brilliant emerald green. Although its eyesight is said to be well developed, it depends largely on its sense of smell to locate its prey.

It stalks silently and its sinuous movements over and around ground obstacles are almost snake-like. When an animal is tracked down, the weasel pounces with lightning speed and usually dispatches it instantly by biting through the vital areas of the head. If it fails to kill instantly and a struggle ensues, the weasel embraces its prey with all four feet until it succeeds in making the fatal bite, either through the brain or through the jugular. On occasion it will pursue a squirrel or chipmunk up a tree, but its ascent (like that of the ermine) is confined to 10 or 15 feet, and this gives the prey a better chance to take evasive action. The weasel's small girth of less than 2 inches (5 cm) enables it to enter tiny openings in fences or crevices when stalking.

The long-tailed weasel is more of a reckless killer than any of the other mustelids, and while it does store some of its food in its burrow, it is often guilty of slaughtering more prey than it can consume. Of all the mustelids it is the most disliked by farmers, for not only does it pilfer nests of their eggs, but it also kills unprotected poultry with wasteful abandon.

M. frenata mixes with others of its kind only during the mating season in July and August. Delayed implantation results in a long period of gestation (anywhere from 205 to 337 days, with an average of 279, according to Peterson). The single litter is reported by some authorities to range from 4 to 9, by others from 1 to 12, and by still others from 3 to 9.

The young at birth are blind, toothless, wrinkled and almost naked, and weigh about 3 grams. At the end of the third week, however, they are well furred and their teeth have developed sufficiently to enable them to chew on meat brought to them by their parents. When they are about 5 weeks old their eyes open, and shortly thereafter weaning begins, and when this process is completed they strike out on their own. Females become sexually mature and are able to mate when they are 3 to 4 months of age, but males do not mature sexually until their second year.

Estimates of the size of this weasel's home range vary from 30 to 400 acres, but whatever the distance of its nightly wanderings back and forth, over and under, it may cover several miles and still be within a few hundred feet of one of its dens. When on the prowl it often lopes, its back arched, and its tail extended. If necessary it will take to water.

The long-tailed weasel is generally a quiet mammal, but when threatened it often screeches. Other sounds are purrs and squeals. Like all mustelids, it has a musk gland on either side of its anus and the secretion is said to be extremely unpleasant.

The pelt of this weasel, especially when in its white phase, has value in the fur trade but, because the animal is not abundant, it is not considered an important species. Man, nonetheless, is a major enemy, although many fall prey to foxes, coyotes, hawks, owls, snakes and sometimes domestic cats.

Mustela nivalis

Least Weasel

The least weasel—6 to 9 inches (15-23 cm) in length (nearly a quarter of which is tail), from 1¼ to 2 ounces (35-58 g) in weight—is the smallest living carnivore and, ounce for ounce, is one of the most pugnacious, aggressive and fearless creatures to prey on the world of rodents. This diminutive mammal, although in virtually every area either relatively scarce or rare, is one of the "good guys" of the Mustelidae family from man's point of view. It helps to control populations of mice, voles, moles, rats and similar species that can cause significant damage to forest or agricultural crops. As Seton wrote, many years ago, "this weasel is never known to attack well-grown poultry, or mammals larger than a rat, so that it must be considered a friend of the farmer; an animal, therefore, that is worthy of full protection."

Because it is so tiny, moreover, it has little to fear from man but has a variety of natural enemies—great horned owls, barn owls, long-tailed weasels, wild domestic cats, foxes and coyotes. Although a fur-bearing animal, it is much too small to be of economic value, and while it is not sought commercially, a few are caught in ermine traps. They are usually mistaken for small ermine and, wrote Peterson, trappers discard them as worthless "younguns."

The least weasel is typically weasel-shaped. Its body is relatively long and slender, its head is small and flattened and about the same diameter as its long neck, and the legs are short, as are the rounded ears. As in all weasels, its eyes are small and beady.

This mammal's summer pelage is chocolate or dark brown above and white below; the white runs the whole length of the underparts from the upper lip to the base of the tail and extends to the feet, the soles of which are sparsely furred. The whiskers show up prominently. In winter the pelage in some individuals changes to nearly all-over brown and in others, particularly where cold and snow predominate, it changes to white, although the tip of the tail may carry a number of black hairs. In winter the soles of the feet are heavily furred. Molting is said to be irregular, but the winter coat probably comes in about November and is replaced by the summer coat about March or April.

The least weasel occurs throughout most of Canada with the exception of the island of Newfoundland, the Maritime provinces, southern parts of Quebec and Ontario, coastal British Columbia and the northeastern part of the Northwest Territories. In the United States it is found in Montana, the Dakotas, Minnesota, Wisconsin, Nebraska, Iowa, Illinois, Indiana, Ohio, Michigan, New York, Pennsylvania, West Virginia, Virginia, Maryland, North Carolina and Tennessee. Some populations occur in the southern Appalachian Mountains.

This mammal requires only sparse ground cover and is at home in meadows, stubble fields and wetlands. It also prospers in barns and other buildings where there are populations of mice. Its home is usually an abandoned burrow or one appropriated from a mole, pocket gopher, ground squirrel or other small fossorial mammal. Sometimes it makes its home in a creek bank. It confines its movements to an area of probably less than 4 acres (1.6 ha).

Because it is primarily nocturnal in habit, its presence may go undetected unless its tracks in snow or soft ground are recognized. Its only noticeable vocal sounds are shrill squeals if irritated, threatened or in pain; in any of these situations it will likely discharge a fetid glandular odor. Young weasels are known to make hissing and chirping noises.

The least weasel, a non-hibernator, is a solitary creature other than during the mating season. Unlike its larger cousins — the long-tailed weasel and short-tailed weasel (ermine) — the female least weasel does not experience delayed implantation after breeding. Consequently it is able to produce two or more litters a year, each litter made up of three or five young. At birth the babies are hairless and their ears and eyes remain closed until they are 3 weeks to a month old. When the kits reach their second week, they carry a good coat of fur and are able to eat solid foods brought to them by their mother. When they are 6 weeks old, they are fully weaned and able to make their own kills. Females are sexually mature by the time they are 4 months of age, and before the year is over they are capable of bearing two litters of their own. The males are not capable of breeding until they are 8 months old.

The nursery den of this mammal is normally underground but may be made in hay or clover stacks. The nest is made of grass and other vegetation and is lined with the fur of animals it has killed for food. Jackson (*Mammals of Wisconsin*) has observed that if a nest

Least weasel

is used frequently the lining of fur may reach a thickness of nearly an inch and become packed like felt.

The least weasel has not been studied as thoroughly as have other small carnivores so the literature on the mammal is limited and often indecisive.

Mustela nigripes

Black-footed Ferret

Perhaps the two best places to see the black-footed ferret (although the likelihood of success is remote) are the Prairie Dog Sanctuary, Grasslands National Park, Saskatchewan, and Wind Cave National Park, South Dakota, where remnants of what was once a widely distributed but never particularly abundant mammal are now rigidly protected. This ferret, North America's rarest mammal, feeds mainly on prairie dogs, and both species have suffered population declines with man's invasion of their habitat, the short-grass prairies. The decline has been especially severe with the black-footed ferret, which for several years has been listed by the Committee on the Status of Endangered Wildlife in Canada and the Fish and Wildlife Service of the United States Department of the Interior as a seriously endangered species.

The black-footed ferret is mink-shaped, but smaller in size than its relative, males being about 19 to 23 ounces (540-650 g) in weight and about 20 to 23 inches (50-58 cm) in length, with a 5- to 6-inch (13-15 cm) tail. Females are always smaller. It is short-legged and has a long, slender neck and rounded ears.

Its nose is black and there is a distinctive black mask from cheek to cheek over its eyes and forehead. The feet and tip of the tail are also black. The body coloring is buffy-white on the belly and throat, and yellowish-brown or buff above with a brownish wash on the back.

Ferrets, like prairie dogs, are fossorial and this species makes its burrow within easy reach of prairie dog colonies. Those who have observed its behavior in the wild report that it often sits in an erect position (as does the prairie dog) to search the landscape for its prey. Once a prairie dog has been spotted it stalks it, body close to the ground, and if necessary speeds up its movements in long leaps. It will often enter a prairie dog tunnel in pursuit of the rodent and kill and consume it on the spot. It is said to bury its victim's remains. If prairie dogs are scarce, it will turn to other fare—squirrels, rabbits, voles, mice, gophers, birds and their eggs, and even small snakes.

The black-footed ferret's marital habits are still under study, but observers report that the female produces an average annual litter of four, which are born in the underground nest in the spring. The young begin emerging from their burrow in summer, mostly at night, and are taught to look after themselves. In the fall, the family unit breaks up and the young go their separate ways.

Although a large prairie area is defined as the range of this species, there is no official record of the number of individuals that may be present in it. In Canada, it is believed to be extinct in Alberta, but there are a few in Saskatchewan's Grasslands National Park. In the United States, where the range given extends from the Canadian border down through the midwest grasslands to Texas, it *may* be present in the Wichita Mountain Wildlife Refuge in southwestern Oklahoma and the area near the Devil's Tower National Monument in eastern Wyoming. This, however, is speculative. In any case, this species is in trouble.

Fore
1 3/8 in (3.5 cm) across
2 in (5.1 cm) long

Hind
3/4 in (1.9 cm) across
1 7/8 in (4.8 cm) long

Black-footed ferret (Former range. Now almost extinct due to agriculture and poisons)

face of black-footed ferret, showing mask

Black-footed ferret

Mustela vison
Mink

This member of the Mustelidae family is the most valued of all North American fur-bearers and makes virtually the whole continent its habitat. The only areas from which it is absent are five states in the American southwest, Anticosti and Queen Charlotte islands in Canada, and the areas of Alaska and the Northwest Territories beyond the treeline. Wild mink, although not native to Newfoundland, were introduced there in 1935 for commercial purposes and have since become established as part of the island's fauna.

The mink, like most mustelids, is a comparatively small mammal with a long, low-slung body and short legs. Its neck is long and its head small and flattened; the ears are short and rounded. Another mustelid characteristic is the musk glands on each side of the anus. These glands contain an evil-smelling substance which is released when the animal is excited (particularly during the breeding season) or when it wishes to confirm its territorial rights.

In the world of high fashion, the fur of this animal is regarded as the symbol of luxury. Long, thick and lustrous, it is almost uniformly dark brown (sometimes almost black) and there are irregular white splashes on the throat, chest and belly. This pelage is molted twice yearly, the first in the spring and the second in late fall and early winter. The summer coat is somewhat lighter and less dense than the winter coat. While mink are still trapped in the wild, many are raised on ranches where selective breeding has produced many color phases. Pearl and albino mutations, however, occur occasionally in wild individuals. Ranch-raised mink may live up to 10 years, but most of those in their natural habitat have a lifespan of about 1½ to 2 years. It is

Mink (Largely exterminated on northern plains)

Left fore
1³/₈ in (3.5 cm) across

believed that a few wild individuals may live as long as 6 years.

Mink of both sexes are "loners" and cohabit only during the mating season, which begins in late February and continues to early April. The males are promiscuous and generally mate with many females before the season ends. Like a number of other mammals the pregnant female experiences delayed implantation. In the case of mink this delay is related to the time of mating: if conception occurs early in the season, gestation may take up to 75 days; if conception takes place late in the season, gestation may take only about 40 days. The average period of gestation is 51 days.

In any case, the young are born during the latter part of April and the early part of May. Four or five kits make up the average litter, although, according to Schwartz and Schwartz (*The Wild Mammals of Missouri*), in exceptional cases there may be as many as 17 —a remarkable accomplishment if attributable to only one mother! The kits are born naked, except for a covering of fine, temporarily white hair. Their teeth do not appear until they are 3 weeks old, and their eyes do not open until they have reached their fifth week. Weaning

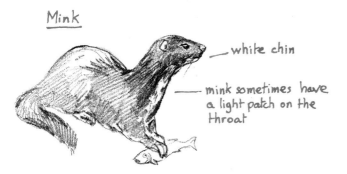

Mink

white chin

mink sometimes have a light patch on the throat

also begins during the fifth week and when they are between 6 and 8 weeks old they are on solid foods and are able to join their mother on hunting expeditions. By the end of August the family breaks up and each animal goes its own way. Not all scientists agree on the length of time required for mink to reach sexual maturity, but most seem to support Banfield's contention that females mature at 12 months and males at 18 months.

While there seems to be agreement that the male mink remains for a time with the last female it bred, there is not agreement that it also remains during the gestation period or that it shares responsibility for the rearing of the young. Some hold the latter view and claim that the parents together take the young on foraging trips and that, in the water, the kits sometimes ride on their parents' backs. Others report different behavior: for example, that the female, when the young are with her, will *sometimes* tolerate the presence of the male. Still others claim that continuing relationships between the two adults are "questionable." Since Nature herself sometimes nods, perhaps there is truth in all three contentions.

The mink makes its home beside or close to water. Dens are made in a variety of places, such as bank burrows, abandoned beaver and muskrat lodges, under roots of trees and in hollow logs. While the main home is the one most frequently used, a number of temporary dens are made throughout the territory. These extra places are often used by other mink when territories overlap. Mink are almost constantly on the move, the male scurrying about over a range that may be as much as 5 miles (8 km) in diameter, the female staying much closer to home and confining her travels within an area of from 30 to 50 acres (12-20 ha).

An accomplished swimmer, the mink can move with ease below the surface of the water in search of fish, frogs, crayfish and wandering muskrats. Muskrats, in fact, are a favorite food and it will not hesitate to invade a lodge, burrow or "push-up" in pursuit of them. Tom Northcott writes that a mink can dive to a depth of 15 feet (4.5 m) and swim 100 feet (30 m) under water. Underwater forages in winter do not deter the mink for, like otter, beaver and muskrat, it takes advantage of air pockets formed when the water level drops below the ice level. Numerous observations have been made of the mink's habit of curling up like a ball and, whether asleep or merely relaxing, floating unconcernedly downstream. Another example of playful moments is

seen when, otter fashion, it slides on its belly down muddy or snow-covered slopes.

Despite its size, the mink does not hesitate to do battle with opponents considerably larger than itself. When fighting among themselves, however, physical injuries are said to be minimal, even though there is considerable shrieking, spitting, hissing and snarling. Fights during the mating season are more serious and may even result in fatalities. If the opponent is of another species, the mink is ferocious and seeks to seize the enemy (or prey) in the region of the neck and sink its teeth into the jugular.

The gait of the mink is quite weasel-like—walking, sometimes running at speeds of 7 or 8 miles (11-13 km) an hour or making low bounds. It often stands on its hind legs to survey its surroundings and, if threatened, quickly seeks the nearest shelter; if necessary, it will seek safety in the nearest tree. Although the hearing and eyesight of the mink are only moderately developed, its sense of smell is acute and it is by the use of this faculty that it finds most of its prey food. The black, beady eyes, incidentally, when caught in the glare of artificial light, appear emerald green.

The standard diet is muskrats and other small mammals, fish, crayfish and other aquatic life, supplemented with reptiles, insects, birds and their eggs or fledglings, and some vegetation. Occasionally (although not as frequently as its cousin, the long-tailed weasel), it invades hen houses and engages in a period of carnage. Banfield, however, writes that it creates greater havoc when it forages about fish hatcheries. The mink is known to take enough food to its den to last for several days, and like the long-tailed weasel it sometimes seems to kill for the sake of killing. When it does kill beyond its needs, it will eat only part of its victim, leaving the remains for others.

Although the mink has only a few enemies, it is preyed upon by red foxes, bobcats, great horned owls, coyotes and sometimes bears. Its constant enemy, of course, is man, for as long as the fashion industry uses the pelts of wild animals in the manufacture of garments, those from wild mink will be in high demand.

Gulo gulo
Wolverine

Has the true identity of the Abominable Snowman of the Himalayas, and presumably that of the Abominable Snowman of North America, been finally revealed? There is no solid evidence to deny or confirm, but hidden away in a book called *Alive in the Wild* is a speculation that perhaps deserves more than passing attention.

William O. Pruitt, biologist and author, makes the case that the wolverine, that rare, bear-like creature whose huge northern circumglobal range includes boreal forests, alpine slopes, high mountain altitudes, and the exposed tundra to the coastal extremes of permanent ice and snow, is none other than the Snowman himself! Dr. Pruitt, one of a number of distinguished scientists whose chapters on various mammals make up *Alive in the Wild*, lived for 12 years in Alaska and during that time had first-hand opportunities to carry out field studies of *Gulo gulo*.

"An interesting comparison," he wrote, "can be drawn between the wolverine tracks in the snow and the published tracks attributed to the yeti, or Abominable Snowman, in the Himalayas. The similarity of the tracks plus the wolverine's penchant for venturing into the permanent snow and ice zone have led me to conclude that the yeti is a large, perhaps undescribed, species of wolverine. Other facts make this a logical assumption—the scarcity of wolverines, their ability to travel far and fast, the few supposed sightings of the beast standing on its hind legs on a distant hill. The peculiar loping gait of the wolverine could be confused through the shimmering heat waves with a bipedal creature running with its knuckles hitting the ground. In short, I suspect the Abominable Snowman to be none other than the wolverine."

Naturalist Roy Vontobel, writing in *Nature Canada*, attributed to Olaus Magnus, a Swedish bishop, what is perhaps the earliest written reference to the wolverine. This cleric published a book in 1555 on the people and animals of the European far north and, says Mr. Vontobel, "he mentioned three newly-discovered species—the wolverine, the giant kraken or cuttlefish, and the sea-serpent—heralding the wolverine's association with monsters in literature."

The wolverine, one of the largest members of the weasel family, is a resident of most of the coniferous forests of central and northern North America. With the encroachment of civilization, however, its range has

Wolverine (Some remnant populations remain in mountains of western states)

Right hind
4 in (10 cm) across
3½ in (9 cm) long

become more and more constricted. While some small populations maintain a tenuous foothold in southern areas, the largest numbers are now found in the Canadian north and in Alaska. Because of its elusive nature, no census count has been or probably ever will be possible. What is known is that it is one of the rarest of all northern mammals. That it has not been placed on the endangered species list is because of its relative abundance in remote areas such as Yukon and Alaska. Its security there seems so assured that trapping is allowed. Yukon, in addition, is a main source of supply of live wolverines for zoological gardens.

So closely does the wolverine resemble a bear cub in size and appearance that from a distance it is often difficult to distinguish between the two. The weight of an adult male ranges from 27 to 55 pounds (12-25 kg) and the length from nose to the tip of its bushy tail is about 40 inches (1 m). The characteristics that contribute to its bear-like appearance are its stoutish body and arched back; its broad head, short round ears and its small beady eyes; its sturdy legs and its large paws with large, light-colored retractile claws.

The pelage of the wolverine is made up of thick

underfur through which grows long, coarse and very smooth outer hair. The over-all coloring of the coat is glossy brown to almost black, although a broad tan or yellow stripe runs along each side from the shoulder to the rump and on to the top part of the tail. There are one or two white patches on the throat or chest. The head and ears are grizzled gray and the muzzle is black. In whisker-like fashion, creamy-white or orange hairs fan outward on the chest and throat. The soles of the feet are furred. This pelage, attractive in prime condition, deteriorates noticeably in summer when shedding occurs.

Because of its scarcity, wolverine fur does not enter significantly into the fur market, but when it can be obtained it commands a high price. The pelt is seldom sold intact, but cut to pattern for use as trim for mitts and for the hoods of parkas. Frost build-up on wolverine fur, caused by the wearer's breath, can be readily brushed off, thus leaving the fur fluffy and retaining its high protective value against wind and cold. Frost accumulation on other furs, such as fox and wolf, tends to adhere and can be removed only by melting it away — hardly possible when the wearer is battling a blizzard or when out on the trail at $-22°F$ $(-30°C)$. Pruitt says that a prime wolverine pelt on today's market might fetch as much as $600.

Wolverines breed in late summer, but because the implantation of the blastocyst does not take place until January, thus delaying gestation, the young are not born until March or early April. Dens are usually made under the roots of a dead or fallen tree or in a rock cave. In Yukon and Alaska wolverines have been known to bring their young into the world in snow-filled ravines, and in one instance a den is known to have been made in an abandoned beaver house.

The babies (normally two or three, but sometimes as many as five) are yellowish-white in color and are covered with fine creamy-white hairs. The tiny paws are darker and there is a suggestion of a dark face mask. The mother nurses her family for 8 to 10 weeks, and then they are weaned. Some writers claim that the young remain with their mother for one year, but Pruitt, after many years studying these animals in their natural habitat, and who remains a recognized authority on the species, reports that they continue as a family unit for *two* years. It is also his contention that they do not become sexually mature until their *fourth* year.

There is an indication that some male wolverines may return to visit den sites and even help in rearing

Wolverine

the young. Whether this is a genuine display of paternal responsibility or a return to a source of good hunting is at the moment unknown. It may be, in fact, that neither of these factors apply; that the males, being polygamous, simply chance on nursery areas while in search of estrous females.

The wolverine may range as much as several hundred square miles in its search for food, but this is probably when it follows herds of migrating caribou. Its home range, however, is probably much smaller, although Pruitt estimates it as anywhere from 50,000 to 75,000 acres (200-300 km²). Whatever the size of its range, the animal identifies it by means of scent stations created by urine and scat droppings as well as by deposits of the acrid musk from its anal glands.

The diet of the wolverine varies with the seasons but its most productive foraging time is during the winter and early spring. While it is capable of killing a caribou if one is immobilized, much of its feeding is on the carcasses or remains left by human hunters or wolves. Examinations of stomachs have shown that in addition to carrion, it consumes fruit (particularly blueberries) and other vegetation, some species of small mammals such as ground squirrels, mice and marmots, birds' eggs and fledglings, and even the occasional porcupine. Wolverines in Alaska have been observed feeding on the carcasses of whales, walruses and seals that have been washed ashore. *Gulo gulo* manages to go without food for several weeks, whereas in similar situations less durable animals would weaken and die.

The mobility of the wolverine is well known, not only in the long treks it makes but in its tree-climbing and swimming abilities. Its normal gait on land is a lope in which all four feet hit the ground at the same time. Because of its broad, bear-like paws, it has little difficulty in traveling over snow. Although its eyesight is poor, its sense of smell is acute and this enables it to proceed unerringly to whatever carrion may be nearby.

A limited folklore relates to the wolverine, such as the story concerning its "gluttony." The animal, so it is said, will so gorge itself that its belly becomes bloated and as tight as a drum. It alleviates this condition by squeezing itself between two trees, thus forcing regurgitation, whereupon it continues to feast! This, being folklore, is perhaps amusing. What is not amusing are the many unfair statements made about the wolverine's personality and behavior. For example, this animal is called "ferocious," but when cornered and threatened so are bears and even a 2-ounce (56 g) Arctic lemming. The wolverine is accused of breaking into a cabin and "wantonly" destroying everything in sight. Perhaps this happens on occasion, but as Dr. Pruitt said in a recent letter to me, "What of the many instances of red squirrels entering a cabin and creating just as much havoc? A red squirrel is just about the most efficient messer-upper there is." The wolverine is soundly condemned for leaving its scent on traps, for fouling other human property and for having a "fierce hatred" of man. The fact is that all mustelids have scent glands and leaving their mark is simply well-established mustelid behavior. Even a domestic tomcat at certain seasons will urinate on furniture, clothes and other household objects that attract its fancy. As for the wolverine's "fierce hatred" of man, this is a normal reaction in all mammals wounded by firearms or agonizingly caught in traps.

Gulo gulo is a solitary, elusive resident of the wild, and it occupies a unique and fascinating place in the natural order of things. Long may it prosper!

Taxidea taxus

American Badger

In the language of the scientist, "fossorial" means "adapted for living totally or partially underground." The term fits a great many North American mammals, but few better than this large member of the Mustelidae family.

The badger is particularly well suited for fossorial life. Its body is short and flat, its legs are short and bowed, and its claws, perfectly designed for digging, are long and strong. A solitary creature of open prairies and farmlands, the badger does more digging than most other mammals. Some is done to create a series of underground dens for its own use, but much more is done in pursuit of its favorite food — ground squirrels, gophers, mice and the like — as it burrows its way into the victims' homes. In fact, Seton wrote that a badger makes a new burrow every day in search of prey food, and this gives a good idea of the pot-holed nature of any area where the animal makes its home. If *forced* to excavate a tunnel, particularly if threatened by an attacker, it digs at a furious rate and, with dirt and stones flying high and wide behind it, can disappear underground in a minute or two. In fact, the badger is said to be able to dig a tunnel faster than can a man using a shovel.

The badger, much larger than its cousin the striped skunk and slightly smaller than the river otter, weighs at maturity 13 to 30 pounds (6-14 kg), females being lighter, and is 26 to 35 inches (65-90 cm) in length. Its coat is a shaggy, grizzled gray above and yellow-white on the belly. The face is brownish and is marked with a white stripe which runs from near the snout back across the forehead to the shoulder. White areas extend from the mouth to the cheeks and a distinctive vertical black bar, sometimes called a "badge," is present in front of each ear. The ears, low and rounded, are brown or black with creamy edges, and the tail, which measures from 4 to 7 inches (10-18 cm) in length, is yellowish-brown. The hair, much thicker and longer on the back than on the head, covers a loose, tough hide, and molts once a year.

Few predators dare to tackle the badger. While it rarely looks for trouble, when trouble does come and there is no means of retreat, it stands its ground with rare courage and determination. It uses to full advantage its exceptionally strong jaws and sharp canine teeth, and its strong sharp claws. (There are five claws

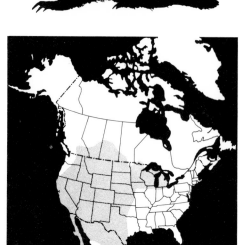

Right fore
3¼ in (8.3 cm) long

Right hind
3¼ in (8.3 cm) long

The badger is a loner and, while it rarely looks for trouble, if forced to defend itself it does so with remarkable courage. While it sometimes is found in forests, it prefers open country such as prairies and farmland. (Photo by Michael McNall)

American badger

on each foot; those on the front feet measure more than an inch in length.) Only a very brave, or foolhardy, adversary will dare to scrap with a badger, and while it may be killed by a pair of unusually capable dogs, it has been known to send a pack of them howling and ki-yi-ing for safety. When fighting or threatened, it hisses, grunts, snarls and growls, and generally releases a strong scent from the pair of glands near the anus. The odor is reported to be relatively inoffensive — to humans, that is — but not all observers agree. Jackson (*Mammals of Wisconsin*) describes it as a "disagreeable, fetid stench." When retreating from an enemy, it tries to back into its burrow, and once the badger is within its protection, most attackers give up and leave. Should one persist in its attack, the possibility would be strong that it would wind up inside the den where it would provide a feast for the badger for several days.

Since this extraordinary burrower prefers to live alone, its association with others of its kind takes place only during the mating season in August and September. As is common in the Mustelidae family, delayed implantation extends the period of the female's gesta-

tion to March and April, when two to five kits are born. The nursery den is usually made in a burrow deeper and longer than usual and in a larger chamber. There is but one entrance (easily identified by the large mound of excavated earth at its mouth) and this is often kept closed off with loose soil.

Baby badgers are born furred, the amount of fur being described by some as "full," by others as "scanty." Their eyes open when they are between 4 and 6 weeks of age, and by the time they are half-grown (about 8 weeks) they are weaned. For some time thereafter the mother brings solid food to them, but when they are two-thirds grown they are taught to hunt small mammals on their own.

From the time they are born until they strike out on their own in early autumn, young badgers remain under the watchful eyes of their mother. There may be exceptions, but it seems evident that the male plays no part in the rearing of the kits. In any event, the mother provides all the care necessary and is fiercely protective of her young, even at the risk of her own life. Young females are capable of breeding successfully as yearlings, but males do not breed until their second year.

The badger is essentially nocturnal, but it has been observed occasionally basking in the early morning sunshine — always close to the entrance of the particular burrow being used at the time. The home range of the male badger is less than 3 square miles (8 km^2), while females confine themselves to about 1 square mile (2.6 km^2). Crossing water is no problem, for it is an accomplished swimmer. There is a report of one badger swimming about half a mile from shore.

Although none of the mustelids are hibernators, they will, like all nesting or denning mammals, seek shelter and sleep for varying periods of time during severe weather. In its northern range, the badger experiences periodic torpidity and will remain within its den for several weeks at a stretch. Unlike true hibernators, however, its body temperature does not become lowered during such siestas.

An involuntary relationship is often reported between badgers and coyotes. This occurs when the coyote, perhaps not altogether to the badger's liking, accompanies the latter on a hunting expedition. This is the game plan, as devised by the coyote. The badger finds, say, the home of a ground squirrel and begins furiously digging its way into the burrow: the squirrel, hearing the rapidly approaching badger, decides to escape and runs along a secondary tunnel that leads to freedom. If the coyote is lucky enough to be stationed at the right exit, it simply pounces on the hapless squirrel. The badger does the work; the coyote reaps the reward. Hawks sometimes freeload in much the same way.

Taxedea taxus, a member of a worldwide group, is a distinctly North American species. In its original Canadian range, it was once common on the Prairies but its numbers there are now greatly reduced. Peterson writes that it is found (but now more rarely) in the "extreme western part of Ontario in the Rainy River region and along the shore of Lake Erie." According to Cowan and Guiguet, it occurs in the interior valleys of south-eastern British Columbia. Its United States range is more extensive and includes most of the western part of the continent, except for the far northwestern mountain regions.

Years ago the European badger was subjected to the disgustingly cruel treatment, thought to be entertaining, of being placed in an open barrel and having to defend itself from dogs. From this idiocy has evolved the verb "badger," meaning to bother, tease, annoy.

The badger, incidentally, which is considered the most beneficial of Wisconsin's mammals because of the large number of harmful rodents it kills each year, is that state's official emblem. Wisconsin is known as the "Badger State."

There is no certain knowledge as to its lifespan in the wild, but captive badgers have lived as long as 15 years.

Mephitis mephitis
Striped Skunk

When Ralph Waldo Emerson, in his essay *Compensation*, wrote that "Nature hates monopolies and exceptions," he used as his analogy the fable about the stag that admired its antlers but disliked its feet. While it was only the fleetness of foot that one day saved it from the hunter, it was the thicket in which the antlers became later entangled that caused its death. This was an example, he said, of the *Law of Compensation* — the law of dualism that seems to govern every facet of life. Emerson's theory (if a little license is taken) is supported by *Mephitis mephitis*, the striped skunk. This well known carnivore/omnivore is an example of "every evil has its good."

On the evil side (from its aggressor's point of view) the skunk has one of the most powerful defense mechanisms bestowed on any creature: two rear jets, each capable of spraying a nauseating repellent as far as 20 feet (6 m), and with devastating accuracy. The composition of this musk, contained in a gland on each side of the anus at the base of the tail, was described by Ernest Thompson Seton as "a mixture of strong ammonia, essence of garlic, burning sulphur, a volume of sewer gas, a vitriol spray, a dash of perfume musk, all mixed together and intensified a thousand times." Small wonder that the scientific name, *Mephitis*, derives from the Latin, "bad odor."

On the good side (from the skunk's point of view) this repellent, if ejected in time, will rebuff immediately almost any predator — man or animal. With one exception even the wiliest of its natural enemies is unable to withstand its overwhelming power. The one exception is the great horned owl. As seems to be the case with most birds, the owl's sense of smell is undeveloped.

Hunger, particularly to the point of starvation, will force any creature to take risks and in such situations a bobcat, fox, fisher or a hawk will kill a skunk, its pungent odor notwithstanding.

Four species of skunk are found in North America. Of the four only two are present in Canada and northern United States—the striped skunk and the spotted skunk (*Spilogale putorius*). The striped skunk has four subspecies, the spotted skunk one.

This amiable, easy-going creature is regarded by many as one of the most handsome members of the Mustelidae family; its thick lustrous fur is particularly attractive in both design and appearance. This also may be said of the spotted skunk. Both are predominantly black, with swatches of pure white running along the back and sides and in the tail.

In the striped skunk the white is shaped like a tuning fork. It begins with a thin white line down the middle of the face. A wide white stripe then runs along the top of the head and branches out at the shoulder into two wide bars which continue along each side of the back to merge into the mostly black tail. The tip of the tail is normally, but not always, white.

This description is a generalization, for the white markings often vary considerably in width and length. The fur of the striped skunk is molted each spring and fall. Other physical characteristics are its small pointed head, its short legs, and hump-like back. Its size is usually compared with that of a large house cat.

The striped skunk is commonly found in agricultural and park lands, but also occurs in open, forested areas. Some (occasionally too many) take up residence in urban areas, often under verandas, in garden sheds, woodpiles and cellars. Unfortunately, in such situations, skunks and humans usually have a decidedly discordant relationship and getting rid of the skunks calls for special skills and experience.

This animal is primarily a night wanderer but often may be seen during the day as it travels in search of food. Its diet ranges from small mammals such as mice, shrews, baby rabbits, chipmunks and gophers to birds' eggs, frogs, grasshoppers, grubs, wasps and carrion. Vegetation is also important, particularly fruits (wild and cultivated) such as blackberries, blueberries, strawberries, apples, persimmons and cherries. Now and again it will raid a henhouse for a feast of eggs, or a beehive for a feast of bees and honey, but these predations are of a minor nature. Because of the large numbers of rodents and insects that are included in its diet, it is considered to be of significant benefit to humans.

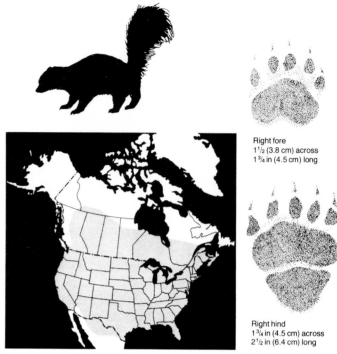

Right fore
1½ (3.8 cm) across
1¾ in (4.5 cm) long

Right hind
1¾ in (4.5 cm) across
2½ in (6.4 cm) long

Striped skunk

Striped skunks, carrying heavy layers of fat built up during the fall period of concentrated feeding, go into semi-hibernation in November and December. The below-ground dens chosen may be those they occupied during the summer and fall, those formerly used by marmots, rabbits, foxes or other small mammals, or those they excavate themselves. Some make their homes in woodpiles or under the floors of buildings. Leaves are used for nesting purposes, and to close off entrances and thus provide barriers against the cold and snow. While most remain in the dens throughout the winter, metabolizing their fat, some emerge for short periods when the weather is mild. Rarely are dens occupied by single skunks. In some instances a dozen or more of both sexes may winter together. Mating takes place sometime during February and early March and the young, averaging four to six in a litter, are born in early May. Males are polygamous and breed with several females during the females' short (3-day) "heat" period.

Baby skunks weigh about half an ounce (14 g) when born. At that time they are virtually naked, although there are markings that show the black and

This night-wandering mammal, while one of the most handsome of the Mustelidae family, has a built-in defense mechanism that is respected by humans and wild creatures alike—its pungent spray. The skunk uses it, however, only in emergencies. (Photo by Mark Nyhof)

white form the fur will take when it grows during the following 3 weeks. It is not until 17 to 21 days later that their eyes open. Although they begin their foraging for solid foods at the age of 7 weeks when they emerge from the den for the first time, they are not fully weaned until they are about 8 weeks old.

Skunks seem to be well aware of the highly offensive quality of their musk, for they are always extremely careful to protect their own fur. In fact they show a reluctance to release the musk at all and only do so as a last resort. At first encounter they usually try to retreat from an aggressor. If still threatened, a skunk, as Miller describes in *Hinterland Who's Who*, will "growl or hiss, stamp its front feet rapidly, or even walk a short distance on its front feet with its tail high in the air." It cannot, as can the spotted skunk, spray from this position. These performances are warnings that any further advance will not be tolerated. If the aggressor does not heed these warnings, the striped skunk, standing on all fours, humps its back and turns so that its head and rear face its opponent. When ready to fire it raises its tail stiffly over its back, exposes the two anal jets, and it's "fire away!"

Each of the grape-size glands contains about a tablespoon of musk and while one brief shot usually is enough to send the enemy in howling retreat, the skunk can, if necessary, fire off four or five more sprays before the supply is depleted. Since it takes about a week and a half to refill the glands, the musk is used sparingly.

The skunk relies almost entirely on this repellent for self-defense, for its movements are slow and lumbering—the very opposite to the swift and sometimes lightning-like reflexes of some others in the weasel group.

Some skunks can be easily tamed and make interesting pets—but only when their scent glands have been removed. Anyone unfortunate enough to be sprayed by one not de-scented will quickly lose enthusiasm for the animal. A number of methods are used to remove skunk odor. Tomato juice is apparently the best for use on the skin and for cleaning dogs. As for clothes, the surest solution is to destroy them. Even the best formulas are themselves unpleasantly odoriferous and there is always the risk that on a damp, humid day the skunk smell will be noticeable.

M. mephitis is North America's most common skunk and is present in every province of Canada except Newfoundland. In British Columbia, however, its range ends east of the Coast Range. Its northern range roughly follows the 55th parallel, although some may be present in the extreme southeastern tip of the Yukon. It occurs in the southwestern part of the Northwest Territories. It is not present in Alaska. It occurs in every other continental U.S. state and south to northern Mexico.

Striped skunk sprays with all four feet on the ground.

Spilogale putorius

Spotted Skunk

This is the smallest of the skunks and is primarily a resident of the United States. Small numbers are present in Canada, but only in the southwestern coastal area of British Columbia. It is not found on Vancouver Island. It is also absent from most of the northern United States.

The defensive capabilities of this mammal are similar to those of its larger relative, the striped skunk, but its shape is a little more weasel-like and its markings are quite dissimilar. The spotted skunk which, in addition to the name spotted stinker, is known as civet cat, polecat, and hydrophobia cat. It carries a coat of short, silky black fur attractively patterned with wide white stripes which run from the front of the ears and across the back and curve into the rump. These stripes are often broken, giving them a spotty look. The tip of the bushy tail is white, and white spots also are present between the eyes. Adult spotted skunks range in length from about 14 to 22 inches (36-56 cm) with 3- to 9-inch (8-23 cm) tails, and weigh about 2 pounds (1 kg).

Seton, who described the projected musk of the striped skunk in colorfully disparaging terms, probably never encountered a spotted skunk, but Banfield, who apparently has, claims it "resembles a highly concentrated onion extract." The smaller skunk, even though equipped with the same weaponry, is not as efficient in its use: the striped skunk can hit a target at a distance of

Right fore
1 1/4 in (3.2 cm) long

Right hind
1 1/4 in (3.2 cm) long

Spotted skunk (Found in Canada only in a small area of extreme southwestern British Columbia)

about 6 yards (5 m), whereas the spotted skunk's longest shot is about 4 yards (3.7 m). Nevertheless the spotted skunk can boast of a unique method of warning of enemies or spraying them if they get too close: it stands on its hind legs, back facing whatever is threatening, and waves its tail; then, if necessary, it shoots its spray in the direction of its hapless victim.

These little creatures are accomplished at climbing trees and will do so if arboreal forage appeals to them or if they are fleeing from predators. Their normal habitat is at ground level, and their living quarters are often expropriated marmot burrows. Frequently they make their dens in hollow logs, brush piles, abandoned buildings and rock slides. They are strictly nocturnal and are seldom seen during the day, and when on the prowl at night they search for mice and other rodents, birds, amphibians, grubs and a variety of insects, as well as fruit. If living near a farm they will occasionally kill hens and eat their eggs.

The spotted skunk is believed to mate in late winter and to give birth in the spring to four or five young. Aside from man, who kills it for its pelt, its most feared enemy is the great horned owl.

Spotted skunk in spraying position

Lutra canadensis

River Otter

".... my purpose is to bestow a day or two in helping to destroy some of those villainous vermin, for I hate them perfectly, because they love fish so well, or rather, because they destroy so much; indeed, so much that, in my judgment, all men that keep otter-dogs ought to have pensions from the King to encourage them to destroy the very breed of those base otters, they do so much mischief."

This condemnation of the river otter, part of a conversation between a hunter and an angler in Izaak Walton's *The Compleat Angler*, was quoted by Ed Park in his engagingly written *The World of the Otter*. The quotation is used again here as a base from which to defend this member of the Mustelidae family against the false allegations that, more than 330 years after Walton's book was published, still persist.

Throughout human history, even up to the present time, different species of wildlife have been unjustly maligned—victims of myths, legends, old-wives tales and sheer ignorance. Many of them, either through hunting pressure or the destruction of their natural habitat, have become extinct or are now on the endangered species list. River otters have not escaped the onslaught.

The river otter has managed to survive largely because of its more isolated land habitat, but its status must be carefully monitored throughout its whole North American range. There is no accurate count of these animals and probably never will be because their furtive way of life makes a census virtually impossible. Probably the only sign of danger will be when the annual kill by fur hunters in both countries goes into a drastic decline.

The angler in Izaak Walton's book reflected an attitude that prevails among many present-day anglers, especially those who pursue trout and salmon: otters are serious predators of these fish and therefore have no place in the same river and lake systems. This, of course, with rare exceptions, has been proved unjustified.

Sufficient evidence has been assembled to prove that trout and salmon constitute only a minor proportion of the fish consumed. While fish do make up a large part of the otter's diet, the species consumed are mainly minnows and other coarse fish such as sculpins, perch, sunfish, catfish and the like. In the Great Lakes

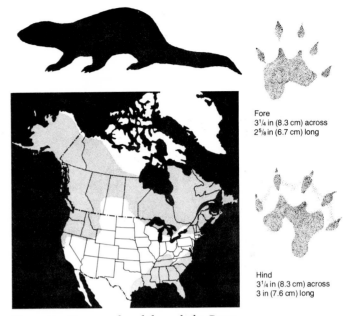

Fore
3¼ in (8.3 cm) across
2⅝ in (6.7 cm) long

Hind
3¼ in (8.3 cm) across
3 in (7.6 cm) long

River otter (Range reduced through the Great Plains and east coast)

region it is known that otters eat lamprey eels, voracious creatures which nearly destroyed the lake trout and whitefish industry there. Occasionally a venturesome otter manages to invade a fish hatchery and a royal banquet ensues. But these expeditions are rare.

Other foods making up the otter diet include water beetles, nymphs, turtles, snakes, worms, mussels, crabs, snails and frogs. Crayfish, as well as ripe wild blueberries, are favorites wherever they are available. There is some evidence that they consume waterfowl and small mammals, but it is doubtful that they can be accused of even minor predation on beavers.

The river otter, *Lutra canadensis*, belongs to a family whose North American members include weasels, marten, wolverine, mink, badger, fisher and skunks. Unlike most of its cousins, however, the otter (like the mink) is semi-aquatic, spending most of its time in or near water but maintaining its permanent residence on land.

The otter is a born playboy whose daily life seems to be made up of fun and games. It is a prankster and an athlete and on the scale of animal intelligence it rates near the top. Not without reason is it frequently refer-

The river otter is a fun-loving creature which enjoys life to the full. It is active year-round, loves sliding down muddy or snow-covered hills, and in water it moves with the grace of a ballet dancer. This species is found only in North America. (Photo by Brian Milne/ Valan Photos)

red to as the "wilderness's good-time Charlie." A family of otters made their home beside Desormeaux Creek, which flowed into Little Whitefish Lake at a time when we had a cottage there. During mid-winter trips to our Quebec cabin, we often skied across the lake in the hope of seeing them frolicking near their home. We were successful on two occasions, when the wind was against us and thus prevented our scent from reaching them.

This story has been told many times by other observers, and it is always much the same. In both of our watches, three otters we presumed to be mother, father and yearling were playing in deep snow near the creek. One would plunge beneath the snow and a few seconds later the other two would sniff around in an effort to locate it. Soon a broad, flattened head with a black, bulbous nose and large brown eyes would appear about 20 feet away. Once spotted, it would immediately submerge and reappear at another spot, and the chase would continue. When "tagged," one of the other two, and occasionally both, would dive beneath the snow and the performance would be repeated. It was a rollicking game of hide and seek, carried out with a good deal of chuckling and bird-like chirping.

Other observers have seen families of otters enjoying what is probably their favorite sport: tobogganing. This is a year-round pastime, but especially popular in the winter. The animals climb to the top of a downhill slide and push themselves with all four feet to get a good belly run down the slope, sometimes right into open water. The runs, sometimes made on their sides and backs as well as on their bellies, are repeated over and over again. Interestingly enough, grizzly bears have been observed disporting themselves in much the same way, as described in Dr. Andy Russell's classic *Grizzly Country*.

Alone or in groups, on land or in water, the otter enjoys life to the full. Its agility in water is remarkable and a delight to watch. Powerful flexing of its body and tail in an up and down motion sends the otter through the water slowly or at fast speeds, but always gracefully. When it frolics, it twists, turns and corkscrews. If it is not traveling beneath the surface, it moves in and out of the water like a dolphin or cruises with only its head showing.

The home range of the otter may be anywhere from 15 to 50 miles (24-80 km) of the stream, lake or coastline where it resides. Periodically it will travel by land and water to the extremities of its range, a journey that may take from 10 days to 2 weeks to complete. During the land portions of its journey it leaves its "mark" by depositing from its two anal glands a few drops of scent—somewhat like that of a skunk, but milder—on tufts of grass or small mounds such as earth and stones. These "marks" are also evident all year round in the immediate area of the animal's home.

Otters breed in late winter or early spring. As a consequence of delayed implantation, the gestation period is extended and is commonly estimated at from 9½ to 12½ months, usually ending in March and April.

There appears, however, to be a marked difference between some North American races. Park, for example, quotes one biologist (K. A. Wilson) as saying that otters in North Carolina have a gestation period of about 61 days, which is comparable to that of the European otter. Cowan and Guiguet (*The Mammals of British Columbia*) use the same figure, but tell of one in captivity that gave birth in 43 days. A male otter may

breed several females during the mating season.

Otters are usually born in dens that were once occupied by animals such as muskrats or beavers. Often, however, adults make their own nursery dens under the roots or in the hollows of large trees, under rock outcrops, in thickets or tall grasses. Sometimes the dens are made in burrows already dug in the banks of rivers or lakes. Wherever they are located, they are always close to water.

The average litter is two or three, but may occasionally be as many as five. The young, when born, weigh about 5 ounces (140 g) and are fully furred. Their eyes do not open until they are about 5 weeks old. Young otters spend an unusually long time in their dens, often 2 to 3 months, before they leave to begin their lives in the open. Surprisingly, although they become the most accomplished swimmers of all land mammals, they have to be taught to overcome their initial fear of *deep* water. Those who have witnessed this training period say that mothers often carry them on their backs, slip away when in deep water, and thus force the youngsters to learn how to keep afloat. Once the fear of deep water is overcome, they quickly, and joyfully, adapt to the new element.

Seton (*Life Histories of Northern Animals*) quotes an observation written by a J. G. Mallais: "She teaches them to dive noiselessly, to circle in deep pools, and how to come up quickly behind sleeping fish or drive them into holes in the banks. Then they are taught to stir the mud with their pads, or turn over stones for hidden miller's-thumbs, and bury their heads in the mud after eels, or how to corner the darting salmon."

From the time the young are born to the time they learn to be independent on land and in the water, the father remains on the sidelines and plays no part in their care or education. It is commonly believed, however, that the male is seldom far away. Reunion does not take place until the cubs are about 5 or 6 months old. Then continues, with even greater vigor, the high-spirited life so typical of the otter family. Other than when sleeping, they are seldom inactive; they are up and about every day of the year.

The river otter is well equipped for the amphibious life it leads, and seems to enjoy land as much as it does water. Water is its favorite element, not only because it is its place of breeding, its primary source of food, and its best protection from enemies, but because it also enables it to attain its greatest mobility.

Structurally the otter is long and streamlined. Its

River otters have a streamlined body to swim and dive.

head is broad and flat, its ears are short, its eyes are small and its nose is bulbous. Like all mustelids, it has whiskers, although these are more prominent in its cousin, the sea otter. Its tail is long and tapered, its legs are short and the toes of its feet are fully webbed. The soles of its feet are furred. The pelage of the otter, highly valued by furriers, is short, thick and lustrous, and is generally dark brown above and grayish brown on the throat and cheeks. A male at maturity may reach a length of nearly 5 feet (1.5 m) and a weight sometimes in excess of 30 pounds (14 kg).

River otters are found throughout Canada and the United States and probably vie with red foxes as the most widely distributed of all the carnivores. The largest specimens are resident on Alaska's Prince of Wales Island and adjacent islands, while the smallest occur in Newfoundland.

River otters mature when they are 2 years of age but according to Banfield, males are not able to breed successfully until they are 6 or 7 years of age. Their longevity in the wild is not well established, but in captivity they have been known to live for up to 16 years.

In a study published in 1972 by the Royal Ontario Museum (*Life Sciences Contributions*), Dr. C. G. van

Zyll de Jong, Curator of Mammals, National Museum of Natural Sciences, Ottawa, wrote that the 20 North American subspecies previously recognized were, on the basis of new analysis, excessive. His new arrangement, which reduces the number to seven, is as follows: *L.c. canadensis*, which occurs in eastern Canada and adjacent areas of the United States; *L.c. lataxina*, which occurs east of the Rocky Mountains in the United States; *L.c. pacifica*, which occurs in western and northern Canada and western United States, as well as Alaska; *L.c. mira*, which occurs along the coast of British Columbia, including coastal Vancouver Island as well as southeastern Alaska and offshore islands; *L.c. periclyzomae*, a fairly large type which is found on the Queen Charlotte Islands; *L.c. kodiacensis*, which is found on Kodiak Island, south of the Alaska Peninsula; and *L.c. sonora*, which occurs along the Colorado River system.

Enhydra lutris
Sea Otter

The sea otter, smallest of all marine mammals, is also the largest of the mustelids. At one time it was abundant around the North Pacific rim from the northern islands of Japan to the Aleutians and Pribilofs and south along the coasts of British Columbia, Washington and Oregon to central Baja California and the Gulf of California. Intensive and indiscriminate slaughter of the creature so threatened its existence, particularly during the last half of the 18th century, that international intervention was necessary to assure its survival. At the same time another valuable fur-bearing mammal, the northern fur seal, was also threatened with extinction. And so, in 1911, a treaty was signed by Great Britain, the United States, Russia and Japan. The treaty (signed by Great Britain on behalf of Canada) outlawed the killing of sea otters and even made illegal the possession of sea otter pelts. It also put an end to pelagic killing of fur seals although it provided for controlled harvesting of them on their breeding grounds.

When the treaty was signed sea otters were so few in number that some scientists believed total extinction was unavoidable. Fortunately a few small northern populations had survived and these slowly multiplied and spread. Populations on Amchitka Island and in Prince William Sound, Alaska, prospered so well, in fact, that between 1965 and 1972 United States authorities relocated 708 individuals from those areas to other habitats at that time unoccupied. All the transplants, except one made to the Oregon coast, have been successful. Canada was also involved in the rehabilitation program and since 1969 scientists of the Pacific Biological Station, Department of Fisheries and Oceans, and the British Columbia Fish and Wildlife Service, arranged for the transplant of 89 Amchitka otters to Checleslet Bay on the west coast of Vancouver Island. This population has since increased and it is thought that the mammal will in time again occupy most of its original British Columbia range. Today the total world population of sea otters is estimated at close to 150,000 individuals, most of them in Alaska.

Sea otter

The sea otter is one of the most interesting of all amphibious creatures. Originally a land mammal, it is related to weasels, skunks, badgers and, of course, to river otters. It took up marine life probably during the early Miocene epoch about 22 million years ago. It was in good company, for the ancestors of other present-day land/sea dwellers — seals, seal lions and walruses, for example — also were terrestrial creatures at that time.

Most adult male sea otters weigh from 60 to 85 pounds (27-39 kg) although a very large individual may reach 100 pounds (45 kg). Most adult females weigh from 35 to 60 pounds (16-27 kg), although one occasionally grows to 72 pounds (33 kg). The length of an adult male may be up to 58.25 inches (148 cm) and that of an adult female may be up to 55 inches (140 cm).

Like the pelage of the fur seals, that of the sea otter is a morphological wonder. Can you imagine a mammal endowed with a coat made up of nearly one *billion* fine, luxurious fur fibers? These fibers, microscopic examinations have shown, grow in tiny bundles and through each bundle, in turn, grows *one* guard hair. (This accounts for the spareness of guard hairs on the animal.) The density of the fur on the otter, in fact, is about twice the density of the fur on the Pribilof seal.

There is, of course, a reason for the sea otter's amazing coat. Unlike the pinnipeds, the sea otter does not have a protective layer of blubber to keep its body warm and buoyant, so nature devised its fur in such a way that air, trapped among the fibers, not only provides protection from the frigid environment, but also provides it with the buoyancy to keep it afloat on the sea's surface.

But this fur has to be kept completely free of foreign elements, especially oil and other industrial effluents, for such pollutants quickly remove the protective layers of air. When this insulation is lost, the animal's body heat is lowered so critically that in a matter of hours it could die of hypothermia. Otter watchers have often wondered why the animal spends so much time grooming or scratching itself. The answer is its need to keep its fur clean and waterproof, not because it is troubled with external parasites such as fleas or lice; in fact, such parasites have never been found in the animal's fur.

The hind limbs of the sea otter resemble those of the pinnipeds in that the feet are webbed and flipper-like, but the fore limbs are more like those of mustelids in that the feet have paws. It is these paws, with retractile claws, that are used for seizing and handling food and for grooming. The rear limbs and flippers are used for swimming. The head is large and blunt, the eyes are small and black, the neck is short and thick, and the ears (like those of the pinnipeds) can be closed when under water. Except for the area around the head, throat and chest, which is grayish or cream colored, the fur of this otter ranges from dark brown to black. In older individuals, the fur around the head, throat and chest often becomes grizzled.

Whereas the teeth of terrestrial mustelids are sharp-edged for cutting, those of the sea otter are broad and flat and designed for crushing. (Seizing and retaining hold of a fish is sometimes difficult). In gathering food the animal dives to the ocean floor, generally down to about 120 feet (37 m), grasps the food in its forepaws

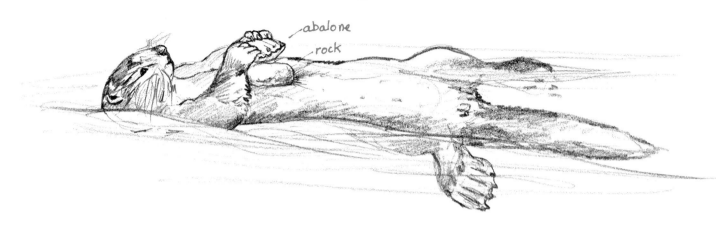

Sea otter feeding. It cracks the abalone on the rock.

abalone

rock

and carries it to the surface under the fleshy fold of its left foreleg. Its dives under water last from 1 to 1¹/₂ minutes. Karl W. Kenyon writes that an otter can carry up to 25 sea urchins as well as a number of clams at one time. Included in this store of food is often a good-sized stone. Once on the surface the otter floats on its back, and if feeding on large clams and mussels, it places the stone on its chest and uses it as an anvil on which to break the shells. Softer foods, such as sea urchins, are simply crushed by the flattened, rounded teeth, while molluscs with soft shells are swallowed whole after being crushed. Abalone, one of its favorite foods, maintains a suction-like grip on underwater rocks and the otter removes them by giving them a hard whack with another rock. Its fondness for abalone, in fact, has brought it into conflict with the commercial fisheries off California. The otter consumes about a fifth of its body weight in food every day.

The sea otter becomes sexually mature at 3 to 4 years of age. Breeding takes place during spring and summer, in the water, and near a rocky beach where both male and female haul out to sleep. Their relationship, however, lasts only a few days. A single pup is born about 8 months later, and weighs about 4.5 pounds (2 kg). It comes into the world fully furred, eyes open and teeth already breaking through. Not until it is several weeks old, however, is it strong enough to overcome the buoyancy of the water and make dives on its own. While it gradually learns to gather food from the sea's bottom, its dependency on its mother continues

for up to a year. To suckle, sleep and to groom (or be groomed) it climbs up on its mother's stomach as she lies outstretched on her back, floating securely on the Pacific swell. Frequently, when resting, the adult otter will wrap strands of kelp around its body to secure its position. The male, incidentally, assumes no responsibility for the care of the young and during the breeding season may mate with a number of females. There is little fraternization between the adults of either sex, although there are accounts (Karl W. Kenyon) of 10 to 50 males sleeping together on Aleutian beaches. Generally speaking, however, adult males choose their own geographical area and adult females their own. The sea otter is not migratory, but it is not unusual for it to travel 30 miles (48 km) or so from its favorite beach before returning.

The sea otter has few enemies now that man is no longer a threat. Whether it is seriously preyed upon by "orcas" (killer whales), white sharks or (when at baby stage) bald eagles is yet to be determined.

The return of the sea otter is a credit to man's concern for the welfare and security of this interesting creature of sea and land. What is not to man's credit is that, in the first instance, indifference and greed nearly caused the sea otter's extinction. This species will survive, and one can but hope that its fellow inhabitants of the oceans—the great whales—will one day also be allowed to roam free, protected and appreciated for the marvelous beings they are.

FAMILY FELIDAE

Felis concolor
Cougar (Mountain Lion)

Of all North American wild mammals, cougars, or mountain lions, are among the most reclusive. These beautiful creatures, once present in virtually every area of the United States and Canada except Newfoundland and the far north, have been so reduced by advancing land use and hunting pressure that they now live in significant numbers only in the western mountains of the two countries. A few may have managed to survive in Florida and possibly in some other eastern states, and some remnant populations may be present in central and eastern Canada. Because they are mainly nocturnal and secretive in behavior, information on their survival is scarce and perhaps inaccurate, except in western areas where they are numerous or inhabit open country. The cougar still maintains a foothold (although in some regions a tenuous one) in Mexico, Central America and from coast to coast in South America south to the Straits of Magellan.

Next to the jaguar, whose northern limit is the southern United States border regions, the cougar is the largest of the North American native cats. It is a slender animal, the males sometimes reaching a length of 9 feet (2.8 m) from nose to tip of extended tail and a weight of around 200 pounds (90 kg). The average length is somewhat less, however, and the average weight is about 125 pounds (57 kg). There is a record of one Arizona male cougar that weighed 276 pounds (125 kg). Females are always much smaller.

The coloring of this animal varies greatly but generally it ranges from reddish-brown and golden yellowish-brown to dull gray. The pelage is uniformly short and coarse in tropical regions, but longer and softer in colder northern climates. Its belly is buff colored and its chest and throat are white. Stripes of black are prominent on the muzzle; the backs of the small, rounded ears and the tip of the tail are also black. Its head, in relation to the size of its body, seems disproportionately small, with eyes placed well in front. Another characteristic is that the hind legs are considerably longer than the forelegs, so at times the animal can look as if it is going downhill when it isn't!

The large front paws contain five toes, and the hind ones four. Each toe terminates in a sharp, strongly-curved claw with a needle-like point. The claws can be extended or withdrawn at will by powerful flexor muscles. When extended they become deadly weapons. All of the mountain lion's senses—sight, hearing and smell—are well developed.

The cougar is a carnivore, or flesh eater, and its long, rapier-like canine teeth can pierce through skin and flesh with ease. Two pairs of cutting teeth, one on each side of the upper and lower jaws, are sharp-edged and, like notched scissors, are capable of quickly severing tough muscle and sinew. With all this equipment, plus its powerful muscles, it is capable of killing elk, moose and other animals beyond its own weight and size.

Whatever their habitat—mountains, deserts, coastal and sub-alpine forests, swamps or prairies—cougars establish and defend territories of their own. The boundaries of these territories, which may extend from 5 to 25 or more square miles (13-65 km²), are marked with numerous mounds of brush, pine needles or other ground cover scraped together and heavily soaked with urine or mixed with scats (feces). Cougars

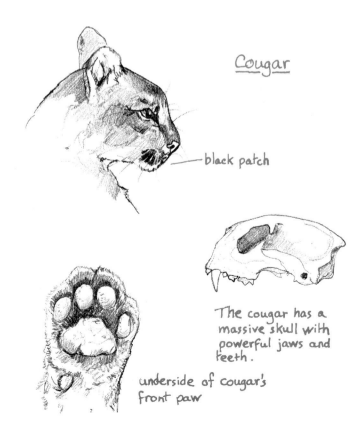

Cougar

black patch

The cougar has a massive skull with powerful jaws and teeth.

underside of cougar's front paw

Although evidence of its presence may sometimes be apparent, sighting a cougar in its natural habitat rarely happens. It is one of North America's most furtive animals. (British Columbia Government Photo)

arriving at identifiable boundaries generally avoid the area rather than risk a confrontation. This policy of "mutual avoidance" assures a reasonable degree of peace among members of the species.

During the mating season, however, boundary lines are disregarded and it is usually the female that leaves her own territory to seek out a partner. Like domestic cats, cougars are polygamous. If, as frequently happens, more than one male courts the same female during the 9 days or so when she is in heat,

vicious fights ensue. The female herself may go on the attack if she objects to courting that becomes too rough-house.

The successful suitor may leave the female within two weeks after mating or may stay with her until parturition is at hand. In any case, after a gestation period of between 90 and 96 days, the female ends the association and seeks out a rocky crevice or some other protected place where she gives birth to one to five kittens.

Most cougar kittens are born in late winter or early spring, although it is known that births may occur in any month. The young, three or four on average, are about 10 inches (25 cm) long and weigh about 12 ounces (340 g) when dropped. Their woolly covering is fawn-colored and dotted with numerous brown spots, their short furry tails are ringed with alternating dark and light brown bands, and their eyes are tightly closed. In about 2 weeks the eyes are fully open.

Nursing by the mother usually ends in about 3 months but can continue for another 5 months or so until they are half grown. At that time they are about 5 feet (1.5 m) long and weigh about 50 pounds (23 kg). When they are 6 weeks old, however, their mother brings them meat and bones from her own kills, their introduction to the protein that will sustain them for the rest of their lives.

Cougars born in late winter or early spring are large and strong enough by autumn to accompany their mothers on hunting expeditions. Before winter ends they are able to kill game by themselves. Although by now well trained and self-reliant, family ties remain strong and it is often several months later, sometimes another year, before complete separation occurs and the young leave to estabish their own territories and, in time, to perpetuate their species.

Just about every adjective has been used to emphasize the secretive, furtive nature of cougars. Most people who have spent a good part of their lives in cougar country have neither seen nor heard the animal, even though evidence of its presence may abound — footprints, remains of a kill or scats. Despite its shyness, however, the cougar has an insatiable curiosity and may follow humans on the trail or sit for hours in some secluded spot to watch people at work or play. Their ability to move silently is uncanny.

The predatory behavior of cougars has been well documented. Normally animals such as deer and elk make up their main diet, but other animals such as moose, mountain goats, coyotes, rabbits, porcupines, raccoons and the like are also on their list of prey species. Domestic animals sometimes are killed and cougars are said to have a particular fondness for horse meat. Occasionally one hears reports of an unusual slaughter of domestic animals, such as one account of a cougar in the United States having killed 192 sheep *in one night!* This, if true, must be regarded as an abnormal slaughtering spree. While cougars have been known to attack and sometimes kill humans, such events are rare. When they do occur, it is usually because the animals are starving or defending their young. They are probably less dangerous to man than grizzlies.

After making its kill, the cougar will generally take it to a sheltered place, sometimes as far as 500 yards away, where it will gorge itself. When sated, it will

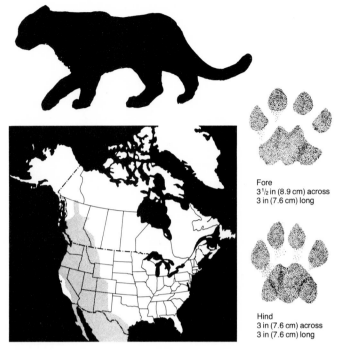

Cougar (Range much reduced. Once found across continent)

Fore
3½ in (8.9 cm) across
3 in (7.6 cm) long

Hind
3 in (7.6 cm) across
3 in (7.6 cm) long

cover the remains with leaves and other ground cover, and then retire for a digestive siesta. If food is scarce, it will return for additional meals, but if plentiful, it may abandon the kill and seek fresh prey. This should not be regarded as wasteful behavior, for the remains of the carcasses provide food for other animals. Instances of what may appear to be overkill, in which deer or elk are slaughtered and only small portions of them eaten, or none eaten at all, have been noted. While this may seem objectionable, it is often nature's way of maintaining a balance. Too large a deer population, for example, could result in heavy depletion of forage, and depletion of forage could result in starvation for the deer.

When stalking large prey, a cougar moves with extraordinary stealth and silence, making full use of cover. Once close to its victim, it leaps on its back, either breaking its neck by a powerful wrench of its paw or by biting deeply into the back of the head. Normally the kill is made quickly. It is characteristic of a cougar to stop pursuing its intended victim if it cannot catch it within two or three jumps.

Much controversy centers upon sounds cougars may or may not make. Do screams that are sometimes

The cougar is very powerful and is capable of killing prey as large as moose and elk. (Photo by Peter Karsten)

Lynx canadensis
Canada Lynx

This member of the cat family is present over a large part of the northern hemisphere. It is found in the forested regions of most of Canada (except coastal British Columbia) as well as Alaska. It occurs in an irregular pattern in continental United States, with populations in Washington, Oregon, Idaho, Montana, Wyoming, Colorado, Minnesota, Wisconsin and Michigan. The lynx is believed to have evolved from ancestors that existed during the Pliocene epoch, which ended about 3 million years ago.

The lynx, like a number of other animals, is frequently referred to in the literature and mythology of the Old World. The European lynx, classified as *Lynx lynx*, was sacred to Freya, the Scandinavian goddess of love and beauty, and according to legend, two of the animals drew her chariot whenever she rode into battle. Greek mythology gave the lynx extraordinary sight and attributed to the animal the ability to see through stone walls. The North American lynx, *Lynx canadensis*, and the European lynx, *Lynx lynx*, are considered by most authorities to be separate but closely related species.

This interesting animal, which looks like an oversized tabby cat, is essentially a forest dweller, preferring areas of thick undergrowth and windfalls. Here it lives on its favorite food, the snowshoe hare, varying its diet when hares are scarce with mice, grouse, ducks, young deer and occasionally young mountain sheep. In the far north, when there are acute food shortages, it will leave the forests and roam the tundra to search for Arctic hare, lemmings and ground birds. Lynx populations, however, are closely related to the cyclic trends of the snowshoe hares. Every 9 to 10 years the hares experience a cyclic fluctuation in population, during which there is a substantial increase in numbers and then a sudden decline. This is most noticeable in northern ranges.

The Ontario Ministry of Natural Resources states that in Algonquin Park, however, the population highs occur from 6 to 13 years apart. It adds that food shortages, diseases and predators have all been invoked to explain the cycle but no theory has won complete acceptance. A recent study, however, suggests an intriguing cause: when there are peak populations of hares, the plants they feed on become severely pruned. This causes the plants to produce a toxic chemical which

heard come from male cougars, or from female cougars during the mating season, or are these spine-tingling sounds the wails of the great horned owl? It seems evident that females do scream at times and that cougars of both sexes and all ages growl, hiss and purr. After all, they are cats! But many of the tales of weird screams and other kinds of caterwauling may be discounted. The cougar for the most part is an unusually silent animal.

Cougars are game animals, and where hunting is permitted (usually on a very restricted, seasonal basis), hounds are generally used to "tree" the animal, from which position it is easily shot. If able to complete its normal lifespan, it can survive in the wild for 10 to 15 years. Captive cougars have lived for 18 years.

Lynx, inhabitants of heavily forested areas, are active all year and are mainly nocturnal. Their favorite food is the snowshoe hare. (Photo by J. C. Holroyd)

Bobcats closely resemble lynx, but whereas lynx prefer northern boreal forests, bobcats like woodlands as well as barren, rocky and swampy areas. Generally smaller than lynx, weighing on average 15 to 20 pounds (7-9 kg), some individuals have reached as much as 68 pounds (31 kg). (Photo by J.D. Taylor/Valan Photos) repels hares. If they continue to eat the plants, the chemical causes a weight loss. Other food to which they might turn usually offers a starvation diet. The hare population consequently dies off and, ergo, so does the lynx population! During the time it takes for hare numbers to recover, the lynx population, dependent on hares for survival, also increases and so the stage is set for another double crash.

A male lynx at maturity weighs 14 to 34 pounds (6.4-15 kg) with the average being 22 pounds (10 kg). It is readily distinguished by its short, black-tipped tail, short body, long sturdy legs, very large, heavily furred paws, well developed side whiskers, and triangular ears which are tipped with long black hairs. Its eyes are greenish-yellow. The coat of the lynx is long, soft and thick and is buffy-gray with a few indistinct dark spots. The belly is lighter in color. Black stripes are prominent on the forehead and around the facial ruff. Molting of the long guard hairs occurs twice a year (October-November and April-May).

These solitary creatures are active all year and silent for most of that time. During the mating season in March and April, their vocal expressions are quite audible. Some observers report hearing shrieks and caterwauling that they firmly attribute to these animals.

Young lynx (two or three usually are born during May and June), weigh 6 to 8 ounces (170-230 g) and come into the world fully furred with a brownish-gray coat; their eyes remain closed for about 12 days. Two months later they are weaned and at about that time their baby coat is replaced with adult fur. As a rule the young remain with their mothers throughout the winter. In about 12 months they reach sexual maturity.

Like the cougar and their smaller cousin, the bobcat, lynx are able to move about with extraordinary silence. In winter, their large furry paws, which serve as snowshoes, enable them to cope with deep snow when other animals such as foxes, wolves, coyotes, deer and elk are barely able to travel.

Lynx are mainly nocturnal, and it is during the hours just preceding darkness and through the night to shortly after daybreak that they are most active, both in travel through the forests and in the search for food. It is not uncommon for a mother and her kittens, when of hunting age, to spread out in a line rather than travel single file when searching for prey. It is said that several families may join forces in this way to track down a kill.

Lynx, which occupy home ranges of up to 8 square

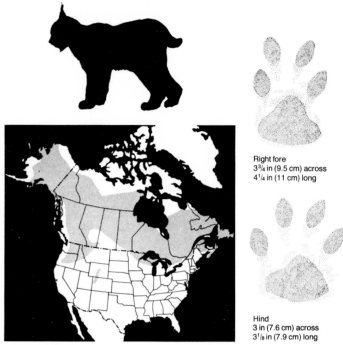

Canada lynx (Once inhabited New England)

Right fore
3¾ in (9.5 cm) across
4¼ in (11 cm) long

Hind
3 in (7.6 cm) across
3⅛ in (7.9 cm) long

miles (21 km²), urinate at frequent intervals to establish communications markers. When necessary they are adept at climbing trees and swimming lakes and rivers, but as a rule they prefer to remain on the ground where protective cover is readily available.

The soft, lustrous fur of the lynx is valued by trappers and the world's fashion houses. Since most of its range has been largely unaltered by man, however, it is still an abundant mammal. This may not always be so, for continuing northern development seems certain.

Lynx rufus

Bobcat

As is the case with cougar and lynx, much remains unknown about the bobcat. Like the other North American members of the Felidae family of carnivores, it is so secretive and solitary in its habits that it is rarely seen. What is known, however, has been well documented by careful, although limited observations by biologists and other wildlife specialists. Bobcats are believed by some authorities to have been present in

North America long before lynx arrived from Asia by way of the Bering Strait "land bridge." They are nevertheless so like the lynx in size and appearance that quick identification is often difficult. One thing is certain: they are *not* crosses between lynx and domestic cats!

The bobcat is generally smaller than the lynx, although an eastern subspecies, *L.r. gigas*, is often larger and heavier. It has shorter and more slender legs than the lynx and its paws are smaller with less fur around the pads. The general coloring varies from reddish-brown to tawny gray on the back, sides and limbs, and whitish on the undersides. Dark spots are prominent on most the body. As in the lynx, the guard hairs are black-tipped and the ruff and forehead carry black stripes. The tail, a little longer than that of the lynx, carries one or two black bars across the top and is black on the upper side of the tip. The ears are rounded, black at the back, but with a noticeable grayish-white spot.

There is, as well, a difference between the lynx and the bobcat in habitat and range. Whereas the lynx prefers boreal forests, bobcats take up residence in more southern-growth woodlands, barren and rocky areas and lower mountain elevations, as well as swampy areas. It is rarely present near farms but when present sometimes preys on poultry and small livestock. Its liking for rodents such as rats—destructive and known carriers of disease—makes it an ally in helping to control such undesirable pests.

Its range (although populations are spotty) is almost all of southern Canada except Newfoundland and Prince Edward Island in the east, and the coastal parts of British Columbia north of Butte Inlet. It is not present on Vancouver Island. It occurs spottily over a wide U.S. range from coast to coast and as far south as southern Mexico.

Bobcats are believed to mate during February and March, producing an average of two or three kittens in late April or mid-May. It is now thought, however, that there may be a second mating period resulting in young being born in August and October.

When she is ready to give birth, the female retires to a well concealed den comfortably lined with grass and moss. The kittens are born blind, fully furred with a dull, tawny-olive coat containing indistinct black marks. Their eyes remain closed for about 9 days and for the next 2 months they are still nursed by their mothers.

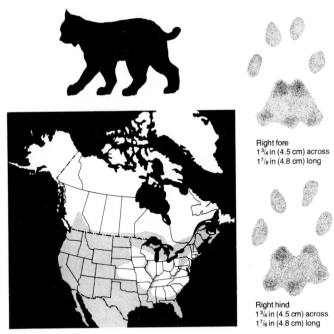

Right fore
1 3/4 in (4.5 cm) across
1 7/8 in (4.8 cm) long

Right hind
1 3/4 in (4.5 cm) across
1 7/8 in (4.8 cm) long

Bobcat

The common belief that males share the responsibility of finding food for the young after they have been weaned, has been brought into question by recent field studies; there seems no evidence that this is so. Kittens born in February or March are believed to be sufficiently trained, and large and strong enough, by fall to look after themselves. Near the end of their first year they go their separate ways.

Bobcats depend largely on sight in seeking prey, although their hearing is well developed. Being nocturnal, they hunt mainly at night, but they are essentially ground-level hunters and stalk their prey much as domestic cats do. The few humans who have encountered live bobcats caught in traps or cornered by dogs report that they fight back furiously and with great courage. Lynx, on the other hand, are more inclined to be submissive when trapped or held at bay. Bobcats climb trees with ease (from which they are sometimes shot) but they enter water reluctantly. Their purrs, meows, hisses and caterwaulings are typically cat-like. In the wild their lifespan is thought to be 10 to 15 years.

Bobcats are also known as "bay lynx" or "wildcats."

ORDER RODENTIA

THE GNAWING MAMMALS

Scientists estimate that in the world today there are about 4,200 species of mammals and that of that number nearly 1,680 species belong to the order Rodentia. These rodents, or "gnawing" mammals, are present in all of the earth's land areas except Antarctica.

But what an odd bag of creatures they are — in size, shape, habitat, lifestyle, importance to themselves and to other mammals, to the total biome and to man himself. While structurally they are remarkably similar, the disparity in size is amazing; for example, the tiniest rodent in North America is the pygmy mouse (*Baiomys taylori*), found in the southern United States, which at adult stage is a little more than 4 inches (10 cm) in length (a third of which is tail) and weighs about $^1/_3$ ounce (8.5 g), while the largest rodent is the American beaver (*Castor canadensis*), found over a wide range in both Canada and the United States, which when fully grown may reach a length, including tail, of about 4 feet (1.2 m) and a weight of more than 100 pounds (45 kg).

Rodents include many mammals well known in North America: squirrels, chipmunks, muskrats, beavers, voles, lemmings, rats, mice, porcupines, gophers, to mention some. Some members of the order are fossorial — adapted to living most of their lives in underground burrows. Some are terrestrial — living more or less on ground level. Some are arboreal — living most of the time in trees. Some are aquatic or semi-aquatic — living most of the time in or near water.

The primary anatomical characteristic of rodents is their two upper and two lower incisor teeth. These incisors never stop growing and, if not kept in check,

Rodents are vital links in the natural food chain and the primary diet of many larger animals. These 5-week-old yellow-bellied marmots, born in the Rocky Mountains, will undoubtedly wind up in the stomachs of wolves, coyotes, badgers or bears — or perhaps satisfy the hunger of golden eagles. (Photo by Mark Nyhof)

The incisors of rodents grow continuously and are kept in shape by wear. If misaligned they will grow uncontrolled. Unable to feed, the animal will eventually starve.

would continue their circular course and eventually turn inward to fatally pierce the creatures' skulls. This horrible tragedy, happily, occurs only rarely, but to prevent it the rodents must maintain a regular gnawing schedule to keep the tips of the teeth from growing beyond a safe length. Beavers, for instance, often pause while felling a tree to gnash the upper and lower incisors against each other. This not only resharpens them, but also helps to keep them at safe and workable lengths. Other rodents, porcupines for example, gnaw on discarded deer antlers, partly because they derive useful minerals from them and partly because the antlers serve to wear down the incisors.

Some rodents, woodchucks for example, hibernate for long periods during the winter. Others, such as members of the squirrel family, experience a state of dormancy that is less intense and is often interrupted by periods of wakefulness. Some rodents are loners, some are colonial, some are territorial and will fiercely defend their "property rights," some are agonistic and some are sociable. Some are even cannibalistic.

Rodents are found in every conceivable habitat: arid deserts, wetlands, dense forests, open meadows, high mountain elevations, Arctic tundra, urban areas and heavily populated cities. Good, bad or indifferent from a human point of view, all of them are essential links in the delicate food chain of so many other species of wildlife.

FAMILY APLODONTIDAE

Aplodontia rufa

Mountain Beaver

This curious creature, the only member of the Aplodontidae family, is unique to North America, and is described as a living fossil—a descendant of rodents that lived on this continent during early Eocene times about 50 million years ago. A western mammal, it is found only in the Cascade Mountain range from southern British Columbia to northern California and east to the Sierra Nevada Mountains of northeastern California. It also occurs in west-central Nevada.

Despite its name, this mammal is not a beaver, nor is it strictly a mountain dweller. In fact, while it does occur at elevations up to the tree line, it is also commonly found in moist, humid forests and meadows at sea level, preferably where there are nearby streams. Some individuals, however, live where water is absent and it is assumed that in such areas sufficient succulent vegetation is available to supply their drinking requirements.

In size and appearance it is more like a small muskrat, but minus the muskrat's long, rat-like tail. A typical specimen measures in length from 12 to 18 inches (30-46 cm) and weighs about 2.5 pounds (1 kg). It has a broad flat head, short legs, small eyes, small rounded ears and long whiskers. Five toes are present on all feet, the fore feet having particularly long, strong claws. Its pelage is grizzled brown above and lighter below and is moulted once a year.

The mountain beaver is a burrower, so much so that some tunnels have been measured to be more than 760 feet (228 m) in length. The burrows are dug at varying depths, but always where the soil is soggy and where it is easy to follow the contours of the land. Numerous side chambers are made, separate ones for the temporary storage of food, for nesting, feeding, disposal of excrement and storage of "earth balls." The latter, either stone or hard clay, are encountered during tunnel excavation. They are often about the size of baseballs and the mammal periodically gnaws on them to sharpen its teeth. The earth balls are also used to block off the nesting-feeding chamber complex to discourage intruders.

The mountain beaver mates during the latter half of February and produces a litter of two or three in late March or early April. The young are weaned when they

Mountain beaver

Fore
3/4 in (1.9 cm) across
1 5/8 in (4.1 cm) long

Hind
7/8 in (2.2 cm) across
2 in (5.1 cm) long

are 6 to 8 months of age and by June are able to forage for themselves. This mammal has a slow rate of reproduction, however, because females do not become mature until they are 2 years old.

This mammal relies heavily on sword fern and bracken to meet its dietary needs, but at certain times of the year will turn to alder leaves and conifers when the protein in those foods is high. Grasses, also rich in protein, are eaten. If its habitat is close to that of humans, it can be a pest for it consumes large quantities of fruits and vegetables and its tunneling damages the subsurface of gardens.

Being fossorial as well as primarily nocturnal, it is seldom seen by man, except in urban areas. It has several natural enemies, however, among them cougars, foxes, lynx, coyotes, mink, fishers and skunks. A nighttime predator is the great horned owl.

Mountain beaver

FAMILY SCIURIDAE

Chipmunks

While research is still being done on the taxonomy of chipmunks, it is believed by some authorities that there are 21 species (some with subspecies) in North America. Only 5 species, however, occur in Canada and the northern states. Of the 21 species, 20 belong to the genus *Eutamias*; the other, the eastern chipmunk, belongs to the genus *Tamias*.

All of the chipmunks are small creatures, ranging in length from about 7 to 14 inches (18-36 cm), a third of which is tail, and weighing at maturity less than 5 ounces (140 g). The eastern chipmunk is larger and more full-bodied than its western cousins and its stripes are broader.

Since the ancestry of chipmunks, like that of other squirrels, can be traced back millions of years, it is to be expected that many legends, particularly of Indian origin, have grown up around them. For example: A chipmunk, weighing about 2 ounces, and the very first of its kind, one day decided to tease a grizzly bear a thousand times its size. After a while the bear became angry and, using its long, sharp claws, it scratched the chipmunk on the back and sides. That is why, to this day, all of these little creatures carry distinctive dark and lighter stripes. While chipmunks have never lost their teasing nature, not one has ever since annoyed a bear.

Chipmunks, depending on geography, live in a variety of habitats. Some are found in forest edges at low elevations, some on alpine tundra and sagebrush plains, and some in grassy areas, in places where there are coniferous and deciduous trees, in valleys where there are low shrubs, rocks and windfalls, in coastal forests and along beaches where there are rocks and piled-up driftwood. Still others are found in urban areas such as parks and residential districts.

Chipmunk burrows are simple tunnels running from small entrances to nesting chambers only a few feet away, as is characteristic of the western species, *Eutamias*; or more elaborate affairs which drop sharply for a foot or so, then continue in sloping fashion for 10 to 12 feet (3-3.7 m) to end at chambers 18 inches (46 cm) in diameter and 14 inches (36 cm) deep, as is characteristic of the eastern species, *Tamias*. The entrances to these burrows may be under rocks, tree stumps or in dense vegetation. Often, however, they are in the open: for example, in a forest floor where there is little or no undergrowth, or even in fields and lawns. These entrances are almost always indetectable in that no mound of earth is seen at the entrance opening; nor are there any noticeable paths leading to them.

Depending on the species, the burrows may have one or more underground alleys for the storage of food. Normally, when a new entrance is made, the old one is sealed off. When a burrow has been in use for a long time, it may have a maze of tunnels leading to the surface, although only one or two will be kept open and in active use. It seems evident, however, according to Dr. B. T. Aniśkowicz, who is an authority on the species, that eastern chipmunks tend to change burrows relatively frequently, rather than keep a burrow for an extended period. "One individual," Dr. Aniśkowicz informed me, "changed burrows three times during one summer. However, a given burrow may be used for a long time by a number of successive chipmunks. A good burrow is valuable and is in constant use, but not necessarily by the same animal." The commonly held belief that the burrows also contain special alleys for the elimination of body wastes has yet to be proven.

At least 7 of the 21 *Eutamias* species, in addition to occupying underground burrows, also live part of the summer in tree nests. Some of the tree nests are made in hollows of limbs or trunks or in abandoned woodpecker holes 10 feet (3 m) or so above ground; others may be as high as 80 feet (24 m). The nesting material both in trees and in burrows is mostly dried grasses and leaves. As studies continue it may be found that more, if not all species of *Eutamias* use tree nests in addition to underground nests, and it is also possible that litters are born in tree nests. The permanent retreats, especially during hibernation are of course underground.

The change of habitat to tree nests occurs near the end of the weaning of the young, when they are ready to begin fending for themselves. It is known that the arboreal nests (which closely resemble birds' nests) are used for only brief periods, such as nursing during the day and resting at night. The movements of the animals to, from and within the nests are virtually silent.

Eastern chipmunks (*Tamias*) are conspicuously active in spring after emerging from hibernation. Then they enter a period described as "summer lull" when they seem to be more furtive and much quieter. This lull may be because of their preoccupation with giving birth to and raising their young. It may also be partly attributable to the summer shortage of hard seeds and

Chipmunks and other ground squirrels have internal cheek pouches.

Right fore

Right hind

nuts, and so gathering food for winter storage would not be part of their activity. The foods plentiful at that time are berries, insects, fungi, green vegetation and the like — none of them suitable for storage — so they quietly search out as much of them as they can eat. The lull ends with the coming of late summer when they are once again commonly seen and heard. When the cold weather returns, they retire to their burrows to begin hibernation. The "lull" phenomenon, which is apparently not characteristic of the *Eutamias* species, is still under investigation.

Since chipmunks occur in warm southern areas as well as in cold northern areas, times and frequency of mating vary. Most northern species breed in the spring and produce a litter of two to seven. In some species — the eastern chipmunk, for example — there may be two annual litters.

Young chipmunks at birth are pinkish, wrinkled, hairless, weigh about $^1/_{10}$ ounce (3 g) and are about $2^1/_2$ inches (6 cm) long. Their eyes do not open until they are about a month old, although within 3 weeks they are almost fully furred. They appear above ground at 5 to 6 weeks of age and by their eighth week they have reached adult length, but not weight. The female and her young remain together as a family up to 3 months, when they go their separate ways.

What happens to young chipmunks when they begin fending for themselves? Do they immediately dig their own burrows, do they establish their own territories, at what stage and under what conditions do they become hierarchial? Once again I turned to Dr. Aniśkowicz:

The lovable, handsome eastern chipmunk, while primarily a ground species, does not hesitate to scamper up large trees in search of acorns and hickory nuts. (Photo by Dr. Donald R. Gunn)

"When they are on their own young chipmunks probably do not dig their own burrows, but move into vacant ones. My experience with *Tamias* is that at first most juveniles scatter-hoard food in a given area and use any available shelter in that area, without having a burrow. Later, they may move into a vacant burrow and store their food there, but few juveniles manage to successfully defend any area around their burrow until the latter part of their first summer.

"*Tamias*, and probably *Eutamias*, are not territorial in the conventional sense of the word. They do not have definite boundaries to their 'territories' that are recognized and respected by non-specifics. Instead, extensive trespassing occurs (home ranges overlap),

though trespassers are chased. In effect, my study shows that dominance hierarchies exist, but are space-dependent. A chipmunk may be at the top of a hierarchy in a given area around its burrow, but be in another, lower position elsewhere."

The home ranges of chipmunks are generally limited to an area only 50 feet (15 m) or so from the burrow system, if the habitat is good, but they may go well beyond that if food is less abundant. Individuals rarely cohabitate, even during the mating season. At that time the male visits a receptive female and mating occurs, but in the female's home range and usually not in her burrow. Even then, the female does not stay long with the male. She may chase him out.

The summer diet of chipmunks ranges from a variety of nuts and seeds to green vegetation, fruits, berries, fungi, invertebrates, slugs, snails, domestic corn, mushrooms and insects and their larvae. Although observations have only rarely been made of chipmunks preying on birds and birds' eggs, one eastern chipmunk was known to have killed a starling and eaten all but its head, wings, feet and feathers. Both *Tamias* and *Eutamias*, however, will eat any animal matter that becomes available. While some hard seeds and nuts may be stored underground, some are also hidden above ground in stumps, hollow logs, or buried in soft ground.

The cached supply of the winter food of both *Tamias* and *Eutamias* consists mainly of the seeds of such plants as knockweed, sedges, thistle and grass. Dr. Aniśkowicz makes the interesting point, however, that while eastern chipmunks do not eat the seeds of conifers, such seeds enter extensively into the diet of the western species. Furthermore, while hard nuts such as acorn, beech, chestnut, hickory and corn kernels are heavy favorites of the eastern chipmunk, they form only a small part of the diet of western chipmunks.

An anatomical characteristic of chipmunks is the paired cheek pouches which they stuff with food for transportation to their burrows. The carrying capacity of these pouches is amazing. Cahalane writes that one individual managed to cram away 145 grains of wheat; another, 31 kernels of field corn; another, 13 prune pits; and another, 7 large acorns. Dr. Aniśkowicz herself says that she once held out 50 watermelon seeds to a tame (but free) chipmunk and it stuffed all of them into its cheek pouches, and still looked for more!

The nursery or sleeping area is the main underground larder. As much as half a bushel of various food items may be deposited in several pits, on top of which is then laid a thick covering of dried grasses and leaves. When the animal retires to its chamber to begin hibernation, its food supply is directly beneath it. While it sleeps a good deal during winter, it awakens every few days to feed; unlike some other hibernators, chipmunks do not store up significant amounts of body fats and so must regularly replenish their supplies of protein.

By the following spring the food pantry is virtually empty. Occasionally, if the weather is exceptionally mild, they will venture into the open for brief periods and then return to their nests to curl up and go back to sleep. The observation of an eastern chipmunk killing a starling was made in mid-winter.

Chipmunks are exceptionally clean and not only maintain a high degree of sanitation in their underground burrows, but also groom themselves regularly, frequently rolling in earth and sand to rid themselves of lice and other parasites. They are subject to infestations of worms; some suffer from botflies, an insect whose larvae burrow beneath the skin. Predators include weasels, pine martens, bobcats, coyotes, badgers, bears, snakes, hawks, diurnal owls, and foxes. Chipmunks in the wild live 3 to 5 years.

The common name chipmunk comes from "chitmunk" or "chitmuk" which is a corruption of the Chippewa Indian name spelled variously as *achitaumo*, *achitaumon* or *adjidaumo*, but does not, as is often believed, come from the "chipping" sounds they make. The scientific names *Tamias* and *Eutamias* have essentially the same meaning, "good steward," considered by most writers as appropriate because of the animals' habit of storing up supplies of seeds.

Tamias striatus

Eastern Chipmunk

The largest of the chipmunk family, this mammal, as its name suggests, is an easterner. The species is found in Canada from Newfoundland (where it was introduced) west to the border of Saskatchewan, and in the United States from the Atlantic west to North Dakota and eastern Oklahoma, as well as south to Mississippi, South Carolina and Virginia. It favors an open woodland habitat (particularly where there are stands of hardwood trees) rather than deep forests, but it is also found where there are brush and rock piles, hedgerows, wooded banks and even refuse dumps where burrows are easily made. If shelter and food are available, it sometimes makes its home in urban gardens and parks.

The eastern chipmunk is reddish-brown overall, but with white or creamy-white underparts. It carries a narrow, dark-brown or black median stripe, on each side of which is a broader grayish stripe (these stripes start on the neck just back of the head), then on each side are two dark-brown to black stripes between which is a white or creamy stripe. As in all chipmunks, its legs are moderately short, as are its ears, which are rounded and erect. Its eyes are large and dark.

Tamias in their southern range may begin mating as early as March, while in their northern range mating generally starts in early April and continues to mid-May. Some chipmunks mate for a second time, but this mating is considered by many (but not all) investigators to involve mainly those females that lost their first litters. Most young chipmunks do not breed for the first time until they are at least 11 months old. In each mat-

Eastern chipmunk

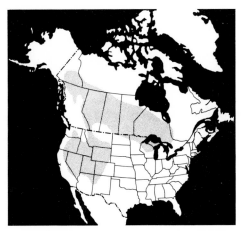

Least chipmunk

ing the gestation period lasts for 31 or 32 days. Two to seven young (four on average) are born.

Although molting data on chipmunks are scarce, it is thought that adult eastern chipmunk males molt twice a year, the first molt occurring in April and May and the second in August and September. Adult females may molt only once a year, in June. Chipmunks born in the spring are thought to molt in June and July; those born during the summer molt in the fall.

The vocalizations of the eastern chipmunk range from a slow, low-pitched *chuck-chuck-chuck* to a rapid, trilling *chip-r-r-r-r* or *chip-chip-chip*. The latter sound has been clocked at 130 "chips" a minute. Remarkably, the calls can be made and heard when the chipmunk's mouth is closed or the cheek pouches are full.

Eutamias minimus
Least Chipmunk

The least chipmunk, the smallest of the family, is also the most widespread. In Canada it is found from the western boundary of Quebec, across northern Ontario (partially overlapping the range of the eastern chipmunk) across the Prairies to British Columbia, then to the Northwest Territories and Yukon. In the United States it occurs from northern Michigan irregularly west to eastern Washington and south to New Mexico. Not every place thoughout this vast area is inhabited by *E. minimus*, but there are probably enough in total to

qualify for another common name—the "most" chipmunk.

The habitat of the least chipmunk is as diverse as its range and, while its favorite places are where new forest growth has followed lumbering operations or fire, and coniferous forests open enough to allow the light and warmth of sunshine to penetrate, it also occurs among the scrub of sagebrush plains and in alpine tundra. It is often found near water, especially along streams or lakeshores where there are tangles of logs, thick underbrush or loose rocks. It is often found at elevations above timberline.

The least chipmunk, as a friend of Seton said, is "the very prettiest," and few would argue with him. Its general coloring is grayish-brown, but it is also colorfully marked by three dark and two light stripes on the sides of the face and by five blackish and four pale stripes extending along the back and sides to the base of the tail. All of the stripes are nearly the same width. The top of the head is brownish and the sides of the body show shades of orange-brown. The underparts are grayish-white and the tail is dark to light-brown on top and yellowish below. The fur, which molts twice yearly, although not silky is dense and fine. The least chipmunk is often mistaken for two other strictly western species, the yellow-pine chipmunk and the red-tailed chipmunk.

Like all chipmunks, *E. minimus* is active from dawn to dusk. Following a day of intense activity, it

Seton wrote of the least chipmunk that it is "the very prettiest," and most observers would agree. It occurs in more parts of North America than other member of the family. (Photo by Wayne Lankinen/Valan Photos)

returns to its nest before dark. Most of its waking hours are spent at ground level, but it also moves about in trees with great agility. Its nest is made in underground burrows but it may also establish a temporary summer tree nest in an abandoned woodpecker hole or a natural cavity; it may even construct a nest in the crotch of a limb.

The least chipmunk's diet is about the same as the diet of other chipmunks — seeds, nuts (but not hard nuts such as beech, chestnut or hickory), fruits, berries, grasses, fungi and animal matter. It is too small to be of much danger to songbirds (even a robin can force it to retreat) but it has been known to steal eggs of the wood pewee. Food gathered for winter use is carried in its twin cheek pouches to its underground burrow. Cahalane, writing about the enormous capacity of the cheek pouches, reported that one animal was found to have in its cheeks at one time 2,100 veronica seeds. Banfield tells of one that had 3,700 blueberry seeds.

Mating takes place in late March and continues throughout the early part of April. After about 30 days, two to seven young are born.

The calls of the least chipmunk are varied, but those most easily recognized are a series of *wop-wop-wop* and *chip-chip-chip* notes. If threatened it utters a high-pitched rapid *chit-chit-chit* followed by a cry that sounds like *tsp-r-r-r* as it scampers away. Some observers say it utters a low-pitched *kik-kik-kik* when communicating with its own kin.

The least chipmunk enters into hibernation with the start of cold weather, but its winter sleep is frequently broken by periods of wakefulness, at which time it disposes of body wastes and refuels itself with food stored in a pit under its nest. This animal in the wild has a lifespan of up to 6 years.

Eutamias amœnus
Yellow-pine Chipmunk

The yellow-pine, or northwestern chipmunk, next to the least chipmunk is the most common of the family to be found in the Rockies. Its range in Canada extends from southwestern Alberta to central British Columbia; in the southern part of the province it extends to the coast, but does not include any of the offshore islands. Its United States range extends throughout the Rockies south to northern California and east to western Montana and northwestern Wyoming.

E. amœnus is found among Douglas fir and ponderosa (yellow) pines in warm, dry valleys and slopes at elevations up to 3,000 feet (900 m), although it sometimes establishes itself in alpine forests. Banfield, in fact, writes that it has been found as high as 14,000 feet (4,300 m) on Mount Rainier, Washington. Its first choice of habitat seems to be open forests, but it also makes its home in mountain meadows and other areas where there is brush and rock, and in logged or burned-over places where there is new growth. It does not like dense forests.

This chipmunk is midway in size between the least chipmunk and the red-tailed chipmunk, but carries more contrasting dark brown and beige stripes. Its background coloring is also more brownish than grayish, the sides having rusty hues of varying shades. The

Yellow-pine chipmunk

tail is comparatively longer and is rusty above and brownish-yellow on the underparts.

Like all chipmunks, the yellow-pine is diurnal, and aside from occasional siestas in cool, shady places if the day is hot, it is active from early morning until dusk. Its burrow is relatively short, at the most about 21 inches (50 cm) deep and about 3 feet (1 m) in length, and generally has a well-concealed entrance. It may also make a summer nest in the forks of trees or against the trunk of trees, in woodpecker holes or hollow logs. Mating takes place in April and the young are born from late May to early June. The litter size varies between four and eight, with six being the average. The offspring reach adult size in the fall.

Yellow-pine chipmunks eat a wide variety of seeds, especially those of the ponderosa pine. Other items in its diet include nuts (not hard nuts), fruit, insects, fungi and corms. It stores large quantities of food in its underground burrow. Dr. Whitaker wrote of one cache that contained 67,970 items, among which was even part of a bumblebee! In colder climates, especially where there are heavy snowfalls, it enters its burrow around the end of October and, except for periodic forays above ground in mild weather, it remains in hibernation until the first part of April.

The yellow-pine chipmunk has a wide repertoire of calls, the most common of which are a shrill *chip-chip-chip*, a sound described as a sharply accented *kwist* and another as *pert-pert-pert*. One vocalization is said to closely resemble a robin's *chirp*.

Eutamias townsendii

Townsend's Chipmunk

This species occurs in Canada only in the southwest corner of British Columbia's Cascade Mountains. In the United States its range runs south along the western slope of the Rockies to central California. In both countries its main habitat is near the edges of dense rain forests, especially where there are lake and stream shores and abandoned roads.

E. townsendii is the largest of the western chipmunks and the darkest in color. Its overall coloring is deep brown, and its longitudinal stripes, although less conspicuous, are the same as in other chipmunks. Its tail, long and bushy, is almost black above and reddish-brown underneath. White-tipped hairs are evident on both sides. The underparts of the body are white to tan.

The Townsend's chipmunk is more timid and less vocal than its cousins. It too is diurnal and, except for inclement weather when it retires to its underground burrow, it is active from dawn to dusk, especially a few hours after sunrise and a few hours before sunset.

The burrow of this species is generally within the root structure of large trees, but it also lives in rock piles and hollow logs. Like many others of the *Eutamias* species, it sometimes builds a summer nest in trees. Its period of hibernation is short and intermittent; for those living at higher elevations where winters are longer and more severe, hibernation is more extended. It often leaves its den for brief periods above ground when the weather is mild.

The Townsend's chipmunk mates in the spring and has one litter which is born in May or June. The offspring number two to six, with five being the average, and they appear above ground in June and July. By August they are adult size and are able to dig burrows and lay in their own supply of food.

The diet of the Townsend's chipmunk includes seeds of various kinds, as well as nuts, berries, insects, bulbs, roots and fungi. It occasionally eats the eggs and fledglings of songbirds. If it escapes diseases and the predation of weasels, mink and other enemies, it may live in the wild for as long as 7 years.

This chipmunk has a range of calls, the most commonly heard being a shrill *chip-chip-chip* and *chuck-chuck-chuck*. Banfield describes its alarm note as a brisk *kivis*.

John Kirk Townsend, a young Philadelphia pharmacist, physician and amateur naturalist, discovered

1. *Townsend's chipmunk*
2. *Red-tailed chipmunk*

this little mammal in 1834 during a trip to Oregon with the famous Thomas Nuttall. The animal was described in Townsend's journal, *Narrative of a Journey Across the Rocky Mountains*. Hence its Latinized name.

Eutamias ruficaudus

Red-tailed Chipmunk

The red-tailed, or rufus-tailed chipmunk, is a creature of the high country and is commonly found in coniferous forests at altitudes from about 6,000 to 10,000 feet (1800-3000 m) (but not above the treeline) in a range that in Canada includes southeastern British Columbia and Waterton Lakes National Park north to Banff National Park. In the United States it occurs in northeastern Idaho, western Montana and Washington. Its range in both countries overlaps that of the yellow-pine chipmunk.

This chipmunk can easily be mistaken for both the yellow-pine and least chipmunk, although it is a little larger. The stripe patterns are the same but are more colorful. The red-tailed chipmunk is deep tawny on the back and sides and cream-colored underneath. The rump is gray and the tail is brown above the brilliant rufus on the undersides; the tail is bordered with black and pale pinkish cinnamon. The five dark stripes are black and the four light ones range from gray to creamy white. Two of the cheek stripes are white and three are brown. The coat is thought to molt twice yearly, first in

June and July, and again in September and October.

This mammal, when mature, is about 10 inches (25 cm) in length, including its 4- to 5-inch (10-13 cm) tail, and weighs about 2½ ounces (70 g).

The red-tailed chipmunk makes its home in underground burrows and, for brief periods, in summer tree nests. While recorded biology of the species is incomplete, it is believed to mate from late April to early May and three to six pups are born about 30 days later. Its diet is the same as that of most chipmunks, although it appears to consume more seeds, fruit, fungi and corms than hard nuts and insects. There is no record of it eating birds' eggs or killing fledglings.

E. ruficaudus is a "light" hibernator and during the winter months it frequently awakens from it torpor to take care of bodily functions and to feed on seeds cached in its burrow the previous fall. If the weather is exceptionally mild, it appears for brief periods above ground. When it returns to its burrow it replugs the entrance with earth—a behavioral characteristic of all chipmunks—and settles down for another sleep.

Its enemies are the enemies of all members of the Sciuridae family, among them being hawks, diurnal owls, weasels, bobcats, coyotes and, where they are present, rattlesnakes. If it escapes death from these predators, and does not fall victim to disease, it may live for about 5 years.

The red-tailed chipmunk is a relatively quiet mammal, but when threatened will utter a series of loud *chirps*.

Marmota monax
Woodchuck

Of all North American wild mammals, those that spend their winter underground in semi- or uninterrupted hibernation perhaps lead the most unassailable lives. Unlike other species—the canids and bovids, for example, which have to cope with the rigors of extreme cold and deep snow, and shortages of food—the hibernators build up heavy layers of nourishing fat during the summer and fall and then retire to well-insulated underground dens where many remain until the arrival of spring.

Some hibernators, among them bears, squirrels, raccoons and skunks, lapse into conditions of prolonged dormancy during which their sleep, while normal, is broken by periods of wakefulness. On such occasions they may leave their dens for brief sojourns outside.

Others, such as the marmots, undergo extraordinary physiological changes in which their body temperatures drop to near freezing; their hearts, normally functioning at the rate of up to 400 beats per minute, are slowed to five beats. In this condition body functions are so curtailed that the animals have all the observable characteristics of death. Deep "sleep" of this kind may last for 6 months or more.

One of the best known of the animal world's Rip van Winkles is the woodchuck, a ground dweller whose other common aliases are groundhog, American marmot, whistle pig and chuck. This outsized member of the squirrel group generally enters its burrow about October and stays there until March or April.

Folklore, however, has it that on February 2 of each year the animal awakens and emerges from its dark underground quarters for a brief spell in the open. The sole purpose of this excursion, according to the legend, is to assess the weather: if it sees its shadow, winter will last for an additional 6 weeks; if it doesn't, an early spring is assured and in that case it ends its slumber.

The woodchuck may be up and about in February in some of its warmer southern ranges, but in the north the animal rarely makes its appearance until late spring.

This mammal is found in every Canadian province except Newfoundland (the island) and Prince Edward Island. It also occurs in lower Yukon and the lower part of the western Northwest Territories. Its United States range includes Alaska and all of the mid- and eastern states as far south as Alabama. A few populations are present in the extreme northeastern part of Washington, the northern tip of Idaho and the northwestern tip of Montana.

Next to its three immediate cousins—the yellow-bellied marmot, the hoary marmot and the Vancouver Island marmot—it is the largest of the North American squirrels. In appearance it is a chunky creature averaging 4 to 5 pounds (1.8-2.3 kg) in weight and measuring 1½ to 2 feet (40-60 cm) in length, including the bushy 4- to 5-inch (10-12 cm) tail. Its height at the shoulders is about 6 or 7 inches (15-18 cm). The weights of woodchucks average about 10 pounds (4.5 kg), although heavier individuals are not uncommon. Woodchucks, of course, are heavier in the fall, the result of intensive eating in preparation for their long sojourn underground. The rich layers of fat laid on sustain them during hibernation, but by the time they emerge in the

No one has settled the question of how much wood a woodchuck can chuck, or whether it is as accurate a long-range weather forecaster as it is claimed to be, but this mammal, in some places better known as "groundhog," is a relatively harmless one that is considered by many hunters as a delicacy. (Photo by Bill Lowry)

spring this fat has been used up and their weight loss may be as much as 50 per cent.

There is considerable variation in color in woodchucks, but the most common is reddish or intermediate brown; occasionally it is cinnamon or chestnut brown. The underparts and legs may be rich reddish hazel, but the feet, eyes, and hairs toward the end of the tail are black, as are the bristle-like whiskers and facial hairs. The tips of the hairs are usually light in color and give the fur a grizzled appearance. Melanistic (black) and albino (white) individuals are frequently encountered. Molting occurs only once a year, starting in late May and continuing until September.

Like all rodents, the woodchuck occasionally has teeth problems. Since the upper and lower incisors never stop growing, they must be kept in perfect alignment so that by constant grinding against each other they are kept sharp and their growth is controlled. Sometimes malformation occurs: the upper incisors go

out of alignment, curve gradually inward and then upward until they penetrate the roof of the mouth. The resulting death is slow and agonizing.

Illinois writer Al Geller once described the woodchuck as a "living periscope" — a rather good description since the animal's eyes, ears and nose are all located at the top of its flat head. This unusual arrangement makes it possible for the "chuck" to size up the world outside its burrow by raising its head just above the surface. If danger threatens, it makes a shrill whistle (which warns others) and then instantly disappears. If the coast seems clear, it emerges cautiously; when it is satisfied that the coast *is* clear, it may amble lazily to a comfortable spot near the burrow and bask in the warm sunshine, or it may wander about to feed on grasses and other low-growing plants and even insects. If near agricultural land it will help itself to green clover, corn and grain and if gardens are handy it will not ignore the appeal of lettuce, carrot greens, cabbage and fruit, especially apples.

Rarely will it travel more than 100 yards from its burrow; even that is a risky journey if dogs, foxes, wolves, coyotes or man are about, for it is a slow-moving animal. Nevertheless, if overtaken, it shows great courage in defending itself. Not infrequently the woodchuck will climb trees to reach fruit or to escape from predators. On other occasions it may, for no apparent reason, sit astride a low branch or fence post. If pursued, it will readily take to water, but swimming is not one of its favorite pastimes.

The woodchuck constructs two types of burrows: one for summer use, which is usually in a pasture, meadow or a rocky slope, but always near sources of green vegetation and other food; the other for hibernating, which is generally where there are fence rows or thickets. The latter is always dug deep enough to assure that the chambers are well below the frost line.

When the winter burrow has been completed and the woodchuck moves in to begin its long hibernation, it closes off the sleeping chamber by building up an earth barrier at its entrance. This protects the woodchuck from predators and isolates it from other animals — skunks, rabbits, raccoons, for example — that may use the tunnel for varying periods during the winter months. When the woodchuck settles down, it rolls itself into as compact a ball as possible and little by little succumbs to the deep sleep that will prevail for the next 4 or 5 months.

I once had the opportunity of accompanying a biologist doing woodchuck studies and assisted in exposing a typical winter burrow. The work started at the main entrance, easily recognized by the surrounding mound of earth. The 10-inch (25 cm) hole dropped at a sharp, narrowing incline for a little more than 3 feet (1 m) and then continued horizontally for another 12 feet (3.7 m); the diameter of the tunnel was 8 eight inches (20 cm). One third along the way a slightly inclined shaft rose to the surface — the animal's "spy hole" from which, hidden from view by the surrounding vegetation, it could survey the landscape or through which if necessary it could make its escape. A short distance beyond that another vertical shaft was found. At the top of this was a chamber of small diameter identified as a toilet. A few feces were found buried in the soft earth, but it was apparent that the woodchuck, a very clean animal, had removed most of the droppings from the burrow. At the end of the tunnel, at a slight incline, was a large chamber, the floor of which was partly covered with dried leaves and grass. This was the hibernation area, or it would have been used as a nursery. Not all woodchuck burrows are alike. Some have as many as ten entrances (or exits) and several dens. Others may be only a few feet in length and have only one den.

The woodchuck does a great deal of burrowing and is well equipped for it. The front legs, which do the hardest work of excavating, are short and strong, and the claws are sharp and very tough. To remove loose soil from the burrow when it is under construction, the woodchuck simply turns around and shoves it outside the hole; the hind legs are sometimes used to kick back the loose soil. Nature equipped it with ears that can be closed, so it can immerse itself in soil and not a grain can get in. Otters and beavers also have this ability; they can close their ears to keep out water.

The woodchuck mates in March, earlier in warmer climates, soon after hibernation ends. At that time, hungry after their long period of sleep and stimulated by the urge to breed, the males are short-tempered and often fight viciously among themselves. Once mated, peace is restored and 28 days later the young, generally four, are born. There is only one litter a year. Blind and naked at birth and weighing barely more than an ounce (28 g), they grow rapidly. Their eyes open in 20 days. Weaning occurs in 5 to 6 weeks, about the time they are ready to explore outside the burrow.

Before the end of the second month the youngsters have learned to forage on their own, and the time of family break-up is at hand. By mid-summer they

Woodchuck

Left fore
2 1/8 in (5.4 cm) long

weigh about 2 pounds (0.9 kg) and there is no longer room for them in the burrow so they leave, either voluntarily or with some encouragement from their parents. Old dens are often used by the youngsters or new ones are burrowed. Although not fully grown until their second year, some are able to mate while still yearlings.

The woodchuck is mostly active during daylight hours. When feeding or basking in the open, it frequently sits upright on its hind legs, squirrel fashion, and scans the land around it. Any unusual movement or noise sends it scurrying to its burrow, but the woodchuck is curious and within moments the "living periscope" reappears to determine the cause of the fuss.

M. monax, a loner and a homebody, is not rated as a particularly intelligent animal, and hunters regard it in one of two ways: either as worth hunting for its value as food, or as worth killing because it is a "varmint." The first attitude is reasonable — it is good eating and many consider it a delicacy. The second attitude is unfair — it is relatively harmless and so has every right to survive. It should not be destroyed simply because it makes good target practice. Left to live its life unmolested, it can reach the age of 6 years, a long time for most small wild animals.

There was a time, before farm machinery became mechanized, that horses drawing plows, wagons or other pieces of equipment suffered broken legs when they stepped into woodchuck burrows. With the virtual elimination of horse-drawn equipment, this danger no longer exists and the woodchuck should be looked upon with less animosity. Other than the small amount of field grain or garden crops it consumes, there is very little to justify rating the animal as undesirable.

The woodchuck, like some other hibernating mammals, may yet prove to be one of the most critical subjects of modern medical science. If the mystery can be solved of its ability to lower its body temperature to near freezing to reduce radically its heart rate and consumption of oxygen, answers may also be found to some human health problems, among them heart disease and related surgery.

The Canadian Wildlife Service reports that nine subspecies of woodchuck are recognized in North America. In identifying subspecies of any form of wildlife, minor differences in size, coloration and skull characteristics are often the determining factors. Such is the case with woodchucks.

Silhouettes and tracks of all marmots are similar.

Left fore
2 in (5.1 cm) long

Right hind (heel not showing)
1½ in (3.8 cm) long

Yellow-bellied marmot

Marmota flaviventris

Yellow-bellied Marmot

The yellow-bellied marmot goes by a number of local names: yellow-footed marmot, yellow groundhog, yellow whistler, yellow belly, rockchuck and, simply, whistler. Like other marmots, it closely resembles the common woodchuck; it is, however, larger than the woodchuck and different in color and markings.

This member of the squirrel family is found in the Rocky Mountains of British Columbia south through the Cascades and Sierra Nevada to California and New Mexico. It makes its home where there are talus slopes, low cliffs and accumulations of boulders. These areas are always close to meadows where vegetation is abundant. While most populations occur at relatively low subalpine elevations, some extend their range as high as 12,000 feet (3,700 m). At lower elevations the marmot is frequently found near abandoned mining or logging camps. It generally favors habitats that are hot and arid.

These marmots form small colonies, each presided over either by a dominant male or less frequently by a dominant female. The marmots, even within family units, are agonistic and those unable to defend themselves are often forced to leave. The ejected ones seek to join another colony, or if they can find a compatible female, to establish one of their own. If they fail to do either and must go it alone, they are generally killed by predators.

The yellow-bellied marmot is abroad during the daylight hours. Most of its time is spent in foraging for food and in sunning itself atop a boulder or rock near its home burrow. Like many fossorial creatures, it is constantly on the alert for danger and when threatened it utters a shrill, short whistle that can be heard for half a mile or so. With this warning young and old gallop to safety among the rocks and, if necessary, disappear into their burrows.

Burrows are of two types: the main or home burrow in which they hibernate and in which families are born, and auxiliary burrows which are used for temporary shelter when the weather becomes unfavorable or for escape from enemies. Entrances to the burrows, especially to the home burrow, are often through narrow openings between boulders or rocks. Rocky fortifications such as these make it difficult for predators such as grizzly bears to dig into the burrow.

The yellow-bellied marmot builds up a heavy layer of fat during the summer by eating large quantities of green grasses and other vegetable matter and in August it enters its den where it remains in hibernation until early spring. Its long sleep is said to be interrupted by occasional but brief periods of wakefulness.

Mating takes place soon after hibernation ends and about 30 days later an average of five pups are born. The young emerge from the den for the first time when they are about 5 weeks old, although for a while their outdoor excursions are of short duration. Eventually, after they have become adjusted to life above ground and weaning is over, they begin regular marmot lives.

The adult yellow-bellied marmot is a heavy-bodied mammal weighing 5 to 10 pounds (2.3-4.5 kg). It is yellowish-brown on the back and sides and noticeably yellowish on the belly. There are buffy-colored patches running from below the ears to the shoulders and light-colored patches between the eyes. The feet and tail are light to dark brown. Melanistic, and to a lesser extent albino, individuals often occur in this species as in other marmots.

Major predators of the yellow-bellied marmot are wolves, coyotes, cougars, badgers and bears. Golden eagles are said to take a heavy toll. The yellow-bellied marmot is commonly a carrier of the tick which transmits Rocky Mountain fever. The mammal, alive or dead, should be handled with care since the virus is dangerous.

Marmota caligata

Hoary Marmot

The hoary marmot, like its relatives the yellow-bellied marmot and the yellow-pine chipmunk, is a resident of the western mountains. Its range extends from Alaska, Yukon, and the Northwest Territories south through British Columbia, Alberta, Washington, northern Idaho and western Montana. It is the largest member of the squirrel family and is about twice the size of its other relative, the common woodchuck. This mammal, which is also known as rockchuck, mountain marmot and whistler, is called "hoary" because of the frosty-white fur that drapes over its back and shoulders like a mantle or stole. The name "whistler" refers to its shrill alarm call.

Because of the hoary marmot's remote and often

Marmots are close relatives of the woodchuck and are all westerners. They are burrowers and live in mountainous country in small, loosely-formed family units. This handsome individual is the yellow-bellied marmot. Marmots make a whistling sound when alarmed, hence their other common name—"whistler." (Photo by Mark Nyhof)

inaccessible habitat, field studies of its behavior have been relatively few, as has written documentation. One of the most comprehensive studies was that made some years ago by Dr. David R. Gray, now Associate Curator of Vertebrate Ethology, National Museum of Natural Sciences, Ottawa. The area of study was Spotted Nellie Ridge, elevation 6,500 feet (2000 m), in the Cascade Mountains of southern British Columbia. References made here to the lifestyle of the mammal are drawn primarily from Dr. Gray's own observations.

The habitat of the hoary marmot extends from fringes of the subalpine treeline up to the point where the high altitude environment ceases to support vegetative growth. It lives in small, loosely organized colonies where there are boulder-strewn meadows, rock outcrops and masses of large rocks at the foot of talus slopes. This type of environment, when it has abundant growth of green grasses and forbs, provides not only

Hoary marmots live as far north as Alaska, Yukon and the Northwest Territories, generally in areas so remote that only backpackers encounter them. This species gets its name from the frosty white fur that drapes over its back like a mantle. (Photo by Michael E. Wooding)

dietary needs but quick escape from ground and aerial predators.

The hoary marmot is strictly diurnal, and even in weather that would keep other small underground dwellers confined to their dens, it is generally abroad most of the day. It occupies two types of burrows: the home burrow, believed to be a complex arrangement of tunnels, where the animal hibernates and where young are born; and auxiliary burrows which serve as daytime sleeping quarters and as quick refuges from enemies, and which the marmot may use as alternate sleeping places at night. Entrances to auxiliary burrows are generally well concealed among rocks. The entrance to the home burrow is readily identified by the large mound of earth and stones removed during excavation.

All four feet are used in burrowing: earth and stones loosened by the forefeet are pushed back under the animal's belly and then kicked out by the hind feet.

This method of excavating is characteristic of another fossorial creature, the badger. If stones are encountered and are difficult to push back, they are carried in the animal's mouth and dropped on the mound outside.

During the warm, lazy days of summer, when not eating, sleeping or playing, the marmot spends much of its time perched on top of a boulder or stretched out on the entrance mound or nearby rocks. Should an enemy approach the alarm is sounded, a shrill piercing whistle which comes not from the lips and mouth but from the throat and chest. Others repeat the alarm and within seconds the whole population within earshot is ready to disappear.

Banfield speaks of this alarm whistle as being "almost exactly the same pitch and duration as the familiar police whistle." But the alarm whistle is only one of several in the marmot scale and sequences vary in length as well as intervals. Gray describes one sequence as "lasting a half hour and consisting of over 900 individual whistles." When uttered where mountain acoustics are finely-tuned, the sound will echo and re-echo in as prolonged and as eerie a way as the bugling of elk or the colliding heads of bighorn sheep.

The community life of this marmot is reasonably harmonious and wrestling seems to be its main recreational activity. The adult males, being polygamous, usually acquire small harems, but in his studies Dr. Gray saw no evidence of a dominance hierarchy. He qualified this observation, however, by noting that the population of the Spotted Nellie Ridge colony was small in relation to the large area available to it, the abundance of food and the numerous burrows. These factors, he suggested, probably accounted for the lack of aggression in the colony. If there is dominance, as some writers claim, it may not be as strong as that of other sciurids such as the yellow-bellied marmot, the black-tailed prairie dog or the Arctic ground squirrel.

Gray writes engagingly of the way in which individual marmots greet each other as they move along the colony trails—the slow approach, nuzzling and the touching of whiskers, the sniffing of each other's head. But it is his description of wrestling matches that does so much to reveal the friendly nature of the little creatures:

"Wrestling usually occurred when two approached each other head on, and, after sniffing, nuzzling, or the more elaborate greeting, one of the pair batted at the other with its front paw. The other marmot either ignored this and continued moving or rose up on its hind legs and began wrestling. They usually held their mouths open and bit at each other's head and throat fur. Often they locked their teeth together while hitting each other's shoulders with their paws.

"Pauses during a wrestling bout were frequent. Sometimes the wrestlers simply stood and stared at each other. At other times they paused while pushing at each other with the forepaws, stretching their heads back, and pointing their noses straight up. During the more rigorous conflicts, if one of the marmots gave a sharp yelp or squeal, they both stopped, shook, sometimes greeted, and then continued wrestling.

"While wrestling, the marmots often tumbled and rolled together down to the bottom of the slope where they broke apart, stopped and looked around for a few seconds before running back up the slope to begin wrestling again. After such a tumble, both animals ran up the slope independently or one chased the other up to a relatively flat area. Here the marmot being chased stopped and turned to face the chaser. Often the chase ended with the one marmot part way down a burrow and the other pawing at it from the entrance. On several occasions, a marmot which had broken away from a fight ran back and looped around his opponent with what seemed clearly to be an invitation to renew the match. . . ."

The hoary marmot, most observers report, always looks fat, especially in late summer. Since it does not store up food in its den, as so many fossorial animals do, heavy feeding especially in late summer is essential to build up the reserves of fat necessary to sustain it during its long period of hibernation. As a consequence, it consumes large quantities and many varieties of green grasses, wild flowers, berries and roots. The marmots of Spotted Nellie Ridge were not seen to drink water even though it was available, nor were they seen to eat snow, and Gray is of the opinion that the moisture in the plants they eat fulfills their requirements.

Hiberation of the hoary marmot depends on geography and begins earlier in the northern than in the southern parts of its range. In British Columbia it begins in September and continues until April, a period of about 7 months; in the south it begins in October and continues until February, a period of about 5 months. Its deep sleep is occasionally broken by short periods of wakefulness.

Mating occurs soon after it leaves the winter den and, after a gestation of 28 to 30 days, four to five pups are born. The youngsters do not emerge from the bur-

1. Hoary marmot
2. Vancouver Island marmot (Vancouver I. only)

row until they are about a month old. Growth of juvenile hoary marmots is slow and they do not attain adult size until after they are into their second year, at which time they become sexually mature.

The hoary marmot, which often reaches a weight of 30 pounds (14 kg), is a handsome creature. Silver-gray above (its hoary mantle), it has a brownish rump and whitish belly. There are distinctive dark and light markings on the head and shoulders. The area between the eyes and around the black nose is whitish. The tail is short, bushy, and brown in color and is occasionally banded with black-tipped hairs. The feet are black. There are two annual molts, and the hoary appearance is most noticeable in its winter pelage.

The enemies of the hoary marmot are mainly wolves, coyotes, grizzly bears and, as some writers claim, golden eagles. Naturalist Bryan L. Sage writes, however, that in his observations of hoary marmot colonies in Alaska, although the mammals became noticeably alarmed at the appearance of an eagle, he neither saw, nor could find through examination of eyries, any evidence of eagle predation. While we await more evidence, perhaps we should assume that the golden eagle in some areas at least does not prey as heavily upon marmots as has been thought.

Marmota vancouverensis

Vancouver Island Marmot

The Vancouver Island marmot, *now seriously in danger of extinction*, is different enough in skeletal construction, as well as coloring, to be recognized as a distinct species within the world marmot group. In the adult stage it is slightly smaller than the hoary marmot and yellow-bellied marmot, and slightly larger than the woodchuck. (The latter, often called groundhog, is also a marmot). In other characteristics, as well as in lifestyle, the Vancouver Island marmot is basically the same as its relatives.

M. vancouverensis is found only on Vancouver Island. Although as yet no one has unraveled the mystery of how it got to the island, the most common theory is that it was originally a hoary marmot. As such it may have crossed from the mainland by means of a land bridge that perhaps existed during the Pleistocene era, and over the years developed into its present form. Another theory is that, as a hoary marmot, it was introduced to the island by coastal Indians. That it simply originated on the island seems highly unlikely. But if the first theory is correct and the island was at one time connected to the mainland, one wonders why other species failed to migrate as well: species such as pikas, mountain goats, porcupines and grizzly bears; all the more strange, in fact, since the environment and ecosystem of both geographical areas are basically the same. The Indian transplant theory seems the most plausible.

It seems certain that the Vancouver Island marmot was once relatively common within its range. This unhappily is no longer the case for its numbers have decreased so radically that it now ranks fourth among North America's most endangered species. Field studies carried out by federal and provincial biologists, as well as by members of the Vancouver Island Marmot Preservation Committee of the Cowichan Valley Naturalists' Club, reveal that there are only six known active colonies and that the total population probably now numbers only slightly more than 100 individuals.

The Vancouver Island marmot weighs 8 pounds (3.6 kg) at most. The average adult is 25 to 28 inches (64-71 cm) in length, with an 8- to 12-inch (20-30 cm) tail. The mammal molts each July and the new pelage is a lustrous black or very dark brown, with patches of white on the forehead, around the nose and mouth and on the breast. Toward the end of summer this color changes to a chocolate-brown shade. During hibernation a further color change takes place, and when the adult mammal emerges from its den, its coat is dullish cinnamon and ragged-looking. The new pelage, after the July molt, is once again black or very dark brown.

This little mammal lives in small colonies at alpine and sub-alpine levels, generally on the side of or at the base of talus slopes with a southerly exposure. Its burrow is made in small crevices among rock piles, under large boulders and occasionally below ground in meadows. The rocks and boulders not only provide protection from enemies but also serve as good observation posts.

In his excellent book, *The Squirrels of Canada*, S. E. Woods, Jr., writes that "Vancouver Island marmots live in relative harmony, even delaying dispersal of the young until their third summer. Agonistic behavior is not a serious factor, but the marmots are territorial, and mature members take care to mark their boundaries frequently by leaving scent from their cheek glands on prominent rocks. They also have a pecking order, or scale of dominance, which is invariably headed by an adult male, followed by the adult females, then the two-year old males, two-year-old females, yearling males, and at the bottom, yearling females. This may appear to be a chauvinistic hierarchy, where the males always take precedence, but by far the most aggressive members are the adult females."

Woods also describes the marmots as very sociable and this, he says, is most noticeable immediately following hibernation. "Most social encounters," he writes, "are characterized by tail-waving similar to a housecat's nose-to-nose greetings, or playfights. Playfights are really shoving matches in which both contestants stand on their hind legs and push their opponent in the chest with their forepaws. Many greetings are brief; both parties continue on their separate ways almost immediately."

The diet of these mammals, after emerging from hibernation, is made up of the berries of Kinnikinnick (a member of the heather family), huckleberry roots and the bark of cedar. By the time July arrives the alpine slopes and meadows support a rich growth of such plants as Indian paintbrush, glacial lilies, lupines, flax and cow parsnip on which they feast. They also consume the ripe and juicy fruit of huckleberry and blueberry plants.

In September or early October members of the colony, their little bodies carrying thick layers of fat

built up after a summer of heavy feeding, retire to their burrows and there they remain in hibernation until the following spring. The young of that year hibernate with their mothers.

When the families emerge from their burrows, they are thin and hungry and, if the snow covering is thick, it is often a struggle to tunnel through it to search for whatever vegetation the spring thaws or strong winds may have exposed on the nearby bluffs. Mating occurs soon afterward and the new litters, each averaging three pups, are born in late May or June and emerge above ground in July. At this time the color of their fur is like dark chocolate.

The Vancouver Island marmot responds to the threat of danger in the same manner as other marmots. Its alarm call is a short piercing whistle which sends members of the colony scurrying to their bolt holes where, before disappearing, they pause momentarily to try to identify the source of the danger. Ground enemies include cougars, black bears, wolves or humans;

This species is only found on Vancouver Island, British Columbia, and is so scarce that it ranks fourth among North America's most endangered species. Thanks primarily to the dedicated work of the Vancouver Island Marmot Preservation Committee, it has been saved from extinction. The youngster shown here will not breed until it is 3 years old, and if it is a female it will only reproduce every second year. (Photo by J. A. Wilkinson/Valan Photos) aerial enemies include golden eagles, red-tailed hawks or diurnal owls. Eventually the marmots return to the burrow entrance, and if the danger seems to have passed, a low-pitched two-syllable call is sounded. Cautiously they return to the open to resume normal above-ground activities.

The scarcity of the Vancouver Island marmots can be attributed primarily to human pressure on or destruction of their environment.

But there is a major natural cause: their own slow rate of reproduction. It is generally believed that young marmots do not breed until their *third* year, and that females only reproduce every *second* year. But this harsh restriction on population growth—a phenomenon experienced also by polar bears—would not in itself lead the species to extinction. If such a tragedy were to occur, it would largely be the result of man's own lack of concern and his callous denial of the right of survival of one of the most interesting and certainly one of the most harmless, of all wild creatures.

Spermophilus richardsonii

Richardson's Ground Squirrel

This prairie rodent is most commonly, though erroneously, known as "gopher," but some people call it picket pin (descriptive of its habit of standing upright and looking from a distance somewhat like the picket pin used to tether horses) or whistletail (flicking its tail to the accompaniment of alarm whistles). It is one of the most abundant of the genus *Spermophilus* and is as characteristic of the prairie lands as golden wheat itself.

The trouble is, few people have a good word to say for it: first, because it consumes large quantities of grain and, secondly, because it has been known to play host to the tick which carries Rocky Mountain fever, to fleas which cause bubonic plague, and to a bacillus which causes tularemia. Fortunately cases of human infection from any of these are rare.

About the only visible benefits that can be attributed to it are that its extensive digging helps to mix the soil and that its underground burrow, which usually consists of a maze of tunnels, galleries and chambers, traps rain water, which in turn helps to irrigate the land. To biologists and other students of wildlife, of course, it will always be an intriguing creature and the object of continuing studies.

This squirrel is a homesteader whose ancestors established themselves on the open prairies of Canada and the United States thousands of years ago. Although not as abundant as it once was, it has managed to hold its own while other creatures, notably the bison disappeared as man advanced across the land. Today it is found in Manitoba, Saskatchewan, Alberta, marginally in Minnesota, but more widespread in the Dakotas, Montana, Idaho, Wyoming and Colorado. It also occurs in a small area where the states of Oregon, Idaho and Nevada meet.

The pelage of *S. richardsonii* is short, gray or yellowish-gray above (with some brown on the back), yellowish on the sides and gray or buff-colored on the underparts. Its tail, short, flat and slim, is brown on top and buffy underneath. There is one annual molt, which occurs in the summer. It has twin cheek pouches characteristic of all sciurids. This plump rodent at maturity weighs from 13 to nearly 16 ounces (370-450 g) and is about 10 to 14 inches (25-36 cm) in length. Males are always somewhat larger than females.

The Richardson's ground squirrel has adapted to several types of habitats, but those best suited to its needs are open, rolling prairie hills where burrows can be readily made in dry sand or gravel. Many colonies, however, are found in grasslands, cattle ranges, cultivated fields, along the edges of grain fields, highways and country roads, always where food is available.

As a rule this mammal, like the black-tailed prairie dog, likes to have a clear view of its surroundings so that should danger threaten it can quickly disappear into its burrow, the entrance to which is seldom more than a few feet away. The approach of a predator—mammal, raptor or human—causes the squirrel to stand bolt upright, squeak repeatedly in high-pitched tones and at the same time flick its tail. These warning signals are given by other sentinels and if necessary a noisy colony of hundreds of squirrels can disappear in an instant. But these are inquisitive creatures and seconds later scores of little heads will pop far enough above the burrow entrances to survey the skies and landscape in search of the enemy that caused their fright.

These squirrels, even though they live in colonies, are more inclined to be quarrelsome than sociable in their inter-family relationships, although they get along well enough with other rodents such as prairie dogs and meadow voles. Whereas prairie dogs openly demonstrate their friendliness toward each other, ground squirrels show hostility, except during the brief mating period in late March and early April immediately following hibernation.

Most members of the Sciuridae family are strictly diurnal. In the case of the Richardson's ground squirrel, its major periods of activity are from 10 a.m. to 2 p.m. and from about 4 p.m. to dusk. During the day it feeds heavily on green vegetation such as prairie grasses, broad-leaved plants, flowers, roots and seeds such as wheat and oats. It also eats insects, particularly crickets, grasshoppers and caterpillars. Carrion occasionally enters its diet. A large quantity of seeds is carried in its cheek pouches to storage chambers underground for consumption mainly in the spring when hibernation is over and before it is time to emerge from its burrow. At that time the squirrel's body fat has been largely consumed and it is hungry.

A large mound of earth commonly marks the principal burrow entrance, although there are other openings that serve as both entrances and exits. The mound, by the way, is used as a look-out when the mammal wants to survey the countryside; in every colony one or more sentinels seem to maintain constant watch for predators. The burrows themselves are complex networks of tunnels, galleries, chambers and passageways, each serving specific purposes and sometimes running at two levels and at depths of up to 6 feet (1.8 m). The whole network may extend underground for as much as 50 feet (15 m). The nests are made in separate chambers, are about 9 inches (23 cm) in diameter and 6 inches (15 cm) high, and are lined with a thick layer of dry grasses and oat hulls.

Underground life begins in some areas in late June or early July when first the males, then a few weeks later the females, enter their burrows. This first stage is known as *estivation*, the forerunner of *hibernation* — the deep sleep which begins when winter sets in and temperatures drop to freezing. The young delay their move until August, mainly because as juveniles they require more time to build up the body fat necessary to sustain them until spring. Some, most of them males, for reasons not yet clear remain topside until October or early Novermber.

Breeding takes place in March and early April and after a gestation period of about 28 days from six to eight pups are born. Naked and blind and weighing about ⅕ ounce (6 g) each, they remain in the nest for a month to 5 weeks. When they are ready to emerge from the burrow they weigh nearly 3 ounces (80 g). By the beginning of September they are adult size. There is only one litter a year.

The enemies of this mammal, aside from man, who

Silhouettes and tracks of all ground squirrels are similar.

Fore

Hind
1 ³/₈ in (3.4 cm) long

Richardson's ground squirrel

keeps up a continuing battle to maintain populations at the lowest level he can, are ground predators such as badgers, weasels, ferrets, snakes, cats, dogs and burrowing owls. Sky-borne predators include hawks and eagles.

The Richardson's ground squirrel was named after Sir John Richardson, a surgeon-naturalist who was a member of Sir John Franklin's first two expeditions into the Arctic.

Spermophilus columbianus
Columbian Ground Squirrel

This burrowing mammal is more than a subterranean house-builder; it also qualifies as an ingenious engineer. Being a member of a family that spends most of its life underground, it must provide for itself a habitat that offers living quarters, storage rooms for food, passageways for the disposal of body wastes, and escape tunnels (often called bolt or plunge holes) for emergency purposes. Most of the ground squirrels create such a system rather efficiently, but the Columbian generally does it with considerably more imagination and style.

Few authorities have described the Columbian's burrow more clearly than has Dr. Banfield. Here is what he says: "This species excavates an extensive tunnel system for summer occupancy. The burrows are situated unprotected on open ground or in banks, usually under boulders, stumps or logs. From the main entrance the burrow leads downward at a forty-five degree grade and then levels off between two and three feet beneath the surface. The tunnels (three to four inches in diameter) vary between ten and sixty feet in length and may have an average of eleven entrances (from two to thirty-five). Piles of loose earth appear at the main entrance, but there are many hidden plunge-holes. There is a central chamber about thirty inches in diameter lined with cottony anemone down or grasses, from which tunnels radiate towards different feeding grounds. Some tunnels lead to feeding grounds; others are 'blind' and serve as toilet areas.

"In late summer the hibernating den is constructed separately off the summer burrow system. It is usually deeper (sometimes up to six feet in depth down to hardpan). It consists of a hibernation chamber with a basal dust mulch and a complete lining of dried grasses. Immediately off the entrance to this chamber is a sump, which varies from one to five feet in depth. This sump drains off any water that might flood the chamber. A plug about two feet long, tamped into place with the squirrel's forehead, seals off the entrance to the hibernation den from the summer burrow. The earth used for the plug comes from the construction of the sump. Leading upwards is a short section of the escape hatch. In spring the emerging squirrel digs directly upwards to the surface, and uses the fresh earth to fill up the sump. The squirrel does not remove the plug to enter the old burrow system."

A burrow such as this would most likely be constructed by a mature and more experienced squirrel. Younger members tend not only to construct shallower tunnels but also neglect to provide for adequate flood control: as a consequence many juveniles are drowned during their first winter of hibernation. Burrows of the type described by Banfield are not uncommon, however, and whether created by conscious design or inherited instinct deserve to be rated as remarkable.

This mammal is a westerner whose range runs from southeastern British Columbia and southwestern Alberta to northeastern Oregon, northern Idaho and northwestern Montana. It is found in a variety of habitats, and while in Canada it occurs most frequently in

Columbian ground squirrel

open country at elevations of between 700 and 8,000 feet (200-2,400 m), in its U.S. range it is also found at lower levels where there are meadows, grainfields and parklands. In Washington state, in fact, it does significant damage at times to wheat and alfalfa crops.

The Columbian ground squirrel is one of the largest of the ground squirrels measuring about 16 inches (40 cm) in length, including its 3- to 4-inch (8-10 cm) tail, and, when ready to hibernate, weighing up to 28 ounces (800 g). Its fur, which is short and fine, is grayish to beige overall. The back and sides are speckled with black and indistinct buff hairs, and its face (including its snout), belly and forelegs are reddish-brown; its hind legs are tawny yellow to yellowish-buff. It carries a prominent light-colored eye-ring. The tail is reddish and edged with white.

Although the Columbian ground squirrel is classified as colonial—and when it is there may be as many as five to a dozen adults to an acre—it also occurs with as few as two to an acre, and even as widely dispersed single pairs. When it is colonial, the area is divided into territories, each under the control of a dominant male. When communicating, the squirrel utters sharp whistles; its presence can also be recognized by its noisy chirping.

Hibernation, which begins first with a period of estivation, lasts from seven to eight months and in some areas begins as early as mid-July. Emergence from the burrow depends largely on altitude, depth of snow covering and availability of surface foods and may

The Columbian ground squirrel is one of the largest of the group. It is a western species whose range runs south from British Columbia and Alberta to Oregon, Idaho and Montana. (Photo by Peter Karsten)

begin as early as March and continue to early May. As is typical of ground squirrels and marmots, the males emerge first. Mating occurs shortly afterwards, generally within 3 weeks, and after a gestation period of 24 days from two to seven pups are born. The young remain in the nest for 3 to 4 weeks and by the end of their first month are weaned. At that time they begin eating tender green vegetation and eventually the wider range of food that makes up the Columbian's regular diet.

The food of this squirrel includes a variety of grasses, leaves, bulbs, seeds, herbs, fruit, plant stems, tubers, and animal matter such as grasshoppers, caterpillars, dead fish, smaller mammals and ground-nesting birds. Large populations living near or in grain fields cause considerable damage to crops and are shot, poisoned or trapped. They can also raise havoc in vegetable gardens. Like other ground squirrels, during the summer the Columbian carries in its twin cheek pouches quantities of seeds and other food which it stores in its burrow for consumption the following spring.

The enemies of this squirrel are the enemies of all mammals living in underground burrows—weasels, badgers, skunks, foxes, coyotes, bobcats, snakes, grizzly bears, golden eagles and large buteo hawks. If it manages to survive, the Columbian may live in the wild for 4 to 5 years.

Arctic ground squirrels are important in the food chain of northern mammals, particularly wolves, ermine, foxes, grizzly bears; hawks, falcons and owls. Native people include these squirrels in their diet and use the fur in making parkas. (Photo by Dr. Donald R. Gunn)

Spermophilus parryii

Arctic Ground Squirrel

Alaskans call it parky, because its pelt is used in the making of parkas, Eskimos know it as sik-sik, an interpretation of its alarm call, and the textbooks list it as Arctic ground squirrel because for the most part the far north is its habitat.

This mammal, the largest of the ground squirrels, occurs throughout most of the Northwest Territories (except the Mackenzie Valley south of Great Bear Lake), northern British Columbia, Yukon and Alaska. It is the only ground squirrel within that range.

Spermophilus parryii at maturity measures about 12 to 16 inches (30-40 cm) in length and has a 3- to 6-inch (8-15 cm) bushy-tipped tail. Males weigh up to 29 ounces (820 g); females are somewhat smaller. The coloring of this species is generally tannish, but more specifically is tawny to reddish (or cinnamon) on the head, cheeks and shoulders, reddish to grayish-brown on the back (diffused with numerous whitish flecks), and yellowish or tawny on the underparts and legs. The eye-ring is buffy or white. Molting occurs twice a year, first in the spring when the molt begins at the rump and continues toward the head, and then in the fall when the molt begins at the head and continues toward the rump. The fall molt leaves the animal with a coat that is noticeably grayer overall.

The Arctic ground squirrel is colonial, and while hundreds of its kind may live within a limited range, a system of territorial control is maintained by dominant males. Each of the dominant ones governs a number of females and diligently defends its preserve against intrusion by other males; most confrontations are settled peacefully, but serious fights sometimes result in physical injury.

Like all ground squirrels, the Arctic form is primarily herbivorous and feeds on a variety of seeds, flowers, fruit, grasses, forbs, leaves, mushrooms and other plants; it will also eat carrion and, as wilderness travelers have discovered, any handout at a campsite. One writer, intrigued by the antics of a squirrel which visited him, thought it "friendlier than the New York City Central Park gray squirrel" but lost his enthusiasm for it when he found it had chewed "undarnable holes" in wool socks left at the entrance to his tent!

The far northern summer seasons are times of almost continuous daylight, but despite the absence of darkness this little mammal adheres to a fairly rigid schedule: it forages actively from about 4 a.m. to about 9:30 p.m., often wandering considerable distances from its burrow as it moves across the tundra in search of food; then it retires to its underground nest to sleep for the next 7 or 8 hours. If the weather is not to its liking, it will remain underground and will feed on the supply of seeds, leaves and the like which it sensibly stockpiles for such emergencies. These stores of foods are also used when hibernation is over and there is still a paucity of new plant life above ground.

Because the tundra has often only a relatively thin blanket of vegetation covering the permafrost, sites that can be successfully excavated for burrows are not always available. As a consequence, once a burrow is excavated it may be used year after year. Most favored areas are meadows where there is sand or gravel, and the soft banks of rivers and lakes. The burrow itself, while it may consist of a maze of tunnels and a number of entrances, is usually no more than 3 feet (0.9 m) in depth. Short secondary burrows are often made within range of the home burrow; these are generally used as escape tunnels when predators threaten.

The Arctic ground squirrel enters its home burrow sometime in September, curls up in a tight little ball, back uppermost and with its bushy tail wrapped over its head and shoulders, and goes to sleep in its nest of grass, leaves and the molted fur of other animals. Brief, natural arousals, however, may occur from time to time.

The hibernation of this ground squirrel is intense. The temperature of its body drops to close to freezing, its respiration rate slows almost to a stop, and its normal heart action of 200 to 400 beats a minute drops to 5 to 10 beats. In this almost death-like state it remains unconscious and unstirring even if dug out of its nest. Rough handling does not disturb it and it can be safely returned to its nest quite unaware of the experience.

Sometime during April or May hibernation ends. The males are the first to make their appearance; then, a week or so later the females emerge. Mating begins after the animals have adjusted to the outside environment and satisfied their hunger; the months of hibernation can reduce their body weight by up to 40 per cent.

Twenty-five days later the new litters, ranging from 5 to 10 pups, are born. The young grow rapidly and are weaned within 20 days. By September they are almost fully grown and ready to begin independent careers. At this time they dig their own burrows, or take over abandoned ones if available. Not all are suc-

Arctic ground squirrel

cessful in finding or establishing safe underground quarters: if burrows are flooded or enveloped in permafrost, the youngsters seldom survive their first winter.

The natural enemies of the Arctic ground squirrel are grizzly bears, wolves, ermine, foxes, hawks, falcons and owls. Eskimos not only eat the flesh of these squirrels but use their fur in making parkas.

Spermophilus tridecemlineatus

Thirteen-lined Ground Squirrel

This mammal, one of the smallest of the spermophiles, is also called striped ground squirrel and striped gopher. At one time it was also known as leopard-spermophile. The name "striped gopher" is incorrect, of course, since "gopher" is the vernacular name of a distinctly separate family of burrowing rodents with rather mole-like habits.

S. tridecemlineatus lives in roughly the same Canadian range as its cousin, the Richardson's ground squirrel — the southern half of the three prairie provinces. Its United States range is much more extensive, however, taking in a large part of the midwest as far south as the Gulf of Mexico. Within the last century its range has expanded as forested areas have been cleared for agriculture, and it is now found as far east as Missouri, Michigan and Ohio.

This squirrel is a handsome creature with alternating stripes, yellowish to white, and blackish to reddish-brown, running from head to rump along the back and sides. The dark stripes are punctuated with a number of light spots. The number of these stripes varies, but the most common individual pattern totals 13 — seven light and six dark. The face and underparts are buff-colored and the tail is yellowish-brown, with a mixture of black hairs with light tips. Adults range in length from 7 to more than 12 inches (18-30 cm). Their weight varies from 4 to 5 ounces (110-140 g) in the spring at the end of hibernation, and from 8 to 9 ounces (220-260 g) in the fall when they are plump with body fat built up for the months of hibernation ahead. Occasionally, albino (white) or melanistic (black) individuals are born, a phenomenon not unusual among animals. The thirteen-lined ground squirrel molts twice during each 12 months, first in the spring soon after hibernation and then in late summer before hibernation.

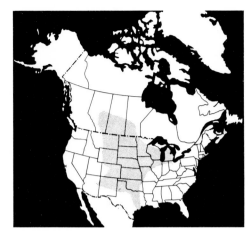

Thirteen-lined ground squirrel

This species makes its home in dry, open fields, open grasslands, along the edges of sloughs and streams, fence rows and woody borders. It particularly likes the lawns of estate properties, does well in the closely cropped fairways of golf courses, and along the mowed borders of superhighways.

On man's economic scale it rates between good and bad. Good, for example, because its burrow digging helps to aerate the soil and encourages an increase of soil-enriching nutrients; in addition, it feeds to some extent on noxious weeds, on insects (especially crickets, caterpillars and grasshoppers), and mice, which damage grain and garden crops. On the bad side, it has a fondness for the heads of ripe oats, wheat and corn, and the roots and shoots of young peas, beets, and other vegetables. There is no record of the number of golf balls that have disappeared down squirrel (or gopher) holes.

The thirteen-lined ground squirrel, like other members of its family, is strictly diurnal. While it is a solitary mammal and agonistic toward others of its kind, it nevertheless often lives in colonies where no doubt an uneasy peace must prevail, especially during the mating season.

Its daytime activities are greatly influenced by light and climatic conditions, and by the seasons. Cloudy and rainy days normally keep it in its burrow; warm, sunny spring days generally bring it topside from about 12 o'clock to mid-afternoon, but as the temperatures rise with the coming of summer it may on pleasant days emerge about 9 a.m. and not retire until about 5 p.m.

Most of the time above ground is spent in either feasting or gathering food for storage in its underground larder. When it is not busy at these chores, it builds new burrows or simply lazes about. It is extremely inquisitive and any interesting sound or smell will cause it to sit up on its hind feet, front feet clasped against its chest, 3- to 5-inch (8-13 cm) slightly bushy tail stretched out to serve as a prop, and quietly scrutinize the landscape, keeping as well a sharp eye on the skies for marauding raptors. If alarmed, it quickly races to its burrow, although seconds later it will carefully raise its head above the tunnel entrance to reassess the situation.

The burrow of the thirteen-lined ground squirrel is seldom easy to find, since the animal removes the earth excavated from the main and secondary entrances, presumably to hide them from predators. This tactic, similar to that of chipmunks, was described by Dr. Harold McCarley in the *Journal of Mammalogy*: "The absence of dirt around long existing burrows was understandable," he wrote, "but the same conditions prevailed around newly dug burrows. Excavation of new burrows was observed several times and it was found that in the excavation process the squirrel brought the dirt to the surface either on top of its head or pushed it out with its forepaws. After the dirt was on the surface the squirrel pushed it away from the burrow entrance with its head and forefeet and then used the hind feet to scatter it away from the entrance." The main entrance, open during the day, is closed at night with a covering of leaves or sod. The secondary entrances usually remain plugged and covered with vegetation but in an emergency can be quickly opened.

There are usually two burrow systems. The first, the summer burrow, is a short one and is generally only a few inches deep; it is most frequently used as an escape tunnel, for eating and resting and for protection against inclement weather. The second, or main burrow, may drop down as far as 6 feet (2 m) and run horizontally, but irregularly, for as much as 20 feet (6 m). This burrow consists of a maze of passageways, some of them leading to "pantries" where seeds and other edibles are stored, some simply leading nowhere, and others leading up to lightly plugged emergency exits. The passageway leading to the hibernating chamber is always below the frost line; the chamber itself is an oval-shaped excavation about 9 inches (23 cm) in diameter and is lined with dry grass. This passageway makes a sharp turn just before the chamber is reached, which makes it very difficult for its archenemy, the badger, to maneuver around since there is no backspace for it to throw the earth as it digs furiously. Ingenious, as well, is the tunnel especially designed as a drain to carry water downward and away from the chamber.

The thirteen-lined ground squirrel is a true hibernator. Beginning in late summer, toward the end of September, or even as late as November (depending on geography) it enters its burrow, seals off the entrance and then retires to the sleeping chamber. There, sitting on its rump, it curls up into a ball and gradually drifts off into a very deep sleep. Its body temperature drops to near freezing and its heartbeat slows down to about five beats a minute. Throughout the whole hibernating period (which ends about the following April) it draws solely on its stored-up body fat for nourishment. By spring, its weight loss will amount to 30 to 50 per cent. There may be some brief, conscious stirring during the hibernation period should unseasonably warm temperatures occur.

The thirteen-lined ground squirrel mates shortly after hibernation ends and in May, after a gestation period of about 28 days, 8 to 10 pups are born, each about 2¼ inches (6 cm) long and weighing no more than ¹/₁₀ ounce (3 g). When they are between 4 and 5 weeks of age, and nearly adult size, they disperse to lead independent lives.

The vocalizing of this mammal is a long, trilling whistle. When alarmed the trills are short, high-pitched and, according to McCarley, "somewhat similar to the alarm call of the killdeer." The mother has a special alarm call for her youngsters and the youngsters have a distress call of their own; the latter has been described as a low "peep" and is frequently heard when the youngsters wander away from their burrow and become temporarily lost. Young squirrels, and sometimes adults, often utter a lower-pitched sound in "distress" situations. Both the alarm and distress calls apparently elicit a prompt response from other squirrels who run to investigate the cause of the problem.

Enemies of the thirteen-lined ground squirrel, in addition to badgers, include weasels, mink, hawks, owls, snakes, foxes, coyotes, skunks and humans. They are also susceptible to infestations of mites, ticks and fleas and suffer particularly from botfly larvae (warbles) which attack the skin in the region of the groin. Automobiles take a heavy toll, as they do of other squirrels living close to highways.

Spermophilus franklinii
Franklin's Ground Squirrel

"Most of the ground squirrels," observed Seton, "are noted for the great variety of the sounds they produce, but this is the musician of the family. It utters the same calls as the others, but expresses them in a fine, clear whistle. Its ordinary note heard in the brushwood is in a high degree musical, resembling the voice of some of our fine bird singers, and has won for the species the names 'Whistling Gopher' and 'Musical Ground Squirrel.'"

This little mammal superficially resembles the eastern gray squirrel. Its primary range includes the three Prairie provinces of Canada and in the U.S. the Dakotas, Nebraska, Kansas, Missouri, Iowa, Minnesota, Wisconsin, Illinois and Indiana. According to Peterson, agricultural land clearing has encouraged it to migrate to Ontario where it is now established as far east as the Kenora, Rainy River and Fort Frances areas.

The Franklin's ground squirrel is most commonly found in dense grassy borderland between forested areas and open prairies. It often frequents places where there are hedges and fence rows and it generally makes its burrow in a well-drained brushy bank or draw; it may also make its burrow close to farmyards, using buildings, shrubs or piled-up waste material to conceal the tunnel openings leading to its underground living quarters.

Except for times of cyclic abundance, which occur

The golden-mantled ground squirrel lives at altitudes of 3,000 to 8,000 feet (900-2,400 m) in the Rocky Mountains. It is a friendly creature and is often encountered by campers. (Photo by Dr. Donald R. Gunn)

every 4 to 6 years, in few places are there dense populations. Peak periods may see as many as 30 animals per acre, but at other times a dense population would be 4 to 6 per acre.

Franklin's ground squirrel, one of the largest of the spermophiles, wears a coat of short, wiry hairs that are brownish-gray and peppered with black; this gives it a spotted or barred appearance, particularly on the rump. The underparts vary in color and may be buff, gray or white. The head is gray and darker than the rest of the back and, as applies to all of the species, the ears are small and a white ring encircles the eyes. The tail is a mixture of black and gray hairs, and while long and bushy, it is not as prominent as that of the gray squirrel for which it is often mistaken. There is one annual molt, which occurs during early summer. This mammal is equipped with three anal glands which, when the creature is excited or frightened, exude a powerful musky scent.

It is one of the most fossorial of the true ground squirrels. Aside from the fact that it dislikes inclement weather (even when it is only windy or overcast) and as a rule is abroad only on warm, bright days, it has a long period of hibernation. In northern latitudes it retires as early as July, while in the warmer southern latitudes hibernation may not begin until October. Since the common time of emergence is late April to early May, the underground sojourn may be anywhere from 7 to 10 months. All told, *Spermophilus franklinii* spends nearly 90 per cent of its life underground.

This mammal is less colonial than other ground squirrels and while it is sometimes found in small family groups of a dozen or so, it usually lives alone. Its burrow is deep and relatively complex, with one main and several secondary entrances. The main entrance is not always well concealed and can be identified by the large mounds of earth surrounding it; the secondary entrances, which also serve as bolt holes, are generally well camouflaged. The underground tunnels branch out to numerous side passages which are used for sleeping, food storage or the elimination of body wastes. The nesting area is generally at or close to the end of a side branch which in turn is located at a higher elevation so as to escape flooding.

Other than short periods spent basking in the sun, most of the time spent outside its burrow is devoted to feeding, for large amounts of body fat must be built up to sustain it during the long months of dormancy ahead. In additon, it carries in its cheek pouches a substantial amount of food of various kinds—seeds, grains and other vegetable matter—which it deposits in its underground larder. Most of this food is eaten in the days following arousal from hibernation. For reasons not fully understood, winter mortality among both sexes and all age groups is high, with a death rate of 40 to 80 per cent.

About three-fourths of this squirrel's diet consists of vegetable matter such as seeds, cultivated grains, roots, berries, grasses and, when available, garden vegetables and the like. The rest of its diet consists of animal matter—insects, frogs, fish, toads, caterpillars and sometimes carrion. In some areas, particularly during peak population years, this mammal is considered an economic pest, for it not only does considerable damage to grain crops; it also kills young poultry and

Franklin's ground squirrel

wildfowl and eats their eggs. Like other ground squirrels it derives most of its water from the moisture contained in plants.

The Franklin's ground squirrel mates soon after hibernation ends and the breeding period, which is marked by much competitive scrapping among the males, lasts for about 3 weeks. After a gestation period of approximately 28 days, from 1 to 12 pups (usually 7 or 8) are born and like most baby mammals come into the world naked and blind. They become fully furred when they are 16 days old, they gain their sight when they are 18 to 20 days old, and when they are a month old they venture outside their burrow. A few weeks later, after weaning, they become independent of their mothers.

Young ground squirrels adapt quickly to their outside environment and, in addition to becoming adept at climbing trees and moving freely among their branches, they take readily to water and soon become strong swimmers. Both sexes are mature by the following spring.

Enemies of the Franklin's ground squirrel include weasels, badgers, coyotes, foxes, snakes, ermine and skunks; raptors such as hawks and owls also take a toll. Parasites and diseases are additional threats to its well-being. Despite the fact that *Spermophilus franklinii* is a shy, nervous animal, it can be readily tamed whenever campers set up their gear close to its burrow. Normally this squirrel seldom ventures beyond a radius of about 300 feet (91 m) from its home.

The Franklin's ground squirrel was named in honor of Arctic explorer Sir John Franklin. It was his companion explorer, surgeon-naturalist Sir John Richardson (after whom the Richardson's ground squirrel was named), who discovered the species.

Spermophilus lateralis

Golden-mantled Ground Squirrel

This attractively colored ground squirrel not only closely resembles the yellow-pine chipmunk but has many of the behavioral characteristics of its little cousin. Where it differs significantly is in its much larger size, up to 10 ounces (280 g) in weight, as opposed to the chipmunk's 2 ounces (57 g) or so, and in its markings: both have prominent light and dark stripes running along the upper sides; the chipmunk, however, has facial stripes as well but these do not occur on the squirrel. The term "golden-mantled" refers to the coppery-red coloring around its head and shoulders.

Spermophilus lateralis is a western mammal that makes its home in the valleys and slopes of the Rocky Mountains at altitudes from 3,000 to 8,000 feet (900-2,400 m). It prospers in pine forests and logged or burned-over terrain, but it favors semi-wooded areas where there are rocky outcrops, fallen trees, talus slides and rocky meadows. The Columbian ground squirrel, the yellow-pine chipmunk and the tiny pika share the same habitat.

In Canada the golden-mantled ground squirrel is found in both Alberta and British Columbia. In the United States its range is larger and extends to southern California and to west central New Mexico. *S. l. saturatus*, commonly known as the Cascade golden-mantled ground squirrel, is a slightly larger but less strikingly colored subspecies found in the Cascade Mountains of south-central British Columbia and central Washington.

The golden-mantled ground squirrel is a "loner" and assembles in numbers only when campers arrive and entice them with handouts. While some of the goodies are eaten on the spot, much is crammed into the mammal's cheek pouches and immediately taken away to its burrow or some other storage place. The squirrel then returns for a refill.

Like other ground squirrels, it spends most of its life in its burrow, but *unlike* most others it makes its home in shallow burrows of varying lengths; some writ-

Golden-mantled ground squirrel

ers say 5 to 15 feet (1.5-5 m), others say up to 100 feet (30 m). The burrow is generally located where there are rocks or tree stumps, although sometimes it is made in open ground where there is a good covering of vegetation. All traces of soil excavated from the main entrance as well as from other shafts or bolt holes are removed so as to provide additional concealment. When the mammal enters its burrow at night, the entrance is generally sealed off with a covering of leaves or other vegetation.

Depending on latitude, it begins hibernation in September and does not emerge until May. There may be periodic awakenings, at which time it would feed on the food cached in a side tunnel the previous summer. The nest of this squirrel is the very antithesis of good housekeeping, for it also accommodates a host of other creatures such as millipedes, fleas, ticks and ants. None of these seem to bother it during hibernation, although when above ground it frequently rolls in dust to remove whatever parasites it can and to freshen up its fur. At such times it grooms itself carefully, using both claws and teeth to comb itself.

The golden-mantled ground squirrel mates shortly after leaving its burrow in May and about a month later from three to seven pups (normally four) are born. Growth of the pups is rapid and by September they are nearly half adult size. Family ties last for only a short time, and once weaning is over and the pups are able to fend for themselves, they go their separate ways. Full maturity and the ability to mate successfully are not reached until the following spring.

Unfavorable weather, especially when it is chilly, windy or rainy, keeps this little rodent underground. In good weather it enjoys basking in the sun but only after its appetite has been satiated. The food eaten by this squirrel consists mainly of green vegetation, seeds, berries, bulbs, mushrooms, buds, leaves and flowers; it also consumes grasshoppers, butterflies, beetles, caterpillars and other arthropods, and will occasionally kill fledgling songbirds as well as consume eggs. It is strictly diurnal.

The golden-mantled ground squirrel is a relatively silent creature and is usually heard only when it is startled or threatened. In such a situation it utters a shrill *tsp-tsp*. If approached, it scurries to safety, turns about for a quick reappraisal of the danger and then disappears, but not without making a last defiant cry. When in family groups or in company with others of its kind, it chatters loudly and if fighting it grunts and sometimes screams.

This little golden-mantled ground squirrel crammed its cheek pouches with food tossed to it by a camper and then scampered off to store it in its shallow underground burrow. (Photo by Mark Nyhof)

Although a ground dweller and most commonly seen scampering along a log or sitting, sometimes bolt upright, on a rock or stump, it occasionally moves about among low shrubs. Now and again it will swim across small streams and will drink from them. Its main source of water is the moisture in vegetation.

The enemies of this squirrel include weasels, bobcats, cougars, bears, foxes and coyotes, as well as hawks and eagles. *S. lateralis* is only minimally in conflict with man, mainly because of its isolated habitat. It loses favor among some foresters, though, because it often kills seedlings and consumes or wastes conifer seeds, thus interfering with reforestation.

Cynomys ludovicianus

Black-tailed Prairie Dog

So highly developed is the black-tailed prairie dog in its behavioral patterns and social interactions that writing about it without anthropomorphizing is almost impossible. This little creature, more a resident of the short-grass country of the American midwest than of Canada, is one of the most intelligent members of the Sciuridae family. A relatively small population occurs in Canada, and that only in the area of Val Marie, Saskatchewan. This mammal, a close relative of ground squirrels, for many years has fascinated scientists and amateur naturalists alike, and an impressive literature has been built up around it.

C. ludovicianus was first identified in Canada in 1927 by Dr. J. Dewey Soper, the distinguished Alberta naturalist, who added to his international fame two years later when he discovered, along the west coast of Baffin Island, the breeding ground of the blue goose. Since that time interest in the mammal has grown and through the efforts of the Saskatchewan Natural History Society the Prairie Dog Sanctuary was created. This sanctuary now forms part of the Grasslands National Park created in 1981. Similar protective measures have been taken in the United States, where it occurs in the Great Plains south to northwest Texas and New Mexico.

Before the turn of the century the population of black-tailed prairie dogs was kept under control by the predation of ferrets, bobcats, badgers, hawks, eagles and owls. As colonization of the Canadian and United States west proceeded, agricultural modification of the land reduced the number of these predators to such an extent that prairie dog populations literally exploded.

Seton wrote that 80-odd years ago the prairie dog population reached a high of about five *billion* animals!

That was about four and a half billion more than the land and the settlers could withstand, for the little creatures, being semi-fossorial, not only pot-holed the ground to such an extent that the well-being of horses, cattle and other livestock was threatened, but they also fed ravenously on a variety of agricultural crops and the forage food of farm animals. All-out war was declared and through the use of poisons, traps and firearms, the species was so reduced in numbers that its survival was actually threatened. That it is not an endangered species today is mainly because of the protection given it.

The black-tailed prairie dog is an engaging little mammal weighing 1½ to 3 pounds (0.7-1.4 kg) and measuring 13 to 17 inches (33-43 cm) in length. Standing on its hind legs, it is about a foot (30 cm) high. It is distinguished from other prairie dogs by the black tip on its 3- to 4-inch (8-10 cm), sparsely-furred tail. Its

ears are short and rounded, and its eyes are large and black. Its short thick pelage is pinkish-brown above, white or buffy-white on the chest and belly.

C. ludovicianus is a superbly organized, socially oriented mammal which lives in "towns"—underground communities of several thousand individuals in an area of 100 or more acres. These towns are made up of neighborhood "wards," which in turn are sub-divided into "coteries"—small family groups of males, females and young. The towns are identified by the large number of 1- to 3-foot-high (0.3-1 m) mounds which mark the entrances to the subterranean passages leading to the family places of dwelling.

The burrow of the prairie dog consists of a shaft about 4 inches (10 cm) in diameter, sometimes with a vertical drop of 10 feet (3 m) or more, sometimes with a sharp incline and sometimes with only a 15 to 20 degree slope. But the subterranean design is much the same for all: a few feet from the surface is a small "listening"

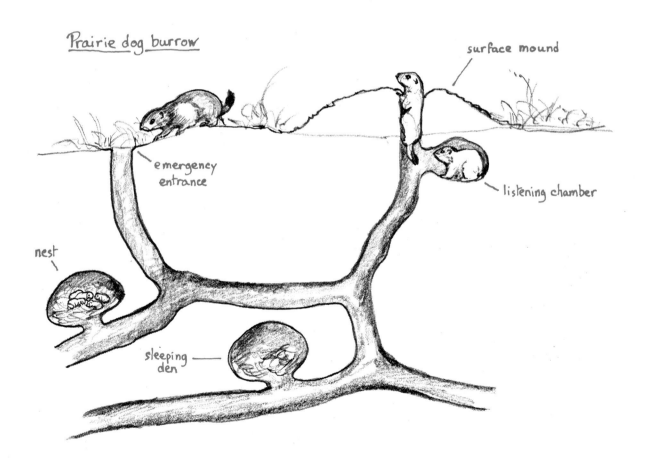

Prairie dog burrow

surface mound

emergency entrance

listening chamber

nest

sleeping den

or "turning around" passage, just big enough for one occupant, then the drop continues to a horizontal passageway which may be 25 feet (8 m) or so in length and from which in turn are one or two side passages leading to nursery areas, a side passage used as a toilet area, and an additional passage in which old nesting or other discarded material may be stored. In most, if not all cases, burrows are interconnected so that in addition to allowing for underground communication with other families, there is also a means of escape if predators or flood waters threaten.

While these burrows may be used by other families within the coterie without any loss of community harmony, difficulties are encountered when burrowing owls, badgers, rabbits, black-footed ferrets or rattlesnakes invade the premises. Of these interlopers, only the rabbit is harmless; the others, especially the

According to Ernest Thompson Seton, about five billion *black-tailed prairie dogs once lived in North America. Today, its numbers have been so reduced that the species is now protected in both Canada and the United States. (Photo by Wayne Lankinen/Valan Photos)*

black-footed ferret, are deadly enemies—as of course are above-ground predators such as golden eagles, hawks, coyotes, foxes and sometimes bobcats.

In addition to living and working together in remarkable harmony, these little creatures show strong bonds of mutual affection for each other. Common gestures are to embrace, rub noses or, by turning their heads sideways, to touch incisors. Some naturalists, while not denying the element of affection, believe such behavior is also a method of establishing identification. Mutual grooming is also a common behavior.

The prairie dog is primarily diurnal and is normally up and about from dawn to dusk. If the day is very hot, rainy or otherwise unpleasant, the whole community will remain underground. When above ground they are vocal and a prairie "dog town" can be a noisy place indeed. Recent studies with a sound spectrogram, according to Whitaker, indicate that the prairie dog has nine different calls. The two most important are the alarm and "all clear" signals. The first is described by most observers as a bark, which alerts the whole colony. If the threat is real, the animals dash for home, yipping as they go. They usually pause at the burrow entrances to confirm the presence of danger and continue to bark, yip or make chirping or wheezing sounds. The second important call, the "all clear," is similar to the territorial call which is commonly heard throughout the day—a bark which is accompanied by thrusting its forefeet upwards with great vigor and bringing them down, as Smith describes it, "like a grand salaam." This is sometimes done with such exuberance that the animal leaps into the air or loses its balance and falls over backwards. Snarls and chatters are also common noises.

C. ludovicianus mates during a 2- to 3-week period once a year, and does so earlier in its southern range than in its northern—anytime during February to April. Gestation takes about a month and the litter is usually four or five pups. The youngsters remain in their nursery for about 6 weeks and are weaned about a week later. They become self-sufficient when 10 weeks of age, but it is not until they are 2 years old that they become sexually mature and able to have families of their own.

The diet of the black-tailed prairie dog is almost exclusively vegetation, although it will frequently eat insects, especially grasshoppers. They do not hibernate, nor do they store food, so they must eat heartily in late summer and fall to build up body fat sufficient to

Fore

Hind
1¼ in (3.2 cm) long

Black-tailed prairie dog (In Canada, only in Grasslands National Park, Saskatchewan)

sustain them during the food-short months of winter. The lifespan of the black-tailed prairie dog in the wild is 7 to 8 years.

Sciurus carolinensis

Gray (or Black) Squirrel

"The ever-varying squirrels were sent, I fear, by Satan himself to puzzle Naturalists." Thus wrote the Rev. John Bachman in a letter to his friend, John James Audubon, in which he urged him to proceed more slowly in the preparation of a prospectus for *The Viviparous Quadrupeds of North America*.

Bachman, who edited the text for the three-volume *Quads*, and contributed much of the written material, was a knowledgeable mammalogist. Audubon, as an artist, was even more accomplished. Together, until the latter died in 1851, they collaborated in what is now considered to be as monumental a work as Seton's *Life Histories of Northern Animals*. Bachman was a careful observer, and while he kept meticulous and accurate notes, he also went to some lengths to discredit many of the myths that had grown up around the animals he studied. Thus: "How do they [gray squirrels] cross broad rivers? It is believed by many people that they carry a piece of bark to the shore and seat themselves on this substitute for a boat, hoist their broad tails as a sail, and float safely to the opposite shore. This we suspect to be apocryphal."

Fanciful though this pioneer belief was, it is nevertheless now accepted that most members of the Sciuridae family are above average in mammalian intelligence. Anyone who has tried to discourage the tree-dwelling varieties from invading bird feeders knows all too well their ability to overcome most obstacles placed in their way. Thwarted at the first attempt to reach whatever nuts or sunflower seeds there may be, they size up the situation — tail twitching furiously and chattering as only a frustrated squirrel can chatter. Their strategy is carefully worked out. They make mental measurements, they consider their options and then, undaunted, they persist until they reach their goal. One gray, which I gleefully thought I had outwitted, walked 10 feet along a taut wire half the thickness of a lead pencil to reach a feeder suspended from it. After a few cautious expeditions it discovered it could *run* back and forth the whole length. The gray's tenacity and remarkable balance were so impressive that no further efforts were made to discourage it. In fact, its presence added a pleasant dimension to our garden and we grew more and more fond of the interesting little animal.

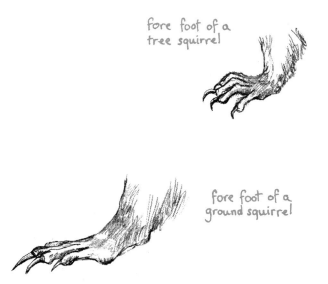

fore foot of a tree squirrel

fore foot of a ground squirrel

S. carolinensis occurs in two major color phases (gray and black) and two uncommon phases (dark brown and red brown). General coloring of the gray and black varies. In the gray it is grizzled-gray above, brownish on the sides, face and feet, and white on the chest, throat, belly and the inner sides of the legs. A prominent white ring encircles the eyes. The long, bushy tail is grayish brown with a number of black bands and a white tip. The outer, or guard hairs, are long and thick, as is the grayish underfur. The winter coat of the gray has on the back and flanks long hairs that have four color bands — a black band at the base, followed by a band of yellow-brown and then a black band and then a band of white at the tip. Six color bands characterize the tail: from base to tip they are black, brown, black, brown, black and white. Many black squirrels are jet black, although their tails may carry white-tipped hairs; sometimes their tails show hairs that are reddish-brown. Molting occurs twice a year, in early May and late September.

As so often happens in nature, there are albinos. Although these are rare, a well-established population is resident in Olney, Illinois, and the story of their survival is a heartwarming example of human compassion. In 1892, relates the American writer John Madson, "a pair of white squirrels was displayed by a saloonkeeper as an advertising stunt. A law was passed to prevent that sort of thing, and the saloon squirrels were set free. The male was soon killed, but the female raised a family and her pale descendants have thrived in Olney ever since. Today there are over a thousand white squirrels in the little town protected by town ordinance and state law."

The perpetuation of this population is remarkable since, as Dr. John A. Livingston points out in his *One Cosmic Instant*, albinism in most animals tends to last only a short time. "Usually these do not survive for very long. They are either so conspicuous that they represent an easy target for predators, or they may not be accepted into breeding populations of their species, and be screened out socially. Even if they find mates, their albinism is usually 'bred out' in subsequent generations."

S. carolinensis, along with others of its kind, is an animal of the Old World, a migrant from Asia that arrived on this continent during the Pleistocene. While one can only speculate as to its original New World range, it is today confined to the eastern half of the United States and occurs only marginally (but plentifully) in the southeastern part of Canada—specifically southern and eastern Ontario, the south corner of Quebec and parts of New Brunswick and Nova Scotia. Small numbers introduced to Alberta and British Columbia are now well established but their range in both provinces has not increased significantly. Some grays are reported to be resident in Saskatchewan, but according to Banfield these are "undoubtedly" escaped pets. It is interesting to note that an estimated 95 per cent of this species in Canada is black.

This animal, a close relative of the larger fox squirrel (*Sciurus niger*), at maturity averages just a little more than a pound (0.5 kg) in weight and measures 17 to 23 inches (43-58 cm) in length, about half of which is the tail. As is characteristic of all tree squirrels, the toes of the front feet carry short but very sharp curved claws, and these enable the animals to scramble up and down trees and leap safely from branch to branch. The equally strong claws on the back feet enable them to hang acrobatically upside down to reach for and eat hickory nuts, fruit and the like. (Since ground squirrels are diggers rather than climbers, their front toes are stockier and their claws are heavier and more flattened). Like all members of the Sciuridae family, gray squirrels have very acute eyesight.

Gray squirrels, which do not hibernate, occupy two types of seasonal homes. In winter, to escape the ravages of the weather, they live in tree cavity dens—usually hollows created by other wild creatures such as woodpeckers. The squirrels often reshape the entrances of these cavities and even enlarge the interiors.

In summer they live in bulkily built nests of twigs, leaves, grass and moss resting on roughly made twig platforms criss-crossed between branches. These "dreys" are generally built about 30 feet (9 m) above ground in high trees. A family of squirrels may occupy a number of such dreys during a summer but these are usually abandoned after a season's use and new ones are built the following year. The cavity dens, on the other hand, are frequently used year after year and are sometimes occupied by more than one family.

In northern regions breeding takes place in January and, after a gestation of 42 to 45 days, from one to six (normally two or three) pups are born. There often are second litters. In southern regions breeding is more irregular and in some areas young are in evidence throughout the year.

At birth the pups are naked and toothless, their

Silhouettes and tracks of all tree squirrels are similar.

Right front
1 ¾ in (4.5 cm) long

Right hind
2 ¼ in (5.7 cm) long

1. *Gray squirrel*
2. *Western gray squirrel*

eyes and ears are closed, and they weigh about half an ounce (14 g). Hair begins to appear in about 2 weeks; during the third week the ears open and the lower incisors break through, and by the end of the fifth week the eyes are open fully. By this time the upper incisors also emerge. The youngsters now weigh 3 to 4 ounces (85-110 g). Weaning begins in the seventh week and ends during the tenth or twelfth, at which time they are capable of looking after themselves. Despite their newly-acquired independence, the young squirrels often remain at home until their mothers give birth to new litters. The mothers, incidentally, assume the whole responsibility for rearing and training the young.

Although to most people squirrels and nuts seem inseparable, the animal's diet is actually quite varied. Here is the way Banfield describes it: "The food of this species varies with the season. In early spring it feeds upon the swelling buds of the American elm, the maples, and the oaks. The palatability of these buds changes dramatically with their development. Next, in June, it feeds on maple flowers and samaras and elm seeds. The summer is a time of plenty; it is then that it lives on a wide variety of fruits and seeds of wild grapes, hazelnuts, cherries, blueberries, apples and mushrooms. In autumn these squirrels turn their attention to their favorite hard nuts, including oak acorns, butternuts, walnuts, beech nuts, and pine seeds. At this season they individually cache a great number of nuts in shallow holes under the ground litter to be dug up later. The wintertime may be a period of stress if there has been a mast failure. Then, until spring arrives, they live under conditions of starvation on pine seeds, and on elm, maple, and sumac twigs and bark. Individual food requirements have been measured to be 470 g per week. They also eat a few insects and caterpillars, and an occasional clutch of birds' eggs if it comes their way."

Like the fox squirrel (whose food preferences are much the same) the gray species can be a nuisance when it takes up residence in urban areas. In this environment it sometimes eats the heads of emerging tulips and crocuses; it has been accused of feasting on garden corn, but in this instance the fox squirrel is the more serious offender. Neither species, it should be emphasized, is a significant predator of birds' eggs or fledglings. Occasionally city-dwelling squirrels, perhaps in need of salt or mineral supplements, have been known to gnaw telephone cables, which sometimes results in disrupted service.

Since they do not hibernate and thus need food throughout the year, squirrels cache as much food as possible to sustain them through the winter months. Great numbers of hickory acorns and beech nuts are hoarded away, most of them in the ground. But these food caches are not always sufficient to meet their needs; they must also build up a heavy layer of fat, not only as a food resource but as a means of maintaining body temperature in cold weather. Because squirrels are desirable animals, sunflower seeds and nuts should be made available when deep snow or ice-encrusted snow covers the ground and prevents them from getting to their buried stores of nuts. Peanuts, incidentally, are said to have ill effects if eaten in quantity.

The gray squirrel is probably the noisiest and "sassiest" of the tree squirrels. When alarmed it utters a long, drawn-out bark described as *kuk ku kuk* and there is vigorous waving of its tail. Perhaps the most common sound is a series of rasping *whicks*. Tail movements apparently are important in squirrel communication. Like all tree squirrels (with the exception of the "flying" species) the grays are diurnal and those living in areas of human populations, where they are often fed

The gray (or black) squirrel may sometimes be a nuisance in urban areas, but no one can deny its intelligence and its ability to entertain. This individual is swinging merrily from a covered coconut shell, suspended from a wire, as it feeds on the sunflower seeds intended for chickadees. (Photo by Dr. Donald R. Gunn)

with the winter birds, are a common sight during daylight hours.

Life in the hardwood forests may be joyous for these fun-loving creatures, but they are not immune from predators. Mink, weasels, bobcats, horned owls, red-tailed and red-shouldered hawks are among their most serious enemies and on the ground they may be outrun and killed by red foxes and raccoons. Human predators also have to be reckoned with, for the gray is rated highly by those who like wild game. Many live to the age of 10 years, and some in captivity have lived for as long as 15 years.

Sciurus griseus

Western Gray Squirrel

This western species is larger than its eastern relative, *S. carolinensis*, and while it does not occur in Canada it is present along the Pacific coast from Washington to California. Its hair on the upper parts is blue-gray and white-tipped. The hair on the undersides is white. The tail is long and covered with bands of gray, white and black hairs which sometimes stand out like a plume.

This mammal is mostly arboreal and builds its nest of shredded bark, sticks, and leaves, often at considerable heights. Its diet consists mainly of pine cones, acorns and other nuts, many of which are stored separately in holes in the ground. It also consumes berries, fungi and insects. In winter it shelters in tree cavities abandoned by woodpeckers and these cavities also serve later as nurseries. The young, from three to five, are born during March and June.

Sciurus niger

Fox Squirrel

Other than a tiny population of perhaps 300 individuals living on Pelee Island, Lake Erie (the descendants of breeding stocks introduced there nearly 100 years ago) fox squirrels do not enter significantly into the world of Canadian mammals, but this interesting member of the Sciuridae family is an important creature throughout a very large range that covers virtually all of the eastern half of the United States. The only eastern states where it is not present are parts of Wisconsin, Michigan, Pennsylvania and nearly all of New Jersey, New York and New England. Were it not for the Great Lakes, its natural range presumably by now would have been extended well into eastern Canada. Transplants, it is reported, are thriving in U.S. west coast parks.

The fox squirrel, although closely related to the gray squirrel, is a distinct species. It is also the largest of all the tree squirrels. While there are several similarities between it and the gray (breeding, nesting, diet, for example) certain differences in lifestyle help to set them apart.

For one thing, although both species make their homes in hardwood forests, the fox squirrel is a dweller of the forest edges and spends a good deal of its time in adjacent open country. It also tends to move about more on the ground and when pursued often runs directly to its home tree even if it is some distance away. The gray squirrel, in similar circumstances, usually runs up the nearest tree. The fox squirrel is diurnal, but is more of a late riser and is not generally on the move until long after sunrise. Although many of its calls and alarm sounds are like those of the gray, it is less garrulous.

There are two other ways of distinguishing between them: the gray squirrel has tiny teeth located in front of the premolars, but these little teeth are lacking in the fox squirrel; in profile, the head of the gray squirrel is more rounded and the ears are larger and less rounded. Both species are considered by many people to be excellent game food and those who have prepared them for the table say that the bones of the gray squirrel are white, while those of the fox squirrel are quite pink.

The pelage of the fox squirrel comes in a wide range of colors, but identification is simplified by the fact that in almost every individual the tip of the tail is tawny or rusty orange; the tail hairs of the gray squirrel are normally white-tipped. But it is the general coloring that is confusing, for in some areas the animal may be beige-gray above, have a buff-colored tail and bright orange and yellow underparts. In other areas it may be black above and buffy or orange underneath. Melanistic fox squirrels (black or dark-brown with white nose and ears) are common in southeastern states. Cahalane describes a gray phase there in which the top of the head is black, while the nose, ears, feet and underparts are white.

In their northern range (which includes Pelee Island) the color of the fox squirrel is commonly beige-gray above (the tips of the long guard hairs are white), the underparts are reddish-yellow, and the long bushy tail is banded black and buff above and reddish underneath. The ears, cheeks and feet are light reddish-yellow.

The main mating season of the fox squirrel in its northern range is from late December to February, but in some areas a second season may begin in May; it is usually confined to mature, healthy adults. Unlike the gray squirrel, which breeds indiscriminately and stays with each female for only a day or two, the fox squirrel is more likely to pair off with a single female while breeding lasts. For all of the tree Sciuridae, mating is a high-spirited, often quarrelsome time and there is much frantic, noisy chasing up, down and around trees and leaping from branch to branch, or tree to tree, in remarkable displays of aerial dexterity.

The fox squirrel, like both the gray and red species, occupies two types of tree homes, both "high rises." One is a winter home which is either a cavity in a tree made by a woodpecker or a flicker, or a natural cavity caused by a limb that has broken away from the trunk, leaving a hole where the decaying wood can be easily removed. After the den has been made the squirrel must periodically remove new growth of bark around the collar of the cavity in order to keep it open. The diameter of the den entrance must not be too large otherwise it might admit raccoons, owls, martens, fisher and other enemies. An opening of about 3 inches (8 cm) is adequate. The average inside depth is about 2 feet (60 cm) and the inside diameter about 8 inches (20 cm). The interior is generally well padded with leaves.

The trees most commonly providing den potential are white oaks and beeches. Hickory trees, which are much stronger and tougher, are less apt to have natural cavities; those that do develop are more quickly repaired by new bark growth. Most nests in tree dens are clean and dry, but infested with fleas. Some observers believe that it is the flea nuisance that forces squirrels to leave the dens in warmer weather to build and live in leaf nests; leaf nests are generally freer of these little insect parasites.

A leaf nest, "drey," is built in the fork of a limb. This nest consists of twigs intertwined in such a way as to provide a platform to hold up the walls of other twigs and branches bearing leaves. While it has the haphazard appearance of a crow's nest, it is actually a compact structure impervious to wind and rain. All of the nesting materials are taken from, or from close by, the same tree.

If the nest is to be a seasonally permanent one, it is given a protective covering of leaves and an opening is

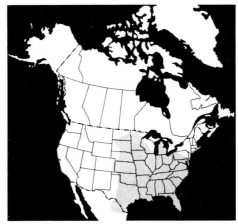

Fox squirrel (Population of about 300 on Pelee Island, Ontario)

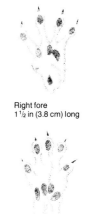

Right fore
1 ½ in (3.8 cm) long

Right hind
2 in (5.1 cm) long

provided as an entrance. If it is to be used only for a brief period (such as a resting place while enjoying a few weeks' feast of nearby ripening corn), it may be nothing more than a casually constructed pile of twigs and leaves. Both types of leaf nests, however, are generally in disarray by the time autumn arrives and are then abandoned in favor of tree dens. New nests are built the following year.

Young fox squirrels, generally a litter of three, are born after a gestation period of between 42 and 45 days. Blind and hairless, except for the beginning of whiskers, they weigh a mere half ounce (14 g) and are about 4 inches (10 cm) long; their claws at that time, however, are well developed. By the end of their second week they have acquired a warm, downy covering of fur, but it is not until their fifth or sixth week that their eyes open. About that time, under the watchful eye of their mother, they begin cautious wanderings outside the nest and start a new diet of tender leaves and buds. When fully weaned sometime during their third month, they begin feasting on green hickory nuts, acorns and other seeds as well as other vegetation. The young usually stay with their mother until the fall, when they quit the nest and strike out on their own. Some, however, do not leave until the new brood is born the following February or March. Females mature as yearlings, while males are not capable of mating successfully until they are 2 years of age.

Few animals are more solicitous of their young than is a mother squirrel. She will courageously defend

174

The fox squirrel is the largest of the tree squirrels and while it occurs throughout most of the eastern half of the United States, it is found in Canada only on Pelee Island, Lake Erie, where it was introduced about 100 years ago. (Photo by Dr. Donald R. Gunn)

her pups against any intruder and, if necessary, will move the whole brood to another nesting site to provide better protection. Even a male that may have remained with her throughout her time of gestation faces banishment from the nursery. Moves from one nesting site to another are often made even when there are no apparent dangers; what prompts them to do this is not always clear.

All tree squirrels are fun-loving creatures and seem especially to enjoy tantalizing other animals. John Madson (*Gray and Fox Squirrels*) relates this story:

"We once spent a riotous half-hour watching two fox squirrels plague a fat Pekinese at the foot of a big soft maple. The lap dog was beside himself with rage. Hanging upside down on the tree trunk six feet above

the ground, one of the squirrels barked, laughed and swore into the raging Peke's face. As this transpired, the second squirrel sneaked around the trunk only a foot or two above the ground, surprising the dog from the flank. The dog came screaming after this squirrel, which climbed six feet up the trunk to chatter and cuss. Shortly thereafter, the first squirrel spiraled low around the trunk and started the whole thing all over again. For over thirty minutes the two squirrels relayed the frothing little dog—never quite endangering themselves but never going so far up the tree that the dog lost interest."

Not being a hibernator, the fox squirrel must cache away great quantities of nuts to survive the long northern winters. These are not stock-piled, but are buried singly just an inch or so in the ground. Nuts of various kinds provide a balance of concentrated fats, proteins, calcium, carbohydrates, minerals and vitamins. But it takes a lot of cached nuts to sustain a squirrel during the lean months of winter, and it requires extraordinary instinct or sense of direction (and perhaps smell) to locate them when the ground is frozen and covered with snow. But, remarkably, it manages to do this.

Trouble, however, is ahead for all tree squirrels if the mast crop fails. At such times survival can be a struggle if the animals are forced to turn to the less palatable seeds of wild grapes, bittersweet, rose hips, blackberry and hawthorn. Squirrels in need of salts and minerals often chew on shed deer antlers and other bones, as well as tree bark and even telephone cables. Experiments have shown that captive squirrels are able to survive for long periods without water. In the wild, if free-flowing water is not available, they derive it from the moisture in acorns, dew on vegetation, rain caught in tree cavities and snow.

Squirrels have an exceptionally long lifespan for small mammals: some fox squirrels in their natural environment have lived up to 10 years. However, throughout their lives they are preyed upon by a number of enemies such as red-tailed hawks (which often hunt in pairs), red-shouldered hawks, foxes, and raccoons. In some states coyotes, snakes and weasels are serious predators. Man is their greatest enemy, for squirrels are among the most important of all small game species, particularly throughout their much larger United States range.

Tamiasciurus hudsonicus
Red Squirrel

The red squirrel is the most abundant of all the Sciuridae family. Unlike the gray and fox species, whose present ranges are almost totally confined to the eastern half of the United States and a tiny portion of eastern Canada, the range of this little rodent covers almost all of Canada and Alaska south of the treeline, a broad western belt running south to New Mexico and Arizona, and an equally large area taking in the northern midwest and northeastern states. It is closely related to, and is about the size of, the Douglas's squirrel, a Pacific Coast species.

The red squirrel is mainly a resident of coniferous forests although it inhabits areas where there is a mixture of conifers and hardwoods. It prefers evergreens because its main diet consists of their cones, especially the cones of spruces, pines and Douglas fir. Included in its menu, however, are many other foods — nuts of the hardwood trees, buds of leaves and flowers, fruit, insects, grubs, birds' eggs and fledglings. In fact, it is the most carnivorous of all the tree squirrels and has even been known to eat mice, voles and cottontail rabbits. It relishes the sap of maple and birch trees, and frequently eats mushrooms, among them the poisonous "fly amanita" — the mushroom made famous in Allegro's *The Sacred Cross and the Mushroom*.

The red squirrel was first described by Jean Erxleben, a German naturalist, during a visit to Hudson Bay in 1777. While the common name given here is most frequently used, there are some areas where it is called pine squirrel, chickaree, bummer or barking squirrel. Its French-Canadian name is *l'Ecureil rouge, un de la Baie d'Hudson*.

The red squirrel, smaller than the gray but twice the size of a chipmunk, is 11 to 15 inches (28-38 cm) in length, including its tail, and ranges in weight from 4 to 8 ounces (113-227 g). There is a pronounced difference between its summer and winter coloring. In summer it is rusty-yellow to orange on the back and sides, and white on the belly, chest, throat, chin and lips. A black lateral stripe, more distinct in some than in others depending on the area, separates the dark fur of the sides from the white fur of the belly. Its tail varies in color from yellowish-orange to red, but remains constant in color throughout the year, as does the conspicuous white ring around the large, dark eyes. The winter coat, which becomes longer and silkier, changes to reddish-brown on the sides, and the back becomes redder to match the tail. The belly color changes from white to gray and with this change the black lateral stripe is lost. There are two annual molts, the first between April and June and the second between the end of August and the beginning of September.

This noisy, saucy and entertaining creature is one of the best known of small wild animals. It thrives in urban areas where there is a suitable environment,

where it can defiantly raid bird feeders, fruit trees and budding flowers, and where it can create havoc with the peace of mind of dogs and cats by its teasing behavior and aerial acrobatics. In its historic element, the evergreen forests, it is a creature whose presence, loudly announced by ratchet-like scoldings, seldom fails to bring satisfaction to the hearts of wilderness travelers. Its effrontery and lack of fear are equaled only by the Canada Jay, or whiskey jack, and when a rapport is developed between it and humans, it is easily tamed.

The red squirrel is more arboreal than either the gray or fox species. It makes its winter nest sometimes as much as 60 feet (18 m) above ground in the cavities of trees. While it does not hibernate, it will spend days at a time in this den if the weather is too cold or blustery. During summer it occupies a nest, sometimes called a drey, which it constructs out of branches, twigs and leaves, and lines with leaves and other vegetation. These nests are made secure in the forks of limbs and are usually strong enough to withstand heavy wind storms and constructed tightly enough to keep out the rain. Leaves and similar vegetation provide a roof and a small hole is made for an entrance.

It is not unusual, however, for some red squirrels to make their homes in other than tree dens or leaf nests. This is particularly so in the case of red squirrels in more northerly ranges. There they often take up residence in rock piles or under stumps or fallen trees. A good, abandoned nest of a hawk or crow may also be renovated to serve the squirrel's needs.

Red squirrels are capable of successfully mating twice a year, but this is more common among those in southern U.S. ranges. Throughout the colder northern ranges mating takes place from late February to the end of March and, after a gestation period of 35 to 40 days, a litter of four pups (on the average) is born. The second breeding season occurs during June and July.

The pups come into the world naked, blind and deaf. About 10 days later, light soft fur covers most of their bodies, in about 18 days their ears open, and in about a month their eyes open. By this time they are active and playful, but they do not normally leave their nest for another month and a half. Weaning is completed when they are 7 to 8 weeks old, and in the interval between weaning and departure from the nest their mother provides them with their first taste of solid food. Red squirrels remain with their mother until they are about 4½ months of age and then strike out on their

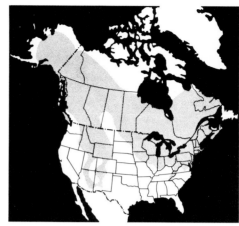

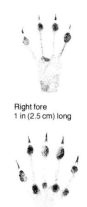

Right fore
1 in (2.5 cm) long

Red squirrel

Right hind
1⁸/₁₀ in (4.6 cm) across
2¹/₁₀ in (5.4 cm) long

own. They become sexually mature and are capable of breeding before the end of their first year.

One of the most interesting behavioral characteristics of the red squirrel is its annual late summer and fall gathering of the green cones of pine, spruce, larch, fir and other coniferous trees. Whereas the gray and fox species laboriously bury nuts of the hardwood trees in the ground (and secrete supplies elsewhere), the red squirrel, after cutting loose and dropping to the ground clusters of cones, moves them to a damp, cool area where they are piled in heaps. The seeds of the cones, protected by the scales, are the winter's main supply of food. By spring all that remains are the scales, in refuse piles known as "middens."

The middens often amount to several bushels of scales, but much larger cones have been recorded. Banfield, for example, writes that "they may measure up to four yards in diameter and one yard in height." Cahalane claims that a midden may be as much as 30 feet (9 m) across and 2 or 3 feet (.6-1 m) deep, while Don Blood reports one midden found in a dense spruce thicket that "was measured at twelve feet in diameter and nine feet deep." Piles as large as this represent annual accumulations going back a number of years.

Like all of the tree squirrels, *Tamiasciurus hudsonicus* is an accomplished mammalian athlete. It displays incredible dexterity in the trees as it races up and down trunks (even running along the underside of limbs!), and makes astonishing long descending leaps between branches. Sometimes it miscalculates and may fall more than 100 feet to the ground. But all tree squirrels are usually able to survive such falls by twisting their bodies to a horizontal position and spreading their tails and legs with parachute effectiveness. In addition, the red squirrel is an accomplished swimmer—probably more so than its cousins—and while water is not its favorite element, it will not hesitate to swim across a river or lake if there is a need to do so.

The lifespan of the red squirrel in the wild is seldom more than 3 years, although some individuals kept in captivity have lived for more than 10 years. Like all creatures it has its enemies—man included. Its natural predators include marten, lynx, bobcat, weasel and several species of hawks. Infant mortality is often high —in some years perhaps as high as 70 per cent—and starvation is largely the cause. The reason for this, as Yorke Edwards points out, is that even those youngsters that survive to leave the care of their parents may still face starvation if they are unable to establish a territory producing an adequate supply of food. "Coniferous trees," he reminds us, "yield annual crops that in some years are heavy, but in other years fail. The years of failure are the years that young squirrels have the smallest chances of survival."

Tamiasciurus douglasii
Douglas's Squirrel

Like certain other small rodents—the black-tailed prairie dog and southern flying squirrel, for example—the Douglas's squirrel occurs minimally in Canada, inhabiting only a narrow strip of coastal British Columbia extending from the Canada/U.S. border north to Owikeno Lake at the head of Rivers Inlet, and east as far as Manning Park (through which runs the Hope-Princeton Highway.) While it occurs on a number of offshore islands, it is not present on Vancouver Island or the Queen Charlottes. Its U.S. range is also limited, being confined to western Washington, western Oregon and northern California. While the Douglas's squirrel is most commonly found in coniferous forests, it also makes its home above the treeline. It also establishes itself in highly populated urban areas where there are stands of coniferous trees and other sources of food. Wherever it lives it is a cheerful little creature whose vigorously twitching tail and loud scolding chatter are as entertaining vocalizations of forest life as the wheezy voice of the boreal chickadee.

Douglas's squirrel

This squirrel, first identified by the Scottish botanist David Douglas, who visited British Columbia in 1825 as a collector for the Royal Horticultural Society, very closely resembles the red squirrel, *T. hudsonicus*. (Douglas is primarily famous for his discovery of the fir which bears his name). For some strange reason, however, even though the red squirrel is found in more parts of North America than any other member of the squirrel family, it is rarely found in the Douglas's squirrel's range.

The Douglas's squirrel, also known as chickaree, and less well-known as yellow-belly, piney sprite, and western red squirrel, has the characteristics of the other tree squirrels, with only slight differences in living and eating habits. Its most commonly used home is in the natural cavity of a tree or an abandoned woodpecker hole. Less frequently than do other squirrels, it will also build a nest in the fork of a tree or modify an abandoned nest of a hawk or crow. Those living at higher wilderness elevations beyond the timberline make their homes within the protection of loose rocks.

Its diet changes with the seasons—in the fall and winter, the seeds of the cones of coniferous trees; in spring, tree fungi and bark; in summer, fresh green vegetation such as alder catkins, ferns, mushrooms, fruits and berries. Insects and grubs also are eaten. But its mainstay is the cones of pines, fir, hemlock, spruce and sequoias, and each autumn it gathers large quantities of them which it stores in moist places (to keep the seeds tender). Some are stored in the forks of trees, but most are cached in depressions on the forest floor.

Unlike the red squirrel, it seems to have no interest in birds' eggs.

The Douglas's squirrel mates in early spring and bears a litter of four to six pups in May or June. In its southern range there may be a second litter. The young are weaned when they are about 2 months old and at that time they strike out on their own. Establishing their own territories and food supply is not always easy, for intrusion into another's area is quickly repulsed. Many of the less healthy and less aggressive, unable to store up an adequate winter food supply, die of hunger. Those that do survive are full grown and sexually mature by spring. As is the case with other tree squirrels, *T. douglasii* does not hibernate although it will remain in its nest for days at a time if the weather is severe.

Distinguishing between the Douglas's squirrel and the red squirrel is difficult unless one gets a close-up view. The most obvious differences are the Douglas's pronounced orange underparts in summer (which change to a buff-orange in winter) and the red squirrel's summer coloring of white or grayish-white underparts (which change to a silvery-gray in winter).

The Douglas's squirrel is believed to have a lifespan in the wild of about 3 years.

The North American range of the red squirrel is more extensive than that of any other member of the Sciuridae family. It is also more arboreal than either the gray or fox species. (Photo by Dr. Donald R. Gunn)

Glaucomys volans and *Glaucomys sabrinus*

Southern and Northern Flying Squirrels

"We recollect a locality near Philadelphia where, in order to study this interesting species, we occasionally strayed into a meadow containing immense oak and beech trees. One afternoon in the beginning of autumn we took our seats on a log to watch their lively motions. The birds had retired to the forest. The Night-Hawk had already commenced his low evening flight. Here and there the common red bat was on the wing. Still, for some time, not a Flying Squirrel appeared. Suddenly one emerged from its hole; another soon followed, and ere long dozens came forth and commenced their graceful flights from branch to bough. One would dart from the topmost branches of a tall oak, and with wide-extended membranes and outspread tail glide diagonally through the air to the foot of a tree about fifty yards off. At the moment we expected to see it strike the earth it suddenly turned upwards and alighted on the body of the tree, then sailed back again to the tree it had just left. Crowds of these little creatures joined in these sportive gambols — there could not have been less than two hundred gliding spirits." John James Audubon, *The Viviparous Quadrupeds of North America*, Vol. 1

It isn't likely that either James Audubon or his friend John Bachman, if alive today, would see such a

Flying squirrels do not really fly—they glide. A loose fold of skin, when stretched taut by extending the front and hind legs, serves as a parachute. (Photo by Wayne Lankinen/Valan Photos)

sight again, for flying squirrels, like so many other little mammals, are now far less numerous than they once were. Both the southern flying squirrel (*Glaucomys volans*) and the northern flying squirrel (*Glaucomys sabrinus*) are, like bats, strictly creatures of the night and to see either in its natural habitat is often more a matter of good luck than of good planning. But all things are possible, and it may be that in a remote woodlot somewhere, 200 "gliding spirits" still go through their acrobatic routines nightly among the oaks, maples and hickories.

While the southern and northern species are closely related, the former may be only half the weight and an inch or so shorter. Both of course have the same loose fold of skin which, when stretched taut by extending the front and hind legs, serves as parachute and sail. The southern flying squirrel can be distinguished from the northern species by the pure white of the underparts; the underparts of the northern squirrel are gray colored. Both species are grayish on the back and sides, but in the southern there is an overlay of tannish fur on the upper parts, while in the northern there are beige-colored hairs. The fur is soft and silky and molts once a year in autumn. Both have large, black eyes and eyelids, and large ears. In artificial light the eyes reflect a brilliant ruby red. Their tails are bushy, flat and

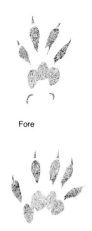

Fore

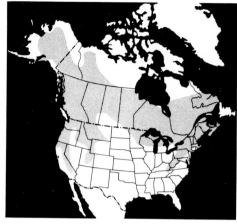

Southern flying squirrel

Hind
3/4 in (1.9 cm) long

Northern flying squirrel

rounded at the tip. They act effectively as rudder and horizontal stabilizer while in flight.

The southern flying squirrel occurs in Canada only in southern and eastern Ontario. It has yet to be recorded in the latitude of Algonquin Park. In the United States its range extends west over nearly two-thirds of the continent as far south as the Gulf of Mexico. It is not found in New England nor in the southern tip of Florida.

The northern flying squirrel occurs primarily in Canada, over nearly a coast-to-coast range. It is present in Yukon and western Northwest Territories, but is not a resident of Newfoundland, Anticosti Island, Vancouver Island or the Queen Charlottes. Its United States range includes parts of northern California, Idaho, Montana, Utah, Wyoming, Wisconsin, Michigan, New York and New England. It occurs as well in the Appalachian Mountains and is also present in Alaska.

As do all squirrels, the flying species make two types of nests: for winter use they utilize a natural cavity in a tree or an abandoned woodpecker's hole; for summer use they may take over an abandoned crow's nest or build a nest of their own in the fork of a tree. The exterior summer nest is also known as a "drey." The tree den, as well as the nest, may be anywhere from 5 to 50 feet (1.5-15 m) above ground.

The southern flying squirrel mates during two periods—February and March, and again from late May through July. The northern flying squirrel also has two mating periods—March and again in May. The gestation period for both is about 40 days and litter sizes range from two to six, with the average being about three.

The young, born hairless, sightless and deaf, weigh less than an ounce (28 g). In about 3 weeks their eyes open, and by their fourth week they are well furred and have gained their eyesight. Nursing continues until their fifth week and at that time weaning begins. By their sixth or eighth week they look exactly like adults, except for their small size. Sexual maturity is reached at the age of 1 year.

Flying squirrels are not only strictly nocturnal, they are also mainly arboreal, preferring to spend most of the time resting in their dens or nests, stretched out in basking fashion on the limbs of trees, feasting on buds, blossoms and bark, or playfully gliding from one branch or tree to another. Considerable foraging nevertheless is done on the ground, especially when hickory nuts and acorns have fallen and when seeds of various kinds as well as fruits, berries, and mushrooms have ripened. Ground foraging also includes insects, birds' eggs and nestlings, and occasionally meat if available. Both species store food for winter use, especially hickory nuts and acorns. Hazelnuts and beechnuts are also favorites. Various places are used as larders—in forks and hollows of trees, in their winter tree dens and sometimes in the ground itself.

Although known as "flying" squirrels, these little mammals do not actually fly: they really glide. Even so, it is a remarkable capability. Ted Kober, a man rich in

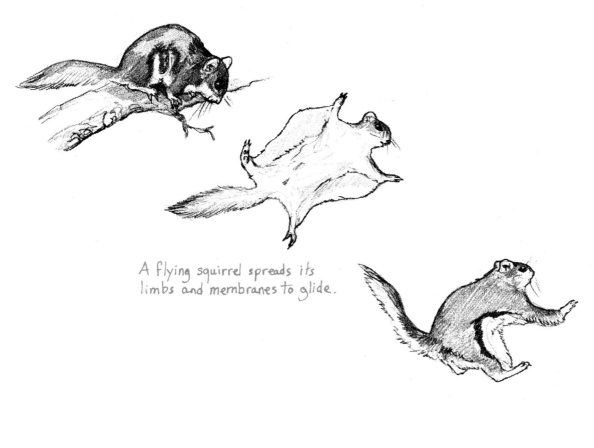

A flying squirrel spreads its
limbs and membranes to glide.

wilderness knowledge, once told me of seeing a squirrel launch itself into the air from a height of about 60 feet (18 m) and glide nonstop at about a 40 degree angle. "When halfway through the glide," he related, "it corrected its course to the left and before it landed it braked, changed its swoop slightly upwards, and settled gracefully on a limb about 10 feet above ground. It was poetry in motion."

Both flying squirrels are considered among the most desirable of all small animals. They have no bad habits from man's point of view (although northerns sometimes try to take bait set in cubbies for marten and often get trapped themselves), and they make remarkably gentle and responsive pets. Their natural enemies include owls, hawks, raccoons, weasels and bobcats. So attractive and harmless are these little creatures, in fact, that any human going out of his way to destroy them should take no pride in the act.

Flying squirrels live for about 5 to 6 years in the wild and perhaps up to 10 in captivity.

FAMILY CASTORIDAE

Castor canadensis

American Beaver

The American beaver is the only North American member of the Castoridae family, and next to the capybara of South America (a sort of outsized guinea pig) it is the world's largest rodent. During the Pleistocene, when woolly mammoths roamed central Alaska and pigs as large as rhinos inhabited Africa, 9-foot-long (2.7 m) beavers, weighing as much as 800 pounds (363 kg), lived in North America.

In the evolutionary process, beavers became smaller and smaller, and today, on average, they weigh 40 to 60 pounds (18-27 kg) and, including tail, are 3 to 4 feet (1-1.2 m) in length. An exceptionally large one would weigh 100 pounds (45 kg) or more. Incidentally, a smaller species of western rodent, 12 to 18 inches (30-46 cm) in length and weighing about 2½ pounds (1 kg), is known as "mountain beaver," but this animal is not a real beaver at all. It is the only surviving member of a family known as Aplodontidae and it looks like a tailless muskrat.

Beavers are remarkable animals in a number of ways. Not only do they alter their environment to meet their own special requirements for survival, but they do it in ways that show skills as tree fallers, hydraulic engineers, land developers and house builders. While they may move from one locality to another, and live in a number of homes during their lifetime, they are devoted and faithful and once mated generally remain with their partners until one or the other dies.

Beavers have other credentials, not the least important being the role they played in the exploration and colonization of the North American continent. When the explorer John Cabot reported that the Grand Banks off Newfoundland were "swarming with fish," European fishermen in increasing numbers braved the North Atlantic to harvest the resource. The rich rewards that came from the fishery beckoned other entrepreneurs and adventurers who were eager to explore the land and to seek the wealth it had to offer. By the time Samuel de Champlain arrived at Quebec, in 1603, as the representative of the French fur monopolists, the fur trade had become more profitable than the fishery—and the animals that were the most prized of all were the beavers.

The search for beavers, coupled with exploration, charting and mapmaking, led men far and wide into the interior of the New World. Some, among them Radisson, Des Groseillers, de la Verendrye and Champlain himself, won permanent places in North American history. It was largely due to the exploits of Radisson and Des Groseillers, in fact, that the Hudson's Bay Company was founded and exploration and colonization of North America began in earnest.

Beavers, although exterminated in some places, inhabit most of North America from the Mexican border north to the fringes of the treeline in Canada and throughout the central and southern parts of Alaska. At one time, as recently as 1930, because of worldwide demand for their furs, they became an endangered species. Fortunately controlled harvesting methods and low fur prices reversed the trend and the animals are now secure in most of their ranges.

There is no accurate estimate of their numbers, but some years ago a helicopter survey crew of the Ontario Ministry of Natural Resources found 425 active beaver colonies in a 184-square-mile (477 km²) area of the northern part of the province. This was a very small study area, and it left to speculation the total beaver population of the whole of Ontario's 412,582 square miles (1,068,587 km²), not to mention the rest of Canada and the United States. One thing was clear: beavers are not only numerically secure, but in some places may even be too numerous for their own good.

Beavers at one time were exclusively land mammals, but as they evolved they adapted to what is now their main environment—lakes, streams and ponds where dams can be constructed and lodges erected, and where trees and other vegetation assure a plentiful supply of food. The extraordinary lifestyle of *C. canadensis* calls for extraordinary physique. I was on the point of also describing them as extraordinarily intelligent. Fortunately Yorke Edwards, who has studied them in their natural habitat, prevented me from repeating that common error. "Their intelligence is a myth," he corrected me. "They are, however, 'remarkable' engineers, but I suspect it is mostly genetic programming—innate behavior patterns. 'Instinct', if you will, but that word is much misused too."

Physically the beaver is chunky, somewhat rotund and high-rumped. Its head is broad and its eyes are small. Its nose and ears have valvular flaps which close when the animal is under water. On each side of the face are long, stiff whiskers. The beaver's senses of

Next to South America's capybara, the American beaver is the world's largest rodent, averaging 40 to 60 pounds in weight (18-27 kg). (Photo by Val and Alan Wilkinson/Valan Photos)

smell and hearing are well developed.

The distinguishing characteristic of the beaver's head, however, is its large orange-colored upper and lower incisors which, as in all rodents, never stop growing and must be constantly ground down to keep them sharp and at "workable" lengths. In the process of keeping growth in check, the animal frequently will pause when cutting down a tree to deliberately resharpen the incisors by gnashing the two top ones against the lower two. If for some reason the beaver is unable to control growth, the teeth eventually curve back into the jaws and the animal dies a dreadful death.

A feature of the beaver is its tail—a paddle-like appendage up to a foot (30 cm) or so in length and 7 inches (18 cm) in width. It serves a number of useful functions.

Most wild creatures have alarm signals. A pronghorn will flare its white rump patch and make it perform like a heliograph, a mountain sheep will suddenly change from a relaxed to a rigid stance, a squirrel will chatter excitedly, and a chaffinch, throwing its voice like a ventriloquist, will make a high-pitched, prolonged whistle when a sparrowhawk is swooping overhead. The beaver, when alarmed, will slap its powerful tail hard on the surface of the water, generally submerging with a splash when it does so. At dusk, in the quiet of the wilderness, the sound is often as loud and as startling as a rifle shot.

The beaver's tail also serves as a very sturdy prop

when the animal stands on its hind feet to cut down a tree. When it is swimming, the tail acts as a rudder, enabling it to steer a straight course or change direction at will. When the beaver is walking upright and using its front legs to carry or drag tree branches, the tail acts as a counterbalance. It does not serve, as some people have been led to believe, as a trowel for plastering mud on lodges or dams.

Most nature writers discredit the suggestion that the beaver uses its tail to carry its young, but this sometimes does happen. In a personal communication, Mme. Françoise Patenaude-Pilote, of the Biology Department of Laval University, Quebec City, stated that occasionally an adult *will* carry its young in that fashion. Mme. Patenaude-Pilote said that she observed such behavior during field studies in Gatineau Park, Quebec, and that the same behavior was noted at least once by an associate, Erwin F. Oertli, during his field studies in Alberta.

The beaver's tail, which on average is about 1½ inches (3.5 cm) thick, is covered with leathery scales, although it is heavily furred at the base. A considerable amount of fat is built up in it during the summer and fall months and provides a source of energy throughout the winter. Beaver tail soup is considered a delicacy by those who like wild game.

Other remarkable features of the beaver's anatomy are its front and hind feet. Those at the front are shorter and are used with great dexterity as it carries out its daily activities, such as holding and turning branches to nibble away at their succulent bark or foliage, or as it constructs or repairs dams and lodges. When the beaver is swimming, either on the surface or under water, the fully-webbed hind feet provide the main means of propulsion and are capable of thrusting the animal forward at 2 or 3 miles (3-5 km) an hour, a speed considerably less than that attained by the otter. When swimming, the forepaws are tucked against the chest as little fists.

The front and hind feet are used for grooming the fur. Two large castor glands and two smaller glands are present in the anal region of both males and females. Whether, as has been stated in some literature, the oil in the smaller glands is released to be deliberately brushed into the fur by the beaver's front paws as a grooming agent is yet to be proved. Mme. Patenaude-Pilote writes that during the Gatineau Park studies she and her associates noted that the animals were only passing their forepaws *close* to the orifices of the anal

American beaver

Right fore
3 in (7.6 cm) across
2¾ in (7 cm) long

Hind
5¼ in (13 cm) across
6½ in (17 cm) long

glands, but that the glands themselves were not systematically touched during the grooming. The importance of the anal glands for the water-repellent quality of the fur is not clear, she noted.

The two large castor glands produce a sweet, musky-smelling yellowish fluid which is released by the beaver at various places to establish its territorial rights. These glands, once thought to have medicinal value, are now used in the manufacture of some perfumes.

It is the dense underfur of the beaver's pelage which makes its pelt valuable. This silky, slightly curly fur, brown in color and about an inch (2.5 cm) long, is protected by guard hairs nearly 3 inches (8 cm) in length. The thickness and color of the underfur, when it is in prime condition (from late fall to early winter) determines its value to furriers.

The beaver as a tree faller in some respects is overrated. While it takes about half an hour to gnaw its way through a 5-inch (13 cm) aspen, it cannot always make it fall in any specific direction. It suits the beaver's needs best when trees fall toward water where branches can be chewed off for easy transportation to

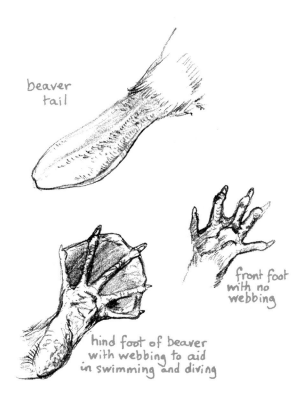

beaver tail

front foot with no webbing

hind foot of beaver with webbing to aid in swimming and diving

the teeth to form a protective barrier, chips are prevented from getting into the animal's mouth. These lips serve the same protective purpose when the beaver is working on wood under water.

Felling trees is a major part of the beaver's life. But there are other important functions — mating, dam building, lodge construction, food harvesting, and the rearing of young. Each spring the 2-year-olds (and sometimes the yearlings) are ejected from the colony or leave voluntarily, to make way for the arrival of the next litter. Since only one colony normally occupies a pond, each of the sexually mature youngsters is forced to find a new habitat. This could be another unoccupied pond or a section of a lake or stream where a dam could be constructed and a lodge built. Inbreeding is not uncommon among beavers, so establishing a home and family is sometimes more quickly accomplished when brother and sister form a union. Beavers generally mate for life.

The dam building begins by embedding sticks, saplings and twigs into the bed of the stream at an angle against the flow of the water. Stones and other pieces of wood are placed at the base on either side for support. Gradually, by adding other sticks as well as mud and stones, a barricade is formed against the current. This work goes on until the dam is completed and, other than a few harmless seepages here and there, the water is impounded and the pond secured.

There is no denying that these dams are engineering marvels. But just as the beaver is unable to control the direction in which a tree may fall, so does it seem unable always to apply logic to its construction decisions. For instance, while dams are always built to stem the flow of water (and thus create ponds), sometimes the widest part of a stream is barricaded rather than a nearby narrows where a dam calling for much less work could have served as useful a purpose. In some cases, dams are built where in fact none are needed. These peculiarities lead to the conclusion that, at least in part, the beaver's working habits are often simply compulsive.

Dams vary in length, height and width. One structure in Teton National Forest, Wyoming, was 1,104 feet (337 m) long. Another recorded by the noted nature writer Sigurd Olson was found in Minnesota and stretched for almost 2,700 feet (820 m). Most dams, even the shortest ones, are extraordinarily strong and to remove them often calls for the use of bulldozers or dynamite. Most, however, have to be capable of holding back enough water to maintain a pond not less than

the lodge or dam, but often they topple the other way, either right to the ground or at angles against other trees. Despite some failures, however, the rate of success is remarkably high.

This industrious little lumberman, working alone, has been known to fall a 100-foot (30 m) tall aspen; in fact, trees 5 or more feet (1.5 m) in diameter have sometimes been cut down, although there is no obvious rationale for tackling such formidable jobs. Not all trees are felled; some are abandoned after being partially cut, perhaps because the beaver was frightened away by a predator.

There is an established pattern for cutting down a tree. Standing on its hind legs, the beaver grasps the tree about shoulder high with its front paws. Then it circles the tree, the lower incisors doing the cutting while the upper incisors act as anchors. Then, still circling, all four incisors wrench off the wood. The chipping usually stops before the core is reached, but the trunk is now so weakened that a stiff breeze, or even the weight of the branches and leaves, is sufficient to topple it. It is a remarkable performance — all the more remarkable in that, by folding its loose lips back behind

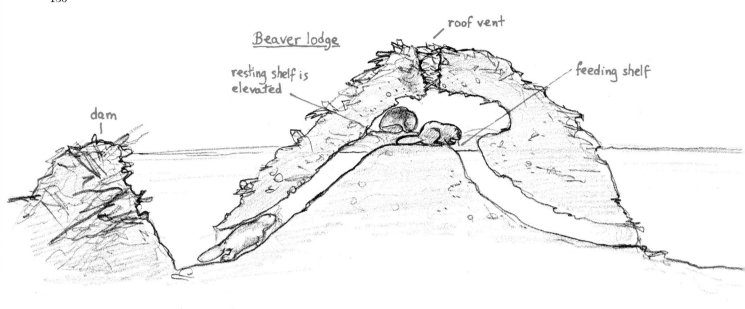

Beaver lodge

roof vent

resting shelf is elevated

feeding shelf

dam

10 feet (3 m) in depth. In the coldest months of winter ponds are covered with several feet of ice and it is essential that enough free water remains to enable the beavers to reach their submerged food supply.

Equally remarkable is the beaver's lodge, which is built in or near the center of the pond or beside the shore; sometimes the lodge is a simple burrow dug into the soft shoreline.

A free-standing lodge surrounded by water resembles a pile of sticks, stones and mud haphazardly heaped together. But underneath this ungainly mound is a cleverly built, insulated shelter. The same materials used to constuct the dam go into the building of the lodge. The floor, constructed on a solid base, sits about 6 inches (15 cm) above the waterline and leading to it are subterranean passageways, one of which is commonly used for movements to and from the pond and the others for escape from predators. The interior of the lodge is generally built on a slight slope. When the animal enters, it first shakes itself free of water and, if hungry, settles down to eat. Water dripping from its body and from the wood it brings in for its meal, runs off into a plunge hole, thus assuring that the ledge-like upper levels, used as sleeping and nursery areas, will remain dry.

While all lodges are roughly similar, not all are the same dimensions. They range from 10 to more than 20 feet (3-6 m) in diameter, and from 6 to 10 feet (2-3 m) in

height. One exceptional lodge was 30 feet (9 m) in diameter.

Busy as they have been in dam and lodge construction, the newly-mated pair must also assemble a supply of food sufficient to meet their winter needs. Throughout the spring and summer they have supplemented their staple diet of bark and leaves from their favorite trees—aspen, willow, poplar and others—with such vegetation as floating duckweed, lilies, green grass and cattails. With the arrival of fall, they stockpile branches of trees under water and close to the main entrance to the lodge. This is done when the leaves have turned color and when the wood contains a good supply of sap and other nutrients. These ingredients prevent leaves and wood from rotting during long periods of submersion. If trees are cut too early, while the sap is still rising, the bark may sour in its underwater storage and become inedible.

Ordinarily transporting branches over rough terrain or through heavy growth of vegetation is a laborious job, so, if creeks are not handy, the beavers frequently dig "canals" along which they can float or pull the branches with a minimum of effort. Canals do not become necessary until the animals have used the trees along the sides of the ponds and are forced to go farther and farther inland. These inland excursions may be for a distance of 500 or 600 feet (150-180 m) from the lodge. At times like these, the animals, slow and somewhat clumsy on land, are most likely to be attacked by predators.

Some of the canals are several hundred feet in length, 3 feet (1 m) wide and 3 feet deep, and are occasionally sectioned off by small dams to assure a proper depth of water. Since the canals are generally formed on flat land and at about the same level as the pond, it is the pond that provides most of the irrigation throughout their length.

Beavers mate *under* water during January and February and the three or four kits (sometimes one or as many as eight) are born in May and June. The infants, fully furred, eyes open and teeth cut, nurse for about 3 months, at which time they are weaned. From then on they subsist on vegetation, although infrequent suckling may still occur.

Man is the beaver's most dangerous enemy and several hundred thousand are trapped each year to meet the demands of the international fur markets. Given a chance to defend itself against natural predators, however, the beaver is a vicious fighter and only the strongest of carnivores (bears, wolves, wolverines, fishers) will challenge it. Otters, living in the same environment, will occasionally attack a beaver and even try to enter the lodge through one of the underwater passageways.

C. canadensis has been accused of being a nuisance, and in some cases this is true. Since the animal is a compulsive dam builder, it frequently constructs them at places where impounded water causes damage by flooding farmlands and orchards and destroying stands of commercially valuable timber. Heavy rains sometimes send these floods on rampages that destroy bridges and wash out road beds. Some streams—migration routes of spawning salmon—are occasionally blocked and must be cleared to allow the salmon's safe passage. But whatever its shortcomings the animal is one of the environment's greatest assets. Wherever beavers take up residence, and long after they have abandoned their homestead, a whole marvelous chain of life benefits. Insects, fish, waterfowl and large and small mammals thrive. In the end, when silt has built up, the pond has been abandoned and the water has been freed to run its normal course, a beaver meadow rich in all the nutrients required for the growth of vegetation remains. Some of the best agricultural areas on the continent owe their superior quality to the multi-talented, industrious beaver.

FAMILY CRICETIDAE

Ondatra zibethicus

Muskrat

Although in a number of ways they resemble and have some of the characteristics of American beavers, muskrats are neither closely related to beavers, nor are they rats. These animals are actually closely related to field mice.

Muskrats occupy more parts of the North American continent than any other mammal, and about the only places they do not occur are the Alaskan and Canadian Arctic tundra, the lower western section of the British Columbia mainland, and the state of Florida. They were introduced to Anticosti Island in the Gulf of St. Lawrence and to Vancouver and Queen Charlotte islands of British Columbia.

In appearance the muskrat is a heavy-bodied animal 16 to nearly 30 inches (40-75 cm) in length, tail included, and weighing 2 to 3 pounds (0.9-1.4 kg). The overall color of its thick glossy fur is dark brown on the back, changing to shades of gray, yellow or red on the sides and gray or white on the belly. A white flash commonly occurs on the throat. Some individuals may be black, fawn or gray, but dark brown is the color that predominates. The underfur is thick and silky.

The muskrat has small beady eyes and small ears, the latter being almost completely hidden by the fur. The nostrils, prominent cheek whiskers, nose, feet and tail are black. Both front feet have four clawed toes and both hind feet have five, those on the hind feet being longer and partially webbed. The forefeet are small and dextrous and, like those of the beaver, are used as hands to hold food and to manipulate materials when building lodges or excavating burrows.

The muskrat is equipped with four $3/4$-inch-long (2 cm), chisel-like incisors which protrude beyond the fleshy, fur-covered lips. When the lips are closed, the animal is able to gnaw on stems and other vegetation without ingesting either water or solid particles. This is also characteristic of the beaver.

Under the skin, close to the muskrat's anus, are two musk glands which become enlarged during the breeding season. These glands contain a very strong-smelling substance that is released in small amounts at numerous points along routes frequented by the animal. As with other animals having comparable glands, the musky smell serves as a means of communication. Their tails, although long and slender, are used as alarm signals much as beavers use theirs. There is not the same resounding smack, of course, but the noise is sufficiently loud to warn others of impending danger.

Although primarily residents of wetlands such as marshes, shallow ponds and quiet streams, these animals sometimes show little fear of humans and if the environment is to their liking will make their homes near heavily populated areas. To casual observers, muskrat lodges may be confused with those of beavers. However, muskrat lodges are considerably smaller and average 3 to 5 feet (1-1.5 m) in height but are very much wider across the base. Muskrats and beavers live reasonably well together and it is not uncommon to come across a pond containing families of both species.

Construction of a muskrat house takes about 3 months and begins in August with the laying of a foundation, or "platform," of mud in the midst of rushes and other marsh vegetation and where the water is a couple of feet deep. When the foundation has been secured, stalks of bullrushes, cattails, pondweed and sedges are then piled up in the shape of a dome. Mud is used as filler and to hold the structure together. As the pile becomes larger the animals work from the underside to excavate one or more channels leading to and through the center of the foundation. This gives them an inside position from which they chew away at the vegetation above until a chamber large enough to serve as family living quarters and nursery is eventually formed. Meanwhile they continue to add to the dome until the roof is completely enclosed.

Not all muskrats build lodges. Many of them live in burrows excavated in the bank of a pond or stream. The entrances to these burrows are always below water level and lead, at upward angles, to chambers large enough to serve as resting quarters and nurseries. Somewhere along the length of each burrow is an inconspicuous ventilation hole which is generally covered with small mounds of vegetation.

Another type of lodge is known as a "push-up". A number of these are made throughout the pond by cutting holes in the ice while it is still thin, then pushing mud and underwater vegetation to the surface where it freezes as a mass and eventually becomes covered with snow. The muskrat shapes a chamber inside these little piles and uses each as a place to renew oxygen, to rest from underwater forays, or to munch on aquatic foods. If necessary, muskrats can stay under water for about 15

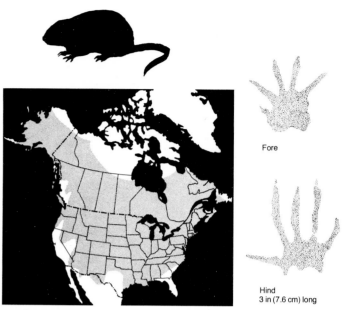

Fore

Hind
3 in (7.6 cm) long

Muskrat

minutes, but the average time of submersion is 3 to 4 minutes. The "push-ups" enable the animal to remain within the pond area for as long as it wishes before returning to the main lodge. They are also used as a means of underwater escape from predators that may invade the main lodge either within or from without. In winter these little resting lodges are often damaged by moose, deer, elk or caribou. The big animals paw at the mounds as they search for food, with the result that the uncovered holes freeze over rapidly. The muskrats must immediately re-open the holes and rebuild the domes.

Muskrats mate in the spring and observers report that at that time the males are competitive and ill-tempered. The gestation period for each mated female is less than 4 weeks, and while the litters vary in size, the average appears to be about six. Tom H. Northcott (*Our Land and Sea Mammals*) writes, however, that in Newfoundland litter sizes may be as few as one or as many as 11. In the northern part of their continental range the animals mate two, and occasionally three times during a season. Dr. Northcott, incidentally, says that in that province muskrat lodges, so common through the rest of the country, are virtually unknown and that the animals there prefer to make their dens in excavated burrows.

The young at birth are naked and blind, but within 2 weeks they have acquired a coat of silky gray fur, their eyes have opened and they are able to take to water. They are weaned at about a month, at which time they become independent of family ties. Kits are mature as yearlings.

Although muskrats do not hibernate, they sleep a great deal during the winter months, and spend the rest of their time in foraging for food in their underwater territory. A typical territory, in both winter and summer, is not much more than 75 to 100 yards beyond the main lodge. In mild weather, if breaks occur in the ice surface, they may move about in the open for short periods, but at such times they are highly vulnerable to attack from predators.

Muskrats are preyed upon by a number of carnivores—wolves, foxes, coyotes, badgers, fishers, mink and otter, for example. Large pike and snapping turtles take an underwater toll, while birds of prey such as eagles and goshawks strike from the air. But the muskrat, given half a chance, fights back ferociously and with great courage in relation to its size, and uses its sharp incisors to advantage.

Man has been, and no doubt always will be, the muskrat's greatest enemy. Each year, under controlled programs, about 10 million prime pelts are harvested in North America and processed into much sought-after fur garments, perhaps traditionally the best known being coats and fur trimmings once known as "Hudson seal." Despite what appears to be an enormous take, there are few if any areas where total populations are endangered. Dr. Northcott, in fact, writes that "if the trapper leaves two pairs of muskrats per acre this will be sufficient to produce next year's crop." Such is the fecundity of *O. zibethicus.*

For reasons not yet fully understood, muskrats experience drastic declines every 7 to 10 years, and it takes 1 to 2 years for their numbers to be restored. In the wild, their lifespan is thought to be 3 to 4 years. Captive muskrats have lived as long as 10 years.

FAMILY ERETHIZONTIDAE

Erethizon dorsatum
Porcupine

The porcupine is slow-moving, bow-legged, and pigeon-toed. It spends almost half of its life in trees. It has a keen sense of smell and touch, its hearing is excellent, it is an accomplished swimmer, but it can see well only at close range. Next to the beaver, it is North America's largest rodent and in its prime can reach a length of 3 feet (1 m) and a weight of nearly 40 pounds (18 kg). Its scientific name, translated literally, means "the irritable back."

A million or so years ago, during the Pleistocene, it crossed the Isthmus of Panama from South America and, in time, took possession of the land as far north as the Northwest Territories, Yukon and Alaska. Today it is found in every province of Canada except Newfoundland and the offshore islands of both coasts. Its northern range extends to the end of the tree line. In the United States it occurs in all states except those in the southeastern part of the continent. It is present in the eastern portions of California and also in most of Alaska.

Like many mammals, its numbers have been drastically reduced and while not an endangered species its future must be watched. This is especially so since it produces only one offspring annually (rarely twins). Its lifespan may be as long as 10 years.

Structurally the porcupine is a chunky mammal characterized by a small head, high-arching back, short legs and thick tail. The whole upper part of the body, including its tail, is covered with quills and these (except for those on the rump and tail) are hidden under the fur. Its feet, equipped with long curved claws, are well suited for climbing. The overall color is black or brown. In most individuals the long guard hairs are yellow-tipped.

The porcupine, primarily a night wanderer, is active all year. It is normally a citizen of forest regions but is found occasionally on the prairies and frequently on farmlands. Ideal porcupine habitat is areas where there are both deciduous and coniferous trees for winter feeding, open spaces with an abundance in summer of edible herbaceous plants, and sheltered places for denning.

The porcupine is not one to be trifled with. There are about 30,000 quills—many of them 3 to 4 inches (8-

Muskrats resemble beavers in many respects and are sometimes mistaken for them. They are not, however, members of the same family. Millions of these mammals are harvested each year and their fur used in the manufacture of garments. (Photo by Mark Nyhof)

10 cm) long—on most of the *upper* body from the eyes all the way to the end of the tail. They lie neatly hidden between the heavy outercoat of guard hairs and the thick, woolly undercoat, and can spring into action in an instant. When attacked, the porcupine erects its quills, stiffens its legs, arches its back, and lowers its head to the ground. Invariably it faces away from its enemy in a close encounter and uses its tail as its main armament.

Long proved false, of course, is the claim that porcupines "throw" their quills. Actually the older tail quills are only lightly attached and are easily dislodged and shot out for a distance of several feet when the tail is thrashed back and forth defensively. Other fallacies are that quills can be easily removed from the victim's skin by cutting the shaft to let out the air, or that quills can be softened by soaking them with solvents. The shaft of the quill is *not* hollow and solvents have no effect. The only sure method of removal is to jerk them out sharply with a pair of pliers. Quills, incidentally, are constantly replaced on the porcupine.

Very few predators, other than the wily fisher, wolverine and bobcat—all excellent climbers—can cope successfully with the porcupine's quills or the animal's method of defense. Most others that try—coyotes, bears, foxes, cougars, dogs, and raptors such as eagles —generally depart in haste with dozens of these needle-sharp, barbed spears imbedded in their heads and other parts of their bodies. While the quills themselves are not poisonous, they are often the cause of death if the victim is unable to swallow food or water, or if infection sets in. If removal is possible, as is generally the case with men and dogs, the operation and recuperation may be painful.

The porcupine is generally a quiet creature but becomes more vocal during the mating season. At this time the male can be heard serenading the female with humming and grunting sounds, the female often responding with resounding squeals. When defending against an adversary, both sexes click their teeth loudly. But the porcupine's sounds are not that easily classified, for they can also coo, whine, sing and screech. Many a camper has heard the spine-tingling screech of an animal that later was found to be a porcupine only a few weeks old.

Porcupines go through a courting performance that few humans have seen. Those who have witnessed the ritual, which takes place during November and December, report that for a week or so prior to accepting a mate the female appears restless, will run for no apparent reason, and will climb up and down trees several times a day. It will make moaning sounds, chatter its teeth and make sobbing noises that are almost human-like. When the male, whining as it goes, finally finds a receptive female, each checks the other's odors and they may even rub noses. All being equal, an understanding is reached, but the female submits only when it is ready, and that may be several days later.

When the great moment arrives, the two perform a love dance. Rising on their hind legs, they approach each other, all the while making low cooing and grunting noises. They may embrace by placing their paws on each other's shoulders, and they may again nuzzle noses. They may even slap each other on the head and sometimes knock one another over with solid body blows. The actual copulation—and beware the impa-

The porcupine is North America's second largest rodent, an adult male often reaching a weight of nearly 40 pounds (18 kg). This mammal, which reached our continent from South America about a million years ago, is widely dispersed, even as far north as Alaska, Yukon and the Northwest Territories. (Photo by Mark Nyhof)

tient male — is made possible by both animals simply relaxing and posturing in such a way as to render the quills harmless. With nature, nothing is impossible.

Along about mid-May and continuing until the end of July, the young are born in caves, in the hollows among tree roots or cavities in rock outcrops. Because of the long gestation period — 209 to 217 days — the babies emerge, eyes open and weighing about a pound (0.5 kg), with a coat of thick black hair and well-developed incisor teeth. Their quills are about an inch (2.5 cm) long, and although soft at first, quickly harden and in a matter of hours are capable of starting the life-time defensive job they were designed for. About a month after coming into the world the young are weaned.

On most charges of being pillagers and nuisances, porcupines would have to plead guilty. Every year they cost the forest industry thousands of dollars by eating the inner bark of, and thus killing, merchantable ponderosa pine, lodgepole pine, tamarack, fir and spruce. Their fondness for seedlings, pine needles and the tender tops of trees adds to the destruction. Forestry people, in fact, will tell you that a lumber camp, operating or abandoned, is the animal's *pièce de résistance*. Doors, steps, tools with wooden handles, boats, toilet seats, even buildings themselves are prey to its beaver-like teeth. This is especially so of anything carrying the salty residue of human perspiration or urine.

Since their food supply, especially in winter, comes largely from trees, the little pellets they evacuate consist mainly of wood fiber. The animals themselves smell somewhat like fermented wood, an odor thought to come from the bark of trees as it goes through the digestive system. The summer appetite of the porcupine, however, is more varied. In its natural habitat it consumes many varieties of ground vegetation as well as the leaves and twigs of trees. It gnaws on discarded deer antlers or bone remains of dead animals for their nutrients. The inner bark, or cambium, of trees, however, is its favorite natural food. In areas close to human habitation it will feast on clover, geraniums, corn, lettuce, cabbage and cauliflower. One individual was seen to consume a bar of soap and there are reports of porcupines tackling automobile tires that have been "cologned" by dogs. One porcupine, in fact, ate a quantity of chloride of lime — and survived! In the summer of 1944, relates Yorke Edwards, porcupines living in an area of Ontario's Highway No. 7 suffered heavy mortality as a result of their liking for the calcium

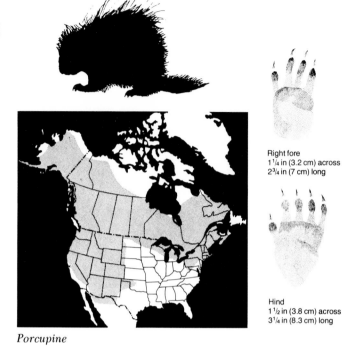

Right fore
1¼ in (3.2 cm) across
2¾ in (7 cm) long

Hind
1½ in (3.8 cm) across
3¼ in (8.3 cm) long

Porcupine

chloride used to lay the summer dust. It was not the chemical that killed them — it was their inability to move away quickly enough from traffic!

While not overly endowed with intelligence, the porcupine gets along well enough in its own environment and is as self-sufficient as any wild mammal. Its relationships with humans also suggest a reasonable degree of comprehension and intelligent reaction, for in captivity it can make an interesting pet and can be taught to respond to its name and to commands. Even old porcupines, when tamed, can be gentle and affectionate.

The porcupine may be one of the most maligned of our wild mammals, but it is part of the natural order of things and so it belongs. The damage it does to our forests and garden crops is infinitesimal in relation to man's predations. After all, the worst crime it can be accused of is pursuing its daily task of survival, and that is every creature's right. The boxes, baskets, moccasins and jackets made by Indians and beautifully decorated with quills are a treasured part of native artistry. For that significant contribution to our heritage, the porcupine deserves thanks.

FAMILY CAPROMYIDAE

Myocastor coypus

Nutria (Coypu)

The nutria (also known as coypu) is of South American origin and was brought to this continent for the purpose of establishing a new fur-farming industry. The venture was not generally successful as only the fur of the belly is marketable, but the mammal itself, largely as a result of its escape from transplant areas, is now wild in a number of places. Today it is found in large numbers in Louisiana (to which it was introduced first in 1938) and in Oregon. At one time, according to Dr. Stephen Seater, the population of nutria in Louisiana totaled some 20 million individuals, but this number was reduced by extensive pelting by the fur industry and by devastation in 1957 resulting from Hurricane Audrey. Nutria colonies later became established in Maryland, New Jersey and Washington. In Canada small numbers occur in extreme southeastern British Columbia and, according to Banfield, "in the Whitefish River drainage of Thunder Bay district, Ontario, and in the Ottawa River drainage of western Quebec and eastern Ontario." Expansion of its population in Canada has been inhibited since the mammal is primarily a creature of warmer climates and is unable to endure the severity of the northern regions.

This mammal is sometimes mistaken for a large muskrat or a small beaver, but what quickly sets it apart is its long, scaly and rounded tail. (The tail of a muskrat is flattened vertically while the tail of a beaver is flattened horizontally). The nutria's habitat — marshes, streams and other wetlands — is similar.

The nutria is a robust creature, generally brownish in color (the tip of the chin and muzzle are white) with a large head and small ears and eyes. Its hind feet are longer than its forefeet, which is also a characteristic of beaver and muskrat. Its incisor teeth, like those of the beaver, extend beyond the lips and are dark orange in color. While the toes of the front feet are not webbed, the first four toes of the hind feet are. Adults, depending on geography, range in length from about 30 to nearly 55 inches (76-140 cm), and weigh 15 to 25 pounds (7-11 kg).

Nutria live in colonies and make their homes and nests in burrows along the banks of water areas where there is an abundance of aquatic vegetation. If the habitat is not suitable for burrowing, nests are often built on shore or even in shallow water. The nests themselves are made of a variety of plant material, and sometimes "platforms," also made of vegetation, are constructed in shallow water and are used for grooming, for feeding or as places to escape from terrestrial predators.

These mammals mate several times annually and each litter consists of 4 to 6 young, although on occasion a litter may be as few as 1 or as many as 11. The young are fully furred when from 7 to 8 weeks of age. Nutria, like all aquatic mammals, are excellent swimmers. Their diet is made up almost wholly of vegetable matter. Like the lagomorphs they re-ingest their fecal pellets, not only to complete digestion of the food but to benefit from the nutrients the pellets contain.

Nutria unfortunately are undesirable in some areas because they compete with muskrats or other more valuable fur-bearing mammals and because their burrowing damages irrigation ditches and dams. If they occur in large numbers, they also deplete the food supply of other mammals. They have a long lifespan, particularly in captivity when they may live as long as 10 years.

ORDER LAGOMORPHA

RABBITS, HARES AND PIKAS

Members of this order are rabbits, hares and pikas. Of these the tiny pika (pronounced "peeka"), which belongs to the family Ochotonidae, is relatively unknown to most people because of its limited range and isolated mountainous habitat. Rabbits and hares, which belong to the family Leporidae, inhabit orchards, meadows, sagebrush plains, forests, swamps and some the Arctic tundra, and are among the most easily recognized of all small mammals. They are known as lagomorphs, a term which means "hare shape."

At one time members of this order were classified as rodents, but taxonomists have found sufficient evidence to support the hypothesis that lagomorphs come from a totally different ancestry. The most visible anatomical difference is their teeth. Adult lagomorphs have two pairs of upper incisors, a smaller pair being immediately behind the pair in front, whereas rodents have only one pair of upper incisors. Scientists now believe that lagomorphs may have evolved from the same type of mammals that gave rise to present-day deer and elk.

Rabbits and hares, while similar in appearance, are structurally different and have different lifestyles and behavioral patterns. The most noticeable structural difference is that hares have longer legs and larger ears and are generally larger overall. Adult lagomorphs molt in the spring and again in the fall. In rabbits the brown fur of summer is replaced with winter fur that is more grayish than brown. The brown fur of most native hares

Lagomorphs, such as this Arctic hare, may have evolved from the same type of ancestors that gave rise to present-day deer and elk. Before dismissing this as far-fetched, consider the fact that some evolutionists believe that humans are descended from tree shrews! (Photo by Dr. David R. Gray)

Rabbits are compact. Legs and ears are shorter than in hares.

Hares have larger ears and longer legs. Hares do not live in burrows as rabbits do, and escape enemies by running.

Pikas are also called rock rabbits. They have short rounded ears.

on the other hand, particularly of those living in cold, snowy regions, turns white.

Rabbits and hares are noted for their prodigious fecundity. In fact, according to Banfield, the eastern cottontail (*Sylvilagus floridanus*) is capable of producing three or more litters a year, with each litter numbering two to seven young (average 5.6). Baby rabbits are born naked and blind, whereas baby hares come into the world fully furred, with their eyes open. Rabbits also build nests that are carefully lined with grass and fur plucked from the mothers' underparts, whereas the young of hares are generally dropped in indifferently scraped-out depressions in the ground.

Pikas, although true lagomorphs, more closely resemble guinea pigs than they do rabbits or hares. They are the smallest of the order, an average adult weighing about 4 ounces (113 g), as opposed, for example, to an adult snowshoe hare which may weigh more than 3 pounds (1.4 kg). Pikas are found in mountainous country of western North America. It is believed they have one litter a year at which time they bear three or four young.

Rabbits and hares are usually more active at night than during the day, whereas pikas are primarily diurnal. While some species of rabbits form into small groups, hares are inclined to be more solitary. Both groups of leporids, however, are often easy prey for predators, although they make good use of their highly developed senses of hearing and smell in detecting danger. When alarmed, they thump the ground with their hind feet as a warning to others, causing vibrations that can be detected for considerable distances. They then try to find safety in burrows, caves or rock crevices. When cornered or captured, they utter shrill screams. Pikas, while diurnal in habit, are less easy to

Rodents have large single sets of incisors (beaver).

Pikas, hares and rabbits have double sets of incisors (pika).

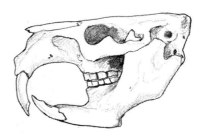

capture for they generally live among talus rocks where they can squeeze for safety into openings too small for most predators to enter. Were it not for the amazing capacity of lagomorphs to reproduce themselves, these creatures would long ago have become extinct. Even so, it is estimated that nearly all die or fall victim to predators during their first year. Few mammals are more important in the food chain.

Lagomorphs have an unusual system of recycling their food. When partially digested, and while the animal is resting, the food is ejected from the anus as soft fecal pellets and then taken back into the mouth, chewed and swallowed. The purpose of this process, known as reingestion, is to enable the creature to derive the greatest amount of nutrients, such as the B vitamins and nitrogen, contained in the pellets. When expelled again they are the round, hard pellets so easily recognized as rabbit or hare scats.

FAMILY OCHOTONIDAE

Ochotona collaris
Collared Pika

Ochotona princeps
Rocky Mountain Pika

These two lagomorphs are the only North American representatives of a family commonly found in a number of Asian countries, among them U.S.S.R., Iran, Afghanistan, Turkey, Tibet and Japan. Twelve species make up the Old World family.

Although the word "lagomorph" literally means "hare-shape" and is therefore a logical classification for hares and rabbits, it doesn't seem to fit this little creature, whose general shape is more like that of a guinea pig. However, the pika possesses sufficient structural characteristics to qualify it for inclusion in the lagomorph group, one being the double set of upper incisors similar to that found in their relatives. For the most part, though, they are distinctive not only in appearance but in size, habitat and lifestyle.

The two North American species closely resemble their Old World counterparts. They are all small, weighing about 4 to 4¹/₂ ounces (113-128 g), and measuring about 6¹/₂ to 8¹/₂ inches (16-22 cm) in length and 3 inches (8 cm) in height; their heads are short and blunt, their ears are rounded and prominent, they have no visible tail and their legs are short. Their fur, which is long, thick and silky, ranges on the upper sides from near-black through various shades of brown, brownish-gray or cinnamon-buff, to grayish or creamy-white on the belly. The soles of the feet, other than the small black plantar pads on each, are heavily furred. Pikas, unlike leporids, which are primarily nocturnal, are most active during daylight hours.

The collared pika is strictly a northern species whose range extends from the southwest corner of northern British Columbia to most of the Yukon (with a spill-over into west-central Northwest Territories) and to southern Alaska. The Rocky Mountain pika is found irregularly throughout the southern half of British Columbia (with a spill-over into western Alberta) and then south to eastern California. It also occurs in Idaho, Montana, Utah, Wyoming, Colorado and northern New Mexico. A small population occurs in the central part of northern Nevada.

These little mammals are colonial and make their

1. *Collared pika*
2. *Rocky Mountain pika*

Fore

Hind

homes among the boulders and rocks of talus slopes, always where there are adjacent alpine meadows. They are commonly found at elevations of 8,000 to 9,000 feet (2,400-2,750 m), although they have been observed in areas as low as 2,500 feet (760 m). In fact, in some coastal fiords they are found at near sea level.

Pikas, as is the case with all lagomorphs, do not hibernate. While food is readily available in the nearby meadows during late spring and the summer, it is generally covered by snow or ice during the winter. To provide for winter sustenance, they begin harvesting green vegetation in late summer, carrying it crosswise in their mouths to their den sites and placing it in layers where the sun can cure it, much as a farmer cures hay. These stacks of food, sufficient to last until the warm sun of spring arouses new growth in the meadows, are jealously guarded and are marked by each owner by means of scent from the mammal's facial glands or by urine. When the vegetation has been cured, it is moved to the pika's den, where it remains dry and handy. Neighboring pikas with designs on another's cache are quickly chased off.

Pikas are believed to mate in late spring and/or

early summer. After a gestation of about 30 days, two to six young are born. It is possible that some produce two litters a year. The babies are born blind and naked and weigh less than 1 ounce (28 g). Their eyes open when they are about 3 weeks old and they start to feed on vegetation when they are 6 to 7 weeks of age.

Travelers who encounter pikas in the mammals' natural habitat are usually captivated by the creatures' ventriloquial capabilities. When alarmed they emit what are best described as nasal squeaks or bleats and with each one they jerk their bodies upward and forward. It is often difficult to determine the direction from which the sounds originate and sometimes they seem to come from a distance when in fact the animal is very close by or almost under foot.

If they escape the predations of their many enemies, pikas may live for about a year. The enemy most feared, besides foxes, fishers, wolverines, lynx, bears, golden eagles and large buteo hawks, is the ermine. This slender carnivore is able to squeeze through openings too narrow to admit most other predators.

In some areas pikas are known as piping hares, rock rabbits, whistling hares, mouse hares, or conies. Most people pronounce pika as *pee-ka*, but the pronunciation *pie-ka* is gradually gaining favor.

The collared and Rocky Mountain pikas are North American representatives of an Old World family. They inhabit western mountain ranges. (Photo by Mark Nyhof)

FAMILY LEPORIDAE

Sylvilagus floridanus
Eastern Cottontail

Were it not for its extraordinarily high death rate, the eastern cottontail rabbit theoretically could long ago have crowded virtually every square mile of the North American continent. In fact, the fecundity of this rabbit is such that, according to Prof. John O. Whitaker, Jr., of Indiana State University, a single pair could begin a line of progeny that could number 350,000 animals in 5 years. Others have made mathematical speculations that are even higher—one (in *Wild Animals of North America*) being an empire within 5 years of 2.5 billion, *all started from one female!*

These, however, are theoretical calculations. The latter, for instance, *might* occur but only if *every* cottontail born during that 5-year period survived—obviously and fortunately an impossibility. Nevertheless, the reproductive capacity of the eastern cottontail, like that of all lagomorphs, can reach staggering proportions. Nature, of course, has provided severe controls.

Cottontails are among the most vulnerable of all wild creatures and their average life expectancy is approximately 6 months. It is estimated that only about 25 per cent survive beyond a year and that only a fraction of these ever reach the age of three.

This high death rate is graphically illustrated by the fact that more than two-thirds of the newly-born are believed to die within their first 2 weeks, mainly from starvation or exposure if their mothers are killed while absent from their nests, by drowning if heavy rains cause flash floods which wash out nests built in low ground, or by being eaten by predators.

The natural predators—hawks, owls, foxes, coyotes, weasels, skunks, badgers, vagrant cats and dogs, for example—take a heavy toll, and many thousands of rabbits fall victim to hunters' guns and snares, die from the ravages of parasites and a variety of diseases, or are killed by automobiles when attempting to cross highways.

It's sad, in a way, that the engaging little cottontail has been assigned such a traumatic role in the scheme of things. But that's looking at things from a human perspective.

Some observers report having spent an hour or so on a winter's moonlit night watching half a dozen

Rabbits and hares have an extraordinarily high rate of reproduction, but also a short lifespan. These mammals experience peak years of abundance, followed by sharp declines. (Photo by Wayne Campbell)

rabbits in what can only be described as fun and games as they hopped over each other, gave chase, and engaged in sparring matches. Comparable antics, it should be mentioned, also coincide with the mating periods which, in the case of rabbits, occur as many as seven times a year.

The different species and subspecies of cottontail rabbits are among the best known of North American wild mammals; but an anomaly exists. Despite their wide range in the United States (the whole eastern half of that country with the exception of New England), the eastern cottontail occurs only minimally in Canada, in southern and eastern Ontario and a small part of southeastern Quebec. A subspecies, *S. f. similus*, is present in southern Manitoba and the eastern corner of Saskatchewan. It has been introduced into southwestern British Columbia and has also recently arrived in southern Vancouver Island.

The eastern cottontail was first described scientifically from a Florida specimen, which accounts for its Latinized species name. It is a medium-sized mammal weighing 2 to nearly 3 pounds (1-1.4 kg) (females are generally a little heavier) and measuring from 14 to 19 inches (36-48 cm) in length. Like all rabbits and hares it has large ears, large hind legs and feet (about twice the size of the front legs and feet), a divided upper lip (which seems to be constantly twitching), large protruding eyes which give the animal a wide range of vision on each side of the head, and of course a white fluffy tail. The iris of each eye is dark brown, but when caught in the lights of an automobile or flashlight reflects a bright red color. Scent glands located on both sides of the anus carry a musky substance which, when left on the ground, serves as a means of social or sexual communication.

The cottontail carries a pelage of thick, soft underfur through which grows an outer coat of dense but coarser guard hairs. The upper parts of the pelage range from dark, buffy brown to grayish brown interspersed with black. The nape and chest are rust colored, there is a white ring around each eye, the ears are grayish and edged with black, and there is generally a white spot on the forehead. The underparts are grayish white and the tail, while brownish on top, is predominantly white. The pelage is molted twice a year, the first molt occurring in late spring and early summer, the second in the fall.

Cottontails prefer open country such as brushy areas, the edges of woodlots, herbaceous fence rows, fields where there is high grass, thickets and brush piles. Although they do not take readily to water, they often make their homes along stream courses. The edges of crop fields, gardens and orchards are also favored but the damage they do by girdling fruit trees, eating vegetables, flowers and other vegetation make them less than desirable tenants.

Unlike Old World rabbits, which are noted for their elaborate underground warrens, the North American species live above ground and give birth to their young in shallow depressions known as "forms." The single exception to this is the pygmy rabbit (*Sylvilagus idahoensis*) of the American west, which digs tunnels or uses those dug by other animals.

All lagomorphs, other than the little pika, are most active from dusk to the early hours of morning. During the day they are content to remain quietly in their nests, or "forms," or wherever there is sufficient cover

Fore
4 in (10 cm) long

Eastern cottontail (West coast population introduced recently by man)

to protect them from predators and the elements. Most of the daylight hours are spent in sleeping and in grooming themselves, although they may often stretch out in the open to bask in the sun, or to seek relief from the heat in a cool, shaded place. An alert observer may occasionally see a cottontail standing upright, forepaws on its chest, viewing its surroundings.

The breeding cycle of the cottontail begins about mid-February but may be delayed until March if snows are heavy and the weather cold. The first of each year's litters is born from 26 to 28 days later and the second is often on the way before nursing of the first one is completed. New litters arrive at regular intervals thereafter until September, when physiological changes in the male prevent further procreation until the following February. During the breeding period of about 7 months, each doe is capable of producing around 60 young.

The courtship of cottontails takes the form of a nighttime dance which appears to have varying routines. Here is Banfield's description: "In the preliminary stages the buck chases the doe in a lively pursuit around the meadow. Eventually she turns and faces the buck and spars at him with her front paws. As they crouch facing each other, a few inches apart, one of the pair suddenly leaps about two feet in the air, and the other runs nimbly underneath it. This performance is repeated several times by either cottontail before actual mating."

Fights between rival males are common but physical damage rarely occurs. The females, in turn, will generally resist advances of amorous males if the approaches are made too soon after they have been bred. At such times the females will attack and may use their sharp incisor teeth to tear fur from the backs and flanks of overly-eager males. Despite these brawling affairs, the cottontail society is a fairly peaceful one. It is the dominant male that does most of the breeding and it is he also that lays claim to and holds the most desirable habitats.

When pregnancy nears its final stages, the female cottontail prepares her form. This is either an existing depression in the ground or one she excavates, and is about 5 inches (13 cm) deep, 7 inches (18 cm) long and 5 inches (13 cm) across. It is lined with vegetation (usually dried), over which is laid fur which she plucks from her breast and abdomen.

The young at birth weigh about 1 ounce (28 g), are 4 to 5 inches (10-13 cm) long, naked except for a thin covering of light-colored guard hairs, and temporarily without sight or hearing. The mother nurses her young at least once a day, either at dawn or at dusk, and while she generally remains near the nursery to defend it from intruders, that is the extent of the attention she gives the babies. To protect them from exposure she covers the form with a layer of grass and fur after each feeding. Nursing continues for about 3 weeks.

By the end of the first week the little cottontails have acquired a full coat of fur and their eyes and ears have opened. When they are about 2 weeks of age, they take their first hesitant but playful hops away from home and a few days later they are completely independent. Sexual maturity comes quickly and most of the juveniles are capable of breeding successfully when they are 2 to 3 months old. Since there are up to seven litters a year, with four or five young in each litter—all capable of breeding while still at the young "bunny" stage—the potential for rabbit population explosions is easily understood.

The home ranges of cottontails vary in size from 1 acre (0.4 ha) to as many as 15 acres (6 ha), depending on the food supply and the amount of good protective cover. These territories, which often overlap, are defended against other trespassing rabbits, and especially so by the does during the breeding season.

A cottontail, if frightened or fleeing from an enemy, takes off instantly, often doing several long leaps at first to gain distance, then changing to zigzagging hops from left to right, high leaps straight into the air, twists, turns—all a great display of body control. Under pressure it can run as fast as 18 or 20 miles (29-32 km) an hour for about half a mile. But for some strange reason, the cottontail follows a circuitous route and will always make its way back to the spot where the chase began, a disastrous maneuver if it is being pursued by a hunter's dogs, for the experienced hunter will simply wait, knowing that the cottontail will eventually return. On other occasions, if it thinks it can outwit its enemy, it will "freeze" by hugging the ground and remaining completely still until the danger has passed.

Field studies have shown that cottontails are relatively quiet mammals, although it is reported that babies in their nest, when hungry, often scream and the mother may utter loud grunts when with them; cottontails will give a shrill cry when fighting and will scream in a harrowing way when being killed by a predator. One characteristic sound, thought to be a method of communication, is made by thumping the hind feet.

The diet of the cottontail varies with the seasons, but is almost entirely confined to green vegetation. The list of food preferences is long and varied and is said, in fact, to include poison ivy. During the winter, when there is an absence of vegetation, they turn to the bark and twigs of trees and shrubs.

Sylvilagus nuttalli
Nuttall's Cottontail

This little rabbit, a close relative of the eastern cottontail, occurs throughout a wide range in the United States midwest from eastern Washington south to New Mexico, but stops before it reaches the Pacific coast. Sometime in the distant past it moved north into Canada and, while it is present in southern Saskatchewan, Alberta and a small southern section of British Columbia, it has never been particularly abundant in any of these provinces.

This lagomorph is light grayish-brown above and white below and has black-tipped ears. The upper side of the tail is gray, the underside white. The hairs across the throat and upper shoulders resemble a buffy-brown collar. The hind feet are whitish above. The weight of this mammal ranges from about 1.5 to 3 pounds (0.7-1.4 kg). Its overall length is about 14 to 15 inches (36-38 cm) with a tail of about 2 inches (5 cm).

Nuttall's cottontail favors sagebrush plains, alpine meadows up to about 10,000 feet (3,000 m), gullies of streams and lakeshores where there are thickets and rock crevices. It is inclined to be fossorial and will often temporarily take over the abandoned burrow of a prairie dog or marmot. It produces two, sometimes three litters each year, each averaging two young. Nests, if not made in a burrow, are generally made in well-hidden pockets under dense thickets. The young are weaned in about a month.

The Nuttall's cottontail generally remains under cover during the day but is active from dusk to dawn. It molts once a year, but there is no marked color change from summer to winter pelage.

This mammal, like all leporids, is a vegetarian and is sometimes a nuisance around gardens. While it is not of particular interest to hunters, it is the prey of coyotes, badgers, foxes, nocturnal owls and large buteo hawks.

Nuttall's cottontail

Lepus americanus

Snowshoe Hare

Snowshoe hare, varying hare, snowshoe rabbit, bush rabbit, gray hare, gray rabbit—these are the names most commonly used in referring to *Lepus americanus*. Officially the first two have preference.

"Snowshoe" (the Canadian usage) relates to the wide, thickly-furred hind feet. "Varying" (a common alternative in the United States) relates to the color changes of the pelage from summer brown to winter white, with a between-seasons mixture of both. Even though there are pronounced differences between hares and rabbits, *L. americanus* is known to most hunters, trappers and other wilderness travelers as "snowshoe" or "bush" rabbit.

Of the seven North American hares (genus *Lepus*), four are found in Canada and the northern United States: the snowshoe hare (*L. americanus*), which is found mainly in boreal forests; the Arctic hare (*L. arcticus*), which is almost exclusively a resident of the tundra and Arctic islands; the European hare (*L. capensis*), which was introduced into eastern North America from Germany; and the northern hare (*L. timidus*), a close relative of the Arctic hare which occurs in Alaska along coastal ranges. To a knowledgeable observer hares are readily distinguishable from rabbits (genus *Sylvilagus*) by their larger ears and much longer hind feet.

A mature snowshoe hare weighs 3 to 5 pounds (1.4-2.3 kg), is 16 to 21 inches (40-53 cm) in length, and is 8 to 9 inches (20-23 cm) high at the shoulder. The hind feet, which are about $5\frac{1}{2}$ inches (14 cm) in length, carry long, heavily-furred toes, the soles of which, especially in winter, are covered with stiff, thick hair. When the animal walks or bounds over the snow, its hind feet spread widely and give it marvelous buoyancy. Even in deep, light snow it can outrun most terrestrial pursuers.

The snowshoe hare is as much at home among coniferous as deciduous trees. The largest populations are found in burned-over areas where there is dense new growth. Young trees provide not only a reliable source of winter food such as tender twigs, leaf buds and bark, but also shelter during and after heavy snowfalls. Throughout the non-winter months the hare's diet consists mainly of herbaceous plants, among its favorites being green grasses, dandelions, daisies, wild strawberries, fireweed and pussy-toes.

Hares, like their cousins the rabbits, when living close to human habitations sometimes invade vegetable gardens; they also have a fondness for the bark of fruit and ornamental trees which, when girdled, usually die. Hares invade areas of reforestation and eat newly-planted conifers and this often causes severe setbacks to regeneration programs.

The snowshoe hare is also known as varying hare, as well as by other names. It inhabits forests where there are coniferous and deciduous trees but is most commonly found in burned-over places where there is dense new growth. (Photo by Dr. Bristol Foster)

Every 9 to 10 years there occur what are known as "peak" periods—a phenomenon experienced by a number of other animals, notably the Arctic brown lemming, which has peak periods every 3 to 4 years. These periods are invariably followed by spectacular declines, caused by starvation due to overcrowding, and diseases which spread rapidly as the animals grow weaker from lack of nourishment. During these months of decline, generally from late winter to spring, the animals are easy prey for predators such as wolves, coyotes, foxes, lynx, bobcats, hawks and owls.

Since most home ranges of snowshoe hares are relatively small in size (anywhere from 4 to 12 acres (1.6-4.8 ha), depending on availability of food, suitable nesting sites and protection from predators) populations within a range in peak years can reach extraordinarily high densities. Banfield estimates numbers reaching 10,000 per square mile in some northern Canadian areas, while the Canadian Wildlife Service reports that in 1970, in central Alberta, densities ran from 3,500 to 6,500 per square mile.

Whenever these sharp declines occur, other animals and birds of prey also generally suffer a severe drop in numbers. The causes of death are much the same: starvation brought about by lack of food, and disease resulting from malnutrition.

The breeding season of the snowshoe hare starts in March or early April and may continue until September. The gestation period is 35 days, and within hours after parturition the females are able to mate again. Like all lagomorphs, snowshoe hares are prolific breeders, although in the case of *L. americanus* reproduction rates vary, not only in the number of litters each year but in the size of the litters. While four litters are normal, as in the mid-west, three are produced annually in Yukon and Alaska, and as few as two in Newfoundland. The number of young in each litter varies from one to as many as 18, depending on the area. In Canada the highest rate of reproduction is in Manitoba, Saskatchewan and Alberta.

The "forms" of the snowshoe hare are usually found in places of dense growth where there is a maximum of protection from predators. Some species of lagomorphs, such as the cottontail rabbit (*Sylvilagus floridanus*), make nests that are lined with grass and with fur from the mothers' bodies, but the snowshoe, like all hares of the genus *Lepus*, simply drops her young on the bare ground.

The babies (known as leverets) are born fully furred with eyes open — unlike rabbits, which come into the world naked and blind. Although they weigh only about 2 ounces (57 g) at birth, they are able within a day or two to make little hops about the form and to start nibbling on green vegetation. Weaning is completed in 3 to 4 weeks and adult size is reached after 6 or 7 weeks. The young are capable of mating the following spring.

The snowshoe hare is active all year and is most commonly on the move from dusk to dawn. It rests in sheltered places during the day and spends a good deal of its time preening itself. Even when it is sleeping, its keen senses of smell and hearing and sensitivity to vibrations keep it in a constant state of alert. If forced to flee, it can travel as fast as 30 miles (48 km) an hour in a springy, bounding gait, with leaps as long as 20 feet

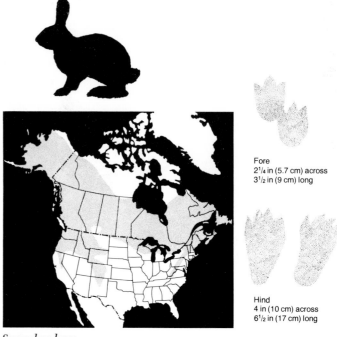

Snowshoe hare

Fore
2¼ in (5.7 cm) across
3½ in (9 cm) long

Hind
4 in (10 cm) across
6½ in (17 cm) long

(6 m). Sometimes, when dodging, it may jump as high as 6 feet (2 m) above ground. If necessary, it will take readily to water and swim without difficulty across narrow rivers and small lakes.

Well-worn trails, used year-round, meander throughout the snowshoe's habitat and are particularly noticeable in winter. Generally the hare keeps to these pathways, for their well-packed surfaces provide not only easy travel but a fast means of escape from predators. There are occasions, however, when the hare leaves the trail to look for a new source of food, or join a group of other hares in a night-time gambol in and out of a clearing. Banfield, referring to such frolics on winter nights, writes that "as many as 25 have been observed flitting silently around a forest clearing... Like small, pale ghosts they appeared and disappeared in the shadows as they fed among the small spruces or chased each other in jerky spasms of movement." The same pathways are often used by other small animals such as skunks, porcupines and weasels.

The lifespan of the snowshoe hare is 4 to 5 years, but very few reach that age. According to the Ontario Ministry of Natural Resources, upwards of 80 per cent of all mature hares in Algonquin Park die each year. Fortunately the amazing fecundity of *L. americanus* enables it to thrive and so it may be expected to continue to play a vital role in the natural food chain and also to be one of the most interesting and abundant of forest dwellers.

Lepus arcticus

Arctic Hare

"Chionophile" is not a word in common use, but biologists sometimes use it when referring to mammals that live in the Arctic. Translated literally, it means "snow loving mammals." This term can be applied to numerous northern species—among them caribou, muskoxen, polar bears, wolves, foxes, lemmings, voles, shrews, and, of course, the Arctic hare, *Lepus arcticus*. And since man is a mammal, perhaps it may also be used (with a little license) to classify northern human residents.

The adaptation by chionophiles to an environment where even in April the temperature can hold well below zero for days or even weeks, where in summer the simmering heat can reach well into the 90s, and where, in some areas, the onslaught of warble flies, nose flies, mosquitoes and black flies causes untold agony, is one of the marvels of the animal world. Equally as remarkable is the ability of the herbivores, particularly large animals such as caribou and muskoxen, to find enough nutritious forage on the windswept tundra and under its snow-covered surface to sustain them throughout the Arctic's 7 to 8 months of winter. All of the Arctic mammals are creatures of immense interest and because of their remote habitat much has yet to be learned of their behavioral patterns and lifestyles.

One well known yet little understood mammal is the ubiquitous Arctic hare, a lagomorph which in Canada occurs from Newfoundland and Labrador on the east to the Mackenzie Valley and Delta on the west, as well as in the Arctic islands. In fact, of all terrestrial mammals, *L. arcticus* may enjoy the distinction of having the most northerly range, for according to Banfield, Captain Markham of HMS *Alert* "observed signs of these hare on the ice 10 miles from the most northern land at latitude 83° 10′ N." The range of the Arctic hare also extends to most of the coastal boundaries of Greenland. A close relative, the northern hare (*L. timidus*),

1. *Arctic hare*
2. *Northern hare*

inhabits coastal Alaska and the northern regions of Eurasia.

While a number of important scientific papers have been published on the general morphology of Arctic hares, relatively little has been written in popular form about the behavioral characteristics of the species. This section, accordingly, is based largely on an article published in *Nature Canada* by David R. Gray and Heather Hamilton, who studied Arctic hares during the course of field work at the National Museum of Natural Sciences' High Arctic Research Station, Bathurst Island, and on Ellesmere Island, Northwest Territories. Additional information was obtained from Dr. Gray through personal correspondence.

The Arctic hare is the biggest member of the hare family and, depending on geography, weighs anywhere from 4 to 15 pounds (1.8-7 kg). Its average weight is about 10 pounds (4.5 kg). The southern snowshoe or varying hare averages only a third that weight. As is typical of hares and rabbits, females are usually larger than males, the opposite being true of most other mammals.

Throughout its whole Arctic range, the pelage in

Arctic hares often stand up on their hind legs to get a better view of their surroundings. When frightened or threatened, they often bound away in an upright stance much in the manner of kangaroos. (Photo by Dr. David R. Gray)

winter of this mammal is completely white except for the thickly-furred pads of its feet (which in all seasons are yellowish) and the black tips of the ears. In summer, depending on latitude, it ranges from overall white (in the *high* Arctic) to grizzled or bluish gray, with mottlings of cinnamon, brown or buff, most frequently on the face, back and ears. Its eyes are large and brown in color, its nose is white, its mouth is pink and traces of black occur around the nostrils. It has strong foreclaws which are capable of digging for food through crusted snow and equally strong incisor teeth which act as forceps in removing plants from rocky crevices.

The coat of this mammal is particularly suited to withstand the most severe winter weather. There are two types of fur, the first a thick layer of soft underfur, the other a thick layer of longer, silky outer hair. Together they act as an insulating blanket so effective that, given the added protection of rocks and snowdrifts, the mammal is able to keep warm even when strong winds rage and the temperature sinks to its lowest level.

A particularly effective way hares adopt to keep warm, as described by Gray and Hamilton, is to "fold their tails down between their hind legs, tuck their forepaws into their chest . . . lower their ears down into the fur on their backs, and settle into an almost spherical shape with only the thick yellowish pads on their hind feet touching the ground. In this position they will sit for hours. . . ."

While more data have to be gathered to establish definite diet patterns, it is known that Arctic willow is the hare's staple food during both summer and winter. Hares also eat a variety of flowers and plant roots, and have a particular liking for the flowers of the purple saxifrage. All of these foods also form part of the diet of caribou and muskoxen.

Arctic hares in ranges north of the treeline are believed to have only one litter a year (Parker), but those south of that (insular Newfoundland, for example) may have two, even three a year (Northcott). Sizes of litters vary according to latitude but data gathered on Axel Heiberg Island indicate that about six leverets appear to be average for that area. On the other hand, in Newfoundland the average number may be as few as four. Time of mating may also vary, but it is believed to occur during April and May, with the young being born in June or early July.

According to Parker, the young are probably born in dish-like depressions made in gravel ridges and

White-tailed jack rabbits are actually hares. They are nocturnal and are rarely seen during daylight hours. (Photo by Peter Karsten)

slopes "usually facing south or southwest and behind, or sheltered by a large rock." Most of the depressions, or "scoops," were previously made as places of protection during severe weather, and thus do double duty as nurseries.

The courtship season is marked by a sort of "boxing" performance, perhaps between males to establish dominance, or between males and females, the female vigorously rebuffing the male. These exchanges are brief and rarely result in injury to either combatant.

Arctic hares have a number of extraordinary behavioral characteristics, all of them recorded by reliable observers; none of them, however, has been or perhaps can be explained. The first is their "spring madness." (Remember the March Hare in *Alice in Wonderland?*). Writing about a particular hare that "befriended" researchers at the Bathurst Island station, an animal affectionately named "Bun," Gray and Hamilton recorded these observations:

"On a July day about five weeks after Bun had left the camp area, he was found six kilometers away sitting very sphinx-like on a patch of mossy vegetation. After a short time, Bun got up and began feeding, seemingly oblivious to the presence of the two observers recording his behavior. Suddenly, and for no apparent reason, Bun began running in wide circles, dashing full speed down the slope, wheeling around and dashing back up to make a full-tilt pass along the ledge of rocks at the top. Then he began interspersing the mad dashes with even madder jumps—not an ordinary rabbit hop, but a leap that propelled him straight up in the air a good meter and a half. As he jumped he kicked his feet and twisted his body in mid-air, so that he came down running, but in a different direction. His ears changed direction in mid-jump too as he flopped each of them forward at a very rakish angle. These tremendous leaps and dashes were broken by short pauses before he set off on the next run. His surprising antics so flabbergasted one observer that she stood camera in hand, so broken up by laughter that she failed to take a single photograph."

Another unexplained behavior is their occasional tendency to gather in enormous herds, and to see 200 or more together at one time is not unusual. Weather station personnel at Eureka have reported herds of several thousand *milling about the station*, and a Canadian Wildlife Service biologist tells of an assembly of about 25,000 hares in an area of 4.8 square miles (12.5 km²)! Pilots flying over these northern regions have told of seeing hills so covered with hares that the hills themselves seemed to be moving. Arctic hares also on occasion follow each other in single file, and on Ellesmere Island, their trails over the years have "worn down the earth and even the softer rocks." Incredible, but inexplicably true!

Except for mid-summer, when they are skittish and generally avoid humans, Arctic hares are relatively easy to approach and, certainly in the case of "Bun," can even make good companions. ("Bun" was once even encouraged to ride on a toboggan!). But when frightened, or threatened by a predator, they stand upright, often bouncing up and down on tiptoes. To escape from danger they bound away, their forelegs held against their chest, in a manner almost identical to that of the kangaroo. They move so fast in that posture that few predators can catch up to them, but during a pursuit they will generally drop to a quadripedal position to continue their escape, generally uphill. Once on high ground, with the enemy safely in the rear, they will assume the upright stance again to get a better view of the terrain and the object of their fright.

The Arctic hare is one of the far north's important faunal resources, not only as a vital link in the natural food chain, but as a source of food for native people. Its natural enemies are Arctic foxes, tundra wolves, ermine on occasion, snowy owls and rough-legged hawks. At the present time there is no data concerning its longevity.

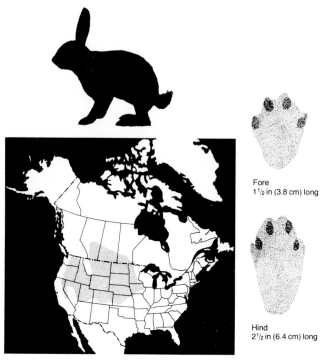

Fore
1 1/2 in (3.8 cm) long

Hind
2 1/2 in (6.4 cm) long

White-tailed jack rabbit

Lepus timidus
Northern Hare

This species is closely related to the snowshoe hare and is found in the open tundra along the western and northern coasts of Alaska. It is also known as Alaska hare, mountain hare, European varying hare and blue hare. It is much larger than the snowshoe hare and smaller than the Arctic hare. Its summer coloring is reddish-brown or grayish-brown above and white below; its ear tips are black.

Other than its present classification, its limited and very remote range and that during the mating season it makes puffing and hissing sounds, little is known about this mammal.

Lepus townsendii
White-tailed Jack Rabbit

This is the athlete of the Leporidae family. Not only can it travel in speeds of up to nearly 45 miles (72 km) an hour in short bursts, but it does so in high leaps of 12 to 20 feet (4-6 m). It can then change its gait to low, grace-

ful glides, but even they may be up to 15 feet (4.6 m) in length. In addition it is an accomplished swimmer and uses all four feet to propel itself; it is also, by using the long, sharp claws of its hind feet as defence weapons, a formidable opponent if forced to defend itself.

Although called a rabbit, this animal is a true hare, with all the hare's physical characteristics. It is large and slim and weighs about 6 to 12 pounds (2.7-5.4 kg) and ranges in length from 22 to 26 inches (56-66 cm). It has very long ears, long slender legs and a relatively long tail. Although the irises of its eyes are yellow, when caught in the glare of a flashlight or a car's headlights the eyes reflect a brilliant red. Its coat in summer is grizzled buffy, except for the underparts and the hind feet and tail, which are white. The ears are dark, grizzled gray in front, white behind and black-tipped, and the outer rims are white. The front legs are buffy colored. In winter the coat turns to pure white, although the ears retain the black tip. It molts twice a year—October to November and April to May.

The white-tailed jack rabbit is a nocturnal mammal and is rarely seen during daylight hours. It is a solitary creature and associates with others of its kind only during the mating season. The time of mating varies according to geography but among northern races it generally occurs toward the end of April and beginning of May. An average of four fully-furred leverets are born in June or early July and are weaned 3 to 4 weeks later. During the mating season the bucks engage in serious fights with each other, biting and using the long claws of the hind feet to inflict wounds. When fighting, and especially if injured, they utter shrill screams, but for the rest of the year they are virtually silent.

In summer the white-tailed jack rabbit feeds on grasses, clover, barley and sometimes the bark of fruit trees; in winter its diet consists largely of buds, twigs and dried vegetation. The enemies of this mammal, aside from hunters who favor its meat, include wolves, coyotes, foxes, bobcats, hawks and owls.

The white-tailed jack rabbit in Canada occurs in Manitoba, Saskatchewan and Alberta as well as in a small corner of northwestern Ontario and a small area of south-central British Columbia. In the United States, however, its range runs from eastern Washington south to northeastern California, then east to include all of the northern states as far as Wisconsin. Its common habitat is open fields and pastures.

Lepus capensis

European Hare

In 1912 seven females and two males of these Old World leporids were brought from Germany to a farm near Galt, Ontario. The following winter they escaped from their enclosures and became free-roving. As is usual with these mammals, they multiplied, and although the increase in their numbers since that time has not been spectacular, they are nevertheless secure throughout the Great Lakes and St. Lawrence River areas of Canada and the United States. Records also show that the mammals had been introduced earlier in New York state and it is probably their progeny that spread to occupy ranges in New England, Pennsylvania and New Jersey.

This is a large hare, abut 25 to 27.5 inches in length (64 to 70 cm), typically hare-shaped with long ears, long front feet, long tail and, overall, a slender body. Its coat is yellowish to gray-brown with white underparts. It molts twice a year, but its pelage, unlike that of the snowshoe hare and the white-tailed jack rabbit, does not turn white in winter.

This is a nocturnal mammal and like other leporids

European hare

is active all year. It is generally solitary except during the breeding season, which occurs during the late winter. After a gestation of 30 to 42 days, three to five leverets are born.

The summer diet of the European hare consists of grasses and herbs and in winter it feeds on twigs, buds, and the bark of shrubs and trees. Its normal habitat is near woodlots and hedgerows. This mammal is a favorite among hunters, but because of its ability to move at fast speeds—up to 30 miles (48 km) an hour in spurts—it is a challenging quarry. Its natural enemies are hawks, owls, foxes, coyotes and bobcats.

This species was classified until recently as *L. europaeus*.

ORDER PINNIPEDIA

SEA/LAND MAMMALS

This order of amphibious carnivores is represented along virtually every coastline in the world. There are 31 species and 16 subspecies comprising a population estimated at between 15 and 25 million animals. The largest populations occur in temperate and polar waters, although one species, the monk seal (found in the Gulf of Mexico), confines itself to tropical areas. Some pinnipeds are found in freshwater lakes.

Three families of pinnipeds inhabit the waters of North America:

The family Otariidae, consisting of four species: the northern fur seal, often called Alaska fur seal; the Steller sea lion, known also as northern sea lion; the California sea lion, the species best known for its performing acts in zoos, circuses and aquaria; and the Guadalupe fur seal, found only on a small volcanic island off the coast of Mexico. These mammals are known as the "eared" seals: their ears, although only about an inch in length, are external and visible.

The family Odobenidae, consisting of but one species—the walrus.

The family Phocidae, consisting of nine species: the bearded seal, harbor seal, ringed seal, harp seal, gray seal, hooded seal, ribbon seal, largha seal and northern elephant seal. The phocids are known as the "true" or "earless" seals. Aside from the fact that they lack external ears (small furls on either side of the head serve as ears), they are taxonomically different from the "eared" group in a number of ways. These mammals are the most abundant and most widespread of all pinnipeds.

Seals, sea lions and walruses are amphibious carnivores known as pinnipeds. This is a harbor seal, a member of the family Phocidae—the "true" or "earless" seals. (Photo by Brian Milne/Valan Photos)

Of the nine species, the ringed seal, bearded seal, spotted seal, ribbon seal and largha seal live most of their lives where sea-ice predominates.

Pinnipeds enjoy the best of two worlds: they spend part of their lives at sea, where they feed on fish and various forms of aquatic invertebrates, and part of their lives on land, where they breed and give birth to their young. Harp seals, harbor seals, and walruses, however, mate at sea and observations of sea-mating by northern fur seals have been recorded in the area of the Pribilof Islands.

Pinnipeds are well equipped for their marine environment, for in addition to their torpedo-shaped bodies, they have powerful swimming flippers, their nostrils and ears can be closed when under water, and (depending on the species) they have the amazing capacity to submerge to depths of up to 2,000 feet (610 m) and to remain submerged up to 45 minutes. Their eyes are very large and are so acutely developed that they can see at depths where vision (at least in human terms) is extremely limited. But there is an exception: the eyes of the walrus are much smaller and have been described as resembling those of a pig.

Seeking food at great depths is no problem for these mammals. Before submerging they exhale and, as they submerge, their normal heartbeat slows down from 55–120 beats a minute to 4–15 beats a minute. As their blood vessels constrict, the flow of blood and oxygen is concentrated around the primary organs such as the heart and brain. This physiological characteristic is much the same in the cetaceans (whales, dolphins and porpoises).

All pinnipeds are graceful, powerful swimmers and most are migratory. Like whales, dolphins and porpoises, they have complete command of their water environment. If frightened, pursued or simply in a hurry, the northern fur seal and walrus, for example, can attain speeds of up to 15 miles (24 km) an hour. Structural differences in the families determine methods of propulsion in water: eared seals and walruses propel themselves by means of their *fore* flippers and use their rear flippers, held together, as a rudder. The earless seals use their *hind* flippers (which are permanently turned backwards) as their main means of propulsion.

On land the pinnipeds seem clumsy and slow-moving, although most of the eared seals and the walrus, despite their size, are remarkably agile. These mammals are able to twist their rear flippers around to be in line with their front flippers and, by using all four, they can move with surprising speed. The earless seals, on the other hand, cannot redirect the position of their rear flippers and so must use the powerful muscular action of their bodies to create mobility. Their progress consequently is slower and seems to require greater effort. Their front flippers, even if they do not aid significantly in achieving motion, are capable of supporting enormous weights. The northern elephant seal, the largest of all aquatic carnivores, illustrates this best: an adult male sometimes reaches a weight of 7,700 pounds (3,500 kg)!

With the exception of the adult walrus (which is quite naked) pinnipeds normally are covered with hair. It is the luxurious warm underfur of the eared seals and the glossy guard hairs of the earless seals that have historically been so much in demand in the garment industry, an industry whose operations in some areas are declining in the face of universal resistance to the slaughter of seal pups. There is also a thick layer of fat, or "blubber," between the body muscles and the tough epidermus; this provides insulation against the low temperatures of northern waters and the severe cold of ice and snow. In addition, the layer of fat provides buoyancy when the mammal is in the water.

The mating season of pinnipeds varies with the species, and may be any time from January to August. Breeding occurs once a year and follows within days, or weeks, the birth of the single pup (rarely twins). Delayed implantation accounts for the long period of gestation. Depending again on the species, the place of birth may be a large land rookery, or an area of ice — often a large, free-moving ice floe. Sexual maturity does not occur in these mammals until they are 2 to 5 years of age.

Aside from man, whose predation in the past has been irresponsibly heavy and has brought at least two species to near extinction, the enemies of seals, sea lions and walruses are large sharks, polar bears and killer whales. Walruses, however, prey on the smaller ringed and bearded seals. Most pinnipeds have long lifespans and some survive in the wild for as long as 40 years.

All of these creatures are descendants of land mammals that returned to the sea in very early times. Some scientists believe that the eared seals evolved from primitive bears, and the earless or true seals evolved from primitive weasel-like mammals. Others suggest all are more closely related to dogs and cats, or that walruses are later offshoots of *both* families of seals. Perhaps one day their true lineage will be established, but it appears certain, as suggested by fossils found along the shores of the Pacific, that the first pinnipeds arose during the early Miocene about 22 million years ago.

FAMILY OTARIIDAE

Callorhinus ursinus

Northern Fur Seal

Northern fur seals, known also as Alaska fur seals and Pribilof seals, occur only in the North Pacific and adjacent Bering Sea, Sea of Okhotsk and Sea of Japan. They are the most oceanic of their family, remaining at sea for about 7 months of the year, rarely touching land during that time, and traveling over vast distances before returning to their historic far northern rookeries to bear their young and mate again.

Highly valued for their thick, fine lustrous underfur, these mammals were at one time in danger of extinction largely as a result of uncontrolled and indiscriminate killing both at sea and on land. In 1911, however, an international treaty* abolished pelagic sealing and set rigid quotas on land harvesting. Since then the population has gradually increased in size and now numbers (an estimate made in 1976) about 1.8 million individuals—about 700,000 less than the population in the mid-1700s. Of the 1.8 million, about 1.3 million breed on the Pribilof Islands, controlled by the United States, and about 463,000 breed on the Commander, Robben and Kuril islands, controlled by the U.S.S.R. A small, apparently non-migratory colony of about 2,000 inhabits San Miguel Island off California.

Although northern fur seals gather in huge rookeries for the breeding season, they are relatively solitary while at sea. Most of them travel alone, but groups of three or four, and occasionally more, are sometimes formed. Most of their feeding takes place at night when squid and various species of fish are close to the surface. There is insufficient evidence to prove that these mammals are a significant threat to the salmon and

Northern fur seal

other commercial fisheries, as is so often claimed. In fact, recent studies have shown that much of their diet is made up of species that *compete* with or are *detrimental* to the commercial fisheries. When feeding, dives of up to 460 feet (140 m) are normal, but rarely do the seals stay submerged for more than 5 minutes at a time. When resting or sleeping they lie on their back or side, with their hind flippers folded toward the head like an arch and held in position by a foreflipper.

The return of these mammals to their rookeries begins with the arrival in May and June of the adult males, or "bulls." These are followed a few weeks later by the mature females. Other seals continue to arrive from July to September in descending order of age, but most of them haul out on areas separate from the breeding grounds. A few days after reaching land, each pregnant female gives birth to a 10- to 12-pound (4.5-5.5 kg) pup (rarely twins) and a few days later is able to mate again. While they remain on the islands, the bulls do not eat, but the females make frequent excursions to sea to feed and thus replenish their supplies of milk. By August most of the adult males leave the islands and they do not return until the following spring. Adult females and juveniles remain on the rookeries until October before migrating south. It is the 3- to 5-year-old, sexually immature "bachelors" that are harvested for their fur.

This harvesting, however, is only a fraction of that of the late 1700s, which saw the start of a decline in numbers to the 1910 low point of fewer than 300,000

*This treaty was modified in 1957 and is operative under the title "Interim Convention on Conservation of North Pacific Fur Seals."

animals. High priority is now being given to research and management programs whose goal is the restoration of populations in some areas where declines have been noted.

Northern fur seals are large animals, adult males weighing 300 to 600 pounds (135-270 kg), and adult females weighing 65 to 100 pounds (30-45 kg). They differ anatomically from other otariids, most noticeably in their unusually long rear flippers. Their color varies according to sex and age, but generally adult males are dark gray to brown above, with gray shoulders and foreneck, and reddish-brown flippers and underparts. Adult females are grayish-brown above and reddish-brown or gray underneath.

During migration, individuals are frequently seen off the North American coast from Alaska south to California. They are often abundant along the coasts of Washington, British Columbia and Alaska, some moving into Juan de Fuca Strait and Puget Sound.

Northern fur seals, as is the case with many forms of marine life, are in serious danger from man's activities, especially from discarded commercial fishing nets, in which they become entangled, and from the discharge of crude oil, even in small amounts. Natural mortality occurs from infectious diseases and parasites, and from the predation of sharks, killer whales and northern sea lions. But if they escape these dangers, males may live for about 17 years and females for about 26 years.

Eumetopias jubatus
Steller Sea Lion

The Steller sea lion, named after the German naturalist George Wilhelm Steller, a member of the 1741 discovery expedition to Alaska, is the largest of the eared seals. Males weigh up to 2,200 pounds (1,000 kg) and exceed 10 feet (3 m) in length; females are nearly four times smaller, weighing as a rule about 600 pounds (270 kg) and reaching a length of about 7 feet (2.1 m). These mammals, which are also known as northern sea lions, occur throughout a range that extends in Asia from the Kuril Islands to the Kamchatka Peninsula and islands in the Sea of Okhotsk, around the Aleutian Islands to Alaska and south along the coast to San Miguel Island off California.

The population of this species is about 250,000 individuals, and while its numbers are stable in the Gulf of Alaska (where they occur in the greatest

Steller sea lion (Major concentration occurs in Gulf of Alaska and along Alaska Peninsula.)

numbers), in some waters (the eastern Aleutians and California, for example) there have been serious declines. The causes of these declines are not fully understood, but may be attributable to new movements of the mammals themselves, diseases, discarded fishermen's nets (in which they often become hopelessly entangled) or to destruction by rifle shot.

Like all eared seals, Steller sea lions spend most of their lives at sea, returning to their rookeries in May, where they remain for up to 3 months. After that time they disperse and do not return until the following year. Where they go remains to some extent a mystery. There is knowledge of north-south migratory movements, but length of migrations or the routes followed are still to be verified before they are accorded scientific acceptance. In any case, the males are the first to arrive at the breeding grounds and there they lay claim to well-defined territories and await the arrival shortly afterwards of the first of the pregnant females. As the females reach the rookeries, they haul out and, to the accompaniment of much bellowing and competitive jostling on the part of the dominant males, are herded to different territories. Within a few days each new arrival gives birth to a single pup weighing 40 to 45 pounds (18-20 kg) and by the end of 2 weeks is ready to breed again—but only once. Before the end of the season, as more and more pregnant females arrive, the males are outnumbered by ten to one.

Almost immediately after birth, the mother lifts the pup up by the neck and places it in a position where

The Steller sea lion is the largest of the "eared" seals, males often weighing up to 2,000 pounds (900 kg). They are also known as "northern sea lions." (Photo by Wayne Campbell)

it can begin to suckle. There is also much nose-rubbing, and vocal exchanges are frequent. This establishes both olfactory and vocal recognition between mother and pup and perhaps visual recognition, making it possible for the mother to identify her offspring when she returns from feeding excursions at sea. Pups that are orphaned or that for some reason cannot be found are rejected by all other adult females and inevitably die, usually of starvation. The pups are born in June and July and at birth are silver-black in color. Half an hour or so after birth they are able to walk and, if necessary, to swim. The mother remains with her young for 5 to 13 days, allowing it to suckle frequently. At the end of that time she begins her nightly excursions to sea, not only to replenish her own food needs but to produce milk for her hungry infant.

When pups are 10 to 14 days old, they are moved to form pods in areas safely away from adults, where they quickly learn to engage in play-fighting and other "fun" interactions and to acquaint themselves with the sea environment.

While most excursions by the mothers are made at night and may take the animals from 4 to 15 miles (6-24 km) from shore, singly or in small groups, scientists have found that at least in Alaskan waters large groups (sometimes as many as several thousand individuals) leave their rookeries in early morning. Once at the feeding grounds they break up into groups of 50 or so to feed, and then reassemble in late afternoon to make their return journey. If large schools of fish are found, especially squid, the sea lions will move *en masse* to feed on them. Their maximum diving depth is about 600 feet (180 m).

Species consumed by sea lions depend to some extent on geography. For example, along the California, Oregon, Washington and British Columbia coasts their diet consists mainly of flatfishes and rockfishes,

Steller sea lions are often seen during their migration along the Pacific coast. (Photo by Wayne Campbell)

while in Alaskan waters they eat capelin, sand lance, rockfishes, flatfishes, salmon, flounder, halibut, cod, pollock, smelt and greenling.

Throughout the 3-month breeding season the males remain within the boundaries of their territories and do not feed. The only sustenance they are able to draw on during their long vigil is the fat of their bodies. This self-imposed "imprisonment"—necessary if territories are to be protected and the rookery held together in some sense of order—results in extreme stress, physical as well as physiological, and this, scientists believe, may account for the fact that few males live beyond 4 years as a harem bull.

While young sea lions up to the age of 2 years do not as a rule migrate to the rookeries, 3-year-old males do but these precocious non-breeders congregate in separate areas. Their's is a carefree life during which their time is spent in play, swimming, feeding and, not infrequently, trespassing into breeding areas—from which they are quickly ejected by the territorial master. Females, however, become sexually mature at the age of 3, and when they migrate to the rookeries they join other breeding females and mate, and then return the

following year to give birth to their first offspring, and then mate again. The males do not reach sexual maturity until they are 6 or 7 years of age, but not until they are 9 or 10 years old are they able to establish harems.

The rookeries generally break up sometime during August with the departure of most of the males. The females linger for a month or so longer, and finally they too depart.

The pelage of this species is light to tan-brown when dry, but appears darker when wet. Adult males have a massive neck and this carries a thick growth of long, coarse hairs. This mammal's enemies are man, killer whales and sharks. A healthy individual may live as long as 17 years.

Zalophus californianus

California Sea Lion

No zoo, aquarium or traveling circus would be complete without one or more California sea lions. These attractive, highly intelligent, fun-loving creatures have won the affection of millions of people with their acrobatic and juggling performances—performances that seem to please them as much as their audiences, provided they are "rewarded" after each act! In their natural environment, however, their popularity is less evident, for many commercial fishermen consider them pests whose consumption of marketable species (they claim) endangers their livelihood.

The California sea lion is a small mammal in relation to the Steller, with which it frequently intermingles in the range they share from southern Vancouver Island, British Columbia, to San Miguel Island, southern California, and Mexico. Male Californians reach a length of up to 8 feet (2.4 m) and a weight of 800 pounds (360 kg), as opposed to the Steller's length of over 10 feet (3 m) and weight of more than 2,200 pounds (1,000 kg). Female Californians are considerably smaller, weighing up to 250 pounds (114 kg) and seldom exceeding a length of 5 feet (1.5 m), as opposed to the Steller female's weight of 600 pounds (270 kg) and length of 7 feet (2.1 m). When together, a further distinguishing characteristic is that male California sea lions utter loud, dog-like barking sounds, while male Steller sea lions make lower-pitched roars.

The California sea lion basks during the day and feeds at night, its diet consisting of squid, octopus, anchovy, hake, rockfish, flatfish, small sharks, salmon and mollusks. It is a very capable swimmer, powerful

California sea lions are the pinnipeds most frequently seen in circuses, zoos and aquaria. (Photo by Fred Bruemmer)

enough to reach speeds of up to 20 miles (32 km) an hour, breaking water in the manner of porpoises, and it can stay under water for as long as 20 minutes. Dives of 2 to 5 minutes, however, are more the rule. It is capable of descending to depths of 450 feet (140 m). These mammals usually remain fairly close to shore, but some individuals have been observed as far as 55 miles (88 km) out to sea.

The breeding season begins in May and continues through June, when adults of both sexes haul out on sandy beaches. Males arrive first to establish their stations and lay claim to territories. A few days after their arrival the pregnant females give birth to a single pup weighing approximately 36 pounds (16 kg), and within

California sea lion (Breeding range is southern California southward.)

10 days mate again. At the conclusion of the breeding season most of the adult and subadult males migrate north, but so many drop out *en route* to their favorite hauling grounds that only a few actually make it as far as British Columbia waters. The females and their young do not migrate but remain as a rule within the area of the breeding grounds. The vocalization of females resembles a quavering wail when calling their pups, but when threatened or angered they bark and growl.

The reproductive biology of the California sea lion is not fully known, and while the age at which males reach sexual maturity has yet to be determined, it is thought that females are capable of breeding for the first time when they are about 4 years old.

The coat of the California sea lion is stiff and the soft undercoat, so characteristic of fur seals, is lacking. When the mammal is on shore and dry, the coat ranges in color from buff to brown but, almost magically, it appears black and glossy as soon as it becomes wet. Some in fact appear black even when out of the water. As is the case with all pinnipeds, its enemies, in addition to man, are sharks and killer whales. This species has a lifespan of 12 to 14 years, although Prof. Bruce R. Mate of Oregon State University, writes of one individual that survived for 31 years.

FAMILY ODOBENIDAE

Odobenus rosmarus
Walrus

Nature may not have been generous as far as appearances are concerned when she designed the walrus, but what was denied it in good looks was more than remedied by remarkable physical attributes — one of them being the paired air sacks in its neck which, when inflated, enable the mammal to sleep at sea in a vertical position with its head safely above water! Then, to help it to haul itself easily onto ice-floes despite its enormous bulk, and to help it to skid head-down through mud while it searches the sea bottom for clams (its favorite food), it was endowed with a pair of outsized upper canine teeth known as tusks. Unfortunately these tusks, which in Atlantic races grow to an average length of 14 inches (36 cm) and in Pacific races to an average length of 24 inches (61 cm), make highly valued carvings and many thousands of the mammals have been slaughtered in years past merely to supply the demand. Today, however, killing of walruses has been restricted to prevent them from becoming endangered. The world population of this species is estimated at about 250,000 individuals, and of these about 200,000 inhabit North Pacific and Arctic waters.

The walrus, the only member of the family Odobenidae, is an "ice pack" mammal whose range takes in the polar ice sheet around the northern hemisphere. For reasons yet to be explained, walruses of the Atlantic region are smaller in size, skull dimensions and length of tusks than those of the Pacific. For example, the weight of an average eastern Arctic adult male is 1,650 pounds (750 kg), while that of a western Arctic adult male has been known to be more than 2,790 pounds (1,267 kg). Cows of both regions are significantly smaller. But even averages are sometimes exceeded in extraordinary degrees, for Dr. Karl W. Kenyon (*Marine Mammals of Eastern North Pacific and Arctic Waters*) writes of one adult female that weighed 3,432 pounds (1,558 kg) and another that weighed 1,500 pounds (680 kg)! The tusks of the male may be nearly 40 inches (1 m) long, which is an amazing length, considering the relatively small head out of which they grow.

Overall the walrus qualifies for one descriptive word — ugly — although perhaps in this case ugliness is only in the eye of the beholder. In any event, the head of the mammal appears absurdly small for the size of the body. It carries a moustache of several hundred, foot-long bristles which cover its broad muzzle; its eyes are small; and the tusks hang down through fleshy lips from the corners of its mouth. All of these are atop a heavy-set, very thick-skinned neck and shoulders which merge into the short-haired wrinkled skin of the ponderous body. The limbs are short and stout and, when the animal swims, it uses its hind limbs for propulsion and its fore limbs for steering. The general color of the walrus on land is cinnamon-brown, but when in water it appears to be nearly white—a phenomenon caused by cold water depriving the skin of blood. There are, however, numerous color variations, depending on age, sex and water temperature.

Walruses are social creatures and whether on ice-floes or on land they are almost always found either in small groups or in herds that may number several thousand. They like close, side-by-side company and few sights are more amazing than acres of these huge mammals so densely packed that maneuverability is reduced to the absolute minimum. Even youngsters (no doubt to avoid being crushed) lie on top of adults. "There is much petty squabbling among the group. . . ." writes Banfield. "When sleeping on promontories, or ice floes, one member of the group will rear up from

Walruses inhabit the polar ice sheet around the northern hemisphere. At one time they were slaughtered by the thousands primarily for their tusks, which make valuable carvings. Killing of the mammals is now restricted. (Photo by Fred Bruemmer)

Walrus have large tusks and hairless bodies.

time to time, peer about, and then flop down reassured." If disturbed, they hunch their bodies forward in caterpillar fashion and, amid huge upheavals of water, plunge into the sea.

Females become estrous every 2 years and mate during April and May—under water, it is believed. But sexual maturity in this species is extremely variable, and scientists have found that it may take from 4 to 12 years before females ovulate for the first time, although 5 to 6 years is average. Fertility in males may not be reached until they are 9 or 10 years of age, although some may become fertile in their seventh year. Dr. Francis H. Fay, University of Alaska, (*Handbook of Marine Mammals*, Vol. 1) writes that it may take an additional 5 or 6 years before males have attained full physical maturity and are able to compete with older males in the breeding process. New scientific studies* also show that there *is* delayed implantation (the period in which pregnancy takes place but the embryo is temporarily prevented from attaching to the uterus) and that this period—3 to 5 months as in other pinnipeds— added to the 11 months of gestation (*longer* than in other pinnipeds) delays birth for a total of 15 months after fertilization of the ovum.

*These findings, as recorded by Dr. Fay in his chapter on walrus in *Handbook of Marine Mammals*, Vol. 1, Academic Press, 1981 ("Implantation and gestation," page 18) contradict previously held beliefs that delayed implantation occurs in all pinnipeds *except* walrus.

While walruses will haul out on rocky islands, reefs, or on the mainland to rest during seasonal migrations, their favorite habitats are packs of moving ice, especially those over the continental shelf where the water is shallow and food such as invertebrates can be readily obtained. While invertebrates make up the largest part of their diet, they also consume crustaceans, tunicates and holothurians. The lips and tongue of the walrus mouth are so shaped that the walrus can suck out the flesh of mollusks after they have been loosened by the stiff bristles on the muzzle. The hard shells are then discarded. Some fish are eaten, usually swal-

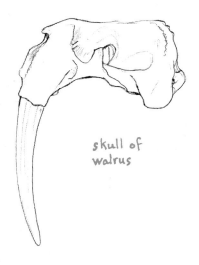

skull of walrus

Walrus

lowed whole. On occasion walruses will prey on seals and will also feast on the carcasses of dead whales. They can dive to depths of 300 feet (90 m) and stay submerged for about 10 minutes.

The walrus gives birth on sea ice to a single calf weighing about 150 pounds (68 kg). The youngster suckles for nearly 2 years before being fully weaned. During its first few months, the calf, if it tires while swimming, will climb onto its mother's back and, on occasion, will even be carried underwater by the mother when she makes shallow dives to feed. When the family breaks up, young females join other female groups and young males join male groups.

Walruses have always been important to native people, although somewhat less so now as southern technology moves north. But even today the mammals' hides are used as sheets to cover boats or umiaks or are cut into strips for lines and ropes; their flesh provides food for human and dog consumption; the blubber provides fuel oil and bones are made into tools. At one time tusks served as sled runners, but today they are made into delicately shaped carvings which have a high market value. The sale of raw or uncarved ivory tusks is prohibited.

Although walruses are now under the protection of governments of several countries, northern oil and gas exploration, as well as other industrial activities, including commercial clam dredging, pose threats for the future and their numbers will have to be monitored carefully.

FAMILY PHOCIDAE

Harbor Seal

Until recently the harbor seal was considered to be one species — *Phoca vitulina*. Studies have shown, however, that significant differences in morphology, physiology and behavior justify the recognition of two species, the other being *Phoca largha*.

Among the major differences are that *vitulina* seals are non-migratory and bear their young on land, whereas *largha* seals are migratory and, while they will haul out on land during ice-free seasons, they return to ice in the winter and it is on ice that their young are born. This affinity with ice has placed them in a group commonly known as the "ice seals." Different, as well, are their pupping and breeding characteristics. *Vitulina* seals, for example, are promiscuous and at breeding time congregate in groups of various sizes (in Alaska sometimes several thousand) made up of mixed sexes and ages; although harems are not formed there are no "family bonds" other than the solicitous and very protective attention the mothers give to their pups during the 2 to 6 weeks period of nursing. Pups of *P. vitulina* are born with a short coat of coarse hair resembling the pelage of the adults (they are at first clothed in the white, woolly "lanugo coat" but this is shed in the womb), and they are able to swim almost immediately. *Largha* seals are monogamous and less gregarious at breeding time and haul out on the ice in small groups. Breeding adults pair off about 10 days before the females give birth to their young, and each pair (along with the new pup) remains together for another month, during which time mating occurs. The *largha* pups, unlike *vitulina* pups, are covered with lanugo fur at birth and retain it for 2 to 4 weeks. At that time it is replaced by a permanent coat of hair which becomes increasingly coarse as the seals grow older; *largha* pups, furthermore, do not begin to swim until they have been weaned.

Both species are timid creatures and move quickly to sea if disturbed; this characteristic, in addition to the fact that when in water they are seldom seen and when on land the herds are usually small and widely dispersed, has made the gathering of accurate population data virtually impossible. The most recent surveys, however, indicate that the world population today is between 760,000 and 950,000 individuals, the *vitulina* making up a little more than half the total.

Until recently only one species of harbor seal was recognized— Phoca vitulina. *Scientists have now identified a second species, P. largha, which in addition to morphological and physiological differences, is migratory and bears its young on ice. Vitulina seals are non-migratory and bear their young on land. This mother and pup belong to the vitulina group. (Photo by Fred Bruemmer)*

Phoca vitulina

This seal has the widest distribution of all pinnipeds. It occurs in both the Atlantic and Pacific oceans, its Atlantic range extending from the eastern Arctic at the top of Baffin Island to Hudson and James bays, Labrador, Newfoundland, Nova Scotia and the Gulf of St. Lawrence. Infrequent sightings of the mammal have been made as far south as Florida. A land-locked population inhabits Upper and Lower Seal lakes in the Ungava Peninsula. Its Pacific range extends from Bristol Bay, Alaska, south along the coast (including the Aleutian Islands) to British Columbia, Washington, Oregon and California. It occurs as well throughout an Asian range which includes the Commander Islands, the Kamchatka Peninsula, the Kuril Islands, and the northeastern part of the Japanese island of Hokkaido.

Vitulina seals are resident in Iliamna, a large freshwater lake near Cook Inlet, Alaska, and in Harrison and Lakelse lakes, British Columbia. Some seals have traveled in winter as far as 25 miles (40 km) up the Columbia River. They are commonly seen around Washington's San Juan Islands and British Columbia's Gulf Islands.

The pelage of this seal at adult stage is variable but may generally be described as ranging from white-gray to dark-brown (sometimes nearly black) with black spots and irregularly shaped white rings and blotches. Males weigh up to 250 pounds (114 kg) and measure from 67 to 75 inches (170-190 cm). Pups at birth are silver-gray in color, with black markings, weigh about 28 pounds (13 kg) and are about 35 inches (89 cm) in length.

Vitulina seals are littoral throughout their range, favoring habitats where reefs, rocks and sandy beaches are protected from the heavy seas of stormy weather. They normally move to land at low tide to bask and rest and leave when the tide returns. They are expert swimmers and are able to dive to depths of about 200 feet (60 m) and remain underwater for up to 23 minutes. Observations made of this mammal's underwater behavior suggest that most dives are in much shallower water and that the seals remain submerged for only 4 to 5 minutes at a time.

Vitulina seals are believed to breed in the water but the time of mating is influenced by their geographical location. Births occur generally from February to September. Mating takes place 6 weeks after the birth of the single pup. Pups are nursed from 2 to 6 weeks and are then abandoned. Following mating implantation is delayed for 1½ to 2 months.

These harbor seals are competitive with the commercial fisheries since much of their diet consists of marketable species such as flounder, salmon, cod, squid, herring and small crabs. Fish caught in commercial nets, such as salmon and mackerel, are often ripped from the webbing and the nets themselves are damaged. The harbor seals also act as terminal hosts of a parasite which infects valuable species of groundfish, thus affecting their sale on consumer markets.

Enemies of the harbor seal, in addition to man, are polar bears, walruses, sharks and killer whales. Golden eagles sometimes prey on basking pups. The normal lifespan of *vitulina* is 30 years.

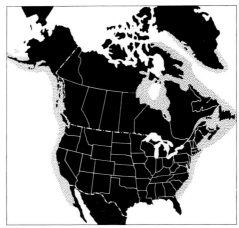
Phoca vitulina

Phoca largha

Phoca largha

Largha seals occupy a western range extending from the Chukchi and Bering seas in the north to the eastern Aleutian Islands, Commander Islands, Kamchatka, Sea of Okhotsk, Sea of Japan, Korea and the Po Hai Sea. They are also littoral in distribution, but haul out on land only when the seas are free of ice during the summer months. As soon as freeze-up begins, they move off-shore to ice floes where they remain until the floes break up in the spring, by which time they may have been carried many miles from their original base. With the coming of winter, however, they migrate north. Their young are born on ice from February to May and within a month following lactation the females mate again. There is a gestation period of about 10 months, including a period of delayed implantation. The pups at birth weigh 21 to 26 pounds (10-12 kg) and are about 34 inches (86 cm) in length. When the pupping and breeding seasons are over, these mammals disperse along the shores of Alaska and Siberia.

Largha seals are excellent divers and some may go to depths of 1,000 feet (300 m) and travel as far as 1,300 feet (400 m) while submerged. They feed during the day, their diet consisting mainly of commercially valuable species such as salmon, herring, capelin, smelt, whitefish and trout. *Largha* seals are preyed upon by polar bears, sharks and killer whales. Under normal conditions they may live 30 years or more.

Phoca fasciata
Ribbon Seal

Because of its remote habitat, its solitary nature and the fact that it seldom occurs near land, the ribbon seal is rarely seen by humans. At one time it was thought that the range of this pinniped was limited to the North Pacific, with populations largely confined to the Sea of Okhotsk, the Bering Sea and, in a more limited way, the Chukchi Sea. Recent surveys, however, show that it also occurs in the area of the Aleutian Islands off Alaska and the Kuril Islands north of Japan. Some, in years of heavy ice formations, have even been sighted along the northern coast of Japan's island of Hokkaido. Despite commercial harvesting of this species in the past, the total population is now estimated at between 90,000 and 100,000 individuals and its future seems secure. The ribbon seal, nevertheless, is one of the least abundant of the so-called "ice seals."

This is one of the most attractive of all land/marine mammals and is especially interesting in that its color and markings change remarkably with every molt until it reaches sexual maturity. It is born with the thick, nearly white, woolly fur known as the "lanugo coat," which is shed about 4 to 5 weeks later and is replaced with a pelage that is blue-black on the upper flanks and back, and silver-gray on the lower flanks and belly. When the next molt occurs the pelage (at that time reddish-brown) becomes black, and the four light bands which characterize the adult seal show faintly. These bands become more and more pronounced until, after additional moltings, they reach their maximum prominence. At that stage the pelage is deep chocolate-brown and the bands are creamy white. One band

encircles the neck and resembles a wide collar, one encircles the body around the shoulders and fore-flippers, and one encircles the posterior trunk. These bands sometimes vary in width and in some seals they come together. Somewhat the same white markings identify the mature females, but because of the females' lighter background they are less pronounced.

Ribbon seals are slender mammals and have one especially interesting morphological characteristic that is not found in other pinnipeds: it is a large air sac in the trachea which, although its true function has yet to be determined, may add to the seal's buoyancy when it is resting in the water. The air sac may also be related in some way to the mammal's underwater vocalizations. Another physical feature is its neck, which is flexible and can be extended to make the mammal appear longer than it actually is.

Seals of both sexes are about the same size—61 inches (155 cm)—but each is heavier in winter when a thick layer of blubber gives them a weight of around 210 pounds (95 kg). There is a significant weight loss (common among pinnipeds) during parturition, breeding and molting. At that time (June) their weight may drop by as much as 50 pounds (23 kg). Weight loss, incidentally, is experienced by terrestrial animals during their winter hibernation.

Male and female ribbon seals occupy similar habitats but are seldom seen, either as individuals or as groups of breeding adults. Their habitat in winter is what is known as "clear" ice—the snow-free area beyond the edges of the floes—along the southern perimeter over the continental shelf. According to Dr. John L. Burns of the Alaska Department of Fish and Game, a scientist who has extensively studied this species, the diet of the ribbon seal is not yet well known. However, samplings of marine life collected from March to June show that pollock, capelin and eelpouts are eaten, and samplings taken during February showed consumption of pollock, polar cod, shrimp and octopus. It is thought that squid may also be eaten.

Ribbon seals live solitary lives except during pupping, breeding and molting, all of which take place on ice from the end of April to about the middle of May. After the pups are born and have been nursed for 3 to 4 weeks, the females mate again. There is a total gestation period of 11 months, including a delay in implantation of 3½ months, before the next pup is born. Each pup weighs at birth about 23 pounds (10 kg) and is approximately 34 inches (86 cm) in length. The pups gain weight rapidly and when weaned weigh on average 65 pounds (30 kg). They are abandoned immediately as nursing comes to an end. During the following three weeks they receive no additional nourishment and their weight drops to about 48 pounds (22 kg). Ribbon seal pups, according to Burns, do not take rapidly to water as do the young of most seals, and proficiency in swimming, diving and finding food is only achieved after 2 or 3 weeks.

While it is now well established that ribbon seals are closely associated with ice when ice conditions prevail, virtually nothing is known about their habitat or behavior during the ice-free months. It is possible that some individuals may haul out on land, but Burns is of the opinion that after the seasonal ice has melted most of the mammals become pelagic and do not haul again until ice reforms in the winter.

An interesting characteristic of ribbon seals is their almost total indifference to intrusion of any kind while they are on ice. It is known that they will sleep for long periods without arousing themselves to survey the landscape. Their lack of fear, Burns suggests, may be related to the fact that their particular habitat is beyond the range of predatory carnivores such as polar bears and Arctic foxes, and so on "land" they do not know the meaning of fear. When there is cause for alarm, however, they can move with remarkable speed across the ice to the safety of the water. They have few enemies at sea but those that prey on them most frequently are probably killer whales and sharks.

Ribbon seals live for as long as 30 years, although the average lifespan is thought to be about 20 years.

Phoca hispida

Ringed Seal

The ringed seal, smallest of all pinnipeds, is in every sense a truly Arctic species. Its range is circumpolar and its habitat is the thick ice which permanently covers the top of the world. Historically the ringed seal has been a mainstay of the native people, although this dependency is diminishing with the encroachment of oil, gas and mineral exploration. Nevertheless there are a number of native communities whose inhabitants still depend on the mammal for food for themselves and for their dogs, and on the hides for clothing, footwear, shelter and covers for boats. Seal oil is burned for both light and heat, and the livers, which are high in vitamin A, are valued as a delicacy. Ringed seals are also hunted

Ringed seal

commercially, although the numbers taken annually are believed to be higher in European than in North American ranges.

Because of its solitary nature, its remote and (to humans) hostile environment, general lack of visibility (especially from ground level) and variation in densities, population counts have always been difficult. The most reliable figure available for the total world population is 2.5 million individuals (a minimum estimate).

The ringed seal, even though it is the smallest of the pinnipeds, is nevertheless an imposing mammal. Adult males weigh between 140 and 180 pounds (64-82 kg) and are 40 to 47 inches (100-120 cm) in length, while females are slightly smaller. Full growth is not reached until the seals are 8 to 10 years of age. Ringed seals are handsome creatures and although color varies, the most common is silver-gray on the flanks and belly and blue-gray on the back. Many irregularly spaced, or fused, creamy-edged dark-centered rings occur on the back and upper sides, and sometimes on the belly; hence this seal's common name. The pelage in some individuals, however, is uniformly dark gray to near-black, and the rings are gray. At the time of breeding, the male's face becomes dark in color.

Female ringed seals reach sexual maturity between 6 and 8 years and males between 7 and 9 years. Mating occurs from April to early May and is believed to take place in the water. Gestation takes about 11 months, which includes a period of about 3½ months delayed implantation.

The ringed seal, like the bearded, ribbon, spotted and largha seals, spends most of its life where sea ice predominates. (Photo by Fred Bruemmer)

Although most of these seals remain within their geographical range throughout the year, some move south with the pack ice on which they have been living. As this ice dissipates, the seals swim north, using stable floes as resting places, until they once again reach their normal range. The southward journey takes Atlantic seals as far south as Hudson and James Bay, as well as Labrador, Newfoundland and the Gulf of St. Lawrence, and the Pacific seals as far south as Point Barrow, Alaska.

The permanent habitat of the ringed seal is thick, shore-fast ice within a few miles of land. This ice covers relatively shallow water in which there is an abundance of schooling fish and bottom-dwelling invertebrates.

Each seal makes a half dozen or so holes, using the strong claws of its front flippers to remove the ice and keep the holes open. Some openings, lightly covered with snow, are only a few inches in diameter at the surface—barely large enough to enable the seal to renew its oxygen. Other holes are large enough for it to climb to the surface and, lying flat, to rest and bask. When on the surface the seal is constantly alert and every few seconds it lifts its head to study its surroundings.

Winter lodgings are made in deep accumulations of snow or in cavities of ice-ridges, and are reached through a hole that is kept open at all times. The seal not only uses this "igloo," generally about 10 feet (3 m) in length and about 2 feet (60 cm) in height, for longer and safer periods of rest, but as a place where the female can give birth to and nurse her single pup. At birth the pup weighs 8 to 10 pounds (3.6-4.5 kg), is about 23 inches (58 cm) in length and is covered with thick, white lanugo, or baby, fur. This fur is shed by the time the 5 to 7 weeks' nursing period is over; the new pelage of coarse, bristly hair somewhat resembles the color and markings of the adult. By that time the pup has more than doubled its weight and, being able to fend for itself, is abandoned. Before nursing has ended, however, the mother will have mated again.

Ringed seals have complete command of their water environment and while they are capable of diving to depths of 600 feet (185 m), it is thought that few dives exceed 300 feet (90 m). They can stay submerged for 15 to 22 minutes. The major predators of ringed seals, aside from humans, are polar bears. In fact, some scientists believe that so great is the dependency of polar bears on ringed seals that should the seals become scarce the bears could not survive. Arctic foxes also prey on newly born and relatively defenseless ringed seal pups. The ringed seal in the wild has a lifespan of up to 40 years.

Phoca groenlandica

Harp Seal

So volatile and unpredictable is the international controversy surrounding the commercial harvesting of harp seals that no attempt will be made in this book to discuss the issues. Suffice it to say that exploitation of the species has been the basis of a lucrative although highly perilous industry since 1750. The annual seal hunt, preceded by the colorful and emotional "blessing of the fleet," is as much a part of Newfoundland's mari-

The large appealing eyes of all young pinnipeds, such as this ringed seal pup, make them among the most attractive of all wild mammals. (Photo by Fred Bruemmer)

time history as the comings and goings of the Grand Banks fishing fleet. Whether sealing comes to an end as a result of growing public opposition to the slaughter of the mammals, particularly the killing of newly-born pups—the "whitecoats" as they are called—remains to be seen; but opposition has become intense, not only in North America but in Europe as well.

The harp seal is indigenous to the North Atlantic and Arctic oceans. There are three distinct breeding populations: one which whelps in the White Sea (an inlet of the Barents Sea), one which whelps in the Greenland Sea north of Iceland, and another (the major one) which whelps off the east coast of southern Labrador, off the northern coast of Newfoundland, and in the Gulf of St. Lawrence. The total world population of this species is estimated at about 2 million individuals, of which approximately 1.3 million occur in Canadian waters.

Harp seals are born during the latter part of February and the first part of March after the herds have completed their migration with the southerly movement of the vast, broken ice fields from the eastern Arctic. Shortly after their arrival at the whelping areas, the

The harvesting of Atlantic harp seal pups—"whitecoats"—has been a major seasonal occupation off Canada's east coast since 1750. Opposition to the killing of these mammals has become intense and the future of the sealing industry is in doubt. (Photo by Fred Bruemmer)

pregnant seals move away from the edges of the floes to places where rough pressure ridges and hummocky snow drifts offer protection from the wind and cold and there, generally during the night or early morning, they each give birth to a single pup between 38 and 43 inches (97-108 cm) in length and weighing about 26 pounds (12 kg). These little creatures are covered with a thick, woolly, lanugo coat which, within a few days, becomes pure white. The pups are suckled for 10 to 12 days, at which time they are abandoned. Within 2 weeks following the birth of their pups, the seals mate again.

The pelage of the harp seal changes color and markings frequently during its early years and some of the changes are known by name. For example, during the first week or so when they are covered with the lanugo coat they are called "whitecoats." As this fur is shed and hairs of gray begin to show they are known as "ragged jackets." When all of the white fur is gone and the pelage of hair is creamy-brown and there are large dark blotches on the flanks, they are called "bedlamers." Pelage changes continue each year until the seal reaches maturity, at which time the male is generally whitish-gray overall, except for the head (which is black just behind the eyes) and the face (which is lighter in color and in some may be black-spotted). The name "harp" seal derives from the fact that the adult male carries on its back a black band which resembles the shape of a horseshoe, or harp; this black band continues along the seal's flanks.

Harp seals are particularly adept at swimming and are not only able to dive to great depths, but to remain under water for long periods of time. Their food intake varies, depending on the season of the year, but it is most intense during the winter and summer. Food also varies according to age groups and habitat. For example, juveniles feed on shrimps and amphipods (the same diet as baleen whales), while yearlings and adults consume prawns, schooling fish such as capelin and herring, and bottom dwellers such as benthic fish and crustaceans. Seals in Greenland waters feed on several species of fish including cod.

Harp seals are gregarious and usually are found in large herds (except for very old males which tend to isolate themselves or to live in small groups). Male seals become sexually mature when they are 5½ years of age, but most do not mate until they are 8. Females reach maturity when they are between 4 and 5 years old, and produce a pup each year. Neither harems nor territorial boundaries are set up at breeding time, although courtship is demonstrative and competitive. Mating occurs during March and there is an 11-week period of delayed implantation. The young are born after a gestation of 7½ months.

Scientists have recorded 15 different underwater vocalizations, some of them resembling gulls' cries, warbles, trills, dove cooing, grunts and clicks. This vocalization occurs only during the whelping and breeding seasons. While the sealing industry accounts for the death of thousands of individuals each year, natural enemies include polar bears, killer whales and Greenland sharks. The harp seal has a lifespan of 20 to slightly more than 30 years.

Harp seal

Halichoerus grypus

Gray Seal

Gray seals are indigenous to temperate North American waters. They are of little economic value and are not harvested commercially. In most parts of their range (Canada being one) their numbers are controlled because of their heavy predation on food fishes and because they damage or destroy nets, lines and traps of commercial fishermen. For example, predation on salmon and cod caught in gill nets in Scotland is often severe, while in Canadian waters the seals commonly cause great damage when they tear mackerel away from set nets and when they strip cod from hooks while lines are being hauled in. To add to the gray seal's undesirable qualities from man's point of view is the fact that it acts as the terminal host for the parasite *Phocanema decipiens*, a worm whose presence in cod fillets makes the product unmarketable.

Gray seals are virtually non-migratory and in our waters are found mainly along the coasts of the Atlantic provinces and most of their offshore islands. Some individuals have been known to move up the St. Lawrence River to about Rimouski, while others frequently appear off the New England coast. One population of about 20 individuals is said to live permanently on shoal islands in Nantucket Sound. This pinniped also occurs in the eastern Atlantic, most of the herds being established around the coasts of Great Britain and outer islands. They occur as well in Iceland waters, in the

While gray seals are not harvested commercially, their numbers are controlled because of their heavy predation on valuable food fishes and because of the damage they do to fishermen's nets. (Photo by Fred Bruemmer)

Baltic Sea and the Gulf of Bothnia and around the coast of Norway as far east as the Murmansk area. Once considered a rare species, the total world population of gray seals is now estimated at 120,000 individuals. Of this total only about 25 per cent are found in Canada.

Gray seals are large mammals, adult males weighing 375 to 685 pounds (170-310 kg) and measuring 77 to 90 inches (193-230 cm) in length; adult females are smaller, weighing 230 to 410 pounds (105-186 kg) and measuring 65 to 78 inches (165-195 cm) in length. Male and female differ in shape, the male, unlike the female, being very massive at the shoulders and covered with skin that is wrinkled and heavy with folds. Of special note is the male's snout, which is long and which ends in a wide and heavy muzzle. It is the odd-looking snout that has given it the other colloquial name "horse-head." Color in both sexes is variable, and while most are silver gray to dusky gray with faint black blotches on the back and sides, others are brown or almost black. The undersides of both sexes are of a light hue. Males are generally darker overall.

Gray seals most commonly frequent mainland shorelines that are rocky or where there are cliffs, often where there are groups of small islands where tidal currents are strong. Some colonies are found on sandy beaches (until recently considered an infrequent occurrence), an example of this being a large colony discovered on Sable Island off the coast of Nova Scotia. Times of whelping and breeding vary and depend on the location of the various colonies, but they generally occur during January and February. Regardless of the size of the colony (some may contain up to 900 individuals), small harems of 8 or 10 females are formed by the dominant males; these males defend their areas, viciously if necessary, against intruders.

Each pregnant female gives birth to a single pup soon after arriving on shore and nurses it for 16 to 21 days. During this period the mothers may make occasional journeys to sea to feed. When lactation is over they abandon their pups and almost immediately mate again, either in the water or on land. Normally cows are bred several times, and often by several bulls, but when the estrous period ends they leave the rookery and do not return until the following year. Meanwhile the pups remain on land for about 2 weeks following their birth and then they too go to sea to live independent lives. Females that have been bred experience an implantation delay of about 3 months and a gestation period of 8½ months, which means a total time lapse of about 11½ months after copulation before the pups are born.

Male gray seals do not mature until they are 8 years of age, but most have to wait until they are 12 to 18 years of age before they are strong enough to compete successfully in the mating process. Females, on the other hand, are sexually mature when they are 4 to 5 years old. Females of this species live in Canadian waters for up to 44 years, while males survive for only about 30 years.

Gray seals are able to dive to depths of up to 480 feet (146 m) and to stay submerged for about 20 minutes. They are thought to be among the few marine mammals that do not have major natural predators, although killer whales and some species of sharks may attack them.

Gray seal

Erignathus barbatus

Bearded Seal

The bearded seal, also known as "squareflipper," is one of the largest of the northern hemisphere's "ice-related" pinnipeds. It occurs throughout a vast circumpolar range and is solitary and seldom seen. Nonetheless the western population of this mammal (Bering Sea to Chukchi Sea), is estimated at 300,000 individuals. While statistics concerning its numbers in waters of eastern North America are yet to be published, the total North Atlantic population (which includes those in European waters) is believed also to be about 300,000. There is no estimate for those in Canadian Arctic waters.

This pinniped is characterized by a head that is disproportionately small relative to the size of its long, thick body and thick neck. Its eyes are large and, like all phocids, it has no external ears. The sides of its snout carry tufts of long, flat bristles, which account for its common name. Adults of both sexes weigh on average from 425 to 550 pounds (193-250 kg), although some have reached a weight of 770 pounds (350 kg), and are 8 to 11 feet (2.4-3.4 m) in length. In some areas females may be slightly larger than males. The color of adult bearded seals, both male and female, ranges from light gray to dark gray, tawny brown to dark brown; the darkest shades occur down the middle of the back. The pelage of short hair is without the mottled and irregular

Bearded seals are also known as "squareflippers," for reasons this photograph makes obvious. They are also known as "ice seals" since they spend most of their lives on fields of drifting ice. (Photo by Fred Bruemmer)

The southerly limit of the western bearded seal is the Aleutian Islands, while the less common eastern bearded seal has been known to be carried by the ice as far south as Newfoundland and Hudson Bay. While most bearded seals (this is noticeably so in the case of the Bering Sea-Chukchi Sea form) maintain a year-round association with ice, in some areas in summer the ice fields recede to areas where the water is too deep to allow for feeding. When this happens the seals will either haul out on shores or remain in the open sea until the ice packs reform in the winter.

Female bearded seals reach sexual maturity when they are 5 to 6 years of age, and males when they are 6 to 7. Mating takes place in May but because of a 2-months' delayed implantation, and a gestation period of about 9 months, the pups are not born until the following April. Each pregnant female gives birth, on ice, to a single pup about 52 inches (130 cm) in length and 70 to 80 pounds (32-36 kg) in weight. The youngsters learn to swim almost immediately and during the 12- to 18-day nursing period grow very quickly, often doubling their weight. The mothers are extremely solicitous and protective, but when weaning occurs the relationship between them comes to an abrupt end and they go their separate ways. About this time the females breed again; in fact, some do so while still lactating. Although these mammals are extremely shy during the winter months and will immediately take to water when disturbed by unusual sounds, they are often indifferent to noise during the warm, basking days of spring and summer. Even low-flying aircraft and men in boats may fail to excite them and, as Dr. John J. Burns points out, "with care it is sometimes possible to crawl across the ice and touch one."

All seals vocalize to a greater or lesser degree both on the surface and under water. This species, while under water, produces a repetitive warbling kind of song of about a minute's duration, each rendition ending in a short moan. At close range the songs can be heard in the air but according to Dr. Burns they can also be heard by "placing a paddle in the water and placing an ear against the butt of the handle." The peak period of singing is during April and May and some scientists suggest that it may be an expression of "sexual excitement."

Bearded seals are important to the economy of the native people, who still hunt them for food for themselves and for their dogs. Their hides make very durable boots, mukluks, household utensils, boat covers

patches common in other seals. The annual molt starts in April, reaches its peak during May and June, and is generally completed in August. In some bearded seals the hair is constantly shedding and there are often visible patches of their black epidermal skin.

Bearded seals spend most of their lives on fields of drifting sea ice which move over the shallow intercontinental shelves. Here, at depths which vary from 165 to 650 feet (50-200 m), they feed on bottom dwellers such as crustaceans, mollusks, worms, hermit crabs and clams; they also consume shrimp and, in lesser amounts, fish. Like other bottom-feeding pinnipeds, they also ingest quantities of sand and gravel. The ice fields, which are kept in constant motion by the force of winds and currents, drift to southern regions during the winter months and the seals move with them. In late spring, as the fields come under the influence of warm currents and weather, they begin to break up and at that time the seals start on their return journey north.

and harnesses and traces for their dogs. The seals' enemies, aside from man, are polar bears, although they are occasionally killed by walruses and killer whales. Bearded seals have a lifespan of up to 23 years. This species is taken in limited numbers each year by United States and Soviet sealers.

Bearded seal

Cystophora cristata
Hooded Seal

The closest counterpart in Atlantic waters of the Pacific's northern elephant seal (*Mirounga angustirostris*) is the hooded seal (*Cystophora cristata*). Like the northern elephant seal, the hooded seal has a large nasal snout which droops limply over the muzzle (it occurs in the male only) but which, during courtship, fighting or when frightened or threatened, can be inflated with air to twice the size of a soccer ball. At the time of mating a bright red nasal membrane (peculiar to the hooded seal) is also inflated and is pushed out of one of the nostrils like a balloon.

The hooded seal is a highly migratory species whose summer molting grounds are on the thick ice pack of Denmark Strait, where, it is believed, more than half a million individuals (probably the world's total population) congregate from mid-June to mid-July. By August, when molting has been completed and the seasonal fast is over, the seals disperse over wide areas of ocean and spend much of their time feeding. Some go south along the east coast of Greenland to Cape Farewell and then north as far as Thule at the head of Baffin Bay, while others go north from Denmark Strait and congregate on the ice pack in the Greenland Sea between Greenland and Spitzbergen.

With the coming of the whelping and mating seasons, the seals migrate again, those in the waters off eastern Greenland going to the ice packs in Davis Strait or to the ice packs off Labrador, Newfoundland, or in the Gulf of St. Lawrence. The populations of hooded seals breeding in our waters are small in relation to the breeding populations of harp seals, but the two species congregate in the same areas and at about the same time. They do not, however, appear to intermingle.

The adult hooded seal is a large mammal, the average male weighing 425 to 775 pounds (192-352 kg) and reaching 102 inches (260 cm) in length. Adult females are smaller, weighing 320 to 660 pounds (145-300 kg) and reaching 80 inches (200 cm) in length. The pelage of this mammal is silver gray with many mottled and irregular patches that are dark brown, brownish-black or black in color. The undersides are lighter. Overall the color and markings are less pronounced in females. When wet the pelage appears more uniformly dark gray.

Whelping occurs during the last 2 weeks of March in areas generally near the center of ice floes. Single pups are born. While the mother is lactating, one or more adult males may court her and, while they remain mostly in the water, should one approach too close to the nursery area the mother will angrily chase the intruder away. At the time of birth the pup, 50 to 66 pounds (23-30 kg) in weight and 34 to 45 inches (87-115 cm) in length, is covered with a coat that is slate-blue on the back and sides and light creamy on the undersides; the face is dark. At this stage the pup is known as a "blueback" and is greatly prized by the fur trade. The mother nurses the offspring for 7 to 12 days, during which time the pup feeds almost constantly and quickly acquires a thick layer of blubber from the extraordinarily rich milk. When lactation has ended, the mother abandons the pup and within 2 weeks mates again. There is delayed implantation of up to 3½ months, followed by a gestation period of 240 to 250 days, after which time, once again on the southern ice packs, a new pup is born.

Male hooded seals reach sexual maturity when they are 4 to 6 years of age, but do not attain what scientists term "true social status" until they are considerably older. Females reach sexual maturity when they are 2 to 9 years of age, but most are mature at 6. Some

When aroused during courtship or when frightened, the large nasal snout of the hooded seal is inflated to about the size of a soccer ball. When mating, a large bright red nasal membrane is also inflated and pushed out of one of the nostrils. (Photo by Fred Bruemmer)

females, however, can mate successfully at 3 years.

Hooded seals are deep-divers and many can remain submerged for periods of up to 18 minutes. Reeves and Ling write about one juvenile, only a month old, diving to a depth of (75 m) 245 feet! The hooded seal is not a constant feeder and is inclined to fast at times other than the breeding and molting seasons. When they are feeding, their diet consists of numerous species of commercially valuable fishes such as herring, capelin, cod, halibut, squid and red fish. Octopus, shrimp, mussels and even starfish are also eaten.

The vocalizations of the hooded seal are not as yet

Hooded seal

well defined, but are said to resemble "grunts," "snorts" and "buzzes." Aside from those harvested commercially, these seals are preyed upon mainly by killer whales. Males and females of the species may live as long as 35 years.

Mirounga angustirostris
Northern Elephant Seal

Next to the elephant seal of the subantarctic, the northern elephant seal is the largest of all pinnipeds. Adult males have been known to weigh more than 2 tons (1,800 kg) and to measure nearly 16 feet (5 m) in length. Adult females are smaller, weighing only 1 ton (900 kg) and measuring about 10 feet (3 m) in length. It is easy to understand why the sight of these massive creatures never fails to arouse excitement and wonder.

During the 1800s this species was heavily exploited by the whaling industry for the oil that could be rendered from its carcass, and by about 1869 so few remained that the mammal was considered commercially extinct. Fortunately a breeding colony of about 100 was found on Guadeloupe Island off the coast of Mexico, and through protective legislation initiated by the government of Mexico and later subscribed to by the government of the United States, the mammal was declared fully protected. These measures, supported also by the government of Canada, have resulted in an incredible recovery of the species. Today the northern elephant seal has increased in numbers to about 48,000

individuals—a remarkable achievement in wildlife management.

As remarkable as that achievement has been, it is no more remarkable than the creature itself. The northern elephant seal is one of the most harmless of all amphibious mammals as far as man's economy is concerned, for its consumption of food is confined to such unmarketable species as rat fishes, spiny dogfish, shark, puffer and cusk eel, although some squid also enters its diet. On occasion, because it is such a deep diver, it gets hooked on bottom-line gear used for the catching of sable fish. "Paddy" Harrison, a commercial fisherman friend of mine, tells of an elephant seal that ran afoul of a hook when he was fishing halibut off Alaska. Killing this mammal, despite its minor unpremeditated sins, is totally unjustified.

The northern elephant seal is typically pinniped in appearance, except in two notable features—the large, grotesque snout which droops over the muzzle (and which becomes inflated during the mating season), and the enlarged, elongated nasal chamber which somewhat resembles that of the elephant (hence the name). Another unusual characteristic is that during the annual molt the outer, or epidermal, layer of skin is also shed.

The northern elephant seal breeds only in southern waters on islands off the coast of California and Baja California where there are good sand or gravel beaches. Adult bulls are the first to haul out and they arrive the latter part of November to establish their dominance over territorial boundaries. Once they are settled in and disputes over land rights have been resolved, the bulls generally stand guard within their territories and only rarely re-enter the water. They draw mainly on their reserves of fat for food. The pregnant females begin to arrive about the middle of December and, either by their own free will, or by being forced or cajoled, they join a dominant bull. Until it can assemble a herd of 40 to 50, the bull restrains its interest in the actual breeding process. If the aggregation of females becomes too large for the male to supervise, other males will arrive to share the "spoils" and so in many cases the rookeries lose their single identity and become a continuous mass of animals. After each female has been on the beach for about a week, it gives birth to a single pup weighing about 65 pounds (30 kg). Nursing begins immediately and continues for about 28 days. By the time weaning is completed the pup may weigh as much as 84 pounds (38 kg).

Once weaning is over the pups, now known as

The northern elephant seal of the Pacific, a huge pinniped weighing sometimes more than 2 tons (2,000 kg), at one time was heavily exploited for its oil and eventually became endangered. International controls, however, have saved it from extinction and today the mammal is numerically secure. (Photo by Fred Bruemmer)

"weaners," leave their mothers and assemble on the beaches in pods where for about a month they live on the fat accumulated during the time of nursing. Eventually, after playing about in the tide pools, learning how to swim and to find food for themselves, they leave the area in small groups and in due course begin their migrations, some of them going as far north as the Gulf of Alaska. During this northward journey some migrants may haul out on beaches to rest; others simply remain at sea. These mammals are occasionally seen in offshore waters, and sometimes on remote beaches along the coasts of Washington, British Columbia and Alaska. In 1981, while a passenger aboard a salmon troller off Vancouver Island's west coast, I saw two elephant seals on beaches in Barkley Sound, east of Ucluelet, but such a sighting is rare.

Northern elephant seal (Breeding islands are circled)

By the time the pups have left the rookery, the females have again become estrous and are ready to breed once more. They may mate with one or more dominant males and when their sexual needs are fulfilled they leave the rookery, very much in need of food after their month-long fast and the strain of feeding the hungry offspring. These females will spend the next few weeks at sea, almost constantly feeding, before returning to the rookery to undergo their annual molt. Here they remain for about a month and then they return to sea, remaining there for the following 8 to 9 months before coming back to bear their pups and mate again. All of the males, including those unable to breed because of immaturity or because of their inability to compete with stronger and more aggressive males, also follow much the same movement patterns, but the breeding males are the first to return the following year.

Female elephant seals become sexually mature at the age of two, while bulls mature at the age of four. Many young bulls, largely because of their smaller size and their inability to infiltrate the well-guarded harems to find receptive females, are unable to mate until they are 7 or 8 years old.

Northern elephant seals, happily now under the protection of conservation-minded governments, are relatively free from the predation of humans, although there are those who will shoot them for the sheer "joy" of killing or in the mistaken belief that the mammals are a threat to the commercial fishery. The only natural enemies of consequence are large white sharks and killer whales. These mammals have been known to live for as long as 17 years in their wild state.

OTHER WILD MAMMALS

This book presents in detail those mammals which, because of their large size, economic value or interesting habits, are best known or most frequently seen. But since many mammals are shy and often very small, they are seen only by rarest chance — except by experienced scientists who, in the course of their field work, seek them out. There are other creatures, however, that are so scarce, or that live in such small geographic ranges, that even the most persistent specialist may never see them.

Most small furred mammals, even though their numbers may be large (shrews, moles, bats, for example) live within the protection of well concealed habitats, and while they flee at the slightest suggestion of danger, they may be occasionally glimpsed. Sometimes they are found dead on country roads or busy highways, or even left on the doorstep by the household cat.

Because there are so many species, it is not possible to deal with them all in detail in this book, but there are a number of fine studies that are available in libraries. Anyone interested in the fascinating history of bats, for instance, would find the Yalden and Morris book *The Lives of Bats* tremendously interesting; similarly, anyone seeking information about lemmings would be well rewarded by reading *The Lemming Year* by Walter Marsden.

Rats and mice that take up residence in homes and other buildings are, of course, a menace to human wellbeing. This is particularly so in the case of the Norway rat (*Rattus norvegicus*), a species that originated in Asia

*Voles are a vital part of the natural food chain and help to sustain other carnivores as well as birds of prey. Their own diet consists mainly of vegetable matter. This female and her new family are heather voles (*Phenacomys intermedius ungava*). (Photo by Dr. Bristol Foster)*

and has since spread throughout the world. This creature, often described as man's worst mammalian enemy, is intelligent, ingenious, aggressive and fascinating. It spreads loathsome diseases and plunders and destroys property. The Black Death of the Middle Ages killed nearly 25 million people; the disease was transmitted not by the rat itself, but by the fleas it carried. Yet despite its dreadful reputation (a 19th-century writer called it "the Devil's lapdog"), the rat has served well in medical laboratories and has, according to one authority, "contributed more to the cure of human illness than has any other animal." A curious paradox indeed!

But mammals, strangely enough, are made much like us, and their daily needs are much like our own. And, as Yorke Edwards says, "they have some astounding special features that often are far more bizarre than man's efforts at science fiction!"

Groups that we dismiss with single words (like "mice" or "rats") have curious and surprising genealogies, including distant relationships with giraffes and barnyard cows. In fact, if we believe in the evolutionary theory, we must then accept the fact that our own primitive ancestors, the primates (which include apes and monkeys as well as humans), are more closely related to tiny tree-shrews that still inhabit the jungles of southeast Asia than to any other mammal. To go one step further, it is generally believed that *all* living mammals are descended from creatures very closely resembling the present-day tree-shrews. And these creatures now —as they probably did in ancient times—weigh, when adult size, about 1 pound (0.4 kg)!

The species that follow are mostly "small fry," many of which unfortunately are regarded with disdain (even, in the case of the tiny field mouse, with apprehension!). Although some of them may be a nuisance around granaries, storehouses and the like, and their numbers must therefore be controlled, they all play a very vital part in the natural food chain of other desirable mammals and, of course, birds. But there are those, such as shrews and moles, that serve man well for they eat insects (among them Japanese beetles and their larvae, cutworms and wireworms) that are harmful to gardens and lawns, while others eat insect larvae and pupae that damage trees. Fortunate indeed is the gardener who can boast having a family of these creatures in residence.

ORDER MARSUPIALIA

Members of this order, which, among others, includes kangaroos, wallabies and anteaters, as well as opossums, are found mainly from Australia west to the Celebes and Moluccas ("Spice Islands") and in North and South America. They occur in New Zealand where they were introduced. There are nine recognized families of marsupials and about 250 species, most of them characterized by the fact that their young, after emerging from the female's cloaca at birth as minute, hairless fetuses (about the size of a bumblebee) laboriously climb up to and enter the mother's pouch where for 9 to 10 weeks they are nourished. The journey of these grub-like creatures, each weighing about $1/2$ ounce (14 g), is one of the marvels of the animal world.

Some marsupials are arboreal, others are terrestrial and/or fossorial, while others are semi-aquatic. There are some that, from a dietary standpoint, are carnivorous, others that are insectivorous, others that are herbivorous and still others that are "everything eaters" —omnivorous.

The one marsupial dealt with in this book is *Didelphis virginiana*, the Virginia opossum, a member of the Didelphidae family. It is an omnivore that occurs throughout a large part of the eastern United States and along a narrow range of the Pacific coast, where it was introduced. In Canada it occurs only minimally in the warmest parts of southern Ontario and British Columbia.

Didelphis virginiana

Virginia Opossum

The Virginia opossum, the only marsupial found north of Texas, is about the size of a domestic cat and is characterized by its long snout, long, almost hairless and scaly tail which (like that of some monkeys) can be used for grasping, and large, hairless and very thin ears. The pelage is long and loose and is made up of a thick undercoat that is gray in color and an outer coat of long, coarse guard hairs with white or black tips. Occasionally reddish, melanistic or albino individuals occur.

This mammal is notably omnivorous and, in addition to feeding on many varieties of insects, also includes in its diet small mammals, birds and their eggs, amphibians and reptiles, berries, nuts and other vegetation as well as carrion. It is a solitary creature and

The mother opossum carries the young on her back once they are too large to be kept in the pouch.

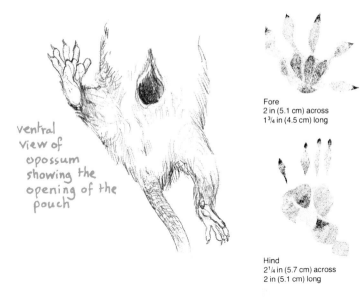

ventral view of opossum showing the opening of the pouch

Fore
2 in (5.1 cm) across
1 3/4 in (4.5 cm) long

Hind
2 1/4 in (5.7 cm) across
2 in (5.1 cm) long

is mostly nocturnal in its forest wanderings. It is active year-round and makes its home in abandoned burrows or in hollows of trees and logs.

Breeding takes place from January to March and may occur again from late May to early July. The young are born after a gestation period of 12 to 13 days. Banfield writes that "as the time for birth arrives, the female carefully cleans the pouch and licks down a pathway in the fur between the cloaca and the pouch entrance. She then props herself up in a sitting position. As the tiny fetuses appear, they are carefully licked dry, one by one. Then they squirm blindly hand-over-hand, with a head-waving motion, up the moistened pathway to topple into the pouch. Inside, the first thirteen seek out the minute teats and fasten on. The litter may consist of up to twenty-five fetuses, but some do not find the pathway and fall to the ground, and others, the late arrivals, finding all the teats taken, are also doomed."

Some may die during the suckling period, but those that do survive (about eight on average) remain in the pouch for 9 to 10 weeks. At that time they emerge, but for the following 3 months they stay with the mother by clinging on her back. They mature sexually as yearlings and with luck may live for 7 years.

The opossum does not hibernate, but is understandably less active during the winter months. "Possum" hunting in some southern states, generally carried out at night with the aid of dogs and flashlights, is a popular sport. Although the mammal exudes an unpleasant odor, its flesh is said to be tasty when roasted. Some opossums are killed for their fur. A strange characteristic of the creature is its tendency to appear dead after being injured or frightened—a performance once believed to be mere play acting. Scientists now believe, however, that the apparent state of unconsciousness is real and is a temporary reaction to shock.

ORDER CHIROPTERA

Bats

Perhaps the least understood yet most disdained of all forms of mammalian life are the nocturnal fliers we call bats. These creatures make up the largest group, worldwide, of mammals—some 900 species, in fact, divided among 18 families. Bats are found in virtually all tropical and temperate regions of the world, except for most oceanic islands, and range in size from the true fruit bats (generally referred to as flying foxes) of southeast Asia to the bamboo bats of the Philippines. The former weigh more than 2 pounds (1 kg) and have wingspreads of 4 to 5 feet (1.2-1.5 m); the latter weigh about 1/20th of an ounce (1.4 g), have wingspreads of only 6 inches (15 cm), and can roost comfortably in the hollow joints of bamboo stems!

Bats, the only mammals capable of true flight, have an ancestry that can be traced back for some 50 million years. The first bat, in fact, was a resident on earth about 45 million years before the first ape-man evolved. Another interesting thing about this particular creature (scientifically known as *Icaronycteris*) is that its fossil remains were found in Wyoming.

As bats developed, their ranges spread to most parts of the world and one can but speculate on the incredible congestion of air-space and the roar of untold thousands of wings as the creatures left their caves to search for food and do whatever else bats do when they keep their nighttime rendezvous. This phenomenon can be experienced even today in Texas, where some caves serve as home for as many as 20 *million* free-tailed bats. With the coming of night, flocks of tens of thousands take to the sky, some of them soaring to heights of 10,000 feet (3,000 m) where, in the erratic flow of air streams, they reach speeds of as much as 60 miles (96 km) an hour. Dr. Merlin D. Tuttle, Curator of Mammals, Milwaukee Public Museum, in his superb chapter on bats in *Wild Mammals of North America*, wrote that "one morning I watched large flocks spiral down from high in the sky. During re-entry into their vertical cave opening, many dived with swept-back wings at speeds estimated at about 80 miles an hour."

The structure of bats is one of nature's architectural marvels, and while their anatomy is much the same as that of other mammals, it is their wings that make them unique. The wing bones are identical to those of human hands, but with these exceptions: the forearms and fingers of bats are very elongated and are joined by two layers of exceedingly thin, elastic membranes (extensions of the skin of the back and belly) which reach out to the tips of the fingers and then continue back past the forearm to join the knee. In most North American bats the short thumb has a hooked, sharp claw which is used for clinging to whatever surfaces the mammal alights on. The toes also have sharp, curved claws. When in flight bats use both their wings and their legs to achieve propulsion; the limbs work in unison in a "swimming" fashion, not unlike the motion of human swimmers.

Bats vary greatly in cranial appearance and superficially create the impression of being horrendously fearsome. Close examination of the face and head, however, (which are generally quite large in relation to the overall size of the body) reveals features that, even though often grotesque, are attractive in some respects —and certainly fascinating in all! Most bats have small eyes and big ears (in the so-called "hammerhead" the reverse is true), fang-like canine teeth and very sharp incisors, cheek pouches in which food is stored when caught during flight, blunt noses, and scent glands containing a strong musky-smelling substance. The pelage of these mammals is normally long and velvety and variable in color.

While the specialized diet of bats, depending on species and where they live, consists of fruit, nectar and pollen, fish, blood and small vertebrates, most live mainly on insects. This is true of those belonging to the family Vespertilionidae, the "evening bats," whose vast worldwide range includes almost all of North and South America (except the cold northern regions) and those belonging to the family Molossidae, the "free-tailed bats," also worldwide and found as well in the United States and South America. At this point it should be mentioned that true *vampire* bats are tiny creatures that weigh only about an ounce (28 g); they feed on the blood of other animals, especially cattle, but there are only three species and they are found only in Mexico and the northern half of South America. Another group of bats, known as "false vampires," found in Africa, India, and the Malayan region to the Philippines and Australia, are large creatures, up to $5\frac{1}{2}$ inches (14 cm) in length, and while some species will drink the blood of small mammals they capture, most consume insects and small vertebrates.

Of the 900 worldwide species of bats only the true fruit bats (flying foxes) are without the complex mechanism associated with ultrasonic echo-location, and therefore they navigate and seek their food visually; false vampires, on the other hand, are equipped with a mechanism comparable to low-intensity sonar and this, along with the relatively well-developed vision of their large eyes, enables them to obtain at least some of their food by sight. For the rest—and this applies to the evening bats in our part of the world—echo-location controls their lives. By means of this remarkable and exceedingly complex mechanism, evening bats send out vocal, high-frequency sounds through the mouth (members of some other families send out sounds through the nose) and these sounds echo back from objects in the bat's path. So sensitive and perceptive are the bat's ears that the mammal can measure the distance, direction and density of what is ahead, and whether in fact it is an obstacle or an insect. Scientists estimate that sound emissions while in flight range from 5 to 20 pulses a second, and that when food is encountered the echo-location sounds increase to as many as 200 pulses a second. Although the high-frequency sounds of bats are beyond the range of human hearing, low-frequency sounds are often heard when the mammal is thought to be communicating or expressing emotion such as fear or anger; bats are also noticeably vocal during the mating season. These sounds are shrill chirps and sometimes screeches.

Bats, when flying—and this takes place from dusk to dawn—catch insects in their mouths. If the insects are small, they are generally eaten while the bat is in

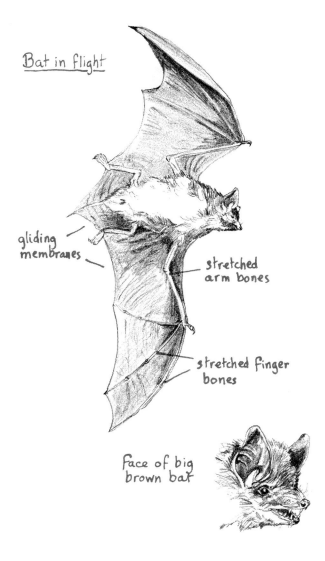

Bat in flight

gliding membranes

stretched arm bones

stretched finger bones

Face of big brown bat

Four families of bats occur in North America: the Vespertilionidae (evening or smooth-faced bats), consisting of 28 species; the Molossidae (free-tailed bats), consisting of 6 species; the Phyllostomatidae (leaf-nosed bats), consisting of 5 species, and the Mormoopidae (leaf-chinned bats), consisting of only 1 species. Only the Vespertilionidae is represented in Canada and the northern United States.

The behavioral patterns of vespertilionids vary according to species. Some are colonial during periods of winter hibernation and while nursing their young in late spring and summer. Others are solitary or, at best, join only in small clusters. While many live during the non-hibernating months in dense, forested areas where there are nearby streams, rivers and ponds and where daytime shelter can be found in woodpecker holes, birds' nests or under bridges, others favor urban areas where shelter can be found in attics, steeples, under eaves, shingles and crevices of various kinds. This is most common in the case of the big brown bat, *Eptesicus fuscus*. One species, the little-known small-footed myotis, *Myotis leibii*, is even reported to have taken shelter behind wallpaper — presumably paper that was pulling away from the wall of a dwelling.

Most bats disperse for a month or so in late summer and come together again in the fall to hibernate. Those in cold, northern climates usually migrate south where winter temperatures are more moderate. Most bats hibernate in mines and caves, hanging head downward by their toes and with their wings folded back; others wedge themselves between crevices or sleep under rocks.

Bats breed from August through October and again in the spring. Litters, depending on species, range from one to four, sometimes twins, but for most species the number is one. Unique among mammals is that the young are born feet first. While the average lifespan is 4 to 8 years, some have been known to live for more than 30 years.

Like all creatures, bats have their enemies and aside from man, they are preyed upon by owls, hawks, skunks, snakes, mink, racoons, cats and dogs, to name a few.

Bats traditionally have been disliked by humans and it may come as a surprise to some readers to learn that these little mammals are not only gentle but actually quite likeable. Bats have long been vitally important to medical science, for much has been learned through microscopic study of the vessels in the mam-

flight. Larger insects are carried to a perch where they are consumed after the wings have been clipped off. At least one species, the little brown myotis, *Myotis lucifugus*, the most common in Canada and one of the most common in the United States, also scoops insects into its wings or into the interfemoral membrane between the hind legs to be eaten at leisure. Banfield estimates that while hunting, the little brown myotis consumes at least one gram of insects each hour. Tuttle makes bat consumption of insects even more amazing; he writes that in Texas large colonies of free-tailed bats require 100,000 *pounds* (45,000 kg) of insects nightly to meet their requirements and that to obtain that amount each may cover more than 100 miles (160 km) in a single night!

mal's fragile wings about human blood circulation, blood cells, wound healing, and the effects of inhaled tobacco smoke. Bat hibernation has led to new findings related to hypothermia as an aid in surgical procedures and in arresting senility. The remarkable echo-location system of bats may yet provide the clues for the development of a similar system for blind people. In short, bats should be respected as friends and allies and we should feel comfortable in their presence.

The name Chiroptera comes from the Greek and means "winged hands," while the family name Vespertilionidae (the family inhabiting Canada and the northern U. S. states) is derived from the Latin word meaning "evening." They are also known as smooth-faced bats, for obvious reasons.

The following, by region, are the bats inhabiting our area. Readers wishing detailed information about the individual species should consult Banfield's *Mammals of Canada* or Whitaker's *Audubon Field Guide to North American Mammals*.

Canada and U. S., coast-to-coast
Little Brown Myotis (*Myotis lucifugus*)
Silver-haired Bat (*Lasionycteris noctivagans*)
Big Brown Bat (*Eptesicus fuscus*)
Hoary Bat (*Lasiurus cinereus*)

Canada and U. S., western
Yuma Myotis (*Myotis yumanensis*)
Long-eared Myotis (*Myotis evotis*)
Long-legged Myotis (*Myotis volans*)
California Myotis (*Myotis californicus*)
Small-footed Myotis (*Myotis leibii*)
Pallid Bat (*Antrozous pallidus*)
Townsend's Big-eared Bat (*Plecotus townsendii*)

Canada and U. S., eastern
Keen's Myotis (*Myotis keenii*)
Eastern Pipistrelle (*Pipistrellus subflavus*)
Red Bat (*Lasiurus borealis*)
Evening Bat (*Nycticeius numeralis*)

Northern U. S., but not Canada
Indiana Myotis (Social Myotis) (*Myotis sodalis*)
Western Pipistrelle (*Pipistrellus hesperus*)

And, by the way, there is no justification for the expression "blind as a bat." While most species have small, weak eyes, they *can* see!

ORDER INSECTIVORA

Mammals belonging to this order are shrews and moles —tiny, furry creatures that, except for their long pointed noses, closely resemble mice. They are found in one form or another in most parts of North America, and in almost every type of habitat: the Arctic tundra, dense forests, alpine meadows, bogs, coastal salt marshes, pasturelands, stream banks and lakeshores, gardens, lawns and golf courses.

Shrews belong to the family Soricidae, and moles belong to the family Talpidae. Worldwide there are about 200 species of shrews and about 20 species of moles. About 11 species of the former and 7 species of the latter occur in North America.

These creatures are the world's smallest mammals, the most diminutive being one that occurs in the Mediterranean area and Africa and that is scientifically known as *Suncas etruscus*. It weighs about 0.07 ounce (2 g). The second smallest is North America's pygmy shrew. It weighs about 0.08 ounce (2.2 g). Either would fit comfortably on your little finger.

While shrews may do some light burrowing, most of them live above ground, but generally under the protection of ground cover such as leaves and low-growing plants. Moles, on the other hand, are better equipped for digging and spend most of their time in burrows. Members of both families are veritable dynamos of nervous energy and are in almost constant motion, day and night, as they scamper about in search of food. Food is vital, in fact, and failure to obtain sustenance within a few hours after eating could result in death from starvation.

A notable characteristic of shrews is their pugnacious nature. If not savagely attacking insects and other food, they do battle with each other. These creatures are loners and are so highly strung that under stress their heart-rate reaches up to 1,300 beats a minute—a rate so incredibly fast that a sudden fright can send them into shock or even cause death. Because of their size and their well camouflaged habitat neither shrews nor moles are often seen by humans. Most of these creatures have a lifespan of only a year and a half.

FAMILY SORICIDAE

Sorex cinereus
Masked Shrew

This is the most common of the shrew family and a species that occurs in almost every part of Canada, Alaska and the northern United States. It is found in a wide range of habitats—forested areas, salt and freshwater shorelines, alpine meadows, grasslands and even the Arctic tundra. It is a small creature, 4 to 5 inches (10-13 cm) in length (one third of which is tail) and weighs about 3 to nearly 7 g. The fur, which is short and velvety in summer, is dull pale brown on the back and pale gray or white on the undersides. In winter the fur is longer but somewhat grayer. The tail is covered with fine short hairs and carries at its tip a black "pencil" tuft.

The masked shrew, depending on geography, breeds from late April to early October. One to three litters, each averaging about four young (sometimes as few as two or as many as 10) are born 17 or 18 days after conception, and each weighs about 0.1 grams. The natal nest is generally an accumulation of dried grasses placed under a log or some other protective covering.

These creatures are beneficial in that they consume large quantities of insects, especially larch and spruce sawflies. Like most of its kind, the masked shrew has a pugnacious temperament.

Sorex arcticus
Arctic Shrew

This shrew occurs mainly in Canada, in an irregular pattern which includes Nova Scotia and the eastern part of New Brunswick, northern Quebec and northern Ontario, most of Manitoba, the northern parts of Saskatchewan and Alberta and most of the western Northwest Territories. It is present in the United States in Alaska and from Lake Michigan to North Dakota.

It is a short-tailed member of the family, about $4\frac{1}{2}$ inches (11 cm) in length. Its coat in winter is glossy black on the back, brownish on the flanks and gray to white on the belly. In summer the color tones are chocolate brown on the back and grayish-brown on the flanks and belly. The tail is cinnamon brown.

The habitat of the Arctic shrew is generally dry places but usually close to bogs and marshes. As far as is known there are two litters during a one-year season, each with an average of about six young. Its lifespan is under 2 years.

Microsorex hoyi
Pigmy Shrew

This rare, diminutive creature is the smallest of all New World mammals, weighing at adult size about 2.2 g. Including tail, it is about $3\frac{1}{2}$ inches (9 cm) long. It occupies a mainly Canadian range and is present in all provinces except Newfoundland (the island, that is). Its

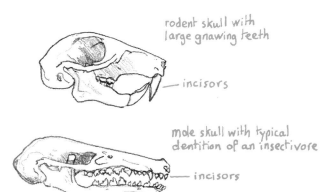

rodent skull with large gnawing teeth

— incisors

mole skull with typical dentition of an insectivore

— incisors

Short-tailed shrew.

Shrews and moles have small eyes and small or no external ears.

United States range takes in the northern states from about North Dakota east to the Atlantic seaboard, as well as most of Alaska. It so closely resembles the masked shrew (a larger species, however) that only an examination of the teeth can establish the difference.

The pigmy shrew in summer is brownish on the upper parts and grayish on the underparts. In winter the brown color changes to a more olive-brown shade.

The pigmy shrew is found mainly in dry, grassy areas of boreal forests; it is also known to frequent wetlands. It feeds mainly on insects, and is believed to bear only one litter a year. Like all soricids its lifespan is less than 2 years.

Sorex monticolus
Dusky Shrew

The dusky shrew inhabits mountainous western North America from Alaska south to California and New Mexico, and favors forested areas where water is close by. It is also found in wet meadows. It is rusty brown on the upper parts and light reddish below.

Sorex merriami
Merriam's Shrew

This species does not occur in Canada but is found in several adjacent northwestern states. Its U.S. range extends throughout the midwest from North Dakota to New Mexico. It is gray above and white below. This little-known species is believed to inhabit dry areas such as deserts, but is also found in open meadows and woodlands.

Sorex vagrans
Vagrant Shrew

This is a western species whose range extends from northern Mexico to Alaska. Known also as "wandering" shrew, it is commonly found in mixed forests near streams, marshes and other moist areas. Some populations live at mountain levels of up to 7,500 feet (2,300 m). The vagrant shrew averages about $4^1/2$ inches (11 cm) in length (of which nearly half is tail) and weighs from $^1/8$ to $^3/8$ ounce (3-10.5 g). In summer its pelage is brownish to grayish on the upper parts and grayish, with brown or reddish hairs, below. In winter its fur is overall grayish or blackish. This species is active all year and lives mainly on insects and their lar-

Shrews are the world's smallest mammals, but despite their size they have a pugnacious temperament and often fight with each other. Most live above ground but generally remain under the cover of leaves and low-growing plants. This is the masked shrew. (Photo by Dr. Bristol Foster)

vae, earthworms, small invertebrates, fungus and green vegetation. It produces one litter a year consisting of anywhere from two to nine young. There is a possibility that some may produce two annual litters, but this would be rare.

The six species above are widespread and similar, with large areas of their geographic ranges overlapping. The next three are also finger-size, but with restricted ranges.

Sorex trowbridgii
Trowbridge Shrew

This medium-sized shrew occurs along the Pacific coastal zone from the extreme southwestern tip of British Columbia to southern California. It inhabits coniferous forests and adjacent wooded areas from sea level to elevations of up to 6,000 feet (1,800 m).

The coat of the Trowbridge shrew in winter ranges from slate black to dark bluish-gray or sooty gray above and paler gray beneath. Its tail is brown on top and white underneath. In summer the fur changes to dark brown. This mammal's diet consists mainly of insects, worms, spiders and the like. A considerable amount of vegetation is also consumed, particularly during the winter. There are believed to be two litters during the mammal's short lifespan, each litter being born in the spring and averaging five young.

Sorex fumeus

Smokey Shrew

Larger than the others, it is found in forests and wetlands in Ontario, Quebec, New Brunswick and Nova Scotia in Canada, and south through the New England states to South Carolina. It is brownish in summer, changing to grayish in winter. It makes its burrows in the leaf mould on the forest floor. The weight of this little creature seldom exceeds $1/3$ ounce (9 g).

Sorex gaspensis

Gaspé Shrew

This species, which weighs about $1/4$ ounce (7 g), is so rare that only a few individuals have been encountered. It is fairly long and thin and is dark gray in color. The habitat of this shrew is usually among rocks and boulders, particularly talus slopes. A closely-related species is the long-tailed or rock shrew (*Sorex dispar*). The Gaspé shrew is found in the Gaspé Penninsula of Quebec and in the mountains of Maine. *S. dispar* occurs throughout the Smoky Mountains of North Carolina and Tennessee.

The nine species just listed are very much alike, so much so that a magnifying glass is usually necessary (along with some museum experience) to identify them.

Cryptotis parva

Least Shrew

This shrew closely resembles the short-tailed shrew but is smaller. While it does not occur in Canada, it is found throughout the eastern half of the United States close to the Canadian border around the Great Lakes.

Sorex palustris

Water Shrew

This little shrew weighs $3/8$ to $5/8$ ounce (11-18 g), depending on geography. It occurs from sea level to mountain elevations up to 7,000 feet (2,100 m) and favors areas that are beside or close to streams and lakes. It is found in every province of Canada as well as the southern portion of Yukon and the Northwest Territories, but does not occur in the dry, western prairie country. In the United States its range is largely confined to the west and is irregular. Some populations occur in the eastern states and in southeastern Alaska.

It is a very dark, even black species on the upper parts and dull white below. The water shrew is appropriately named. An excellent swimmer, it can submerge to the bottom of a stream but when it stops swimming the air caught in its water-resistant fur provides such buoyancy that the creature immediately shoots back to the surface. Hair on the hindfoot also traps air bubbles and enables the shrew to actually run on water—for short distances!

Blarina brevicauda

Short-tailed Shrew

This is a mouse-sized, mole-like creature that occurs in moist areas of hardwood forest in eastern North America from the Gulf of Mexico north to southeastern Saskatchewan and Manitoba, the southern half of Ontario and Quebec and all of the Atlantic provinces except Newfoundland.

The fur of the short-tailed shrew is short and velvety, slate black on the uppersides and gray beneath. It is more fossorial than other soricids and is not agonistic. There may be as many as three litters during the mammal's lifespan, each averaging about five young. While some individuals may live until their third spring, most die when they are about 18 months of age. The major cause of death is starvation.

The short-tailed shrew is noted for its poisonous bite. When it attacks other mammals such as mice, a mixture of venom and saliva enters the wound and is strong enough to subdue or kill its prey. When experienced by humans, the bite has been known to cause shooting pains and swelling. This shrew, however, feeds primarily on insects and other small invertebrates.

Sorex bendirii

Bendire's Shrew

This is North America's largest shrew, an average adult being about $6^{1/2}$ inches (17 cm) in length, tail included. It inhabits only the warm Pacific coast from the Fraser Valley in British Columbia south to California.

While its range is similar to that of the Trowbridge shrew, its habitat is different in that it does not occur at the same high elevations. It does, however, favor coniferous forests where there are streams and wet areas and it is commonly found on beaches. This creature, if forced to escape to water, is a good swimmer. Much yet remains to be learned of its behavioral patterns.

FAMILY TALPIDAE

Fortunate, indeed, is the person who sees a mole in the wild, for of all species of fossorial mammals this creature is by far the most constantly subterranean. Rarely does a mole venture out of its burrow system and when it does it scampers back, if for no other reason than that its small, weak eyes are extremely sensitive to light. This mammal, generally larger than a shrew, is elongated and cylindrical in shape. Its long, pointed snout projects over the margin of the lower lip, is fleshy and movable, and with its whiskers is its primary sensory organ. The neck of the mole is short, and the eyes are minute and generally hidden in the fur. A particular characteristic is its disproportionately large, broad front feet which are equipped with long, flattened claws. The feet are permanently turned outward and are ideally suited for burrowing and for moving through soil with ease. The thick plush-like fur is grainless, which enables the mole to move as easily backward as forward.

Moles make two types of burrows—one running just under the ground, which is used for feeding and resting, the other much deeper, which is used as a nurs-

ery as well as for shelter. Provision is also made in side passageways for the disposal of body wastes. In constructing tunnels the mammal pushes excess earth upwards to the surface and in doing so creates little piles that are commonly referred to as molehills. Since moles prefer to remain underground, there is little need for surface openings, but when these are excavated they are invariably plugged.

Moles are active year-round and during all hours of the day and night. They mate in the spring and after a gestation period of 4 to 6 weeks produce an average of four young; the young moles, blind and naked at birth, are self-sufficient when about a month old, at which time they leave the nest and construct their own burrows. They breed for the first time the following spring. Moles are solitary and will fight each other whenever they chance to meet.

These mammals are heavy eaters, and while worms and white grubs are probably their favorite food, they also consume many kinds of insect larvae as well as snails, slugs and, on occasion, voles and garter snakes. Small amounts of vegetation also are included in their diet.

Neurotrichus gibbsii

American Shrew-Mole

This creature, the smallest of the North American moles, about 4 to 5 inches (10-13 cm) in length and about $1/4$ to $3/8$ ounce (7-11 g) in weight, is the only member of the Talpidae family that has arboreal capabilities—even though these capabilities are confined to climbing low bushes in its search for food. It is a western species that inhabits only the warm Pacific coast from Vancouver, British Columbia, south to California. It is called shrew-mole because its forefeet are similar to those of the shrew: they are not adapted to digging. (There are cranial differences, as well). Its habitat is mixed forests where the soil is deep, moist and soft. The American shrew-mole is overall gray in color.

Scapanus townsendii

Townsend's Mole

This is a large black mole nearly 8 or 9 inches (20 cm) in length whose range is similar to that of the American shrew-mole. Its habitat is most frequently open places such as meadows and fields. It sometimes makes its home in lawns, in which case it is a nuisance.

Moles have powerful front limbs and large digging claws. Although moles resemble rodents in their habits, their diet does not consist of plant material. Moles and shrews feed on insects, their larvae, and other invertebrates.

Scapanus orarius
Pacific Coast Mole

This mole is found in the range occupied by the shrew-mole, but it is also found in Oregon and Idaho. It makes its home in the moist ground of deciduous forests. It is from 6 to 7 inches (15-18 cm) in length and black in color.

Scalopus aquaticus
Eastern Mole

Sometimes referred to as the "common mole," this mammal is found in the eastern half of the United States south from the Great Lakes and is found in Canada only in Ontario's Essex county. It prefers open woodlands, pastures, lawns and gardens. Its length ranges from about 4 to 9 inches (10-23 cm) and in its northern range it is overall gray in color.

Parascalops breweri
Hairy-tailed Mole

This creature is distinctive among moles because of its hairy tail. It is a forest species and inhabits Ontario and Quebec. In the United States it is found from New England south to North Carolina and Tennessee, as well as west to eastern Ohio. Its length is from $5^{1}/_{2}$ to nearly 7 inches (14-18 cm).

Condylura cristata
Star-nosed Mole

The star-nosed mole is remarkable in appearance because of a ring of fleshy little "fingers" surrounding the end of its snout, all quite pink and bare. The tentacles are always in motion and are used as "direction finders" and to search out food. The tentacles close up when the mammal is eating. The most northern by far, it inhabits woodlots, swamps and sometimes dry areas of the northeastern states as well as Ontario, Quebec and northeastern Labrador.

ORDER RODENTIA

The major rodents occurring in Canada and the northern United States have already been dealt with, but there are other less well known members of the order that must be mentioned.

There remain differences of opinion whereby some taxonomists still retain most species such as rats, mice, voles, lemmings and muskrats in the Old World family Muridae. Other taxonomists place these species in the New World family Cricetidae, leaving only the black rat, Norway rat and house mouse (all introduced to this continent) in the family Muridae. In this book what seems to be the most commonly used classification has been followed.

Because of differences in morphology and behavior, the family Cricetidae is divided into two groups: the cricetines and the microtines. The cricetines make up the largest group since it consists of all members of the family except the lemmings and voles. In addition to differences in body structure (particularly in the nature of their teeth) the distinguishing characteristics of the two groups are:

Cricetines: These mammals have long tails, large eyes and ears, and are nocturnal. They are omnivores, and while vegetable matter, fruit, insects and invertebrates make up most of their diet, some will also kill and eat mammals their own size.

Microtines: These mammals have stout bodies, short legs and tails, and their eyes are almost concealed under their thick fur. Unlike the cricetines, microtines are active day and night. They eat many kinds of vegetation, needles, twigs and bark of trees, to mention only a few of their favorites.

Both groups share two important characteristics: they breed throughout the year and produce several litters annually.

FAMILY GEOMYIDAE

Pocket Gophers

Sixteen species of pocket gophers make up this strictly North American family of small, fossorial rodents, but only four occur within the geographical scope of this book. They are the northern pocket gopher, the plains pocket gopher, the western pocket gopher and the camas pocket gopher.

These creatures spend virtually their whole lives in burrows and on the rare occasions when they do appear above ground it is generally to gather surface food or to establish new burrows in more desirable areas.

The burrowing systems of the pocket gopher are of two types: one system of tunnels runs from a few inches to a foot or more beneath ground level and is used primarily for easy access to the roots and tubers of vegetation; the other system is deeper and consists of tunnels providing side areas for nesting, food storage and disposal of body wastes. The tunnels are only a few inches in diameter and run in haphazard directions, sometimes for considerable lengths. When a burrow is constructed the mammal works mainly at night, using its strong foreclaws to loosen the soil, which is then pushed to the surface through an inclined vertical shaft. If necessary the mammal uses its large incisors to loosen hard soil, remove stones or to cut through roots. Numerous entrances are made at different places along the burrow's length, but these are usually closed off with earth; the entrances are detectable by the mounds of soil on the surface.

Often, when feeding on vegetation that penetrates the roof of the upper chamber, the gopher will pull the whole plant down rather than just eat the roots or tubers. Some of this food is eaten on the spot, some of it is dragged to the pantry, but most of it is cut into small pieces and carried in the cheek pouches to the food storage area. These cheek pouches are external fur-lined pockets which extend from the front of the face back to the shoulders. To remove the food the gopher places its front feet at the back of the pouches and pushes forward. When emptied the pouches are turned inside out to be cleaned and then, by means of a special muscle, are returned to their original position. This mammal's lips can also be closed behind the upper and lower incisors, which enables it to keep earth and other material from entering the mouth. If dirt gets into its

Unlike chipmunks, pocket gophers have <u>external</u> cheek pouches with openings to the front.

eyes, they can be cleaned by releasing a fluid contained in the lachrymal glands.

The pocket gopher is strictly a loner and is content to live out its mainly underground life in the darkness and solitude of its burrows. Normally, tunnels that intersect those of other gophers are sealed off, but should the barrier be freed and the mammals meet, a vicious fight, to the accompaniment of loud squeals and hisses, generally ensues. This antisocial behavior is relaxed only during the mating season in April and early May (pocket gophers in mountain areas, according to Banfield, may not mate until July or August) and any demonstrations of goodwill occur only between male and female. When copulation is completed to each other's satisfaction, the mammals return to the pitch-black security of the burrows and the connecting tunnels are again sealed off.

The female gives birth to a litter of from 2 to 7 young (4 on average) after a gestation period of 3 to 4 weeks. The young stay with the mother for about 2 months and then leave to create their own burrows and to lead their own solitary lives.

Pocket gophers can be pests if they occur where vegetables, fruit trees or flowers are grown, or where there are field crops such as corn or alfalfa. They have been known, as well, to gnaw the covering of underground cables, even, claims Banfield, if it is lead or copper sheathing. They do, however, help to aerate the land and to enrich it with the humus that forms from excreta or from uneaten vegetation.

Pocket gophers do not hibernate and so must continue to find food during the winter months to supplement whatever it earlier cached away. If the ground is soft enough, even though snow-covered, the mammal will burrow to the surface and make tunnels through the snow itself, often lining these elongated "igloos" with earth to prevent their collapse. Surface vegetation helps to sustain them until spring brings on new root and tuber growth.

Structurally the pocket gopher is a fairly stocky creature with short legs, a short naked tail and a sparsely haired body. Its eyes and ears are small. It has two very distinctive characteristics: the pair of prominent external cheek pouches which extend from the mouth backwards to the shoulders, and the large, exposed orange-colored incisors. Weights vary according to species, but range from 5 to 18 ounces (141-510 g). Color also is variable but is generally light to dark brown, even blackish, on the back and sides. Albinos are not uncommon.

Pocket gophers are preyed upon by badgers, weasels, foxes, skunks and snakes (and no doubt other animals). It is evident that they spend more time on the surface at night than was previously thought, but they are not preyed upon by owls. This lack of owl predation has been borne out by examination of the pellets regurgitated by the birds. These pellets contain indigestible matter and thus far there has been no significant evidence of gopher remains. The lifespan of pocket gophers can be about 3 years.

Thomomys talpoides
Northern Pocket Gopher

A western species, its range in Canada includes southern Manitoba, Saskatchewan, Alberta and British Columbia. In the United States it occurs south to California and New Mexico, including the states of Washington, Oregon, Nevada, Arizona, Utah, Idaho, Montana, Wyoming, Colorado, New Mexico, Nebraska and North and South Dakota.

This is a small creature, weighing about 3 to 5 ounces (85-140 g). It is about 9 inches (23 cm) in length. Its color varies from brown to yellowish-brown, with white patches under the chin. It is commonly found in meadows and other areas where the earth is loose and moist, such as along river banks. Some occur in rich grasslands of mountains of both Canada and the United States.

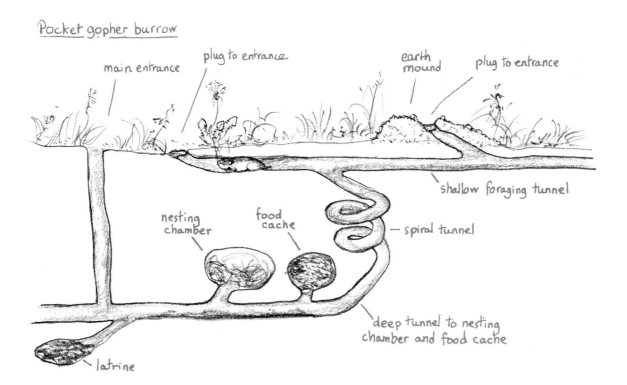

Pocket gopher burrow

main entrance — plug to entrance — earth mound — plug to entrance — shallow foraging tunnel — spiral tunnel — nesting chamber — food cache — deep tunnel to nesting chamber and food cache — latrine

Geomys bursarius
Plains Pocket Gopher

This species is fairly large, weighing 4½ to 12½ ounces (127-354 g) and measuring about a foot (30 cm) or more in length. Its color varies, ranging from light to dark brown on the back and sides (sometimes near black on the upper parts). There may be white on the throat and on the back. The feet are whitish or pale brown.

This species is found in the eastern Great Plains region of the United States and occurs only marginally in Canada, in a small pocket of southern Manitoba east of Emerson. In the United States its range includes eastern North Dakota and South Dakota, Minnesota, Wisconsin, Illinois, Indiana, Missouri (where it is common), Arkansas, Louisiana, Wyoming, Colorado, New Mexico and Texas.

It prefers grasslands and meadows where the soil is moist. It is often found in lawns and in gardens where its tunneling and eating habits make it a decided nuisance.

Thomomys mazama
Western Pocket Gopher

This species occurs only in the United States, and its range is limited to western Washington (to the Pacific coast), northwest Oregon and northern California. It is a small mammal about 7 to 9 inches (18-23 cm) in length weighing about 2 to 3½ ounces (57-100 g). Its color varies from reddish-brown to gray or even black, the shades often being directly related to the soil in which it makes its burrows. This species is believed to be less fossorial than other gophers, but its occurrence above ground is mostly at night.

Thomomys bulbivorus
Camas Pocket Gopher

A rare, little-known species which occurs only in an area near Portland, Oregon. Whitaker says that this mammal is the largest of all gophers occurring in that state and that it has a particular fondness for the bulbs of the camas lily, hence its common and Latin names.

FAMILY HETEROMYIDAE

Pocket Mice and Kangaroo Rats

These little creatures are what biologists often refer to as the "different mice," mostly because instead of being mice and rats they are actually related to pocket gophers (family Geomyidae). One especially common morphological characteristic is that, like pocket gophers, heteromyids have external fur-lined cheek pouches that are used for transporting food to underground burrows. When the job is done, the pouches can be turned inside out to be cleaned and then returned to their original position by the action of a special muscle. The pelage of these mammals is generally soft and velvety, although in some it is harsh and spiny. All are burrowing mammals, are nocturnal in habit, eat the same foods (mostly seeds and vegetation, but sometimes insects and other invertebrates), store food in underground "pantries" and derive most of their moisture from the vegetation they eat. They give birth to one to eight young in underground nests. All are active throughout the year.

These mammals have a short lifespan, sometimes only a matter of months, since they are heavily preyed upon by coyotes, badgers, skunks, weasels, snakes, hawks and owls, and are thus particularly important in the natural food chain.

This family is made up of about 70 species, but the only ones present in Canada and northern United States are the olive-backed pocket mouse, plains pocket mouse, Great Basin pocket mouse, hispid pocket mouse (genus *Perognathus*); dark kangaroo mouse (genus *Microdipodops*); and Ord's kangaroo rat and chisel-toothed kangaroo rat (genus *Dipodomys*).

The *Perognathus* group travel on all four limbs, and when foraging stand in a bipedal position. Those belonging to the *Microdipodops* and *Dipodomys* group move only by the use of their hind feet with the tail acting as a balance and as a prop while standing. These latter two groups jump in much the same manner as do kangaroos, hence their name.

Perognathus fasciatus
Olive-backed Pocket Mouse

This soft-furred pocket mouse is found in a small midwest range which takes in the extreme southwestern tip of Manitoba, the southern part of Saskatchewan and the extreme southeastern tip of Alberta. Its United States range takes in the states of Montana, North and South Dakota, Wyoming and northwestern Nebraska, northwestern Colorado and extreme northeast Utah. It inhabits arid grasslands and lives primarily on seeds, along with some insects. It is grizzled gray on the upper parts and white below, weighs about $3/8$ ounce (10 g) and is no longer than $5^5/8$ inches (14 cm).

Perognathus flavescens
Plains Pocket Mouse

This mammal occurs only in the United States in a range that runs from southeastern North Dakota south to the Texas panhandle and east to southern Minnesota and northern Iowa. It lives in burrows in arid to semiarid habitats and feeds mainly on grasses and sedges; in farming areas it often consumes large amounts of grain. It is a small, slender creature with a soft, velvety pelage, pale-yellowish to grayish-buff on the upper parts and white below. The plains pocket mouse weighs $1/4$ to $1/2$ ounce (8-14 g) and is $4^1/2$ to $5^1/8$ inches (11-13 cm) in length.

Perognathus parvus
Great Basin Pocket Mouse

This pocket mouse is similar to the olive-backed pocket mouse, but its range extends from south-central British Columbia south through eastern Washington to California. Populations are found in the northern states of Oregon, Idaho and Wyoming. Unlike most of its kind, it experiences a state of winter dormancy and remains in its nest for 3 to 4 months, waking up periodically to eat seeds stored earlier. This species is gray on the upper parts and white below. It weighs $5/8$ to $1^1/8$ ounces (16.5-31 g) and is $5^3/4$ to $7^3/4$ inches (15-20 cm) in length. Its tail is long—almost the same length as its body.

Perognathus hispidus
Hispid Pocket Mouse

The hispid pocket mouse occurs in the United States midwest, the most northerly part of its range being mainly North and South Dakota. Its pelage is harsh and spiny, brownish (with some yellowish hairs) above and buff on the underparts. It has a short tail. It inhabits sparsely covered prairie lands where it lives on seeds and insects. This pocket mouse sometimes reaches a weight of $1^5/8$ ounces (47 g) and a length of $8^3/4$ inches (22 cm).

Dipodomys ordii
Ord's Kangaroo Rat

Only the sand hills of southeastern Alberta and southwestern Saskatchewan are the Canadian habitat of this handsome rat-sized rodent, but its United States range is an extensive, although somewhat irregular one. In the U.S. its most northerly range includes Washington, Oregon, Idaho, Montana, Wyoming and South Dakota. The Ord's kangaroo rat is nocturnal and spends most of its day in its burrow, emerging at night to feed on grasses and forbs as well as grasshoppers and other insects. Like the dark kangaroo mouse, it can survive by drawing on the water in succulent plants and the water in their food as it is metabolized. Banfield writes that the Ord's species is also able to reabsorb water from its urine. This species has a long, silky pelage which is tawny colored on the upper parts and white below. It weighs up to $3^3/8$ ounces (96 g) and measures up to $11^1/8$ inches (28 cm) in length.

Microdipodops megacephalus
Dark Kangaroo Mouse

The most northerly range of this United States species is the southeastern part of Oregon. The rest of its range is confined to a small part of northwestern Utah, most of Nevada and a small part of northeastern California. The dark kangaroo mouse lives in burrows in arid sagebrush country and feeds mainly on seeds; it will eat plant leaves and insects when they are available. This little creature is one of the few rodents that relies almost entirely for water on drops of dew or the moisture in plants. Most of its moisture is obtained from its food as it is metabolized. The dark kangaroo mouse is brownish to grayish-black on the upper parts and pale grayish to white on the underparts. It weighs $3/8$ to $5/8$ ounce (10-17 g) and is $5^3/4$ to 7 inches (15-18 cm) in length.

FAMILY CRICETIDAE

New World Rats and Mice

Reithrodontomys montanus
Plains Harvest Mouse

This mouse occurs in prairie country, especially where bluestem and other grasses are prevalent. Its range includes western Wyoming and North Dakota. It generally nests above ground, but will sometimes build its nest in a burrow which it uses as a permanent resting or sleeping area and for raising its young. It weighs about ¼ to ⅜ ounce (7-10 g) and is 4 to 5½ inches (10-14 cm) in length. Pelage is brown on upper parts and white below. This mouse does not occur in Canada.

Reithrodontomys humulis
Eastern Harvest Mouse

This mouse is indigenous to the eastern United States. In its northern range it is found in Pennsylvania, Delaware, Maryland, Ohio and Kentucky. It lives in weedy areas such as marshes and meadows and feeds (mostly at night) on seeds and various grains. Like other "harvest" mice, its name comes from the fact that it stores food in its nest. Some of these mammals hang their tiny nests (made of woven plant materials) on the stalk of a sturdy plant. The nest is round and has a very tiny entrance. This mouse is brown on the upper parts and lighter below. It weighs ⅜ to ½ ounce (10-15 g) and is 1¾ to 3 inches (4.5-8 cm) in length.

Reithrodontomys megalotis
Western Harvest Mouse

This mouse is primarily a resident of the United States, where it occurs over a wide western range. In Canada there are small populations in extreme southern British Columbia, Alberta and Saskatchewan. In its northern United States range it is found in Missouri, Iowa, Oregon and Washington. It inhabits fields, fence rows, marsh borders and other areas where there is good ground cover. Some live in dry valleys and plains where moisture is obtained from the juices of vegetation. In other areas it likes to be close to water. Its main food consists of seeds, but it also eats berries, flowers, fruits and insects. Brownish above, buffy on the sides and white underneath. Weighs ⅓ to ½ ounce (9-14 g) and measures 4 to 6⅛ inches (10-16 cm) in length.

Peromyscus maniculatus
Deer Mouse

The deer mouse is abundant in both Canada and the United States. In Canada it occurs in every province except Newfoundland and is present in most offshore islands; it is well-known in the Yukon and western Northwest Territories. It occurs in all of the northern states and some Alaskan islands. There are many subspecies, but most look alike and can be identified only by close examination by specialized scientists. Deer mice live in a variety of habitats, some of them as unlikely as an old shoe or pocket of a coat hanging from a wall in a deserted cabin. They are omnivores, and will eat seeds, berries, nuts, insects, fungus, caterpillars and birds' eggs. Some make their nest in burrows, some in hollow logs, and some in the cavity of a tree root. This is a pretty little creature about 1 ounce (28 g) in weight and 4⅜ to 8 inches (11-20 cm) in length, including its 1¾ to 4¾ inch (5-12 cm) tail. It is reddish-brown (sometimes grayish) above and white below. A close relative is the Sitka mouse (*P. sitkensis*), a slightly larger creature which is found in British Columbia's Queen Charlotte Islands and islands of southern Alaska.

Despite the distaste with which many people regard mice, those belonging to the New World family, such as this deer mouse, are immaculately clean and, in fact, quite attractive. (Photo by Wayne Campbell)

Fore
³/₈ in (1 cm) long

Hind
⁷/₈ in (2.2 cm) long

Deer mouse tracks

White-footed mouse

Peromyscus leucopus

White-footed Mouse

This mouse, also known as "wood mouse" and "wood gnome," is similar to the deer mouse. It is common over the eastern half of the United States and occurs also in Ontario, southern Quebec and southern Nova Scotia. It is one of the climbing species and often makes its nest in tree cavities, abandoned nests of birds and squirrels, fallen logs, abandoned burrows or haystacks. It feeds on insects, seeds, fruits and often caches food near its nest with the approach of winter. Its color ranges from reddish-brown to tawny, and is white underneath. It reaches an average length of about 7 inches (18 cm) and a weight of ²/₅ to 1 ounce (11-28 g).

Onychomys leucogaster

Northern Grasshopper Mouse

This species occurs mainly in the United States midwest, with populations in Washington, Oregon, Montana, Wyoming, North and South Dakota, Minnesota and Iowa. Its Canadian range includes southern Manitoba, Saskatchewan and Alberta. Its habitat is the dry prairies and the low valleys and deserts of the Great Basin, where it feeds on insects (particularly grasshoppers) and occasionally other mice. It lives in burrows where it normally caches food. It is fairly heavy-bodied and is grayish, sometimes cinnamon-colored on the upper parts and white below. It weighs 1 to 1⁷/₈ ounces (27-52 g) and is from 5¹/₈ to 7¹/₂ inches (14-19 cm) in length.

Woodrat

Neotoma floridana

Eastern Woodrat

A United States mammal, it occurs in the eastern part of the continent with its northern range extending to Pennsylvania and New York in the east and South Dakota in the west. It lives in rocky, treed areas, as well as open lands where the terrain is swampy. It feeds mostly on a wide variety of vegetation as well as fungi and insects. This mammal is brown or grayish on the back and sides and white or grayish on the belly. It weighs 7 to 16 ounces (200-455 g) and may be as long as 17³/₈ inches (43 cm).

Neotoma fuscipes

Dusky-footed Woodrat

This mammal occurs along the United States west coast, its most northerly range being in western Oregon east of the coast. It builds its nest on the ground as well as high up in trees and feeds mainly on green vegetation as well as seeds, nuts and fruits. It is buffy-brown on the upper sides and grayish to whitish (sometimes with touches of tan) on the belly. It weighs 8 to 9 ounces (225-255 g) and is about 13 to 19 inches (33-48 cm) in length.

Neotoma cinerea

Bushy-tailed Woodrat

Anyone who backpacks, pitches a tent or builds a cabin in the western mountains, sooner or later stands a good chance of encountering one of the wilderness' most famous rodents—the bushy-tailed woodrat. This large mammal is at times a kleptomaniac, whose habit of stealing human belongings (especially objects that are shiny, such as razor blades, watches or eating utensils) and hoarding them in its den is legendary. It occupies a large range that extends from the lower part of the Yukon to southern California and new Mexico, and is also found in Washington, Oregon, Idaho, Montana, Wyoming and North and South Dakota. In addition to British Columbia (excluding offshore islands) it is found in the Rocky Mountains and foothills of Alberta. Its habitat ranges from sea level to high alpine regions and it makes its home in caves, cliff crevices, log cabins, abandoned mines and often coniferous forests. It feeds on green vegetation, but will also eat nuts, seeds, fruits, mushrooms as well as insects and the flesh of dead mammals. This mammal weighs $5\frac{1}{2}$ to $15\frac{1}{2}$ ounces (156-439 g) and is $11\frac{1}{2}$ to $18\frac{1}{2}$ inches (29-47 cm) in length, about half of this length being tail. Its long, dense pelage ranges from pale gray to black on the upper parts and white below. Its tail is fairly bushy and resembles that of a squirrel. Whenever the woodrat is present, there is a strong musky odor; this is most evident at its den and nesting site—usually hidden in a crevice behind rocks.

Clethrionomys gapperi
Southern Red-backed Vole

This mammal, also known as Gapper's red-back vole, is common throughout Canada and all of the northern states. It is a creature of cool, damp areas such as swamps and bogs and forested areas where there are decaying tree-trunks and moss-covered ground. It often occurs above the timber line where there are mossy talus slides. In open prairie country its habitat is generally in coulees where there is shrubby vegetation. It lives on a varied diet of vegetation, fruits, seeds, buds of plants and the bark and stems of shrubs and trees. This vole varies in coloration but a typical specimen may be rust to reddish or gray to yellowish-brown on the upper parts and white or gray on the underparts. A distinguishing mark is the broad stripe which runs from the forehead to the base of the tufted tail. This mark varies in hue and may be reddish-brown, sooty-gray or bright chestnut. While it uses surface runways, it constructs its nest underground; occasionally, however, it will nest in logs. The southern red-back vole is a tiny mammal weighing $\frac{5}{8}$ to $1\frac{1}{2}$ ounces (16-42 g) and measuring $4\frac{3}{4}$ to $6\frac{1}{4}$ inches (12-16 cm) in length, nearly two inches (5 cm) of which is a slender tail.

Clethrionomys rutilus
Northern Red-backed Vole

The northern red-backed vole (sometimes called tundra red-backed vole) is holarctic in distribution and occurs on this continent in Alaska, Yukon, Northwest Territories and northern British Columbia. It inhabits open forest or scrub as well as rocks and talus slopes. Its diet consists of various shrubs, berries, leaves, twigs and heaths. This mammal uses surface runways and during the winter follows runways under the snow. It makes its summer nest in underground burrows and its winter nest above ground. Its color varies according to

the season and the age of the mammal but may generally be described as light-brown to yellow or pale brownish-yellow; usually, in summer, it has a bright reddish-brown dorsal stripe which runs from the forehead to the bushy tail. This mammal weighs $\frac{3}{5}$ to 1 ounce (18-28 g) and is about 6 inches (15 cm) in length.

Phenacomys intermedius
Heather Vole

The heather vole occurs in every Canadian province except the Maritimes and Newfoundland; its range also extends into the lower part of the Northwest Territories and the Yukon. In its northern United States range it occurs in Washington, Idaho, Utah, Montana, Wyoming and Minnesota. Its habitat primarily is dry forest areas, where it feeds on vegetation. This mammal is grizzled-brown on the upper parts and silvery on the underparts. It weighs $\frac{1}{2}$ to $1\frac{3}{8}$ ounces (15-39 g) and its length is $5\frac{1}{8}$ to 6 inches (13-15 cm).

Phenacomys albipes
White-footed Vole

The rarest of all North American voles and one which occurs only along the coastal areas of northern California and Oregon. It feeds on vegetation. It is a burrowing mammal, is overall brown in color, weighs less than 1 ounce (28 g) and ranges in length from $5\frac{3}{4}$ to $7\frac{1}{4}$ inches (15-18 cm).

Phenacomys longicaudus
Red Tree Vole

This species is found along the coastal regions from northern California to Oregon. It lives most of its life in trees, where it builds its nest and where it feeds mainly on the needles of Douglas firs. It is reddish on the upper parts and white on the belly. It seldom exceeds $1\frac{5}{8}$ ounces (47 g) in weight and $8\frac{1}{8}$ inches (20 cm) in length.

Vole

Microtus pennsylvanicus
Meadow Vole

This is by far the most common and most widely distributed of the many species in the genus *Microtus*. This is the "field mouse" for all of Canada except for the Pacific Coast and northern Northwest Territories, living also in the southern half of Alaska, and the northern half of the United States except in the far west. The meadow vole lives, as its name suggests, in meadows, where it feeds on vegetation. While its color is variable, a typical specimen would be grizzled, rusty-brown above and grayish below. It reaches a maximum weight of 2½ ounces (70 g) and a maximum length of 7¾ inches (20 cm). It uses both surface runways and underground burrows. It sometimes makes its summer nest on the surface if there is sufficient ground vegetation, such as grass hummocks, or suitable rocks to provide adequate protection. In winter the nests are more commonly made under warm blankets of snow. The nests, globular in shape and about 6 inches (15 cm) in diameter, are made of woven grass.

Microtus montanus
Montane Vole

This little-known vole inhabits the arid Great Basin and high elevation grasslands from southern British Columbia to Arizona. It is found in Washington, Oregon, Montana and Wyoming. It lives on vegetation. The montane vole, also known as "mountain vole," is brown to near-black on the upper parts and gray or white below. It weighs up to 3 ounces (85 g) and measures up to 7½ inches (19 cm) in length.

Microtus townsendii
Townsend's Vole

A western species, it occurs along a coastal range from Vancouver Island and the Fraser Valley in British Columbia south through Washington and Oregon to northwestern California. It is grayer in color than most *Microtus* species. It feeds on vegetation and when living near gardens or nurseries frequently becomes a pest by eating the bark of young trees, thus killing them. This vole is fairly large, weighing up to 3⅝ ounces (103 g) and measuring as much as 9⅜ inches (24 cm) in length.

Microtus oeconomus
Tundra Vole

The tundra vole occurs over a wide range across the top of Eurasia and is found throughout Alaska and the Yukon as well as in a large part of the Northwest Territories. It is also present in a small area on the coastal slope of the St. Elias Mountains in northwestern British Columbia. This mammal inhabits marshes and wet tundra areas adjacent to streams or lakes. It is sometimes found in thick grass at higher, drier elevations. Its food consists mainly of green grasses and sedges, and it is especially fond of knotweed and licorice roots. The coat of this vole is grizzled brown above and buffy-gray beneath. The mammal weighs ⅞ to 2¾ ounces (25-80 g) and measures in length from 6 to 8⅞ inches (15-23 cm).

Microtus longicaudus
Long-tailed Vole

The long-tailed vole is somewhat colonial and is common in forest openings throughout the mountains of the west from a small area in Alaska through most of the Yukon, most of British Columbia and south in the United States to California. Some populations occur in the southern part of Alberta as well as in western South Dakota.

Its habitat is dry, grassy areas ranging from sea level to Alpine meadows at about 4,000 feet (1,200 m) and its diet consists of green vegetation. Its pelage is made up of sparse, coarse hair, grayish to dark brown on the back, grayish on the flanks and silvery-gray on the underparts. This vole weighs ¾ to 3 ounces (21-85 g) and is 6¼ to 10⅜ inches (16-27 cm) in length.

Microtus chrotorrhinus
Rock Vole

This seldom-seen vole is an easterner, occurring in Canada in the northern moist forest of Ontario, Quebec and New Brunswick, and in the United States in Maine and New York, and south to North Carolina. Some populations occur in Minnesota. It feeds mainly on green vegetation. The pelage of this mammal is brown above and gray on the underparts. Its nose and face carry an orange hue. The rock vole, which closely resembles the meadow vole, weighs at most 1⅜ ounces (40 g) and is seldom longer than 7½ inches (19 cm).

Microtus xanthognathus

Yellow-cheeked Vole

This mammal is similar to the rock vole although larger, and occurs across the northern halves of the Prairie provinces, much of the Northwest Territories and Yukon and part of central Alaska. It is colonial in habit and prefers forested areas near streams and marshes. Lichens and horsetails make up most of its diet, although it will also eat wild fruits such as blueberries. This vole is brown on the upper sides and gray below and its nose and face are orange colored. It weighs 4 to 6 ounces (113-170 g) and is 7$\frac{1}{4}$ to 8$\frac{7}{8}$ inches (19-23 cm) in length.

Microtus oregoni

Creeping Vole

The creeping vole is a Pacific Coast species found from British Columbia's Fraser Valley south through Washington and Oregon to northwest California. It inhabits forest edges where there are brushy and grassy areas. Its diet is made up primarily of green vegetation, although berries and fungi are also eaten. In coloration it is brown on the upper parts and silvery below. It is semi-subterranean in habit. The creeping vole reaches a maximum weight of about 1$\frac{1}{8}$ ounces (31 g) and a maximum length of about 6$\frac{1}{8}$ inches (16 cm). It is also known as the Oregon vole.

Microtus gregalis

Singing Vole

The singing vole, also known as the Alaska vole, occurs in both Alaska and the Yukon. It prefers dry tundra areas, where it feeds on green vegetation. This species tends to be colonial and is noted for its vocalizations — a series of high-pitched trills which are sounded at the approach of danger. The singing vole is buffy or pale gray on the upper parts and gray below. It weighs at most 2$\frac{1}{8}$ ounces (60 g) and its maximum length is 6$\frac{1}{4}$ inches (16 cm).

Microtus ochrogaster

Prairie Vole

This species occurs in Canada in eastern Alberta, Saskatchewan and Manitoba. In the United States it inhabits much of the midwest and is found in the following northern regions — Montana, Wyoming, North and South Dakota, Minnesota, Wisconsin, Iowa, Illinois, Indiana and Ohio. It is similar to the closely-related meadow vole but has a shorter tail. The upper parts are grayish to very dark (almost black) brown, the sides are lighter and the belly is tan or grayish. Its favorite habitats are upland herbaceous fields, shrubby borders of wooded areas, and fields of grain, bluegrass and clover. Well defined runways are made on the surface and under the ground, where it spends most of its life. Nests are made both above and below ground and are woven of grass. The diet of this mammal consists of grasses, sedges, roots, tubers, seeds and bulbs. It is known to eat insects, small invertebrates and other mice. The prairie vole weighs $\frac{3}{4}$ to 2 ounces (21-56 g) and measures 4$\frac{5}{8}$ to 7 inches (12-18 cm) in length.

Microtus pinetorum

Woodland Vole

This vole occurs in Canada in only a tiny section of Ontario north of Lake Erie, but its United States range is enormous — almost all of the eastern continent except Maine and possibly New Hampshire. Its most northwesterly range only extends to Minnesota and Iowa. Its southerly range includes all states as far as the Gulf of Mexico. The woodland vole is somewhat colonial and lives in burrows in forested areas where there is good ground cover. It also inhabits orchards and gardens. Like most voles, this creature derives much of its food underground from tubers, roots, bulbs and stems of plants, but it will also venture above ground to feast on berries, nuts and seeds. If an apple is lying on the ground, the vole will dig a tunnel under it and consume it from the bottom up. The woodland vole is reddish-brown on the upper parts which shades to a lighter color on the sides and belly. Its maximum weight is about 2 ounces (56 g) and length about 5$\frac{3}{4}$ inches (15 cm). This mammal is also known as pine vole.

Arvicola richardsoni

Richardson's Water Vole

Richardson's water vole is related to the water vole, or "water rat," of Eurasia and has often been featured in English children's stories. Well isolated now from Asia, it inhabits two small ranges — one on the Coast and Cascades mountains from Oregon to British Columbia, the other down the Rocky and Selkirk mountains from Mt.

Robson, B.C., to Wyoming. It looks like a very large meadow mouse and lives in underground burrows in Alpine meadows close to streams and other wet places. It is an excellent swimmer and will not hestitate to enter water to escape terrestrial predators. Its food consists mainly of a wide variety of vegetation, as well as willow buds and twigs. The water vole is dark grizzled reddish-brown on the upper parts and gray (sometimes with white spots) on the underparts. This is the largest of North American voles, being as much as $10^1/4$ inches in length (26 cm).

Lagurus curtatus
Sagebrush Vole

This vole is a medium-sized creature whose Canadian range is limited to southern Alberta and southern Saskatchewan and whose northern United States range includes eastern Washington and Oregon, southeastern Idaho, eastern Montana, and North and South Dakota. It is colonial and prefers arid areas, where in summer it feeds on grass heads and green plants, and in winter on roots and the bark and cambium layer of sagebrush. In coloration the sagebrush vole is pale gray on the upper parts and white, silvery or buff on the underparts. A typical specimen weighs $5/8$ to $1^3/8$ ounces (17-38 g) and measures in length $4^1/4$ to $5^5/8$ inches (11-14 cm). Most voles have long tails, but in this mammal the heavily-furred tail is generally less than 1 inch in length (2.5 cm).

Lemmings

From the very beginning of their relationship with lemmings, humans have responded to these diminutive mammals with feelings of fascination, mystification and, often, downright disgust. Even today, in both North America and Europe, ancient legends persist and there are still those who believe that lemmings "fall from the sky," that their flesh is poisonous, that they cause a fever, that at certain seasons they pass through a stage of madness so severe that they lose all sense of fear and will attack anything in their path, that they engage in *planned* mass migrations and will plunge to their death over cliffs or into the sea on missions of deliberate suicide. It is reasonably certain that lemmings do not "fall from the sky" (although a sudden surge of high wind would lift them from the ground and

drop them elsewhere, just as a tornado can do to buildings). As for the other beliefs, research is still too inconclusive to make positive statements. For example, at least two highly-respected Canadian scientists who have carried out extensive field studies on collared lemmings, which experience population fluctuations just as dramatic as the fluctuations of brown lemmings, remain unconvinced that they are caused by disease, predation, over-crowding or even food shortages, and they also discount the established beliefs about mass suicides. Yet the actual reasons for the phenomenon are yet to be determined.

Generally speaking, lemmings are relatively stout little creatures with very short tails, weak eyes, short legs and very soft fur. When feeding above ground, they move in hesitant, jerky trots and pause every few seconds to look around for the presence of enemies. Two types of submerged runways are used — one under vegetative mold, the other short tunnels excavated in soft soil about 6 inches (15 cm) down. Most lemmings live in colonies and are often agonistic toward each other. They are active day and night throughout the year, which is about their average lifespan.

Although these creatures are being studied in their habitat and in laboratories, much remains to be learned about their morphology and lifestyles. What is certain is that, like other small rodents, they are essential elements in the food chain which assures the survival of so many terrestrial animals and raptorial birds.

Dicrostonyx groenlandicus
Collared Lemming

The collared lemming, sometimes called varying lemming, is a tundra dweller whose range includes Alaska, Yukon and the Northwest Territories including virtually all the Arctic islands. A closely related species is the Ungava lemming, *D. hudsonicus*, which inhabits the tundra zone of northern Quebec and Labrador.

The collared lemming weighs 2 to 4 ounces (57-113 g) and measures 4 to 7 inches (10-18 cm) in length. The pelage of this mammal varies according to its geographical range, but may broadly be described as buffy-gray above with a dark dorsal stripe, and buffy-gray to white on the underparts. It is the only rodent that turns white in winter.

The collared lemming lives on a summer diet of vegetation, such as grasses, sedges, cottongrass and bearberries, and on a winter diet of twigs and willow buds. It breeds over an extended period, sometimes as early as January, but normally from March to mid-May and from mid-June to September. The litter sizes average about five young, although some may consist of as many as seven. Like all lemmings, the collared and Ungava lemmings live in summer in shallow underground tunnels, in this case under the tundra sod. In winter they make their home in runways beneath the snow.

Every few years populations reach enormous numbers and the lemmings begin a migration that results in heavy mortality. The population then slowly rebuilds, only to "crash" again—and thus the cycles are repeated. Predators include carnivores such as ermine, wolverine, Arctic foxes, wolves, owls, hawks, falcons and gulls.

Lemmus sibiricus

Brown Lemming

This species is now believed to be the same as the Siberian lemming. Its North American range covers Alaska, Yukon and a large part of the northern Northwest Territories, including most of the Arctic islands from Baffin Island to Banks Island. It occurs also in a small area at the extreme northeastern part of Manitoba bordering on Hudson Bay, and in the Coast and Rocky Mountains of northeastern British Columbia and northwestern Alberta.

The brown lemming weighs about 2^1/$_2$ to 4 ounces (70-113 g) and measures 5 to 6^1/$_2$ inches (13-17cm) in length. Its coat is brown on the upper parts and gray below. It is grayer overall in winter. This mammal generally lives in large colonies and makes its summer home in shallow tunnels under moss; in winter it uses dried grass to make round surface nests, the center of which is lined with lemming fur. Woven balls such as this provide good insulation but lack durability. When soiled or damaged they are abandoned and new ones are built. The nest balls are usually found on hummocks of grass or among rocks.

Breeding occurs throughout the year with the exception of the period of mid-May to mid-June. One to three litters, each consisting of 4 to 9 (usually about 7) young are born annually. Brown lemmings are famous for their long migrations when populations reach peak numbers, and for their cyclic "crashes." When these crashes occur the land seems almost devoid of them, but gradually their numbers are

The collared lemming is the only rodent that turns white in winter. These mammals are active day and night throughout the year. In winter months they live in tunnels under the snow. (Photo by Dr. David Gill)

restored and eventually the phenomenon repeats itself.

The summer diet of the brown lemming consists of grass shoots, sedges, and the tender leaves of plants. In winter it feeds on bark and twigs of both willow and birch trees. The enemies of this lemming are tundra carnivores such as least weasels, ermine, Arctic foxes, wolves, grizzly bears and wolverines. Raptorial birds such as snowy owls and short-eared owls, gulls, ravens, and hawks also take a toll.

Synaptomys cooperi

Southern Bog Lemming

The southern bog lemming looks so much like its relative, the meadow vole, that even an experienced observer would have difficulty in quickly distinguishing between the two. It is, however, longer than the vole and its pelage, to use Banfield's term, is "shaggier." This is a small mammal weighing from ^{1}/$_2$ to 2 ounces (14-57 g) and measuring from 3^3/$_4$ to 6 inches (10-15 cm) in length. Its coloration is brownish on the back with a mixture of gray, yellow and black; its underparts are silvery.

Its range runs from southeastern Manitoba to the Maritime provinces, except Prince Edward Island. It is not found in Newfoundland or Anticosti Island. In the United States it occurs south to Kansas, Arkansas, North Carolina and Virginia.

This species, whose abundance throughout its range varies from year to year, inhabits thick stands of marsh grass, but, as its name suggests, it also occurs in spongy bogs and mixed woodlots where leaf mold is thick and damp. Burrows are excavated under heavy leaf mold and consist of a maze of side tunnels. The nest is usually located in a protected area, often under sphagnum moss, and is made of dry leaves and grass and then lined with fur, generally from the animal itself. Mating occurs throughout the year, the peak periods being spring and fall, and several litters may be produced annually. The usual number of young in each litter is 3 to 5, but occasionally it may be only 1 or as many as 7. So prolific is this creature that a female may be pregnant while still nursing its last brood.

Southern bog lemmings feed mainly on leaves, sedges, and seeds of several types of grasses. Also included in its diet are berries and insects, as well as fungus, moss and bark. The enemies of this lemming are weasels, foxes, coyotes, short-tailed shrews, skunks, hawks, owls, crows and snakes.

Synaptomys borealis

Northern Bog Lemming

This mammal is so similar in appearance to the southern bog lemming (*S. cooperi*) that identification can be established mainly by laboratory examination of the teeth, although an experienced observer might be able to identify it by minor differences in coloration; for example, unlike its relative, it has rust-colored hairs at the base of its ears. It is about the same size as the southern bog lemming, weighing from $3/4$ to $1^1/4$ ounces (23-34 g) and measuring from $4^3/4$ to $5^1/2$ inches (12-14 cm). It is generally brown on the upper parts and grayish below. Some males carry a patch of white hair on the flank.

The northern bog lemming occurs mainly in Canada, its range taking in all provinces (with the exception of the Maritime provinces and Newfoundland) as well as the Yukon and Northwest Territories. It is not found on offshore islands. Populations occur in Alaska, while in continental United States the species is present in Washington, Idaho and Montana. Its habitat includes bogs, spruce wood, subalpine meadows and tundra where there is moist ground cover and soft surface soil. Its food consists mainly of sedges, grasses and leafy plants.

This mammal, like its relatives, uses runways made under surface leaf mold and other vegetation during the summer, and under snow in winter. Its main home, however, is in short underground burrows. Its nest is made of grass woven into balls about 8 inches (20 cm) in diameter. In winter the nest is located above ground, usually in a place well protected from the elements, and in summer it is kept underground. Mating takes place from May to August and there are usually four litters, each averaging four young.

Like other small rodents, this creature is preyed upon by several species of carnivores as well as by hawks and owls.

FAMILY MURIDAE

Old World Rats and Mice

Of all species of alien mammals to take up residence in North America, the three least desirable are the black rat, the Norway rat and the house mouse. These creatures, which are native to Asia, spread throughout the world as humans set forth on ships from the Old World as explorers, traders or settlers. Scurrying aboard while the vessels were in home ports, these rodents scurried off at hundreds of ports-of-call and established themselves in their new environments. Today they are mainly found wherever humans congregate—seaports, cities, towns, villages and farms.

Although albino strains of two species (the Norway rat and the house mouse) bred especially for the purpose, have played an important role in medical and other forms of scientific research, in their wild state they are pests and enemies of society. It is estimated that world-wide they cause billions of dollars of damage each year by destroying crops and property and they cause untold suffering as a result of spreading disease and poisoning food. Whatever good may be ascribed to the Norway rat (and this is only when it is held in controlled situations in laboratories), the species will always be infamous as the mammal that spread the horrible bubonic plague which raged throughout Europe in the mid-1300s and killed millions of people. The same rodent caused plagues which occurred in this century in California. Even today the rat plague breaks out on this and other continents, but thanks to medical science it can be controlled and those afflicted can be cured.

Although these three species have similar morphological characteristics (particularly coloration and their large ears and long, scaly and nearly naked tails), they are dissimilar in size, the black rat weighing 5 to 10 ounces (141-283 g) and measuring $12^7/8$ to $18^1/2$ inches (33-47 cm) in length, the Norway rat weighing from $6^7/8$ to 17 ounces (195-485 g) and measuring $12^3/8$ to 18 inches (32-46 cm) in length, and the diminutive house mouse weighing $\frac{1}{2}$ to 1 ounce (14-28 g) and measuring 5 to $8\frac{1}{8}$ inches (13-20 cm) in length.

These creatures are active both day and night throughout the year. They are omnivorous and will eat almost anything; their fondness for human food, especially when collected in garbage cans or removed to dumps, is well known. Grains, seeds and other plant materials also enter their diet, as do invertebrates, eggs and nestling birds. One of their most serious offenses is that their droppings contaminate other foods and objects and this makes them a menace to human health. They are all prolific breeders and produce several litters every year. These creatures prefer warm climates and, while they are all too common in the southern parts of Canada (the house mouse is the exception), they occupy very large ranges in the United States.

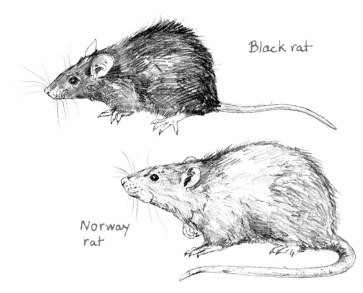

Black rat

Norway rat

Rattus norvegicus
Norway Rat

This rat is also known as brown rat, common rat, sewer rat and water rat. It occurs in the southern areas of all Canadian provinces from Newfoundland to Vancouver Island, and in every U. S. state. Unlike the black rat, which prefers high elevations in which to make its nest, this species is a burrower and lives in the dark recesses of buildings and in sewers. Some, however, live during the summer in fields where seeds and grains are abundant. The Norway rat is colonial and lives under a hierarchical system in which a dominant male rules. The dominant rat generally commands the best nesting area and the one closest to the best supply of food. If the choice could be made, the Norway rat would confine its eating mainly to grains, meat, fruit and other select items, but when hungry it will consume anything. It becomes super-cautious, however, if confronted with poisoned food prepared for its extermination. This rodent has an extremely high degree of intelligence, as well as a remarkable resistance to anticoagulant poisons, and despite the best efforts of science to eliminate it, it often manages to prosper wherever it is present. In addition, it is a prolific breeder, some females being able to produce as many as 12 litters a year, each litter being 2 to 20 young. The average, however, is more likely to be 5 or 6 litters each with 7 to 10 young. The Norway rat is brownish-gray on the upper parts and grayish on the underparts. It is more robust than the black rat. This mammal is a disease carrier. It contam-

inates food, water and the land, and it destroys property by its gnawing habits. It even causes disastrous fires by gnawing away the covering of electrical wiring. Most references to this species make a point of claiming that more human lives have been lost because of it than have been lost in all the wars in history.

Rattus rattus
Black Rat

Known also as the roof rat and ship rat, this mammal is commonly found around coastal waterfronts where it lives in colonies in the attics of warehouses and other buildings. It is an excellent climber and for that reason prefers higher elevations than does the basement and sewer-dwelling Norway rat. The black rat occupies a range that extends around the coastal United States from Maine in the east to Washington in the west. It also occurs in some inland areas served by waterways traversed by ocean-going vessels, St. Louis and Kansas City being cities where its presence has been noted. In Canada it occurs in such maritime areas as the Fraser River delta and Vancouver Island. This rat is grayish-black on the upper parts and light yellow or white on the belly. It is not as thick-bodied as the Norway rat and has larger and broader ears. The tail is longer than the body. The black rat is much more abundant than the Norway rat.

Mus musculus
House Mouse

This miniature version of the Muridae rats is the most common of all rodents. In Canada it occurs in all provinces, fortunately only in the southern sections, although populations are found in the west as far north as the Mackenzie Delta. Every U. S. state has them, as does Mexico and other countries to the south. The house mouse is a creature we could well do without, for like its larger relatives it is a destroyer of property, a contaminator and a disease spreader. Most of them live in close association with humans—in houses, buildings and barns. When grain is ripening, they move to the fields and will commonly be found in fence rows and weedy roadsides. While it prefers grain, fruits and vegetables, it, too, will eat anything edible and will leave unsanitary traces of its presence. Colonial in habit, it makes itself eerily known as it scurries about in attics, behind walls or under floors, generally in the hours of darkness. The house mouse is a prolific breeder and is capable of producing as many as 14 litters a year, each consisting of 2 to 13 young; the average is 5 to 10 litters, with 5 to 7 young per litter— enough, in any case, to assure its perpetuation as a species. While repellents will discourage them and poisons will kill them, the safest method of control is by the use of baited traps. Few control measures are more productive, however, than the hunting capabilities of the domestic cat, although many are killed by rats, small carnivores, hawks, owls and snakes. The pelage of the house mouse is grayish brown on the back and sides and buffy colored on the belly. To an untrained eye it may be mistaken for a plains pocket mouse or harvest mouse.

House mouse

FAMILY ZAPODIDAE

Jumping Mice

These tiny nocturnal creatures, whose jumping and hopping movements are curiously similar to those of the kangaroo, belong to a family of 11 species that occurs in northern and eastern Europe, middle and eastern Asia, and North America. Of the 11 species, the western jumping mouse (*Zapus princeps*), the meadow jumping mouse (*Zapus hudsonius*), the Pacific jumping mouse (*Zapus trinotatus*) and the woodland jumping mouse (*Napaeozapus insignis*), are resident in both Canada and the United States.

Jumping mice, to those fortunate enough to observe them in their natural habitat, are among the most fascinating of the woodland's "little people." Ranging in size from ½ to 1⅜ ounces (14-38 g), they are readily distinguished from other mice by their extraordinarily long, tapering tails, which are twice the length of their bodies, and by their long hind legs and large outward-splayed hind feet. These outsized hind feet provide propulsion powerful enough to enable them to jump, from a standing start, for distances of up to 8 feet (2.4 m). In fact, Schwartz and Schwartz tell of some meadow jumping mice that when frightened "have been reported to leap as much as 10 or 12 feet at a time," and of one jumping mouse that "was timed to travel at the rate of 8 feet per second."

Zapodids, sometimes called "bigfoot" mice, are among the most beautiful of all rodents, although each species has distinguishing color characteristics. As a family, they prefer habitats where moist grasslands are abundant, often around sloughs, marshes and borders of streams. All are accomplished swimmers and are able to float on water; at least one species, the meadow jumping mouse, can swim under water. These creatures feed mainly on seeds, green vegetation and insects, although the woodland jumping mouse adds various kinds of fruits and berries to its diet.

Jumping mice are hibernators, and beginning about mid-September and continuing until the end of October, they retire underground where they remain for 6 to 8 months. Nests of grass are made in tunnels excavated in mounds of earth, in hollow logs, under clumps of grass or in other mammals' abandoned burrows. After sealing off the entrances from inside, they shape their nests to their liking, curl up in little balls and with their heads and front legs tucked between their hind legs and their tails encircling their bodies, gradually go to sleep. Since they do not store up food for winter use, they must feed heavily before hibernation to build up reserves of fat sufficient to sustain them throughout the winter months and to maintain body temperatures at levels that prevent freezing. It is believed, however, that only about one third survive hibernation. Those that do, emerge late the following spring. Soon after leaving their nests they breed and within 18 to 23 days, depending on the species, two to eight young are born. The number of litters ranges from one to three a year. The pelage of all jumping mice is thick but short and wiry.

Jumping mice are of no economic importance, either favorable or unfavorable, but they are significant in the natural food chain. They are preyed upon by several species of carnivores—weasels, mink, skunks, for example—as well as hawks and owls. Snakes take their toll, as do bullfrogs. When swimming or floating in water they may quickly disappear into the mouths of fish. Jumping mice are not believed to live for much more than a year.

Zapus hudsonius

Meadow Jumping Mouse

This is the most widely distributed of the family Zapodidae, occurring in its northern range from the Atlantic coast to Alaska. It is present in all northern states as far west as eastern Wyoming. Its range does not include the southern halves of Saskatchewan, Alberta or British Columbia, although some populations are present in an area of central B.C. This mammal weighs from $1/2$ to 1 ounce (14-28 g), is brownish on the back, yellowish on the sides and white on the belly. It often produces three litters a year (June, July and August), each consisting of five to six young.

Meadow jumping mouse

Zapus princeps

Western Jumping Mouse

Found in Canada from Manitoba west to the lower part of Yukon, in the United States over an irregular midwest and western range south to New Mexico. Its upper parts are olive-brown (often with a dark dorsal stripe), sides yellow and belly white. It weighs from $1/2$ to $1^3/8$ ounces (14-38 g) and produces one litter a year, averaging five young born between the last of June and end of August.

Zapus trinotatus

Pacific Jumping Mouse

The range of this mammal is limited to southwestern British Columbia south through the Pacific coastal states to northern California. According to Banfield, it is the most primitive of the three zapodids, and is considered the prettiest. It is black on the back, ocherous or tawny on the sides (the fur there being streaked with black). A narrow but prominent orange stripe borders the ventral side. The underparts are white. The Pacific jumping mouse weighs from $1/2$ to $1^3/8$ ounces (14-38 g). It is believed to produce one litter a year, averaging four to eight young.

Napaeozapus insignis

Woodland Jumping Mouse

This is an eastern species whose range in Canada extends from the extreme southeastern part of Manitoba east to central Ontario, southern Quebec and the Maritime provinces. While it does not occur in Newfoundland, it is present in southern Labrador. In the United States its range takes in almost all of the country north of West Virginia and as far west as northeastern Minnesota. Some populations are found in the Alleghenies south to northeastern Georgia. Slightly larger than the meadow jumping mouse, it weighs from $5/8$ to $7/8$ ounce (17-25 g). This is a brightly colored species with a brownish back, orange or golden-yellow sides with scattered dark hairs, and a white belly. A long jumper, it often reaches distances from a standing start of 8 or more feet. The woodland jumping mouse is thought to produce two litters in the summer, each averaging four to six young.

MAMMAL WATCHING

Man's relationship with mammals has changed significantly since the pioneering days in North America. Where mammals were once viewed either as useful sources of food or clothing or as competitors to be destroyed, now mammals are more often valued for their own sake as part of the natural world around us.

It should not be surprising that of all the animals in the world our fellow mammals seem to us the most intriguing. Because we too are mammals, we share the basic biological systems and the basics of communication with the wild mammals that we enjoy watching. Biological closeness is perhaps a starting point in explaining the great satisfaction we receive from watching the backyard antics of squirrels or the industry of beavers.

For most of us, opportunities for observing mammals in the wild are limited. A quick glimpse of a furry form dashing across a road at night or a bedraggled creature brought to our doorstep by a hunting cat may be the closest we come to wild mammals in our day-to-day lives. Unlike birds, most mammals, especially the smaller species, are rarely seen. They are wary of man, secretive, and often nocturnal in habits. There are exceptions; some mammals, because of their size or abundance, are the dominant feature of their home ground. Barren-ground caribou on migration and herds of bison are hard to miss — if you happen to be in the right spot at the right time.

As a boy growing up on the outskirts of a city, my interest in mammals was frustrated by both my lack of basic knowledge and the apparent lack of suitable wild habitat for observing them in. My enthusiasm for the mammals that I could not see led me to the unusual hobby of collecting skulls. Soon family, friends and relatives began directing various kinds of mammals to me —in all states of decomposition—and I slowly developed a reasonable collection. It became obvious that mammals were indeed around. I can still remember the feelings of a new world opening to me on my discovery of the handbook, *The Mammals of British Columbia* published by the British Columbia Provincial Museum in 1956. Finally I knew the range of possibilities for my area and where I might expect to see what. Soon after that I joined the junior branch of the local natural history society and the guidance and knowledge offered there completed the picture for the local mammal scene.

For anyone interested in watching mammals, these two important steps are basic prerequisites: First, determine what species are in your area, and second, consult the local museum, naturalist group or hunters and trappers for advice and more precise information on good localities for seeing mammals.

For most mammals, you have to work to obtain the pleasure of watching them. There are several techniques that are so simple and yet generally satisfying that many people have used them without really being conscious of setting out to look for mammals.

Following mammal tracks in sand, mud or winter snow can teach a great deal about the behavior of the mammal being tracked. As Ernest Thompson Seton said, "The trail is an autobiographic chapter of the creature's life." As well as the Seton type of woodcraft book, there are modern field guides to animal tracks which can help in identifying the often confusing marks left by mammals. Tracking or trailing can also lead you to an area where the chances of seeing the mammal are much greater, such as a den site or a regular source of food. Regular tracking can provide a schedule of animal movements that will help in planning the best time to wait for the mammal to appear.

One of the unexpected pleasures of tracking in

snow is the discovery of mammals using your own tracks to make their way more easily through deep or loose snow. If your own trail takes a fairly direct route and is not in a well-traveled area, inevitably mammals will use your trail. In fox country, foxes will use ski or snowshoe tracks to enable them to cover more territory in their constant search for food. So it is wise to repeat your route regularly to see what mammals may have followed *your* tracks.

Wolves will also use ski or snowmobile tracks to their advantage when the snow is soft. Their use of human trails is a natural thing for animals who often travel so precisely in single file that a small pack can leave a track that seems to have been made by, at most, a pair. This reminds me of the delight I felt one day, when slogging through deep melting snow in the Arctic, to find a set of muskox tracks heading in the right direction and of a stride length just right for me. After enjoying the ease of traveling in someone else's tracks for some time, I discovered the reason why the tracks were so suitable. The muskoxen had been following the tracks I had made on the trip away from camp that morning!

A simple yet effective method for seeing mammals is known as "still-watching." You choose a spot during the day, away from a road or trail, house or campsite, where some feature suggests possible mammal activity. The spot should have at least a small clear area for viewing, plus a comfortable rock, log or stump for sitting and to give the watcher some concealment. The ideal situation is to be above ground in a tree platform or "high seat" where your presence is less likely to be detected. Just before dusk, armed with appropriately-colored warm clothes or blankets, you establish yourself in as much comfort as possible and sit quietly, waiting. For the experience to be most rewarding, you have to let your mind settle into the appropriate mood of watchfulness and quiet patience. Dusk is a time of activity for many animals, and even if no mammals are seen, most people find "still-watching" a memorable experience.

If finding an appropriate place for still-watching mammals is a problem and there is a no local source of information, there are books that can help. Most references are directed at hunters or trappers but the same information can be used for those who just want to see mammals. A standard source book first published in 1932 but still readily available is R. M. Anderson's *Methods of Collecting and Preserving Vertebrate Animals*, published by the National Museums of Canada. It gives many suggestions for finding mammals and for attracting them.

Feeding stations set up to attract birds are also visited by some mammals. Squirrels are the most common mammal visitors, but with care in selection of food items offered other species will visit too. In many greenbelt areas close to cities, feeders are visited by gray and red squirrels, chipmunks, flying squirrels, snowshoe hares, raccoons, pine martens, and even fishers in the more remote locations.

Trappers often use specially prepared scents to attract fur-bearing mammals to their traps. Some of these scents or baits are concoctions with secret lists of ingredients. Anderson's book gives some standard recipes for which the main ingredients can be obtained at some pharmacies. Some examples: anise oil for muskrats and raccoons, oil of rhodium for weasels, and oil of catnip for lynx and bobcats.

In most situations with mammal-watching possibilities, a major problem is the timidity of mammals in the presence of humans. Often as soon as the watcher is scented or sighted, the mammal flees. To cope with this problem, watchers have to become more aware of wind speed and direction in relation to themselves or the bait, and have to conceal themselves as much as possible. In many cases the site itself has to be used for hiding. Make use of logs, rocks, trees and bushes. For chance encounters, canoes, tents or vehicles can be used as effective blinds enabling relatively long periods of viewing. A person fully visible but in a canoe or car is usually less frightening to mammals. In a less temporary situation an effective blind can be made from fiberboard or cheap plywood and carried to the site.

Blinds are obviously most useful at sites where mammals can be expected. Mammals living in colonies, such as ground squirrels or sea lions, or those that live in dens, such as red foxes or wolves, can be more readily observed from a well-established blind. In setting up a blind at a den site or colony, care must be taken to ensure that the mammals are not unduly disturbed by the human intrusion. Just as over-zealous photographers can drive nesting birds to abandon their nests, so careless mammal watchers can cause the abandonment of a nursery den. It is always better to observe more from a distance than little or nothing from too close.

To help in viewing mammals from a distance, binoculars or spotting scopes are important assets. Although it can be hard on the eyes after prolonged observations, a single eyepiece spotting scope on a light tripod is about the best combination for long periods. Though it is often hard to resist trying to photograph mammals, I have often regretted the attempt. I find that a fleeing glimpse of an unusual mammal registers a much stronger impression on the brain if it is not hampered by an attempted photograph. Unless the photograph is excellent, the encounter is in effect lost when photography interferes with careful and intent watching.

For recording observations, the most important tool is the notebook. Any pocket-sized bound book will do to record the sighting or a series of observations. A written record of mammals seen and the circumstances surrounding the observations not only makes pleasant reading in later years but may provide a useful scientific record of an unusual event.

Other equipment to help in mammal watching can be borrowed from the bag of tricks used by mammal hunters. Several types of predator calls are available for about $5 at hunting supply outlets. These little gadgets make a sound like a squealing mouse or a wounded rabbit and can be effective in calling in curious predators such as foxes, coyotes, weasels or bobcats, and even other mammals such as squirrels and deer. With the ever-wary predators, such a call can make the difference between a fleeting glimpse and a prolonged look at the animal. Even the squeaky calls made to attract birds can attract weasels and foxes. Although I would hesitate to use a moose call in hunting or breeding seasons, they too are available and "guaranteed" to bring moose into view.

The records and tapes of mammal sounds available to help hunters attract their prey are probably more numerous than those mammal records made simply for enjoyment by naturalists. Just as mechanical calls could be useful in attracting mammals for observation, so too could these records and tapes. They are certainly worth a try, again bearing in mind the possible disruption they could cause and the hazard of calling in large mammals during the rutting season. Among the many recordings of bird songs, frog and insect calls, and other sounds of nature on the market, there are a few published recordings solely of mammal vocalizations, notably those of wolves and humpback whales.

You do not have to be in the true wilderness to see mammals. A few years ago my wife and I were paddling a canoe amid the marine traffic and miscellaneous flotsam in Victoria's inner harbor and were followed by a curious harbor seal who repeatedly swam up to our paddles and gave us a good look-over. I have watched beavers at work along major highways, within 100 yards of occupied lakeshore cottages, on the banks of the North Saskatchewan River where it passes through Edmonton, and on Ottawa's Rideau River within a few miles of the Parliament Buildings. Beavers are ideal subjects with which to begin the hobby of mammal watching. They can be found throughout much of North America below the tree line and, because of their alteration of the habitat by building dams and lodges, they are easy to locate. An active beaver colony can be recognized by the freshly chewed branches or trees in the area and the trails left as they move from the pond in search of food. By quietly watching at dawn and dusk you are almost assured of seeing them.

Backyard encounters with raccoons and woodchucks are other common introductions to wild mammals. With raccoons especially, these encounters can lead to a prolonged arrangement of feeding on demand. For other nocturnal mammals, using a red light enables you to see them without the intrusion of bright lights.

Bat watching is a relatively easy activity to arrange. In the time of year when insects are flying, bats can usually be seen at dusk. They are most easily watched over open areas near the edge of a woods, along roads, lakeshores or streams. Flying bats can be attracted by tossing handfuls of fine gravel high into the air in front of the approaching bat. The small particles are perceived as possible food items and bats will follow the falling gravel down to head level. Though it is not easy to find roosting sites of hibernating bats, it is worth checking inside old buildings where individuals of the more solitary species can be found hanging from attic ceilings.

National, provincial and state parks provide opportunities for seeing more wild animals than just the ever-present highway or campground panhandlers seen by most tourists. Naturalist programs which provide information and guided hikes with a naturalist can lead to regular sightings of certain mammals. In the western mountain parks, hikers can be assured of seeing chipmunks, ground squirrels, pikas and hoary marmots. In Ontario's Algonquin Provincial Park and national parks in Saskatchewan and Manitoba, visitors can take part in organized wolf-howling excursions which have a good rate of successful vocal contact with wolves.

Whale watching as an organized activity is becoming popular on all three coasts. On the St. Lawrence River since 1970, late summer and early fall boat excursions have been organized by several different societies to allow large groups to see blue, finback and beluga whales. On Pacific, Atlantic and Arctic coastlines too are locations where colonies of sea mammals, such as sea lions, walrus and seals, are accessible by small boat or by hiking. With these mammals it is important to avoid driving them into the sea by getting too close.

Mammal watching can be most successful when combined with activities such as hiking, camping and canoeing. Some time for mammal watching should be planned as part of a holiday and the trip schedule should be kept flexible enough to allow you to make use of unexpected opportunities. A canoe trip may present good opportunities to see mammals, but if you cannot stop to watch otters because you have not yet paddled the required number of miles for that day, you may remember the trip more for what you did not see than for what you did. Watching river otters fishing as you sit motionless in a canoe, or drifting slowly down a wandering stream following a foraging mink, can make paddling even in flat water an exciting experience.

The nature of mammals and the relatively small amount of research that has been done in the wild mean that amateur mammal watchers can make significant contributions to the science of mammalogy. There is still a great deal to be learned about many of the common species. Even basic records of occurrence and distribution, particularly in areas away from major centres and without local museums, can be of great value to scientists. Records of interesting behavioral observations can be published in the newsletters or magazines of state, provincial or local naturalist clubs.

By adopting a mammal that needs help, mammal watchers can make important progress in the conservation of rare or endangered species. A shining example of such a contribution is the work done by the Vancouver Island Marmot Preservation Committee of the Cowichan Valley Naturalists' Club. The dedicated naturalists in this group have done an excellent job of bringing the plight of this rare mammal to the public's attention. They carefully monitor the accessible colonies and even patrol the more accessible sites to educate the public and protect the marmots.

Other naturalist groups have taken up the cause of locally endangered or potentially endangered mammals. In Saskatchewan the black-tailed prairie dogs at Val Marie are protected by the new Grasslands National Park after years of pressure from conservationists. A killer whale park is a good possibility in British Columbia waters, and Ontario already has its Polar Bear Provincial Park. But in general mammals have not always received the concern that they deserve. In the north, national park boundaries have been established that leave out important mammal ranges. The first of the many International Biological Program ecological reserves proposed in 1975 still does not offer the muskoxen and threatened Peary caribou of Polar Bear Pass on Bathurst Island any permanent protection. The Thelon Game Sanctuary, one of the few sanctuaries established specifically for mammals, in this case muskoxen, is threatened by growing pressure to open the area to mineral exploration.

For mammal watching to continue as a source of pleasure to ever-increasing numbers of people, those same people will have to adopt conservation as the vital tool in making this pleasure a continuing reality.

David R. Gray
National Museum of Natural Sciences,
National Museums of Canada

BIBLIOGRAPHY

Aniśkowicz, B. T. *Social and Spatial Organization of Tamias Striatus Communities and Related Aspects of Behaviour.* Ph.D. thesis, October, 1977.

Anon. *Mammals of Algonquin Provincial Park.* Ontario Ministry of Natural Resources, 1978.

Anon. *Wolves and Coyotes in Ontario.* Ontario Ministry of Natural Resources, 1968.

Banfield, A. W. F. *The Mammals of Canada.* National Museum of Natural Sciences, National Museums of Canada. University of Toronto Press, 1974.

Bergerud, A. T. *The Annual Antler Cycle in Newfoundland Caribou.* Canadian Field Naturalist, Vol. 90, 1976.

——— *Caribou.* Big Game of North America, Wildlife Management Institute. Stackpole Books, 1978.

——— *Decline of Caribou in North America Following Settlement.* Journal of Wildlife Management, 38 (4), 1974.

——— *The Population Dynamics of Newfoundland Caribou.* The Wildlife Society, 1971.

Bigg, Michael A. *Harbour Seal* — Phoca vitulina and P. largha. Handbook of Marine Mammals, Vols. 1-2. Academic Press, 1981.

Bonner, W. Nigel. *Gray Seal* — Halichoerus grypus. Handbook of Marine Mammals, Vols 1-2. Academic Press, 1981.

Broadbooks, Harold E. *Tree Nests of Chipmunks with Comments on Associated Behaviour and Ecology.* Journal of Mammalogy, August, 1974.

Bruemmer, Fred. *Encounters with Arctic Animals.* McGraw-Hill Ryerson, 1972.

Burns, John L. *Bearded Seal* — Erignathus barbatus. Handbook of Marine Mammals, Vols. 1-2. Academic Press, 1981.

——— *Ice Seals.* Marine Mammals, Pacific Search Press, 1978.

——— *Ribbon Seal* — Phoca fasciata. Handbook of Marine Mammals, Vols. 1-2. Academic Press, 1981.

Burt, William H. *The Mammals of Michigan.* University of Michigan Press, 1946.

Cahalane, Victor H. *Mammals of North America.* The Macmillan Company, New York, 1947.

Cosco, John. *Mountain Beaver: Its Biology and Implications to Forestry in British Columbia.* B.S.F. thesis, University of British Columbia, April, 1981.

Cowan, I. McT. *Nesting Habits of the Flying Squirrel.* Journal of Mammalogy, 1936.

De Long, Robert L. *Northern Elephant Seal.* Marine Mammals, Pacific Search Press, 1978.

Dunford, Christopher. *Summer Activity of Eastern Chipmunks.* Journal of Mammalogy, February, 1972.

Edwards, R. Yorke. *Fire and the Decline of a Mountain Caribou Herd.* Journal of Wildlife Management, 1954.

Ewer, R. F. *The Carnivores.* Cornell University Press, 1973.

Fay, Francis H. *Walrus* — Odobenus rosmarus. Handbook of Marine Mammals, Vols. 1-2. Academic Press, 1981.

Fiscus, Clifford H. *Northern Fur Seal.* Marine Mammals, Pacific Search Press, 1978.

Ford, Alice. *Audubon's Animals: The Quadrupeds of North America.* Studio Publications, Inc. 1951.

Fuller, W. F. *Behaviour and Social Organization of the Wild Buffalo of Wood Buffalo National Park, Canada.* 1960.

Geist, Valerius. *Mountain Sheep: A Study in Behaviour and Evolution.* University of Chicago Press, 1971.

——— *Adaptive Strategies in the Behaviour of Elk.* Faculty of Environmental Design, University of Calgary.

——— *Behaviour.* Big Game of North America. Wildlife Management Institute. Stackpole Books, 1978.

——— *Mountain Sheep and Man in the Northern Wilds.* Cornell University Press, 1975.

——— *On the Behaviour of the North American Moose in British Columbia.* 1962.

——— *On Weapons, Combat and Ecology (from Aggression, Dominance and Individual Spacing).* Plenum Publishing Corporation, 1978.

——— *The Relation of Social Evolution and Dispersal in Ungulates during the Pleistocene Period, With Emphasis on the Old World Deer and the Genus* Bison. Quaternary Research, 1971.

Gentry, Roger L. *Northern Fur Seal* — Callorhinus ursinus. Handbook of Marine Mammals, Vols. 1-2. Academic Press, 1981.

Gray, David R. *The Defence Formation of the Muskox.* Musk-Ox, 1974.

——— *The Marmots of Spotted Nellie Ridge.* Nature Canada, Jan/Mar, 1975.

——— *Movement and Behaviour of Tagged Muskoxen on Bathurst Island, N.W.T.* Musk-Ox, 1979. (The status of the muskox and Peary caribou on Canada's Arctic islands, in "Proceedings in the Symposium on Canada's Threatened Species and Habitats." Special publication, Canadian Nature Federation, 1977).

——— *Muskox.* Hinterland's Who's Who, Canadian Wildlife Service, 1975.

Harington, C. R. *Quaternary Vertebrate Faunas of Canada and Alaska and Their Suggested Chronological Sequence.* National Museum of Natural Sciences, Ottawa, 1978.

Harington, C. Richard. *Denning Habits of the Polar Bear.* Canadian Wildlife Service, Report Series No. 5.

Heard, D. C. *The Behaviour of Vancouver Island Marmots.* M. Sc. thesis, University of British Columbia, 1977.

Henry, J. David. *Fox Hunting.* Natural History, November, 1980.

Herrero, Stephen M. *Conflicts between Man and Grizzly Bears in the National Parks of North America.* Third International Conference on Bears — Their Biology and Management, International Union for Conservation of Nature and Natural Resources. Morges, Switzerland, 1976.

——— *Human Injury Inflicted by Grizzly Bears.* American Association for the Advancement of Science, Vol. 170, 1970.

——— *Man and the Grizzly Bear.* BioScience, 1970.

——— *People and Grizzly Bears: The Challenge of Coexistence.* Reprinted from the John S. Wright Forestry Conference Proceedings, Purdue University, 1978.

Hewlett, Stefani and K. Gilbey. *Sea Life of the Pacific Northwest.* McGraw-Hill Ryerson Limited, 1976.

Hoefs, M. *Ecological Investigation of Dall Sheep and Their Habitat.* Ph.D. thesis, University of British Columbia, 1975.

Holroyd, John C. *Observations of Rocky Mountain Goats on Mount Wardle, Kootenay National Park, British Columbia.* The Canadian Field Naturalist, Jan/Mar. 1967.

Ingraham, Bob. *Why Save Them from Extinction?* Endangered Wildlife in Canada, Canadian Wildlife Federation, Ottawa, 1970.

Jackson, Hartley H. T. *Mammals of Wisconsin.* University of Wisconsin Press, 1961.

Jonkel, Charles. *The Behaviour of Captured North American Bears (With Comments on Bear Management and Research)* BioScience, November, 1970.

Kastner, Joseph. *A Species of Eternity.* Alfred A. Knopf, 1977.

Kelsall, J. P. *The Migratory Barren-Ground Caribou of Canada.* Queen's Printer, 1968.

Kenyon, Karl W. *Sea Otter* — Enhydra lutris. Handbook of Marine Mammals, Vols. 1-2. Academic Press, 1981.

Kolenosky, George B. *Hybridization Between Wolf and Coyote.* Journal of Mammalogy, May, 1971.

——— *Season of the Black Bear.* Ontario Naturalist, Summer, 1978.

Kopas, Leslie. *The Kermode Bear of British Columbia.* Wildlife Review, Summer, 1979.

Krebs, Charles J. *The Lemming Cycle at Baker Lake, N.W.T. During 1959-62.* Arctic Institute, North American Technical Paper, No. 15, 1964.

Lemon, Enid K. *Forest Habitat: The Island Whistler.* Forest Talk, B.C. Ministry of Forests, Fall, 1981.

Livingston, John A. *One Cosmic Instant: A History of Human Arrogance.* McClelland and Stewart, Ltd. 1973.

Lorenz, Konrad. *On Aggression.* Harcourt, Brace and World, Inc., 1966.

Madson, John. *The Cottontail Rabbit.* Olin Chemical Corporation, 1963.

——— *Gray and Fox Squirrels.* Olin Chemical Corporation, 1964.

Marsden, Walter. *The Lemming Year.* Chatto and Windus, 1964.

Mate, Bruce R. *California Sea Lion.* Pacific Search Press, 1978.

Milne, Lorus and Margery. *The Cougar Doesn't Live Here Anymore.* Prentice-Hall, 1971.

Munro, W. T. *Vancouver Island Marmot.* Committee on the Status of Endangered Wildlife in Canada, Ottawa.

Murray, Allan. *The Wild Dogs: A Story of Wolves in Manitoba.* Province of Manitoba, 1973.

Newby, Terrell C. *Pacific Harbour Seal.* Pacific Search Press, 1978.

Northcott, Tom H. *The Land Mammals of Insular Newfoundland* Government of Newfoundland, 1974.

Novak, Milan. *The Beaver in Ontario.* Ontario Ministry of Natural Resources, 1976.

——— *Recent Status of the Wolverine in Ontario.* Ontario Ministry of Natural Resources, 1975.

Novakowski, N. S. *Endangered Wildlife — Mammals.* Endangered Wildlife in Canada, Canadian Wildlife Federation, Ottawa, 1970.

Odell, David K. *California Sea Lion.* Handbook of Marine Mammals, Vols. 1-2. Academic Press, 1981.

Parker, Gerald R. *Morphology, Reproduction, Diet and Behaviour of the Arctic Hare* (Lepus arcticus monstrabilis) *on Axel Heiberg Island, N.W.T.* Canadian Field Naturalist, 1977.

Peterson, R. L. *The Mammals of Eastern Canada.* Oxford University Press, 1966.

——— *North American Moose.* University of Toronto Press, 1955.

Pimlott, Douglas H. *Wolf Control in Canada.* Canadian Audubon Magazine, Nov/Dec, 1961.

Pruitt, W. O., Jr. *Animals of the North.* Harper and Row, 1966.

——— *Alive in the Wild* (The Wolverine). Edited by Victor H. Cahalane. Prentice-Hall, Inc., 1970.

Rand, A. L. *Mammals of Yukon.* National Museum of Canada, Bulletin No. 100, Biological Series No. 29, 1945.

Roe, F. G. *The North American Buffalo.* 2nd Editon, University of Toronto Press, 1970.

Rogers, Lynn L. *Shedding of Foot Pads by Black Bears During Denning.* Journal of Mammalogy, Vol. 55, No. 3, 1974.

Russell, Andy. *Grizzly Country.* Alfred A. Knopf, 1972.

Sage, Bryan L. *Alaska and Its Wildlife.* Viking Press, 1973.

Scotter, George W. *How Andy Bahr Led the Great Reindeer Herd from Western Alaska to the Mackenzie Delta.* Canadian Geographic, Oct/Nov, 1978.

Schusterman, Ronald J. *Steller Sea Lion* — Eumetopias jubatus. Handbook of Marine Mammals, Vols. 1-2. Academic Press, 1981.

Schwartz, Charles W. and Elizabeth R. *The Wild Mammals of Missouri.* University of Missouri Press and Missouri Department of Conservation, 1981.

Seton, Ernest Thompson. *Life Histories of Northern Animals.* Vols. 1-2. Scribners Sons, 1909.

Soper, J. Dewey. *The Mammals of Alberta.* The Hamley Press, Ltd., 1964.

Stirling, Ian. *Midsummer Observations on the Behaviour of Wild Polar Bears* (Ursus maritimus). Canadian Journal of Zoology, 1974.

Stonehouse, Bernard. *Animals of the Arctic — The Ecology of the Far North.* Holt, Rinehart and Winston, 1971.

Theberge, John B. *Wolf Management in Canada through a Decade of Change.* Nature Canada, 1973.

——— *Wolf Play.* Ontario Naturalist, June, 1972.

van Zyll de Jong, C. G. *Food Habits of the Lynx in Alberta and the Mackenzie District, N.W.T.* Canadian Field Naturalist, Jan/Mar, 1966.

——— *Differentiation of the Canada Lynx* Felis (Lynx) canadensis subsolanus *in Newfoundland.* Canadian Journal of Zoology, No. 6, 1975.

——— *The Distribution of the Wolverine* (Gulo gulo) *in Canada.* Canadian Field Naturalist, 89 (4), 1975.

——— *A Systematic Review of the Nearctic and Neotropical River Otters* (Genus *Lutra*, Mustelidae, Carnivora). Life Sciences Contributions, Royal Ontario Museum, No. 80, 1972.

Whitaker, John O., Jr. *The Audubon Society Field Guide to North American Mammals.* Alfred A. Knopf, Inc., 1980.

Woods, S. E., Jr. *The Squirrels of Canada.* National Museum of Natural Sciences, Ottawa, 1980.

Aspects of Predations of Seals by Polar Bears. Ian Stirling and W. Ralph Archibald. Journal of the Fisheries Research Board of Canada, Vol. 34, 1977.

The Clever Coyote. S. P. Young and H. H. T. Jackson. Wildlife Management Institute, 1951.

Comparative Hunting Abilities of Polar Bear Cubs of Different Ages. Ian Stirling and Paul B. Latour. Canadian Journal of Zoology, 1978.

The Great White Bears. Ian Stirling and Charles Jonkel. Nature Canada, Vol. 1, No. 3, 1972.

Hare Revelations. David R. Gray and Heather Hamilton. Nature Canada, Jan/Mar, 1982.

Harp Seal — Phoca groenlandica. K. Ronald and P. J. Healey. Handbook of Marine Mammals, Vols. 1-2. Academic Press, 1981.

Hooded Seal — Cystophora cristata. Randall R. Reeves and John L. King. Handbook of Marine Mammals, Vols. 1-2, Academic Press, 1981.

Immobilizing and Marking Wild Muskoxen in Arctic Canada. Charles J. Jonkel, David R. Gray and Ben Hubert. Journal of Wildlife Management, 1975.

The Mammals of British Columbia. I. McT. Cowan and C. J. Guiguet. Provincial Museum Handbook No. 11, 1966.

Mammals of the World. Ernest P. Walker et al. Vols. 1-2, Johns Hopkins Press, 1964.

Migrations of Caribou in a Mountainous Area in Wells Gray Park, British Columbia. R. Yorke Edwards and R. W. Ritcey. Canadian Field Naturalist, 1959.

Muskoxen at Bathurst Island. David R. Gray and Donald B. Cockerton. The Beaver, Winter, 1974.

Northern Elephant Seal — Mirounga angustirostris. Samuel M. McInnes and Ronald J. Schusterman. Handbook of Marine Mammals, Vols. 1-2. Academic Press, 1981.

Ringed, Baikal and Caspian Seals — Phoca hispida, P. sibirica and P. caspica. Kathryn J. Frost and Lloyd F. Lowry. Handbook of Marine Mammals, Vols. 1-2. Academic Press, 1981.

Steller Sea Lion. Roger L. Gentry and David E. Withrow. Marine Mammals, Pacific Search Press, 1978.

The Survival of the Wood Bison in the Northwest Territories. A. W. F. Banfield and N. S. Novakowski. Natural History Papers, National Museum of Canada, 1961.

Vancouver Island Marmot. Allan R. Hawryzki and Maxime Carpenter. Wildlife Review, Winter, 1978.

Wild Mammals of North America. Edited by Thomas B. Allen. National Geographic Society, 1979.

The World of the Wolf. Russell J. Rutter and Douglas H. Pimlott. The Ontario Naturalist, March, 1968.

The Wolves of North America. S. P. Young and E. A. Goldman. American Wildlife Institute, 1944.

Proceedings of the First International Mountain Goat Symposium. Kalispell, Montana, 1977.

Marten Ranges and Food Habits in Algonquin Park, Ontario. G. R. Francis and A. B. Stephenson. Ministry of Natural Resources, Ontario, 1972.

The Social Ecology of Coyotes. Marc Bekoff and Michael C. Wells. Scientific American, April, 1980.

INDEX TO MAMMALS

INDEX TO PEOPLE, PLACES AND THINGS